# Chicago After Stonewall

A History of LGBTQ Chicago
from Gay Lib to Gay Life

St Sukie de la Croix

Copyright © 2021 St Sukie de la Croix

All rights reserved.

No part of this publication may be reproduced, distributed, or transmitted in any form or by any means, including photocopying, recording, or other electronic or mechanical methods, without the prior written permission of the publisher, except in the case of brief quotations embodied in critical reviews and certain other noncommercial uses permitted by copyright law. For permission requests, write to the publisher, addressed "Attention: Permissions Coordinator," at the address below.

Rattling Good Yarns Press
33490 Date Palm Drive 3065
Cathedral City CA 92235
USA
www.rattlinggoodyarns.com

Cover Design: Rattling Good Yarns Press, front and back cover photographs courtesy of the Richard Pfeiffer Archives

Library of Congress Control Number: 2021935161
ISBN: 978-1-7341464-9-3

First Edition

To all the GLF radicals, wherever you are.

# CONTENTS

| | | |
|---|---|---|
| | Introduction | vii |
| 1 | The Cops, the Mob, the Gay Bars | 1 |
| 2 | Chicago's Gay Liberation Front vs. Police Sgt. John Manley Jr | 14 |
| 3 | GLF Dances vs. the Gay Bars | 21 |
| 4 | GLF Branches Out | 26 |
| 5 | University of Illinois Urbana-Champaign | 32 |
| 6 | GLF and the Mainstream Press | 41 |
| 7 | GLF and the Vietnam War | 44 |
| 8 | Ortez E. Alderson, the Black Panthers, and the Killing of James Clay | 49 |
| 9 | The *Chicago Seed* Gay Supplement and *The Boys in the Band* | 58 |
| 10 | Gay Pride Week 1970 | 62 |
| 11 | GLF vs. the Psychiatrists | 65 |
| 12 | The GLF Split | 82 |
| 13 | GLF Around Town | 88 |
| 14 | The Aldermanic Candidates | 91 |
| 15 | Midwest Regional Gay Liberation Convention | 94 |
| 16 | The 2nd Gay Pride Parade, the Kiss-In, and the Fiery Flames Collective | 101 |
| 17 | The Bijou Adult Movie Theater, the Cops, and the Mob | 105 |
| 18 | The Gay Community Center on Elm Street | 112 |
| 19 | Lavender Woman and the Daughters of Bilitis | 116 |
| 20 | The Tom Foran Zap | 121 |
| 21 | Venceremos | 124 |
| 22 | The National Gay Convention in Chicago | 128 |
| 23 | Michael Bergeron and the Democratic Convention | 132 |
| 24 | Rev. Charles Lamont | 134 |
| 25 | Mary Houlihan and the Gay Catholic Mass | 138 |
| 26 | Women's Caucus/Music and Linda Shear | 142 |
| 27 | Gay Pride 1972 | 151 |

| 28 | Gay Bars and Discos in the Early 1970s | 156 |
| 29 | Trouble at Dugan's Bistro | 167 |
| 30 | A Handful of Artistic Delights | 180 |
| 31 | Three Dicks: Nixon, Ogilvie and Daley | 187 |
| 32 | Hippies, Yippies and Gays | 190 |
| 33 | Legislative Action | 197 |
| 34 | Cruising | 204 |
| 35 | The Gay Teachers Association | 208 |
| 36 | The Case of Rev. David Sindt | 211 |
| 37 | Protest at the Athenaeum Theater | 216 |
| 38 | State Rep. Webber Borchers | 218 |
| 39 | Gay Pride Week 1973 | 223 |
| 40 | Gay Pride Week 1973 Women-Only | 232 |
| 41 | The Anti-Drag Law | 236 |
| 42 | Gays Fostering Teens | 243 |
| 43 | The Houston Murders | 248 |
| 44 | Gay Anthropologists and "Homophobia" | 251 |
| 45 | Trans-Issues and "Gender Bending" | 253 |
| 46 | Lady Baronessa and Shaun Luis Win Miss Gay America 1974 & 1975 | 262 |
| 47 | TV Stereotypes | 265 |
| 48 | More God and Gays | 269 |
| 49 | Loyola U Gay Group and Rogers Park Gay Center | 276 |
| 50 | Women's Coffeehouses and More Women's Music | 281 |
| 51 | Lesbian Separatism | 284 |
| 52 | Charles "Chuck" Renslow, Bathhouses, the Gold Coast, and the Dewes Mansion | 288 |
| 53 | Columnist Mike Royko | 293 |
| 54 | Beckman House and Gay Horizons | 298 |
| 55 | The 5th Annual Gay Pride Parade | 306 |
| 56 | The Case of David C. Gardner | 312 |
| 57 | Lavender Woman Splits | 315 |

| | | |
|---|---|---|
| 58 | The Lesbian Writers Conference | 321 |
| 59 | The Howard Brown Memorial VD Clinic Pre-AIDS | 323 |
| 60 | Racism at the Lesbian Bars | 329 |
| 61 | The 1st Issue of *Chicago Gay Life* and the 6th Annual Gay Pride Week | 332 |
| | Afterword | 341 |
| | Bibliography | 342 |
| | Index | 370 |

On January 20, 1974, in the *Chicago Tribune*, Darrell Sifford asked Mrs. Ruth Osborne, a handwriting expert:

"Can you tell a homosexual by his handwriting?"

"If he's coping well with his homosexuality, if he doesn't feel guilty about it, it's hard to determine. But, as a rule, the homosexual will have a full loop below the line but instead of being rounded it'll be pointed.

"What the homosexual is doing, of course, is drawing a penis. I can spot a lesbian almost every time. I've rarely known it to fail. She'll square the loop on her Y."

# INTRODUCTION

*Chicago After Stonewall: Gay Lib to Gay Life* is a detailed account of how LGBTQ's in Carl Sandburg's "City of the Big Shoulders" responded to the Stonewall Riots. This book pulls together jigsaw pieces of information from many sources, including a wealth of documents held in the McCormick Library of Special Collections at Northwestern University, Evanston, IL, to reveal a picture of a raggle-taggle band of dysfunctional rebels with one cause.

In post-Stonewall Chicago, several attempts were made to publish a gay newspaper, but none lasted. The longest was the *Chicago Gay Crusader* with twenty-six issues, between 1973-1975. However, the paper was irregular and a hangover from the 1960s hippie underground press in style. It wasn't until June 20, 1975, when Grant L. Ford published Volume 1/Number 1 of *Chicago Gay Life*, that Chicago boasted a professional gay newspaper. The headlines on the front page of the first issue read: "GAY PRIDE!! Manford, Segal to speak during GP week"; "Women plan special events"; "Associate Editor speaks out"; "Religious radio station grants gays equal time," and; "Gay military men to appear on radio."

After that first issue, a seamless thread of gay newspapers continued to the present day, a goldmine for researchers of LGBTQ history: *Gay Chicago* (1976-2011); *Windy City Times* (1985-present); *Outlines* (1987-2000); and *Chicago Free Press* (1999-2010).

However, from the Stonewall Riots until the publication of *Chicago Gay Life*, there was no reliable source for local gay news, only irregular gay publications like *The Paper*, *Mattachine Midwest Newsletter*, or hippie underground/alternative rags, *Seed, Kaleidoscope, Reader,* and *Second City*, and college newspapers like *Maroon* and *Roosevelt Torch*.

As with my other two history books, *Chicago Whispers: A History of LGBT Chicago Before Stonewall* and *Out of the Underground: Homosexuals, the Radical Press and the Rise and Fall of the Gay Liberation Front*, I stay very close to my sources. I quote extensively from newspapers and magazines because I want the reader to experience what it was like "in the moment." I also quote from what gay activist Frank Kameny called "the country's most influential opinion-molders" – newspaper advice columnists.

This book begins with Henry Weimhoff, a University of Chicago student, and ends with the first issue of *Gay Life* on June 20, 1975 and an impassioned editorial by Valerie Bouchard for the community to "come together, unite, and focus on similarities and not differences."

# 1
# THE COPS, THE MOB, THE GAY BARS

Within days of the June 1969 Stonewall Riots, the newly formed New York Gay Liberation Front fanned the dying embers of the '50s and '60s homophile movement, igniting a fireball of radicalism. No other oppressed minority rallied so quickly around one incident, a seemingly insignificant clash between homosexuals and police at a Greenwich Village gay bar. The Stonewall Riots received little media coverage at the time they occurred: two articles buried deep in the *New York Times*, two more on the front-page of the *Village Voice*, the *New York Daily News* headlined "Homo Nest Raided, Queen Bees Are Stinging Mad," and a couple of eyewitness accounts in the underground press. However, there was no mention of the Stonewall Riots in Chicago's mainstream press. The only coverage of it appeared in the July 1969 *Mattachine Midwest Newsletter* when William B. Kelley, a veteran activist, wrote:

> "In an unprecedented display of brute 'gay power,' hundreds of young people angered by the New York police's treatment of the Stonewall bar and its patrons rioted outside the bar on June 28, threatening police, trying to overturn a patrol wagon, chanting and chalking slogans on walls. The next night, crowds gathered again and attempted a demonstration, but police tactical forces eventually broke them up.
>
> "The Stonewall is in Greenwich Village and is very popular with quite a young clientele. The police had entered reportedly to seize illegally sold liquor, not to arrest patrons. Judging from the complete havoc their visit wreaked inside the bar, their behavior may have been a bit provocative, and it seems there was a citizen over-reaction. The *New York Times* of June 30, the *Village Voice* of July 3, and the *Berkeley Barb* of July 4 carried a variety of fuller accounts, with pictures in the case of the *Voice*."

Kelley mentioned the riots again the following month, in his "Gaylimaufry" column:

> "NEW YORK's gay riots of June were followed by more organized drum-beating for the homophile cause. Daughters of Bilitis and Mattachine of New York led a rally and march by 500 from Washington Sq. to the Stonewall Inn, site of the police-provoked disorders, in what was billed as 'this city's first gay-power vigil.' Craig Rodwell's Homophile Youth Movement (HYMN) also pamphleted the neighborhood. Even blasé Greenwich Village couldn't repress some gasps ..."

In June 1969, gay nightlife in Chicago was thriving. The Trip, a three-story bar and restaurant at 27 E. Ohio St., had just reopened after a notorious raid a year earlier. The bar featured the talents of Arthur Blake, famous for his impressions of movie stars and political figures. An ad in the *Mattachine Midwest Newsletter* claimed he was returning from the East Coast with "mad, mad props." Blake impersonated both male and female celebrities, among them Charles Laughton, Charlie Chaplin, Talullah Bankhead, and Bette Davis. His impersonation of Eleonor Roosevelt led to an invitation to the White House to perform for the First Lady and FDR. Blake died of pancreatic cancer on March 24, 1985, in Fort Lauderdale, FL. One obituary read, "Mr. Blake is survived by Irving Cohen, his manager, director, and close friend who was at his side at the time of his death; also, with him for the last 42 years."

Other Chicago gay bar entertainments in June 1969 included Romi Blue and his "Guys Are Dolls Revue" at the Blue Dahlia, a drag bar at 5640 W. North, and Tony Dee and his guitar at the King's Ransom, 20 E. Chicago, with hosts Danny and Stan. In the June 1969 *Mattachine Midwest Newsletter*, Mark Howard in his "Chicago Gay Scene" column describes Kitty Sheon's bar at 745 Rush St. as "a P.E. [Piss Elegant] joint with the biggest closet in Chicago. Ribbon clerks, wall-trolley operators and pedal-wares pushers line the walls, acting out like celebrities."

The Stonewall Riots in New York City had no effect on the Chicago Police Department's ruthless tactics. A year earlier, police brutality against anti-Vietnam War demonstrators at the 1968 National Democratic Convention revealed Chicago police to be brutal, corrupt and out of control. Nothing had changed. The Vice Control Division of the Chicago Police Department continued raiding, beating, blackmailing, and arresting homosexuals in parks and gay bars. In the July 1969 *Mattachine Midwest Newsletter*, in Jim Bradford's column, "The President's Corner," he wrote:

> "The scene has shifted back to the streets. We have numerous reports of the old 'prostitution' game being played. To recap, the cop acts gay,

wants to have sex, introduces the question of money. He insists on paying you (yes, Mary!), and you get pinched under the prostitution statutes whether you accept or not. Legally there is no case unless you accept, but the story always gets changed on the way to the stationhouse. Once he decides you are gay, you are guilty, since he is enforcing his personal fucked-up morality and not Illinois law. Who but a cop offers $10 to a 40-year-old?"

Another twist on the "prostitution game" was explained to the author by female impersonator Tillie the Dirty Old Lady, arrested at the Chesterfield, 2829 N. Clark St.:

"I was at the Chesterfield about a year and a half and it got raided in March of 1966. It was all Mafia-owned, you know. There was a murder, and they found a guy in a trunk of a car, and everything the Mafia had anything to do with got raided and closed down. I went to jail for nine hours, and I was fingerprinted like I robbed a bank. The guy just jumped on stage and said, 'The house is under arrest.'

"They let the customers go, but everybody else had to stay. All they wanted was the people who worked there, the bartenders and the owner. We went to jail and all I did was wear a dress. Then they took us to court, and it was thrown out. I did not talk to the vice cops because they spread money all over the bar and they asked all the show girls to come up and have a drink with them. Well, they reversed it in court and said the girls were hustling them. So that's what they got them on, was hustling. I was sitting in the back and I didn't join them. All I was arrested for was being a member of a house of ill-repute.

"Back then it was terrible. You didn't dare touch anybody, on the shoulder even, or send a drink across the bar. You couldn't walk around with a drink in your hand, you had to be seated. If you wanted to move somewhere else, the bartender had to take your drinks wherever you were going. These cocksuckers today think all this came on a silver platter."

Nick D'Allesandro "owned" the Annex, 2835 N. Clark St., and the Chesterfield. Jim Henritze, a manager at the bar, described "payoffs" to the author:

"I was never in a raid. I did get busted once at the Chesterfield when I started. That was because Nick hadn't paid off. I was working a split shift from 4-8 and from 10-4 and I came in early and was setting up the bar and these two kids came in and ordered a beer. I served them a beer and all of a sudden two cops came in and went right over to them and checked their IDs. They were, supposedly, underage. The cops closed the bar and took me to the Town Hall. My statement was already written for me before I ever got there, because in those days you had to pay off. Nick had a bad habit of saying, 'I'll catch you tomorrow,' or he was going out the back door and they were coming in the front. He never wanted to pay his bills. He just stalled for long enough and he owed so much money that the only way to get him to pay was to bust him. Of course, it was all thrown out, it was just a set up deal.

"In fact, one time I was just starting work and a big black Cadillac pulled up outside and four or five guys from the outfit came in and they all walked back to the office. They emptied all the registers, the only thing they left was change. Then they all left. Nick hadn't been paying off his partners. That's how they got their money."

At 3:30 a.m. on September 8, 1969, police raided the Annex. In that month's *Mattachine Midwest Newsletter*, Kelley wrote:

"The lone patrolman arrested a 20-year-old whose name is unknown, and although he was apprehended while leaving the bar, he did not resist arrest, yet was handcuffed and led outside. Meanwhile, other officers, including at least two with gold braid indicating sergeant's rank or above, in three cars had mysteriously arrived. Some entered the bar, which in 5 minutes had almost emptied, and soon some customers emerged and cried, 'They're beating the shit out of some guy in there.' This reporter, who was then observing on the sidewalk, re-entered the bar to find two officers dragging a screaming customer from his overturned bar stool. His clothes were torn, but I witnessed no beating. The customer was kicking and yelling, 'What have I done? I haven't done anything,' and the officers were forcibly removing him. Once outside he continued resisting while being placed in a squad car, and an officer did aim several nightstick blows at him as he was trying to kick his way out.

"(At that hour, the customer may have been intoxicated and was obviously terrified of police in any case. Subsequent inquiry indicated that the only thing he appeared to have 'done' was to refuse and maybe argue when ordered by police to pick up his change and leave the nearly-deserted bar).

"In the meantime, a sergeant was trying to calm both the customer and the over-excited patrolman, who was yelling 'cocksucker' at the victim while wielding his nightstick. Having little success, the sergeant then called for handcuffs, and the original patrolman threatened me and other bystanders with arrest if we were still there when the paddy wagon came."

Again, on September 20, the cops raided the 21 Club (Legacy), 3042 W. Irving Park, arresting twelve and charging them with public indecency – defined in the October 1969 *Mattachine Midwest Newsletter* as "lewd fondling of the body in public," a law Chicago police applied to same-sex dancing, and even two men with their arms over each other's shoulders. In an interview with the author, one "Anonymous Gay Man" at the 21 Club raid, said:

> "I was talking to people and all of a sudden, 'Turn the lights up. Turn the lights back on.' Everybody's standing around. They come down and say, 'You over here. You over here. You on this side. You on this side. The rest of you get out.' So, we left. We watched across the street and the paddy wagon ... they put them all in the back."

Woodrow "Woody" I. Moser, the gay owner of the Legacy 21 Club, bailed all his customers out of jail, where they had languished for twelve hours. Moser then started a defense fund, holding a benefit cocktail party on October 12. Moser opened the Legacy 21 Club in 1961 and ran the bar with his partner, Jose Rodriguez, until he passed away on October 12, 1992. Rodriguez continued running the bar for a few more years. It's now long gone.

In the October 1969 *Mattachine Midwest Newsletter*, Jim Bradford and William B. Kelley wrote that a week after the 21 Club raid, the Blue Pub at 3059 W. Irving Park was also hit. Four men, including a bartender, were arrested. This was followed on October 9 by a raid at the Alameda Club, 5210 N. Sheridan Rd., another syndicate-connected bar. It was recently opened by Howie and Burt, who previously ran bars Club 69 and The Place, both closed down due to urban renewal.

The Blue Pub was a piano bar, famous for "The Two Black Georgia's." Old Marlene, a regular at the bar, told the author:

> "There was Georgia Owens and Georgia White. Georgia White was a thin woman that used to forget wearing underpants, and she'd pull up her dress and show everything that God gave her. That's the way it was! She was at Louis Gages, and the Blue Pub, well both Georgia's worked at the Blue Pub.
>
> "Georgia White died on a Sunday and her nephew picked her up late on a Saturday night, because she always stayed over time sitting around the piano. Then the bar [The Blue Pub] got a phone call the next morning that Georgia had passed on, so then we got the other Georgia [Owens]. She was working right by the Chicago Theater ... a long skinny bar, I can't think of the name of it. Anyway, Georgia Owens worked in a lot of gay bars over her lifetime too, but she was a jazz pianist. She didn't stay at the Blue Pub long because her boyfriend at the time ... they had a big car accident. When she came in, they had to have a mic for her because she didn't have a voice, whereas Georgia White you could hear her every place. But Georgia Owens didn't have a voice ... she's still alive, so I shouldn't say that, but she wasn't as good an entertainer as Georgia White. She was

raunchy and she was down to earth, where Georgia Owens was basically blues.

"Georgia White had a massive heart attack, she had cirrhosis of the liver and everything else. God knows that woman could out drink more than you and me and ten other guys in the bar. I didn't go to the funeral, Tom went ... that was the owner of the Blue Pub at the time ... he went, and the head bartender went. That was the only two.

"With her family, she had the nephew that used to pick her up in the car, drive her there and picked her up. Well, I assume her family knew what kind of bar she worked in. During the war she worked in factories, but after the war she started entertaining again."

Dr. Thomas Erwin Gertz remembers the Blue Pub:

"The guys would get in there and get a couple of drinks. They would sit around that bar and some of them would even sit on the bench with Georgia and say let's do *Hello Dolly* and how 'bout *Sound of Music* and we would just ask for a song and Georgia would just do them and, of course, when she had a few drinks she would do *Bye Bye Blackbird*. ... *Back your ass against the wall, here I come balls and all, bye bye cherry*. She'd say, 'It's too early, I need more to drink,' and I'd say, 'I'll buy you a drink.' And it'd be, 'It'll take more than one drink. No no, wait a while, later, later.' She obviously had to have a few drinks in her before she was comfortable singing and playing that, but you know ... well, when she did that, you could be walking down the street outside and it sounded like a choral group inside, and that would be outside on the street, just coming from inside. The guys were just ... it was just a fun place as far as Georgia went."

In response to the bar raids, Jim Bradford, the Mattachine Midwest president, wrote in the *Mattachine Midwest Newsletter*, "THE NEW MILITANCY EMERGES":

"In addition to our letter to the new head of the vice squad, I wrote to Police Superintendent Conlisk and Mayor Daley, restating our position that 'these raids are harassing techniques and not legitimate law enforcement activities. They cannot be explained away on any legal or legitimate basis. ... We will not be put off with attempts to justify these raids; we demand their end, now.' Furthermore: 'We are prepared to force the Department legally to restrict its activities to legitimate, non-harassing enforcement acts. We hope that the same equitable result can be accomplished by reason, short of legal action, but we also wish to serve notice that the time has come for us to say that the harassment and abuse are at an end.'

"I am quite serious about following through on this. If we do not get satisfaction from the Mayor and the Police Department, we will have to file suits and engage in public picketing."

After the October 1969 bar raids, the harassment ceased. Old-timers put this down to the fact that one of Mayor Richard J. Daley's sons was allegedly scooped up in the raid on Legacy 21. Not his first arrest at a gay venue, but his third. Eyewitnesses claim he was also arrested at a raid on Louis Gage's Fun Lounge on February 25, 1964, and May 3, 1964, at a private party at 20 E. Goethe Street. Whatever the truth, Mayor Daley's son was never charged, and the gay bar raids stopped for a while.

The raid on the Legacy 21 Club made it to the courtroom seven months later. The following article, written by David Stienecker, appeared in the June 1970 *Mattachine Midwest Newsletter*:

"A long-delayed trial of 12 persons arrested September 20, 1969 at the Club 21 (Now Legacy) began on May 18. The first 1 1/2 days were spent trying to pick a jury. By noon of the second day only eight jurors had been chosen. It was then decided to waive the jury and go ahead with the case. An MM Officer was in court to hear the testimony of one of the vice patrolmen. The crap that was spilled forth went something like 'He had an erection, I could tell because of the bulge in his pants.' It was pointed out by attorney Paul Goldman that the officer could not tell if the man in question had a bulge unless he had seen the size of the arrestees genitalia beforehand. Another example of such questionable testimony occurred when a policeman testified that a man 5' 2" was rubbing genitals with a man 5' 10." There's a neat trick if you can do it.

"The case against the bar owners and the employees (keeping a disorderly house) was dismissed. Eight patrons had been charged with public indecency. One, a sailor, had his case dismissed (the Navy took over). Another, a German immigrant, had his case reduced to 'disorderly conduct,' then pleaded guilty and was fined $100. Of the other six, five pleaded guilty to the public indecency charges and fined $100. One stood it alone and pleaded innocent, but in the absence of witnesses on his behalf, and because of the police testimony, he was found guilty and fined like the others. The last defendant still has the option of appealing.

"According to Goldman and the MM observer, the judge in the case, Irwin Field, was fair in his conduct of the trial and distinguished himself by his restrained demeanor. What a shame the defendants didn't stick together and beat this rap. We hope that those who pleaded guilty realize that they are furthering the corrupt system under which we are subjugated.

"The bar owner now has to appear before the liquor commission June 1. We wish him the best of luck."

In the spring of 1972, police brutality again hit the headlines, this time against African Americans and other minorities. On April 6, the Rev. Ralph Abernathy, national president of the Southern Christian Leadership Conference, called for "an investigation of and nonviolent action against police brutality in Chicago." He went on to say, "Studies have shown Chicago to be the worst city in the nation for police brutality. This has meant that more black people are killed by police in Chicago than in any other city in the United States." Some black leaders called for the resignation of Police Supt. James B. Conlisk, including Andrew C. Barrett, an official of the National Association for the Advancement of Colored People, and Renault Robinson of the Afro-American Patrolman's League. In a series of raucous "police-citizen community meetings," the *Chicago Tribune* wrote that Conlisk faced "serious accusations that policemen harass and brutalize citizens, take bribes, and prey upon those who cannot speak English," and that "police are derelict in responding to calls, fail to curb street gangs and dope, lack adequate racial and ethnic representation in their ranks, and need more foot patrolmen."

On June 1, Conlisk presided over a community meeting in the heavily gay Town Hall District. The following day the *Chicago Tribune* headline read, "Youth Harass Conlisk." An estimated 100 of the 400 people in the gymnasium of St. Andrew's Catholic Church, 110 W. Addison, were young protestors from a group called Rising Up Angry, who repeatedly shouted "pig, tell us about brutality, that's a pack of lies," and demanded an end to police harassment of longhairs and gays. Ronald Rae, commander of the Town Hall District, didn't help matters when he suggested gays should be called "sads" because their suicide rate was twice that of the rest of the population. Rae was a retired army reserve colonel, a former head of the police bomb and arson squad.

The *Chicago Tribune* reported that a slender, bearded young man, jumped to his feet and screamed, "I demand you apologize. The reason the suicide rate is so high is that we are being denied our constitutional rights."

Six months later, the front-page headline on the *Mattachine Midwest Newsletter* read, "Justice 24, Cops 0":

> "The gay community should rejoice at the news of the indictment of 24 policemen from the Chicago Avenue District for two reasons: The alleged activities have been a major source of intimidation and exploitation of patrons of gay bars in that district for some time and the list of names included in the indictment contains at least three cops who have become well-known to Mattachine Midwest and the gay community as a result of persistent complaints about them from people who claim that they had

been falsely arrested, usually for alleged 'solicitation for prostitution' and usually in the same geographical area of Chicago (LaSalle Street – Division Street – Chicago Avenue – Michigan Avenue).

"These policemen are Patrolman Edward McGee, on the force since 1956, now assigned to the Jefferson Park District; Steve L. Seno, a patrolman since 1955, who was suspended in November 1972; and Confesor Troche, a patrolman since 1961, still assigned to the Chicago Avenue District."

The scandal and cleanup of the Chicago Police Department remained in the headlines for the rest of the year. Chicago's gay community had been a lucrative cash cow for corrupt police and politicians for decades. The cash now dried up as, for the first time, gay bar owners fought back. A headline in a December 1972 *Chicago Tribune* read, "Take set at 'hundreds of thousands.' Traffic Chief Braasch among 24 in graft indictment." ... "Twenty-four present or former Chicago policemen, including Traffic Chief Clarence E. Braasch, were named yesterday as members of a police extortion racket that allegedly solicited payoffs of 'hundreds of thousands of dollars from at least 53 taverns in the Near North Side Chicago Avenue district in recent years."

Braasch and the others were suspended effective 12:01 p.m. January 1, 1973. The following day the *Chicago Tribune* noted the investigation was extended to include the Brighton Park and Town Hall Districts. The latter included the gay neighborhood on Clark Street north of Diversey Parkway.

It was no secret in Chicago's gay community that the mob had a stake in most of the gay bars and the cops were shaking them down. Patrolmen were handed packages openly in front of customers. In the early-1960s, Blondina worked at the Shoreline 7 at 7 W. Division. In an interview with the author, he said:

"I did drag, and I did the payoffs. I always had white envelopes, since I had the front door, the police captains and the police officials and the politicians would come in and I would hand them their envelopes. I never looked inside but I knew it was a lot of money, there were a lot of payoffs there. We had big names come in there, a lot of them. The back was more reserved for syndicate men and their girlfriends, or cops or politicians."

However, it wasn't until 1973, when US Attorney James R. Thompson investigated tavern shakedowns, that cop pay-offs became public knowledge. (Thompson later became Governor of Illinois 1977-1991). In the *Chicago Gay Crusader*, William B. Kelley reported forty-seven cops from three districts had been indicted. Many of the taverns involved were gay-owned or had a gay clientele.

The trial of Braasch and his co-conspirators from the East Chicago Avenue Police District began in August. Braasch, charged with extortion and perjury, denied any knowledge of the shakedowns. US Atty. Thompson gave four officers immunity in return for evidence: John Cello, Edward Rifkin, Lowell Napier, and Salvatore Mascolino. Cello told the court he conducted shakedowns of bars in the nightclub-heavy Rush St. area beginning in 1964. The payoffs were dubbed the "vice package" and tavern owners were referred to as "members of the vice club." The "club" dated back to previous East Chicago Avenue Police District Commanders John McDermott and Walter Maurovich, with a brief hiatus of eight months in 1966 when Comdr. James Holzman took over and cleaned up the district. In August 1966, Police Supt. James B. Conlisk Jr. appointed Capt. Braasch who, at the request of his underlings, approved the "vice club" reinstatement on condition he had final approval of its members.

The vice club worked like this: After a tavern was targeted, police visited several times in one evening brandishing shotguns, checking liquor licenses, and lining customers up against a wall to check IDs. Later the owner was invited to join the "vice club" and told the harassment would end, and police would "slant" reports of any trouble on the premises. The tavern owners had no choice. Each bar paid upwards of $100 a month, with the profits shared between the vice cops, Capt. Braasch, and deputy superintendents at police headquarters. Although not mentioned in court, there was a suspicion a percentage went to Supt. Conlisk himself. The beat vice cops each raked in up to $250 a month, while Braasch's share was estimated at $3,710 a month. Mayor Daley defended Conlisk, and suggested payoffs were a two-way street and tavern owners should take some of the responsibility. In September, the *Chicago Tribune* reported that State's Atty. Bernard Carey accused Daley of hatching a plan to intimidate the tavern owners by revoking their liquor licenses:

> "'It is one more example of Daley's technique of thwarting and downgrading the work of my office and the United States attorney's office to end corruption, and it will not work,' said Carey. 'I am pledging full protection to any witness who will come forward to testify about illegal activities by police. I can and will see that such a witness need fear no retaliation from the crooked police or from their political pals. I urge the citizens of Chicago to cast aside fear and come forward to join us in this effort.'"

Assured of their safety, tavern owners, or their representatives, came forward to testify. One exception, according to the September *Chicago Gay Crusader*, was Ira Gruenberg, the owner of the Nite Life, 933 N. State St., who was indicted for perjury after he denied making payoffs. As this mob-controlled nightclub had hosted drag shows going back to the 1940s, his claim seemed unlikely. Gruenberg later testified and the charges against him were dropped. Nearly every gay bar on the Near North Side from 1966-1970 was named as a victim, including the popular King's Ransom, and New Jamie's, 1110 N. Clark St. On August 17, the *Chicago Tribune* updated the growing list of taverns lined up to testify, including the gay/straight bar Hayride (Wagon Wheel), 1001 N. Clark St., and the gay Ifs, Ands or Burt's, 5 W. Superior St. – amusingly misspelled Ifs, Ands and *Butts* by the *Chicago Tribune*. Norbert Springer, a bartender at both bars, told the court of regular payoffs of $100 a month at the Hayride and between $150-$300 at Ifs, Ands and Burt's.

Salvatore Strazzante, a former assistant state's attorney who resigned his post when called to testify, said he paid $100 a month, over a three-year period, on behalf of his father, the owner of the King's Ransom. Myron Minuskin, a former Chicago assistant corporation counsel, admitted he acted as lawyer and payoff conduit for Claudia Murphy, owner of the Inner Circle. He also admitted charging Murphy fees for making the shakedown payments and failing to report the money on his tax returns. Others who came forward were Charles "Chuck" Renslow, who told of his payoffs at the Gold Coast, 501 N. Clark St., and Gerry's Club, 2265 N. Lincoln Ave; Julius and Walter Fleishman, brothers who operated Sam's, 1205 N. Clark St. and the Normandy, 744 N. Rush St.; Nick Argiris, former assistant manager of Bently's, 640 N. State St.; and representatives from Alfie's, 900 N. Rush St.; the Baton, 430 N. Clark St.; the Haig, 800 N. Dearborn; Togetherness, 61 E. Hubbard St.; the Croydon Circle Lounge, 616 N. Rush St.; and the Baron Lounge, 629 N. Clark St. Argiris of Bently's, who paid $100 a month to Salvatore Mascolino, told the court, "The way the laws are in Illinois, they can close you up any time they want to. They call it a setup." He explained that he paid up because he didn't want police harassing his homosexual clientele, "If any police officer would walk in, everybody would walk out."

As the trial of Capt. Braasch and his crooked vice officers continued, the extent of Chicago police corruption became all too clear. State's Atty. Thompson expanded his investigations into police districts in Austin, Town Hall, Englewood, and Foster Ave. On October 5, 1973, Braasch was found guilty of extortion and perjury, along with eighteen of his former cops. Two months later Braasch was sentenced to six years in prison. On October 10, Mayor Richard J. Daley announced the resignation of Police Supt. Conlisk for "personal reasons." In his place, Daley promoted Act. Supt. James M.

Rochford, who created a new Office of Professional Standards, staffed partly by civilians, to investigate brutality and corruption charges.

In February 1974, Austin district former police Capt. Mark Thanasouras was sentenced to 3 1/2 years in prison and fined $20,000 for his part in tavern shakedowns. He served eighteen months. In July 1977, he was gunned down on a Chicago street execution-style. Thirteen of Thanasouras' men were convicted of extorting $150,000 from thirty taverns and $125,000 to permit gambling in the district. Only one gay bar was mentioned in that case, the Blue Dahlia, who paid $300 a month from 1966-1970. US Attorney Thompson continued his investigations in the Town Hall district. Though no gay bars were mentioned in the case, in the 1960s, at least three were paying off the police: the Chesterfield, the Annex, and the Orange Cockatoo, 2850 N. Clark St.

On April 18, 1974, Eugene J. Benjamin, former vice-coordinator for the Town Hall district, was indicted, pleaded guilty to extortion charges and sentenced to one year in prison. No tears were shed in the gay community, as Benjamin persecuted gays as far back as 1968. According to the *Mattachine Midwest Newsletter*, on May 31 of that year, Benjamin and another officer raided Molly's, a popular non-alcoholic teen hangout at 2935 N. Broadway. The owners and patrons were charged. The crime was same-sex dancing. When the defendants appeared in Holiday Court, all the charges were dismissed. Undeterred, Benjamin returned to Molly's the following night and warned the owners he would return later, and if he saw two boys dancing together he would raid the premises again.

An October 1973 article by Bob Wiedrich in the *Chicago Tribune* begins:

> "SCHOLARS SEEKING a textbook example of the unholy alliance between crooked police, politicians, and mobsters need look no farther than Chicago's North Side.
>
> "For there, in a network of 20 nightclubs and bars catering to the specialized recreational needs of homosexuals, the mutually avaricious interests of these groups are interwoven in a tragic tapestry of corruption.
>
> "In short, thieving lawmen and politicos have joined forces with crime syndicate gangsters to prey upon some of society's most vulnerable members – the gay people.
>
> "...THRU TWO years of surveillances, investigators have identified Joseph DiVarco as the crime syndicate's overlord of the growing maze of gay bars on the North Side. Repeatedly, he has staged meetings with hoodlum backed tavern operators at the same locations at which he has also rendezvoused with corrupt police."

## CHICAGO AFTER STONEWALL

Wiedrich goes on to suggest that "other hoodlum groups in the gay bar business" included members of the Boulahanis clan of mobsters on the West Side.

# 2
# CHICAGO'S GAY LIBERATION FRONT VS. POLICE SGT. JOHN MANLEY JR.

While Mattachine Midwest considered picketing, the seeds of a more radical gay liberation group germinated on the South Side of Chicago. On October 3, 1969, Henry Weimhoff, a student at the University of Chicago, placed a classified ad in the ROOMMATES WANTED section of *Maroon*, the student newspaper. It read, "2 Gay Students Wanted to Share 5 Rm Unfrn. Apt. (53$^{rd}$ & Harper) $52 & Utils. 955-7433. (Keep Trying)." The handful of students who answered the ad, in turn, collectively placed another ad in the October 24 *Maroon*, "GAY POWER IN 69-70 Anyone interested in joining the Hyde Park Homophile League write Box 69, c/o Maroon. Replies kept confidential." Two months later the group renamed itself the University of Chicago Gay Liberation Front (UC-GLF). However, Gay Lib wasn't the first homosexual student group. *Time*, on May 12, 1967, reported on students at Columbia University in New York who formed the Student Homophile League (SHL), the first gay organization to receive university recognition. The SHL, who claimed not to be a social group, but purely educational, argued homosexuals were "unjustly, inhumanly and savagely discriminated against" in the US. They planned to fight for the right of homosexuals "to live and to work with his fellow man as an equal." Organizers of SHL remained anonymous. As one of them reasoned, "We would be losing jobs for the rest of our lives."

*Time* noted other students were tolerant of the group. One sophomore commented, "As long as they don't bother the rest of us, it's O.K." However, the anonymity of the group's members caused problems, as some students asked, "How do you treat them equally when you don't know who they are?" It later transpired that a bisexual student named Stephen Donaldson founded the League two years earlier. The organization received an official charter on April 19, 1967. Publicity given to SHL led to a similar group forming at Cornell University in March 1968, then others around the country. After the Stonewall Riots, Columbia's Student Homophile League changed its name to the Gay Liberation Front.

After two weeks of meeting for lunch at the Blue Gargoyle café, the newly formed UC-GLF went public on January 21, 1970, when members participated in a 45-minute round table discussion on WHPK, 88.3 FM. The topics included "the oppression of the homosexual in society, the gay student on campus, and the formation of a militant gay organization." Two days later the first direct action took place when nine UC-GLF members danced with members of their own sex at a "straight" campus dance. Reactions from the "straights" ranged from mildly amused to staring and pointing, but there was no violence. Though it seems tame now, same-sex dancing was revolutionary in Chicago, where police considered it "indecent behavior," reason enough to be arrested for obscenity.

The next UC–GLF action was against Police Sgt. John Manley Jr., a notorious cop who for years lurked in the dark urinals of restrooms in Lincoln Park, entrapping hundreds of gay men. In the September 1969 *Mattachine Midwest Newsletter*, David Stienecker, the editor, penned a humorous piece suggesting Officer Manley might be "getting off" on the toilet arrests. In the next issue a photograph of the undeniably handsome cop appeared and another warning about his nefarious activities. On February 7, 1970, Manley arrested Stienecker at his home and charged him with "criminal defamation." At Foster Avenue police station Stienecker was denied a phone call to the ACLU and spent four hours being processed, then released on $25 bond. By all accounts, Manley was visibly shaken when Stienecker pleaded innocent and fought the charges; homosexuals never fought back in Mayor Richard J. Daley's Chicago. On May 6, after three Kafkaesque court appearances, Stienecker and Renee Hanover, his lesbian lawyer, turned up a fourth time to be told the case was dismissed.

The day before Stienecker's arrest, a headline in the *Maroon* read, "Gay Lib Protests Talk by Detective." The article, written by Nancy Chisman, began, "Gay liberation front, a registered student activity group, has drafted a letter of protest to the Women's Bar Association (WBA) of Illinois over the appearance of Police Detective John Manley at a forthcoming meeting." Manley was giving a talk on juvenile crime. Copies of the GLF letter were sent to Ralla Klepak, attorney at law, and chairperson of the legal education committee of the WBA of Illinois, and M. Lois Dierstein, the president. It read:

"Dear Friend:

"It has come to our attention that Officer Manley of the Chicago Police Department is to address the Women's Bar Association of Illinois on February 25, 1970. We are concerned that your organization may have extended this invitation to Officer Manley without knowledge of his activities in relation to the gay community of Chicago.

"In addition to his work with the Youth Division of the Chicago Police Department, Officer Manley has been engaged, in recent summers, in the arresting of homosexuals in the Lincoln Park area. His devotion to duty has often resulted in the arrests of in excess of a dozen people per day on charges of public indecency. Many arrestees have reported that Manley falsely arrested them, charging them with public indecency when nothing more than a conversation had occurred. According to arrestees, events leading to their arrests have followed this pattern: Approaching his intended victim inside Lincoln Park restrooms, or in some cases outside of them, Manley would behave suggestively, engage his victim in conversation and then charge him with 'public indecency.'

"After making a conquest Officer Manley is free to go on to his next, but what of his victims? For the victims of Officer Manley's over-zealous and twisted crusade against the city's homosexuals, their arrest doesn't simply end with a costly legal defense, a jail term or fine. For those who are forced by social stigma to lead double lives, the consequences are often devastating as loss of job, severed family ties, and even apartment eviction (no legislation protects the civil rights of homosexuals).

"The Women's Bar Association would be well advised to concern itself with the problem of how society's degrading attitudes and irrational fears in regard to homosexuality can be corrected, rather than to honor a man who gets his kicks through the persecution of the victims of this oppression. Harassment of homosexuals by the police should not be tolerated.

"In militant resistance to our oppression, Gay Liberation appeals to the Women's Bar Association to rescind its invitation to Officer Manley and stand with us in oppressing the injustices that homosexuals suffer at the hands of society at large and specifically at the hands of the Chicago Police Department.

"In the struggle for Gay Liberation.
Nancy Garwood, Co-Chairman
Step May
William Dry"

## CHICAGO AFTER STONEWALL

The night before Manley spoke, UC-GLF held a supper meeting at Ida Noyes Hall, a three-story neo-Gothic building on the university campus, to map out a strategy for the following day's protest. Among those attending was George Mandrenas, an activist from San Francisco's ONE Inc., a more conservative gay group. Mandrenas called UC-GLF's Step May, said he was in town and would like to make contact with Gay Lib. May invited Mandrenas to the meeting. There, Mandrenas spoke to a woman called Alice, who explained Manley's history of arresting and fabricating evidence against homosexuals. It wasn't until the following day on the picket line they realized George Mandrenas was an infiltrator, none other than the target of their protest, Police Sgt. John Manley Jr. In the April 1970 *Chicago Journalism Review*, Ron Dorfman wrote:

> "Mandrenas was greeted cheerily next day when he arrived in front of the Bar Association building on La Salle Street, until older gays informed the students that Mandrenas was the hated Manley himself. Upstairs, after his speech, Manley informed reporters: 'I don't have anything against these people. Why, I even had dinner with them last night.'"

When asked to comment on UC-GLF's concerns, Manley told the *Chicago Journalism Review*, "I'm honored, that they feel I have the compelling personality to induce people to commit public indecency."

On March 3, 1970, the *Maroon* noted that after "Mandrenas" left the meeting at Ida Noyes Hall, Police Officer Charles Glass, Manley's sidekick, walked in and asked UC-GLF members for the names of people Manley had falsely arrested. Angered by the incident, and a little shamefaced, UC-GLF wrote to Capt. Harry Ervanian, director of the police internal inspections division, questioning the legality of Manley's covert infiltration of their meeting and Glass' attempt to collect members' names and addresses.

Manley had an "in" with Mayor Daley's political machine. He was the son of John J. "Cap'n Jack" Manley, the director of the Port of Chicago. After only four years as a cop, Supt. James B. Conlisk promoted Manley to sergeant. He had already made the news under the headline, "Hippie Killed by Policemen in Old Town." On August 22, 1968, Manley fatally shot seventeen years old Native American Dean Johnson of Sioux Falls, SD, after the youth allegedly fired a .32 revolver at Manley and officer Frank Szwedo after being stopped for a curfew violation. Johnson, described by the *Chicago Tribune* as "dressed as a hippie with long hair and beads," was in Chicago to protest the Vietnam War at the 1968 Democratic National Convention. The shooting occurred at North and Wells Sts., a few blocks from protestors gathered in Lincoln Park, the epicenter of the first night of riots. A year later, Manley was again involved in a shoot-out with a youth in the same area. An article in the *Chicago Police Star* (the official publication of the Chicago Police Department) reads:

> "In the early morning, Youth Officers Frank Szwedo, * 10968, Youth Area # 5, and John Manley, *2427, Youth Area #6, stopped two youths for curfew investigation at North and Wells. One youth produced a draft card to prove that he was 18. The other youth reached into a duffel bag, drew a gun and fired point blank at the officers and then ran. Manley received a powder burn on his arm. The officers shouted for him to halt. Instead, the youth turned and again aimed his gun at the officers but was fatally wounded before he could shoot. The other youth was arrested and searched and found to be carrying a large bowie knife. He was charged with unlawful use of weapon."

According to the *Chicago Journalism Review*, even Manley's fellow cops didn't like him. They resented his rapid rise to sergeant, thought to be the result of his father pulling strings. One colleague said Manley was "hung up about being a cop and will lie and phony-up arrests to make a record." After UC-GLF picketed Manley's WBA speech, parents of two GLF members received anonymous letters outing their children to them. The poison pen writer suggested that hassling a Chicago police officer was "a dangerous activity." Also, the UC Student Activities Office began receiving threatening calls from "a man from San Francisco" asking for names and addresses of UC-GLF members.

In 1993, John Manley was in the news again. On March 2, a *Chicago Tribune* headline read, "City cops taking on sex harassment":

> "A film in production by the Chicago Police Department explores sexual harassment, with officers of both sexes acting out such misconduct.
>
> "The 15-minute video, to be shown this spring at shift roll calls in all 25 police districts, is the latest of three initiatives by Police Supt. Matt Rodriguez to inform and sensitize the department's 12,434 officers to the problem.
>
> "It may seem too much of a touchy-feely method for such an iron-fisted profession, but sexual harassment is becoming a serious issue for many law enforcement agencies. The Chicago-area office of the federal Bureau of Alcohol, Tobacco and Firearms recently announced plans to give nearly 200 agents sensitivity training after a controversy over a sexual harassment complaint led to the transfer of the agent in charge.
>
> "...Allegations of sexual misconduct filed by a female police lieutenant surfaced last month after she complained to the department's internal

affairs division that her watch commander, a male captain, had made unwelcome and lewd sexual remarks to her.

"Capt. John J. Manley, a 27-year veteran, has responded to the internal enquiry by suing Lt. Vickie Huber [-Zoch] in Cook County Circuit Court, charging she defamed his character. He seeks an injunction and $2 million in damages from Huber [-Zoch], a 12-year veteran. Both officers are assigned to the Foster Avenue District.

"While Manley is acting as his own lawyer, Huber [-Zoch] is represented by attorneys Candace Wayne and Wayne's husband, John Jemilo, a former first deputy superintendent of the Chicago Police Department."

According to a *Chicago Tribune* article on April 28, 1994, this was the first case of sexual harassment charges aimed at a ranking member of a large Midwestern police force. A hearing was held in front of a Civil Service judge at police headquarters in response to a petition by Supt. Rodriguez to seek the firing of Capt. Manley:

"Among the accusations against Manley ... are that he frequently engaged in sexually explicit language to loudly harass female officers, solicited them for sexual favors and crudely joked about sex while presiding at change-of-shift roll-call formations at the Foster Avenue District.

"...Four female officers, led by Lt. Vickie Huber-Zoch, testified how fear of reprisal kept them silent about Manley. They remained quiet, they said, even when he rebuked them as 'bimbos, bitches and whores'; solicited them for sex; or threatened to shoot one of them, claiming she had been late to roll call when she wasn't.

"Huber-Zoch, a 13-year veteran, said the final straw for her came when she said Manley shoved a clipboard into her stomach, after asking her to have sex with him and getting rebuffed.

"'He very commonly referred to a woman as a psychic bitch; he loved to attack (women's) mental capacity,' Huber-Zoch told Manley's prosecutor, Assistant Corporation Counsel Paulette Petretti."

In August, the situation escalated when "Six Chicago police officers filed a sweeping series of sexual harassment charges against the Chicago Police Department seeking $14 million in damages. They placed blame on the inadequate response to the charges by Supt. Matt Rodriguez and two dozen top brass rank-and-file officers." In the *Chicago Tribune*, Jan Ferris wrote:

"The suit, filed in federal court on behalf of four female and two male officers, alleges ongoing harassment by certain members of the Marquette and Foster Avenue District stations, and a list of retaliatory measures against those who have spoken out against the alleged abuses.

"The harassment has ranged from crude sexual jokes to explicit posters and other pornographic materials, the suit charges. Retaliation against whistle-blowers has included poor job reviews, a reassignment to clean toilets, suspensions and threats of termination ...

"...The lawsuit accuses Rodriguez and other top-ranking officers of failing to adequately train and supervise employees."

Capt. John Manley was fired in 1995 after an internal police investigation into the harassment allegations.

In 2015, a 72-years old Manley was again in trouble for impersonating a government official. Jason Meisner in the *Chicago Tribune* wrote:

"...Manley had parked his blue Dodge in the media parking lot (near the Dirksen U.S. Courthouse at 219 S. Dearborn St.) ... and left the vehicle unattended for more than two hours with police-style lights flashing in the rear window, records show.

"Confronted by security officers when he returned to the car, Manley claimed he was a 'special agent' with the U.S. Maritime Service responsible for seizing boats on the Great Lakes, according to court records. He produced a gold badge that turned out to be a fake, prompting U.S. Marshals to take him for questioning."

# 3
# GLF DANCES VS. THE GAY BARS

On February 17, 1970, UC-GLF increased their public profile when four members, Libby, Richard Chinn, Michelle Brody, and Stephen "Step" May appeared live on the *Stan Dale Show*, WBBM-FM, answering two hours of questions from listeners. Dale was a radio broadcaster, author of books on sexuality, and founder of the Human Awareness Institute in 1968. Two days later, UC-GLF's Henry Weimhoff joined Mattachine Midwest's Jim Bradford and lesbian author Valerie Taylor on Studs Terkel's one-hour radio program, *Wax Museum* on WFMT-FM. The latter was the first joint action between Mattachine Midwest and the Gay Liberation Front, the new radical kid on the block. Mattachine first noted UC-GLF in the November/December 1969 *Mattachine Midwest Newsletter*:

> "The Homophile Liberation Alliance [Later UC-GLF)] announces its formation as an organization 'composed mostly of young liberal/radical homosexuals/bisexuals' ... .We will involve ourselves not only in the fight for homophile rights but also for all oppressed peoples, i.e. Blacks, Chicanos, Puerto Ricans, Indians, Asian-Americans, etc. The HLA will take definite positions on questions such as the war in Vietnam, urban renewal, pollution, corrupt politics, and all matters which affect our community as well as the heterosexual majority."

For more information, *Mattachine Midwest Newsletter* urged readers to contact Richard Chinn, 2510 S. Sawyer Ave.

In the *Chicago Seed* "Gay Liberation Supplement" in the March 1970 issue, UC-GLF activist Murray Edelman writes:

"We must work toward creating a gay consciousness, a realization of suppressed desires and feelings. Adjusting to homosexuality means habitually denying the desires to dance or even to be completely honest with others. We must not allow specific issues like the right to dance in public or even in our own bars to remain ignored. We could focus our efforts on one specific issue – DANCE!"

The first GLF dance took place on February 21 at Pierce Tower on the University of Chicago campus. Six hundred and sixty people attended. On April 4 a second dance drew twice that number. Both proved a huge success, bringing in much needed cash for the newly set-up bail fund. The March 1970 *Chicago Seed* wrote of the first dance, "It was a far cry from the cold, crowded, and impersonal North-Side gay bars. If you give gay people a chance to dance, touch each other, and talk freely, they behave like 'respectable' human beings."

Sadly, two on-campus gay dances didn't sit well with the university authorities. An editorial in the April 14, 1970 *Maroon* began, "We were disturbed by the recent announcement by Edward Turkington, director of student housing, that Gay Liberation will no longer be allowed to hold dances in University residences as student activities. The reasons given for the decision were that Gay Lib dances attract too many non-University people."

The paper noted there were no security problems at either dance – no fights, no stolen coats or property. The university's decision to eliminate the dances is "weak-willed at best, discriminatory at worst," wrote the *Maroon*:

> "There are scores of University functions that attract large numbers of non-University personnel. Are we to eliminate films, concerts, religious services, etc. that attract non-University personnel? All dances and similar social events attract people from Hyde Park; we do not feel that this is reason for prohibiting these events, nor do we think Gay Lib should be specially penalized rather than the other campus groups that sponsor dances.
>
> "We must feel that the University is either not thinking clearly in this matter, or that they are actually afraid of something other than what they state, such as a raid by the Chicago vice squad. Members of Gay Lib are fighting an uphill battle for acceptance of a way of life our society condemns. We have been heartened by the enthusiasm and tolerance exhibited so far by all students both gay and straight, and think that it would be a great shame if the University were to cast the first stone."

In a letter to UC-GLF's Step May, Turkington estimated 70 percent of those attending the two on-campus gay dances were non-students. He pointed out the University's policy that dances were restricted to those affiliated with the University and other events like films and concerts held at Rockefeller Chapel or Mandell Hall were open to the public. In the April 17, 1970, *Maroon*, Turkington was backed-up by Skip Landt, the director of student activities, who said:

> "The lack of facilities on campus for large crowds requires restricting events to those which would draw an audience primarily from the University community. There are tax problems involved that necessitate the use of University facilities only by members of the University. Because it is an educational institution, the University receives a tax discount on their buildings."

Landt told UC-GLF if they wanted to hold dances on-campus, the leaders would have to sign a pledge promising not to advertise off-campus. They would also have to devise a security plan to ensure that non-university people couldn't gain entry. In response to the ban, UC-GLF canceled an upcoming event. Spokesperson Susan Tosswill explained, "We decided to drop it because we can't deal with another hassle right now."

In the April 24 *Maroon,* Murray Edelman wrote a letter to the editor:

> "What is the evidence that non-UC people attended this dance? Neither of our oppressors – Turkington or Landt – attended the dance. Are they basing their judgment on just gossip? ... Landt said in the *Maroon* that he 'would be concerned if a very substantial minority of the audience in any on-campus event were non students.'
>
> "Why is he only concerned about Gay-Lib activities? A substantial portion of the audience is non-University for services at Rockefeller Chapel and concerts at Bond Chapel and Mandel Hall. (Perhaps Gay Lib should check ID's at these events).
>
> "We demand some evidence why our activities deserve special restriction. The University should check all ID's at either ALL of the campus events or at NONE of the campus events."

The unofficial UC-GLF response was to hold a guerilla dance in the Fred Hampton Gym on May 16. Organized by Step May, the dance was a protest against the oppression of all people and half of the 600 who attended were non-University guests. UC-GLF's third dance was held at the Coliseum Ballroom, 1513 South Wabash Ave., on April 18 and was the first city-wide Gay-In. It was a huge success, with 2,000 gay men and lesbians attending. However, organizing the event was fraught with problems, one being that the Coliseum required insurance. David Thierry explained in the April 28, 1970, *Chicago Gay Liberation Newsletter,* "Insurance was denied us by companies throughout the United States. A faggot dance was too big a risk! ... Thanks to a black broker, a brother, we got the insurance and the hall on the 17th, the day before the dance. The policy came from California, from the company that insured the Black Muslim convention."

Thierry thanked lawyers Jonathan Smith, Renee Hanover, and the ACLU, for dealing with the Chicago vice squad who, supporting the bar owners who paid them kickbacks, threatened to raid the dance and charge everyone with "public indecency." The lawyers pointed out that same-sex dancing wasn't illegal and that it wasn't indecent. In preparation for a possible raid, lawyers, law students, and the press attended the dance "in drag as gays" to act as witnesses. The first openly gay public dance in Chicago went off without a hitch. There were no arrests.

The Coliseum dance was a protest, a boycott of the Mafia-owned gay bars. The GLF gave the bar owners a list of demands, that they should allow same-sex dancing and drop their drink prices – gay bars charged more for drinks than straight bars. David Thierry continued:

> "We asked those at the dance to boycott the bars for one night. Instead, they went to the bars after the dance, willing and eager to suck their oppressor's cock, begging to be screwed again. They'll continue to go to the bars until they realize that gay = faggot = nigger. They'll get themselves together when they're ready to be recognized as men, not the nigras they are to the bar owners. Uncle Tom it to the bars, brothers, but remember what you are in the eyes of the vice, the bars, the syndicate. End self-hatred. Think about what you mean to yourself, to those of us who offer freedom. Forget your massa's voice and listen to your own. It's telling you to come out. The revolution has just begun."

The primary focus of GLF was to force gay bars to allow same-sex dancing. The Normandy Inn on Rush St., the largest gay bar in the city, held 500-600 people. On April 24 and 25, 1970, the Normandy was picketed. The protest emptied the bar. On April 29, the Bar Committee of GLF met with Wally and Jerry Fleischmann, the owners of the Normandy. They promised to "do everything in their power" to obtain a dancing license. They would apply for it on April 30 and, if granted, the bar would allow dancing. If not granted, they promised to fight for it. In Northwestern University Special Collections, a GLF leaflet entitled "What the hell does Gay Lib think it's doing?" reads, "The oppressive atmosphere of the Normandy must be removed. The right to dance, any tempo, any style, is thus a crucial step towards our personal and collective liberation."

The boycott was suspended until May 15. On May 14, both parties met again, by which time the bar owners had acquired a license and agreed to allow same-sex dancing, both slow and fast. They also threw out the draconian dress code. Customers could now wear sunglasses, sleeveless T-shirts, and shorts in the bar. All were previously banned. Other concessions included banning discrimination against women, a pledge that drink prices would remain the same. There would be no minimum, no cover, and no pressure on customers to buy drinks. Prior to this, customers at the Normandy were required to cradle a drink in their hands at all times.

The following night, gays danced together for the first time in the Normandy. Still, when a slow number was played and couples drew closer, security stepped in and separated them. The owners reneged on the deal and the no-touching rule was reinstated. The Fleischmann brothers explained that a new district police commander started that morning and they were waiting to see where he stood on the matter. The call went out from GLF, "Now it's time for some gay power! This Friday night (22nd) is D-Day! Invade the Normandy! Join us and dance (any way you want to)! ... Do it! Dance! Brothers and sisters, dance!" On May 21, the Fleischmanns backed down and permitted slow dancing. The final action against the Normandy occurred July 31, 1970 when GLF and the newly formed Black Caucus (later renamed Third World Gay Revolutionaries), picketed the bar after the owners initiated a $2 minimum to keep out the "riff-raff," interpreted as meaning blacks. The $2 minimum was dropped immediately.

Two months later, bars were advertising that they allowed same-sex dancing. In the *Chicago Gay Liberation Newsletter*, a full-page ad for Up Your Alley, 5748 W. Chicago at Central, read, "Live entertainment, dancing, gals and guys are welcome." For the first time ads for bars and businesses in Chicago gay publications boasted "GAY OWNED AND OPERATED."

# 4
# GLF BRANCHES OUT

In March 1970, the *Chicago Seed* reported on a North Side Gay Liberation Front forming off-campus. "We want to sponsor dances, talks, and rap sessions, movies, getting it together with local churches, schools, and other groups," the new GLF told the *Chicago Seed*. "If you're interested in getting your head together about male and female homosexuality, we're interested in talking to you."

Another GLF had already formed at Northwestern University in Evanston. The *Daily Northwestern* student paper on February 23, 1970, reported the group had thirty-five members. Among the early NU-GLF actions was to join UC-GLF at the protest against Sgt. Manley's appearance at the Women's Bar Association and the boycott of the Normandy. On March 8, NU-GLF hosted a "Teach-Out" in the University's Business Building, in conjunction with Women's Liberation and Men's Liberation – the latter group headed by Prof. Jack Sawyer to examine male chauvinistic attitudes toward women and gays. There were two speakers at the event: psychologist William Simon, from the Institute for Juvenile Research, who spoke on the subject of misconceptions about homosexuality, and lawyer Renee Hanover who spoke on homosexuals and the law. In the March 3, 1970, *Daily Northwestern*, NU-GLF co-founder, Bill Dry, urged the straight, as well as the gay community to attend the "Teach-Out." Over 300 showed up. Two days later, Baran Rosen in the *Daily Northwestern* published the first in a series about "the philosophy behind the increasing openness and spirit of protest of homosexuals." The paper interviewed NU-GLF's four founding members: Robert Birch, a graduate student in German; Maher Ahmad, a speech junior; Bill Dry, a graduate student in religion; the fourth student, a CAS freshman, called himself John, a pseudonymous name. He lived in a dorm and didn't know how his dorm-mates would react to his being gay. Birch told the paper:

> "The primary reason for establishing Gay Lib groups, is that members hope to liberate themselves and other homosexuals from the social, political and economic prejudice directed at them by heterosexual society, and to liberate heterosexual society from the ignorance and fear that cause prejudice. Our society forces the homosexual to ask himself, 'Why should the guilt be intra-punitive? Why is the society so messed up that it feels it necessary to pressure homosexuals?'"

Dry, who the paper noted was wearing a Gay Lib button reading, "Out of the closets and into the streets," added, "The homosexual must stop internalizing the guilt that society imposes on them and begin taking pride in themselves."

On April 1, NU-GLF issued the following statement:

"Dear Faculty Member

"Male and female homosexuals at Northwestern have recently organized a Gay Liberation movement on campus. We would like to take this opportunity to explain to you the purposes of our group.

"Homosexuals are economically, legally, and socially discriminated against. Gay people who are open about their homosexuality often cannot find work; gay people who keep their homosexuality hidden live in constant fear of being exposed and losing their jobs. Some laws openly discriminate against homosexuals; others, such as public indecency laws, are applied on a double standard so that things that a heterosexual can do legally, a homosexual cannot do without fear of arrest. Fear of social ridicule and prejudice forces the homosexual to hide his identity; this, in turn, prevents him from reaching his full potential as a human being.

"The objectives of Gay Liberation are three-fold:

"To educate the heterosexual community about homosexuality in an attempt to overcome, through education, the degrading stereotypes, irrational fears, and outright discrimination that homosexuals are subject to;

  1) To secure equal rights for all homosexual men and women and to protest all laws of sexual morality, whether they affect homosexuals or heterosexuals; and
  2) To provide social and intellectual activities for the homosexual student.
  3) There is a lack of activities at Northwestern that specifically fulfills the needs of gay students.

"We wish to make members of the faculty and student body aware of the fact that there does exist a large homosexual community, both at

Northwestern and in society in general, that is no longer willing to hide an essential part of its identity in order to enjoy the rights that a supposedly free society should grant to all its citizens. Gay Liberation intends to actively oppose the oppression of homosexuals.

"We hope that you will support us and do all that you can to help us. You can demonstrate your support for our goals by signing a petition that will be circulated among the faculty and students during the next few weeks. The petition asks the university to take a public stand opposing all forms of discrimination directed at homosexuals. You might also wish to write a personal letter to Chancellor Miller expressing your support for our goals.

"Sincerely yours

William Dry
Maher Ahmad"

The NU-GLF's first public meeting took place on April 2, 1970, at Parkes Hall, Room 214, and the first on-campus dance was held May 2 at the Patten Gym. For one-dollar, gay men and lesbians danced to the sounds of a band called Buckshot. In contrast to the problems that beset the UC-GLF dances, the Northwestern administration permitted non-University students to attend the gay dances.

Soon after the founding of NU-GLF, another group started at Roosevelt University. After Lois Shelton wrote about the formation of UC-GLF in the March 9, 1970 *Roosevelt Torch*, "The group is composed of liberal to radical thinkers who find the classroom, court room, and meeting hall appropriate places for presenting their case. One member has suggested that the group call themselves the 'Pink Panthers,' to emphasize their predisposition to action."

Shelton added that RU-GLF meetings were held weekly at 1:00 p.m. on Wednesdays in Room 774. The following month, the *Roosevelt Torch* advertised an RU-GLF meeting:

> "[That] ... concerns itself with what are the oppressions homosexuals face in the Chicago metropolitan area and what feelings homosexuals at Roosevelt University have toward the University and whether or not they have experienced repressive or suppressive conditions. Have courses taught in the fields of anthropology, sociology and psychology treated homosexuality as a normal part of social and sexual development or has the subject been relegated to a position founded on individual prejudices either from the researcher or on the part of the instructor?"

Roosevelt GLF's concerns about how homosexuality was treated in college courses may, or may not, have been addressed later in the year. The December

## CHICAGO AFTER STONEWALL

1970 *Chicago Gay Alliance Newsletter* reports that Roosevelt University was offering a credited college course in homophile studies. However, in an email from Laura Mills, Roosevelt University archivist, to the author, dated January 14, 2010, she writes, "I've looked through all the course catalogs for the 1969-70 and 1970-71 academic years and there was no course like the one described. It's possible that it was proposed but never implemented. It's also possible it was done independently of the official university curriculum."

Two years later, the *Chicago Gay Alliance Newsletter* reported on a skirmish between RU-GLF and the university authorities. The college bookstore announced it would no longer sell copies of Peter Fisher's *The Gay Mystique*, considered, at the time, to be one of the best books on gay life. The reason given was that it sold poorly, but a bookstore employee insisted that when the book was displayed in the window, it sold well. The book was removed when a "directive from the 8$^{th}$ floor" banned gay books. The outcome of the clash is unknown to the author.

On April 9, 1970, yet another GLF was founded at the University of Illinois Chicago-Circle Campus (UIC-CC). The group declared May 7 Gay Liberation Day on campus. The May 4, 1970, *Daily Illini* wrote:

> "On this day male and female homosexuals will circulate leaflets, hold a panel discussion in CCC, and speak in classrooms. This is an attempt to educate the heterosexual and homosexual community about the reality and not the myth of homosexuality. Beginning Monday, May 4, Gay Lib will inaugurate an answering service for individuals in need of information about Gay Liberation and homosexuality."

Foreseeing an adverse reaction from some students, Alfred Woods, UIC-CC-GLF president, told the *Daily Illini*, "For those in this academic community who see this as a prime opportunity to practice that one bad joke that they have been saying all year, we ask you not to waste your breath and our time."

On May 15, UIC-CC-GLF held their first dance in the Illinois Room, with the Chicago rock band, Second Coming, who had just released an album and had two hit singles on Mercury Records: *Requiem for a Rainy Day* and *747*.

Three days after UIC-CC-GLF formed, another at Northern Illinois University-DeKalb received recognition as an official student organization by the NIU Students Association. This group started after four NIU students attended GLF meetings in Chicago: Dennis, Carl, Guy, and Stephen (first names only). They first tried to recruit members by placing an ad in the

*Northern Star* student paper, but the ad was rejected as "dubious." Undaunted, the NIU-GLF dispatched speakers to public forums, like anti-war marches and as guests on local radio shows.

Over the next two years, other gay groups formed in schools and colleges in Chicago. The *Chicago Gay Alliance Newsletter* reported that on November 19, 1971, the Gay Activist's Coalition was formed at the Loop College of the Chicago City Colleges (Loop College was later renamed the Harold Washington College after the election of the first African American Chicago city-mayor). Forty-five people attended the meeting and officers were elected: Richard Pfeiffer, president; Paul Stensland, vice-president; and Eileen Wicker, Treasurer. One of its first actions was to distribute questionnaires to teachers asking if they would like Coalition members to speak to their class about sexism and the lifestyle problems of gays. According to the June 1972 *Chicago Gay Alliance Newsletter* the response was favorable. On May 12, the Coalition presented the movie *Les amitiés particulières* to students and staff. The film, an adaptation of the 1943 novel by Roger Peyrefitte, tells the story of the relationship between two boys at a Roman Catholic boarding school. In the film, the boys' love affair is destroyed by a zealous priest who sets out to save their young souls from eternal damnation. It was filmed on location at the 13th-century Royaumont Abbey, 50 km north of Paris and was produced by Christine Gouze-Rénal, whose sister, Danielle, was the wife of French president François Mitterrand.

In December 1971, Robert Reinhold wrote in the *Chicago Tribune* about the national rise of GLF student groups:

> "In defiance of taboos that have prevailed for generations, thousands of students are proclaiming their homosexuality, and openly organizing 'gay' groups on campuses around the country.
>
> "No one knows exactly how many are involved. In growing numbers, they are forming cohesive organizations for educational, social, and political purposes. Often, they receive official sanction and remarkable acceptance from fellow students."

Reinhold goes on to write:

> "... gay groups have found little difficulty in achieving recognition as official campus organizations on such diverse campuses as Boston University, Columbia, Cornell, Illinois, Colorado, Stanford, and the various University campuses of California campuses. ... But at a handful of schools, there have been official obstacles, mostly from older administrations and trustees. The organizations have been barred from the University of Texas at Austin, San Jose and Sacramento State Colleges in

California, the University of Kansas, Pennsylvania State, the University of Florida at Tallahassee, University of Southern California. In San Jose, a California judge ordered the college to accept the group, and lawyers are preparing suits in most of the other cases."

Meanwhile, in Chicago, there were developments at Mattachine Midwest. On August 8, 1970, a headline in the *Chicago Tribune* read, "'Gay' President Quits; 25-Year-Old Takes Post":

"Mattachine Midwest announced the resignation of Jim Bradford as its president, to be succeeded by Tom Erwin, vice president for the past one and half years of the five years of the five-year-old homophile organization. ... Prior to his involvement with the homophile pro-homosexual-movement, he [Bradford] was active in New York's campaign to abolish capital punishment and has taken leadership positions in the Chicago peace movement."

Tom Erwin is described as, "the organization's youngest president and the first native Chicagoan to hold the post":

"Mattachine Midwest, a not-for-profit Illinois membership corporation, celebrated its fifth anniversary July 20, 1970, as the first Midwestern group working for homosexuals' legal, social and economic equality and welfare. A banquet to mark the occasion was held at the Trip restaurant, 27 E. Ohio St., site of a notable legal battle in behalf of homosexual's right to congregate in places of public amusement."

# 5
# UNIVERSITY OF ILLINOIS URBANA-CHAMPAIGN

One university GLF group founded soon after the Stonewall Riots was at the University of Illinois Urbana-Champaign (UIUC). Jeffrey Graubert was an early member. He told the author:

> "I began school in the fall of 1970, so I missed out on the informal GLF that began in the 1969-1970 school year. During registration, I met William Stanley who was passing out flyers for the informal GLF. I joined him and felt that our first action should be to become an official student organization. I proposed it at our first meeting of the 1970-'71 school year (held at the Red Herring coffee house) and it passed. There was no objection from the university, or student government, and it was almost anti-climactic. From then on we met in the Illini Union."

However, three years earlier, an article by Jim Bradley appeared on the front page of the *Daily Illini* student paper on June 3, 1966. The headline read, "THE HOMOSEXUAL: A Stranger in Society ... 'I Can Never Be Happy.'" It began:

> "The person we'll call John Richard was sitting at one of the tables in the Illini Union Tavern. 'I don't think that I or any other homosexual can ever be totally happy,' he's saying, '– here at the University or any other place.'
>
> "John Richard is about 22 years old. He's not bad looking; medium height, dark, well-groomed hair and slender build. He looks a great deal like many of the other students that crowd into the Illini Union Tavern and Commons during the late afternoon and evening hours.
>
> "The one thing that sets Richard apart from most students is that he is homosexual – a self-proclaimed 'stranger in our society.'"

According to Bradley, Richard eschews therapy. He tells him, "I'm not sure why I'm a homosexual." Then he adds, "I'm a homosexual now, and I guess I'll always be a homosexual. I'm not interested in being helped. I only want to be left pretty much alone."

Bradley continued:

> "Richard is at the same time typical and different from the 40 or so homosexuals that make up Champaign-Urbana's 'gay' society. Together with many of the other homosexuals studying at the University, Richard is desperately trying to maintain a kind of life that has no meaning for most students.
>
> "He is one of dozens of students living within – yet apart from – our heterosexual society. His world is vastly different from that of most University students. His entire life is estranged from our society. He sees things differently – and he reacts differently.
>
> " ... If he finds that you're interested, he's anxious to talk about himself and his friends. He'll introduce you to others in the 'crowd,' and then wait around until the ice is broken and you can talk to them.
>
> "The 40 students, instructors and 'one nighters' who make up the community are not easily typed. They come from all kinds of backgrounds – rich, poor and middle-class. Their interests range widely, but generally they stick to 'arty' subjects.
>
> "They're [sic] personalities span the full spectrum of diversity. Like their heterosexual counterparts, some are easy to like, while others take more time to understand.
>
> "The 'community' is bound together by more than their sexual deviance. Through the years they have established close bonds in living habits. The community has currently 'taken over' two or three blocks along a street in northeast Urbana. Here most of them have rooms or small apartments. This is the center of the 'community.'
>
> "Members of the 'community' like to think of themselves as a social unit."

How organized or unorganized this 1966 "community" was is unknown to the author, but as early as February 1970, there was a GLF at UIUC. It was led by Ed Lisowski. In an email to the author, dated December 28, 2020, Lisowki wrote:

> "I was aware of various Gay Liberation Fronts forming in 1969-70 around the US, particularly on college campuses, because of my association with the underground newspaper the *Walrus* and maybe through national gay publications such as the *Advocate*. I had a good friend and mentor who had a close association as a theoretician with the Socialist Workers

Party and their youth group Young Socialist Alliance. I was loosely affiliated with the Communist Party USA and their youth group W.E.B. Du Bois Clubs of America. I may have been one of the original members of the W.E.B. Du Bois Club chapter at UIUC when it formed to challenge a state law, the Clabaugh Act, which prohibited university officials from extending university facilities 'to any subversive, seditious, and un-American organization, or to its representatives.'

"These old-left organizations had policies that prohibited active homosexuals from membership, so Bill [Stanley] and I saw the need for a gay rights organization with ties to the far left at UIUC. The 'Liberation Front' part of GLF was to show solidarity with National Liberation Fronts, including the Viet Cong, around the world. I have some memories that the 'Gay' part was also controversial because some of the gay people in Urbana-Champaign preferred to be called 'homosexuals.'

"The U of I recognized registered student organizations, so we formed a Gay Liberation Front at UIUC so we could have meeting space on campus. 'We' included several other people who were considerably more moderate in their political views than Bill [Stanley] and me. The University required membership of at least ten students, faculty, or staff, but I don't remember giving a list of members to the university when we applied for recognition. At the time, I was a staff member (offset press operator) who worked at the Student Union, so I may have been listed as an officer (President). We started having regular meetings, which were mostly discussion sessions focused on gay issues. About half the attendees were women, so feminist theory guided many of those discussions.

"The only other activity I remember from the early years was hosting gay dances in the student union. At the time we had two quasi "gay" bars that periodically welcomed or discouraged gays, but neither bar permitted dancing because they lacked a cabaret license. Once we had a gay-owned bar with dancing, the need for the campus dances waned.

"GLF was always a moderate gay rights group despite its name. It went through various name changes involving Lesbian, Bisexual or Queer in parallel with national gay politics. At some point Liberation Front became Alliance."

One of UIUC-GLF's first public events was advertised in the *Daily Illini* and read, "FREAK-GAY ROCK CONCERT ... *Walrus* and Gay Liberation Front will present a folk and rock concert from 11 a.m. to 7 p.m. Saturday in the Sunken Garden and at the Sun Singer of Allerton Park."

Lisowski remembers:

"Back then I was part of *The Walrus* collective that published an underground newspaper called *The Walrus*. We had a subscription to a wire service (like UPI or AP for the left anti-war movement) called Liberation News Service, so I was aware of GLF activities around the country. It helped stimulate me to form a GLF at U of I UC. Also, at the time, I knew some people in local rock bands. In the spirit of the Yippie movement, I thought Allerton Park would be the perfect place for a gay rock concert because of its possible gay connection with Robert and John [Allerton. See below] and the naked statues in the formal gardens. I asked one or two bands agree to play for free with the understanding it would be a practice session for them. This was the extent of the planning.

"I thought the day of the concert was fun but uneventful. From what I can see in my old photos, maybe 40 people showed up at the Sun Singer for the music. I also knew someone who had a business painting radio/TV antenna towers. At the time he was painting the FM/TV antenna tower for WILL (the campus radio and TV station) in a secluded area on the Allerton property and he was staying in his van with his girlfriend at the base of the antenna. A few days later he mentioned that on the day of the rock concert, the U of I Alumni Association had 'Mothers' Day" bus tours at Allerton Park and that busloads of mothers were driven around the Sun Singer and were shocked to see mostly men dancing to a rock band at the base of the naked male statue. ... I thought it was a funny coincidence, but did not think much about it. The painter also mentioned that the head groundskeeper had a heart attack a few days later and died.

"I decided to try a second concert at Allerton Park about a month later. Again, it was minimal planning, and I did not think to ask for anyone's permission, since the park, except of the mansion, was treated as a public space. This time the Allerton Park groundskeepers and the Piatt County sheriff were there telling us the concert was not going to happen. It could have turned into an ugly situation, especially since one or two busloads of people came down from Chicago. (I may have distributed some concert flyers at a gay dance at the Chicago Coliseum a few weeks earlier.) Fortunately, the antenna tower painter was there, and he negotiated with the groundskeeper and sheriff to allow the rock concert in the secluded area at the base of the radio tower. It lacked the charm of the Sun Singer area, but at least no one ended up in jail."

Allerton Park is a 6,000 acres nature reserve and mansion bequeathed to the University of Illinois in 1946 by Robert Allerton, farmer, industrialist, and heir to the First National Bank of Chicago. Allerton was a gay man who made Illinois history by legally adopting his lover. An article in the March 5, 1960, *Chicago Tribune* read, "A decree was entered in Platt county court in Monticello ... in which Robert Allerton, 87, millionaire farmer and art patron, legally adopted John Wyatt Gregg, 59, who has had the status of a son for 30 years." The *Chicago Tribune*, never using the word gay, homosexual, or lover, went on to say Allerton tried to adopt his son a few years earlier, but Illinois law did not permit the adoption of an adult. The Illinois legislature changed the law in 1959 after Allerton pulled some strings, or so the story goes. The official reason for changing the law was to allow a man marrying a woman with adult children to adopt those children. Allerton and Gregg met in 1922 when the former was invited to a Zeta Psi fraternity house in Champaign for the Dad's Day football game. In a 1984 interview with Nancy M. Becker, archived at the University of Illinois at Springfield Norris L. Brookens Library, Gregg recalled, "Robert Allerton was invited over there for lunch before a football game and he didn't have a son and I didn't have a father so we were paired off and lived happily ever after." Gregg was an orphan, both his parents died years earlier.

On October 16, 1971, the *Daily Illini* published an article by Margaret Bicek headlined, "Laws inhibit homosexual activity," about state and city laws:

> "Illinois is almost the only state in which homosexuality itself is not illegal, but a variety of state and local laws impose penalties of imprisonment and fines for many gay actions.
>
> "In Champaign and Urbana, a female impersonator or 'drag queen' may be jailed or fined simply for appearing in public.
>
> "Two persons, neither of whom were students, were arrested in Champaign two weeks ago after a Gay Liberation dance on the charge of indecent conduct. The Champaign ordinance reads, 'It shall be unlawful for any person to commit any indecent or immoral act; or to appear in any public place in clothes properly belonging to the opposite six [sic] or not properly or decently garbed.'
>
> "According to police reports, the suspect was stopped 'because officers suspected a female impersonator. The subject's hair was normal, but his voice sold him out and he was arrested.'
>
> "Harvey Shirley, Champaign police chief, said he could not remember a woman ever being arrested on such a charge and that he did not feel it was directed against conventions of dress such as women wearing pants.
>
> "He said indecent conduct or disorderly conduct are the usual charges brought against homosexuals in the city. The penalty for the offense is a fine of not more than $500."

In Urbana, the penalty was a fine of up to $200 or six months in jail. The Urbana ordinances prohibit actions "tending to debauch the public morals" and stated that no person may "appear in a dress not properly belonging to his sex or in any indecent or lewd dress."

## CHICAGO AFTER STONEWALL

Three months later, UIUC-GLF set about changing the draconian Champaign-Urbana laws. In January 1972, Ronald L. Knecht wrote in the *Daily Illini*, "Urbana dress code hit":

> "The campus Gay Liberation Front, (GLF), apparently challenged the Urbana dress code law in a letter to Mayor Charles M. Zipprodt, Friday.
>
> "The letter, which followed a successful fight against a similar ordinance in Champaign, asked the city council to revise the city code. Zipprodt said Friday afternoon that he had given the letter to Jack Waaler, city attorney and corporation counsel, and asked him to draft an amendment to the code.
>
> "According to GLF the code as it now reads is a 'direct attack upon the homosexual, lesbian, transsexual men and transvestite members of the Champaign-Urbana community.' The letter added, 'Laws which prohibit any indecent or lewd act or behavior' and appearance 'in a dress not belonging to his sex' are frequently used to harass the gay community.
>
> "... If the amendment were passed, both cities would be rid of laws which prohibit women from dressing in men's clothes and vice versa. Conceivably, women could be arrested in Urbana under the current law for wearing blue jeans or pant suits, if an officer judged those 'dress not belonging to the sex of the wearer.'"

The next target for the UIUC-GLF was the Wigwam restaurant, 708 S. Sixth St. Jackie Zimmerman wrote in the *Daily Illini*:

> "The Gay Liberation Front claimed that the Wigwam's management has embarked on a deliberate plan to discourage homosexuals from coming there and change the climate of the bar.
>
> "Jeff Graubert, a member of Gay Liberation, said, 'So many 'accidents' have occurred at the Wigwam that it's disgusting. We have been shoved around and had drinks spilled on us. We are asking people to boycott the Wigwam and intend to prove that we have the same right to be served as anyone else.'
>
> "Tom Cochran, owner of the Wigwam, denied any deliberate mistreatment of homosexuals. 'I'm running a business,' he said. 'If people come in here and act like ladies and gentlemen, we serve them.' According to Graubart, most of the abuse has come from the Wigwam's manager, Larry Birkey. Graubart said he was sitting in the Wigwam with friends April 9, the manager, who was not working that night, arrived with two companions.
>
> "'It was horrifying,' Graubert said. 'Birkey walked in in his Army uniform and just walked around glaring at us. All the gays got scared and started leaving.'

"I was left alone at my table, and Birkey came over, picked up a glass of beer on the other side of the table and threw it at me. There was no question about it. He didn't clear off any other tables.

"Graubart called the police and tried to press charges against Birkey. However, two of his friends who had gone to the station as witnesses refused to testify.

"'They didn't really see it happen,' Graubart said. 'Birkey's two friends claimed it was an accident, so there really was no case.'"

The UIUC-GLF tried to enter into an agreement with the Wigwam that there will be no future incidents and Larry Birkey be fired. On April 18, 1972, Jim Gehring in the *Daily Illini* wrote:

"Members of the Gay Liberation Front (GLF) continued to picket the Wigwam this weekend with only one incident occurring.

"Jeff Graubart, a GLF member, said two 'thugs' came out of the Champaign restaurant-bar and grabbed leaflets and signs held by some of the picketers. Graubart said the two also threw two GLF members, Bill Warren and Bill Stanley, into the street.

"Champaign police were called, but the two had left before they arrived, and no arrests were made."

Cochran refused to sign the agreement "because the Wigwam does not discriminate." He also claimed the boycott hadn't hurt the restaurant. Graubert disagreed, saying it looked "like a tomb."

The Wigwam was remodeled and renamed the Round Robin by the same management.

In May 1973, the Champaign City Council tentatively approved dates for public meetings on, among other things, to incorporate a Homosexual Bill of Rights into existing city statutes. Not all councilmen were on board. On May 9, 1973, Greg Miller wrote in the *Daily Illini*:

"Councilman Kenneth Dugan, 3rd, said he could not morally condone such an ordinance. 'We cannot, I think, legislate that that God is very plain about.'

"Citing scripture, Dugan explained his opposition to amendments concerning homosexuals. 'According to this,' he said, 'it's a sin.'"

The gay rights proposal was soundly defeated. In the *Daily Illini* Greg Miller wrote, "Several homosexuals and two psychiatrists addressed the nine-member council prior to the vote in support of the resolution. Dr. Morton S.

Tabin, 705 W. Park Ave., said failure to pass the resolution 'would add pressure and anxiety to what is already an unfortunate individual.'"

Councilmember Mary Pollack said she was extremely disappointed by the vote, saying, "denying people their civil rights is incredible to me."

The UIUC-GLF had more luck with the Urbana council. On the cover of the *Daily Illini* on August 28, 1972, an article begins:

> "The long-debated and highly controversial 'Homosexual Bill of Rights' was finally passed out of the Urbana City Council Committee on Legislation Monday night.
>
> "The ordinance, which would guarantee equal rights for all Urbana residents, regardless of sexual preference, will go to the full council at its next meeting, Sept. 4., with no recommendation from the committee.
>
> "The committee voted 2-2, with chairman Kenneth Appel, D-7, abstaining. Ald. John Peterson, 1-2, and Edward Harris, D-4, voted to recommend the bill for passage, while Ald. Paul Hursey, D-3, and George Eighmey, R-6 voted against it.
>
> "Monday night's action ended almost four months of debate over the issue, highlighted by both Bible-wielding ministers and empassioned [sic]supporters of the legislation."

On September 4, 1973, the Gay Bill of Rights was voted down by the Urbana city council, 7 to 6. However, on September 7, Jane Fritsch wrote in the *Daily Illini*:

> "Urbana's proposed 'homosexual bill of rights' may not be a dead issue ... Mayor Hiram Paley said Thursday he drafted a letter to the city's Human Rights Commission asking that it 'review the entire issue' and determine whether such an ordinance should be passed by the city council.
>
> " ... After the ordinance was rejected Tuesday night, about 20 of its supporters gathered outside the Urbana City Building to decide on future action, and suggested methods of retaliation ranging from a 'kiss-in' in the City Council chambers to a march on [Committee Chairman Kenneth] Appel's house.
>
> "Many of the bill's supporters seemed to feel that Appel, who voted against the ordinance in the final council vote, had betrayed them.
>
> "In the wake of Tuesday night's meeting, Appel sent a letter to Paley requesting that the Human Relations Commission 'study in some detail the problems of the homosexual in Urbana.'
>
> "Appel said in the letter that the legislation should have been 'more carefully tailored to the problems of this community,' and that a clause should be inserted to 'restrict the ordinance's applicability' in the area of housing.

"The defeated ordinance would have guaranteed equal housing opportunities to all citizens, regardless of 'sexual preference.'

"Appel also said that based on the commission's findings, it should draft 'appropriate legislation to reduce as far as possible the indignities that it finds they (homosexuals) suffer.'

"In response to Appel's letter, Paley said he will ask the commission to:
- Determine through hearings and research whether homosexuals have special problems with respect to equal opportunity and equal treatment under the law;
- Determine whether the legislation should be enacted at the city level;
- Draft a carefully prepared ordinance; legislation.
- Detail all possible ramifications of any such legislation."

Urbana passed the Human Rights Ordinance on November 17, 1975. The new law outlawed discrimination on the basis of sexual orientation in employment, credit transactions and public accommodations. Violators were fined up to $200.

On July 21, 1977, the *Pantagraph* reported on Champaign adding gays to the city's Human Rights Bill:

"Mayor William Bland, who cast the deciding vote as the city council adopted a human rights ordinance that includes protection for homosexuals, says he was caught between many of his prejudices and a good Christian conscience.

"... It passed on a 5-4 vote, with Bland breaking a 4-4 deadlock.

"'I don't think my decision is going to be popular,' Bland said. 'I had parents call me very concerned that a homosexual could teach their children in school ... and it really goes against my upbringing and many, many of my prejudices.'

"Bland said, 'a good Christian conscience and a disposition toward all of those people who might benefit' led to his affirmative vote.

"He also said he knew 'a lot of competent, contributing members of the community are homosexuals,' another factor in his decision.

"Urbana passed a similar ordinance two years ago and both were approved at the urging of a broad coalition which included persons connected with the University of Illinois."

# 6
# GLF AND THE MAINSTREAM PRESS

The new post-Stonewall militant homosexual first registered in the local mainstream press on February 22, 1970, in *Chicago Today* with Paul Sampson's article, "The 'gay' life in Chicago: Homosexuals today refuse to remain submerged and oppressed by the 'straight' world." It begins:

> "OPENING NIGHT of *Boys in the Band*; it's clear from the first joke that there are two audiences present. They both laugh at the funny lines, but one group starts laughing sooner and chuckles longer and more knowingly. In the cigaret-fogged lobby between acts, there's the same split. Some of the people trade a certain kind of look – a bit conspiratorial, certainly not campy, nothing theatrical, you understand, but – tonight it's O.K. to 'come out.' All the straights in the audience have been looking at the gays on the stage and they like them. So let them look at some gay people who aren't acting – it'll do them good.
>
> "Tomorrow it will be back to the straight old world for most of these people, back to a life of secret agent duplicity for some – but not for all. Homosexuals are less and less willing to live submerged lives, more and more ready to take a visible position to improve their legal and social status."

Sampson goes on to paint an accurate portrait of the trials and tribulations of gays in Chicago: the bar raids, police harassment, extortion and entrapment. He writes, "So Chicago, always known as a swinging city, is hardly a wide-open town where homosexuals are concerned. One young man revealed that he heads for Milwaukee when he's in the mood to 'cruise' – Chicago is too repressive. Milwaukee!"

Civil rights lawyer, Renee Hanover, told *Chicago Today* why the city was bad for gays:

"Since the model criminal code was passed in 1961, inroads have been made against it, making convictions easier to obtain. The police control most of the proceeding in such an arrest: they make the charges, recommend bond, and their word is generally accepted in magistrate courts. It makes it very difficult to win such a case on its merits, even when the charges are not justified."

Hanover described a typical client:

"In one case, the victim was informed he was under arrest, then reminded that it would cost him 'a couple of hundred dollars' for bail. The kindly policeman offered to call the man's parents or his employer to get the money. Needless to say, when the supposed cop suggested that the matter could be settled right there for $20 or $30, the victim coughed up."

Capt. Raymond Carter, director of the vice control division, refused to take allegations of harassment seriously. He told *Chicago Today* that "Some officers are better at arresting burglars or stickup men; some are good at these cases." He suggested complaints be directed to the police department's internal investigation division.

Sampson interviewed an unnamed University of Chicago student (it was Henry Weimhoff) who is "typical of the new homosexual." Sampson wrote:

"He's convinced that his is a perfectly valid sexual orientation, one that makes as much sense as anyone else's. He sees the 'problem' of homosexuality as coming entirely from outside – it's only a problem because society chooses to make it one. 'Sure, some gay people have personality problems. If everyone tells you there's something wrong with you, your self-esteem falls apart. That's the real problem.'"

The University of Chicago GLF isn't mentioned by name. Sampson ended with:

"This young man and people like him see a parallel between their situation and that of the blacks. Both are minorities with legitimate grievances against the majority culture. Some homosexuals have adapted more or less militant tactics or at least rhetoric – 'Gay Power' buttons, a New York group called the Gay Liberation Front – and some have been moved to support other minorities because of the lessons learned from their own clashes with the straight world. Meanwhile, life for homosexuals in Chicago may be gay, but it isn't always cheerful."

Another article, "Homosexual Revolt" by Susan Root appeared in March 1970 in *Chicago Daily News*. She wrote:

"Gay Liberation is a new and growing campus phenomenon. Several chapters have been or are being formed on Illinois campuses. One such group was organized at the University of Chicago in January and is now accredited by the university. ... Informal groups of homosexuals at Southern Illinois, Illinois State and Illinois Wesleyan universities have written the UC chapter and expressed an interest in organizing. Members of Gay Lib explain their new militancy as a logical extension of their involvement in progressive causes. 'I was very active in civil rights,' said Henry [Weimhoff], the soft-spoken organizer of Gay Lib at UC, 'and then it dawned on me that I was fighting for the rights of other oppressed minorities when I was a member of an oppressed minority myself.'"

Root described members of UC-GLF:

"Sitting around a long table they look no different from the 'straight' students around them. The girls range from plain to delicate and pretty; the men, from hirsute revolutionary to clean-cut fraternity types. There is no exaggeration of dress, manner or speech to set them apart. Yet, they are the real avant-gardes of homosexuals because they have 'come out.'"

# 7
# GLF AND THE VIETNAM WAR

In mid-February 1970, the Student Mobilization Committee (SMC), an anti-Vietnam War organization, held a three-day national conference at the Case Western Reserve University campus in Cleveland, OH. Three thousand activists attended the largest anti-war conference to date, certainly the most diverse. Organizations represented ranged from Quakers to Black Panthers. The main focus was the upcoming international anti-Vietnam war protests, but those attending also voted in support of Gay Liberation. The Chicago SMC met on February 28 and again March 7 at the University of Illinois Circle Campus to discuss local participation in the mass anti-war protests. They planned a week of actions from April 13-18 that included a gay event – UC-GLF's Step May proposed Thursday, April 16, 1970, as Gay Liberation Day in Chicago. The proposal passed. This was in addition to UIC-CC-GLF declaring May 7 Gay Liberation Day on campus.

On April 15, 1970, in Copenhagen and Rome, violence broke out as thousands of anti-Vietnam War protestors clashed with police. In the US, riot squads and tear gas were used to quell skirmishes in Boston, Detroit, Washington DC, Madison, and Berkeley, CA. In Chicago, the protest was peaceful. The police surprisingly subdued considering the brutality of two years earlier at the 1968 Democratic National Convention. Nobody was arrested in Chicago, not even those marching with Viet Cong flags, though they did get their names taken. The April 16, 1970, *Chicago Daily News* estimated 10,000 people crowded into Civic Center Plaza for the "taxpayer protest" against the Vietnam War. The April 15 rally was timed to coincide with the deadline for paying federal income taxes. US Sen. Charles Goodell (R-NY), the keynote speaker, called for an end to "seven years of folly." He declared, "Let us make the painful choice, the right choice, the moral choice for this country – to get out of Vietnam now." Rep. Abner Mikva (D-IL) also spoke out against the war. After a concert by a little-known Champaign-Urbana rock band, REO Speedwagon, a year before the release of their first album, the protestors marched down State St. to join another rally outside the Federal Building. Prior to the Civic Center Plaza rally, the Student Mobilization Committee to End the War in Vietnam held a demonstration outside the Board of Education, demanding "basic student rights"; GLF members from Roosevelt, Northwestern, UI-CCC, NUI-DeKalb and UC were in attendance.

At 3:00 p.m. at Civic Center Plaza, gay anti-war protestors marched together to the Federal Building under a banner that read: "POWER TO ALL OPPRESSED PEOPLES – GAY LIBERATION." One of the speakers was NU-GLF's Bill Dry. This was the first-time homosexuals marched openly on the streets of Chicago. After the rally, some lesbians joined Women's Lib picketing Hugh Hefner's Playboy Mansion, where a $100 a ticket celebrity anti-Vietnam War fundraiser was taking place. While Women's Lib shouted, "Don't go into Hefner's Playboy mansion. His girlie magazine makes women into sex objects," anti-war celebrities crossed the picket line, including Dennis Hopper currently riding high on the hog from *Easy Rider*, Candice Bergen, and science fiction writer and director Rod Serling, who commented on the Women's Lib protestors, "It's a matter of priorities. Women aren't getting killed. The men in Vietnam are."

The April 16 Chicago Gay Liberation Day began at noon with a rally in Grant Park. There was music and dancing and a long list of speakers: Bill Dry (NU-GLF), Martha Shelley (New York City GLF), Renee Hanover (Lawyer), Henry Weimhoff (UC-GLF), David Stienecker (Editor of Mattachine Midwest newsletter, on trial for the "criminal defamation" of Police Sgt. John Manley), Jim Bradford (President, Mattachine Midwest), Rennard Cordon "Rennie" Davis (New Mobilization Committee to End the War in Vietnam), and Lee Weiner (Political activist). Davis and Weiner were among the Chicago 8, along with Abbie Hoffman, Jerry Rubin, David Dellinger, Tom Hayden, Bobby Seale and John Froines, all accused of conspiracy and incitement to riot, charges stemming from the anti-Vietnam war protests at the 1968 Democratic National Convention in Chicago. At the time, Weiner was working on his Ph.D. in sociology at Northwestern. According to Baran Rosen in the April 17, 1970, *Daily Northwestern*, NU-GLF's Bill Dry told the crowd, "What society calls us is not what we are but what the ruling class needs to say we are in order to affirm what it is. THAT IS, THE POWER elite can only define itself and keep its power by defining by class, race and sexual role stereotypes who shall or shall not participate in the fruits of society."

After the rally, the protestors walked along sidewalks through the Loop to the Municipal Court Building of Chicago, 321 N. LaSalle, waving flags and chanting "2-4-6-8 gay is just as good as straight" and "Gay power to gay people." Outside the court, they denounced police harassment and the arrest of *Mattachine Midwest Newsletter* editor, David Stienecker. Coincidentally, their arch-nemesis, Police Sgt. John Manley, was leaving the building as they arrived and, on seeing them, made a hasty escape. The protestors crossed over to Michigan Avenue, where they "liberated" the Tribune Building from the paper's biased coverage of gays – ironically, the following day, the *Chicago Tribune* was the only mainstream paper to cover the rally. They wrote:

> "One hundred members of the Gay Liberation Front, protesting alleged harassment of homosexuals by police and society, staged a noon rally yesterday in Grant Park .... The rally's theme, 'out of the closets and into the streets,' was demonstrated by the group as they held hands while sitting on the grass in the park. ... Another 150 persons, mostly office workers on their lunch hours, stood nearby, attracted by colorful flags and signs proclaiming Gay Power and Gay is Beautiful."

While some homosexuals protested the Vietnam War, others campaigned against their exclusion from military service. In May 1966 in the *New Republic*, David Sanford wrote "Boxed In":

> "Borrowing the tactics of earlier civil rights workers, homosexuals in several parts of the country plan to demonstrate on Armed Forces Day, May 21, to protest their categorical exclusion from military service. Many homosexuals *do* serve in the military, and without scandal. But they must dissemble, hide their sexual tastes from draft boards and in pre-induction screening. The last of 70 items on the medical history form prospective draftees must fill out when they report for physicals reads, 'Have you ever had or have you now ... homosexual tendencies?' If a homosexual checks the 'no' box, he violates a federal law and risks a fine and imprisonment. If he checks 'yes,' he is disqualified, and he may be permanently handicapped in getting or holding a job."

In the May 1966 *Mattachine Midwest Newsletter*, an anonymous author dubbed it "A Moral Dilemma":

> "Personal prejudice is one thing. But when popular ignorance becomes embodied into law and policy that summarily and without regard to individual merit affects millions of citizens the course is clear. Honorable men protest. Legislation regarding homosexuals is hodgepodge law based

on widely and responsibly disputed myths. The target example is the draft."

The "moral dilemma" was explained further in April 1970 in the *Chicago Sun-Times*, with a question answered in "The Draft Counselor," a twice-weekly column telling young men about their rights under the draft:

> "Question: I am a homosexual. I hold an II-S student deferment now. Are you rejected for being a homosexual? Is there any way in which you are tested? Answer: The Army's medical standards list 'overt homosexuality' as a cause for rejection. Your local board may classify you I-Y or IV-F if you are rejected, depending on what the physicians at the examining station recommend.
>
> "To obtain a physical deferment you must submit a letter from a psychologist or psychiatrist describing your condition, outlining its history, and detailing how it would interfere with your functioning in the military. If you have had psychological treatment, this should be indicated.
>
> "The author goes on to warn the questioner that government agencies, prospective employers and schools, will have access to this information. Meaning, if you admitted you were gay, you could be denied work and an education in the future. The author continued:
>
> "You should also consider carefully whether, by in effect having yourself 'certified' as a homosexual, you may be reinforcing tendencies which are not truly permanent. Some men are able to reach a bisexual or even heterosexual adjustment through therapy. Whether you want to do this is your own decision, of course.
>
> "For these reasons, you should fully discuss your situation with a psychiatrist or psychologist before he writes a letter. You are also advised to contact an experienced draft counselor to see whether you may be eligible for some other deferment that would cause fewer potential complications."

One man who went that extra mile to prove his homosexuality to the draft board was James Michael McClain from San Francisco. Under the headline, "Organist Fined $250 for Photo to Draft Board," an article in the *Fort Worth Star-Telegram* begins:

> "A young organist who pleaded homosexuality to avoid military service was fined $250 Thursday for sending explicit photographic proof of his sexual bent to his draft board.
>
> "The fine was levied in federal court here against James Michael McClain 20, after the prosecution charged that the pictures so shocked an unsuspecting female draft board clerk that she had to take five days leave to recover."

In court, McClain claimed that his draft board in Louisiana turned down his request to be rejected because he was a homosexual. His draft status was currently uncertain. The article ended, "The court was told that mail reaching the Baton Rouge board was now being opened by a man as a precaution."

# 8
# ORTEZ E. ALDERSON, THE BLACK PANTHERS, AND THE KILLING OF JAMES CLAY

One GLF member who took direct action against the Vietnam War was African American Ortez E. Alderson. Born in Buffalo, NY in 1952, Alderson grew up on the South Side of Chicago. At age eighteen, he was a striking figure in his red bellbottom pants, yellow sweater, maxi-trench coat, floppy black hat, a necklace with a black fist on it, and Gay Liberation Front button. Alderson was chairman of the Black Caucus of Chicago GLF, later renamed Third World Gay Revolutionaries. On July 29, 1970, he and three companions – Phyllis J. Burke (27), Kevin M. Clark (19), and Patricia J. Pottinger (23) – were arrested and charged with seizing and destroying Selective Services records in the Livingston County Draft Board office in Pontiac, IL. According to the *Chicago Gay Liberation Newsletter*, the police caught up with them in the nearby town of Minonk, after they made an illegal U-turn and fell into conversation with the cop who stopped them. (In fact, they were stopped because all four were sitting in the front seat). They were charged with breaking into the draft board office and removing draftee records, along with cards listing all men registered in Livingston County since 1922. They left behind the records of those with draft exemptions. The FBI also accused the "Pontiac 4," as they became known, of pouring cans of orange paint over two desks and tearing an American flag off the wall and draping it over a filing cabinet.

On July 29, 1970, *The Times*, a newspaper out of Streator, IL, reported:

> "Allan Rohn, Minonk chief of police, stopped a car carrying four persons on a minor traffic charge and the county draft records were discovered in the auto.

"The Minonk police, assisted by Dist. 8 state police, arrested the four and took them to the Woodford county jail in Eureka.

" ... Garbage sacks containing the records from the office were found in the back of the car and were traced to the Pontiac headquarters."

The *Times* article described the damage:

"Entry was made by prying open a side door. Orange paint was thrown throughout the interior of the office, damaging the floor, walls, equipment, furniture. Twenty-eight file drawers containing records were emptied, as were all the file boxes containing cards of all the men who have registered since 1922. ... The empty 3 by 5 inch file boxes were piled on a table in the back room with the U.S. flag spread over them. The flag had been torn from a wall in the front office.

"Everything was taken except classifications that would be ineligible for induction into the armed services.

"A recruiting poster was placed flat on the floor, covered with paint and three artificial flowers were placed on it."

A headline in the November 17, 1970 issue of *The Times* read, "Four Defendants Fail to Appear in Peoria Court":

"Failing to appear in the court of Federal Judge Robert D. Morgan in Peoria, Monday morning, were four defendants accused of ransacking the Livingston County Draft Board office in July.

" ... Selection of a 12-member jury was to begin Monday morning and 50 prospective jurors were on hand.

"Attorney Ronald L. Barnard, who previously represented the four at the preliminary hearing was present as their attorney and stated he had no idea where they were."

Judge Morgan issued bench warrants for their arrest. On November 28, in *The Times*, it was reported that, "the quartet surrendered to the Federal Bureau of Investigation in Chicago," where a bond was set for $50,000 each. They were placed in the custody of US Marshalls. Two days later, June Simpson wrote in *The Pantagraph*:

"The 'Pontiac 4' pleaded guilty in U.S. District Court Monday morning to charges of damaging government property and interfering with the administration of the Selective Services Act.

"Judge Robert D. Morgan indicated that he will set the sentence at one year in jail on the first charge and three years probation on the second, as proposed by U.S. Asst. Atty. Max Lipkin."

Alderson, represented by ACLU lawyer, Ronald L. Barnard, was the last to be released on bail of $5,000. He was sentenced to one year in prison, spending the first three months in Peoria County Jail. In an interview with *Motive* magazine, Alderson described his incarceration in Peoria:

> "When I was there, I was the only black on the tier for a long time. The rest of the people seemed to be poor whites from around that area and they also seemed to be – or were – racist; something I put up with at the time. There were quite a few hangups going around at that time about whether or not I was actually gay. I of course am ... and very proud of it. And then being a black man, too, everyone was rather afraid to try and hassle me or try to do anything with me. I guess this had something to do with that All-American black male myth."

Alderson served the rest of his term in the federal prison at Ashland, KY, a medium-security facility near the town of Summit. The same federal correction center where gay civil rights leader Bayard Rustin was incarcerated during World War II. Rustin violated the Selective Service Act requiring adult males under 35 to register with local draft boards. While in Ashland, Alderson and three other gay prisoners, Craig (Puerto Rican), Green (Black) and Davis (Sioux Indian), tried to organize a Gay Pride Day on June 28, 1971, in prison. Not surprisingly, prison officials denied their request and the three were thrown in the hole.

This wasn't the first time Alderson had been jailed. He told *Motive* that in April 1968, after the Martin Luther King riots, he spent five months in Cook County Jail on a trumped-up charge, "I was only fifteen at the time and I didn't know Martin Luther King had been shot. I didn't know what the show was when I was walking down the street, but I got thrown into jail with this ridiculous charge of arson."

Alderson's role in Chicago's Third World Gay Revolutionaries led to his selection as one of GLF's representatives at the 1970 Black Panther Revolutionary People's Constitutional Convention in Philadelphia. In September 1970, the *Chicago Tribune* reported the focus of the convention were the twin themes of socialism and solidarity. There were "6,000 delegates, onlookers and street people" attending fifteen workshops hosted by churches and community centers, on topics ranging from sexual self-determination, drugs, health, the military, schools, and political power. Black Panther co-founder Huey Newton addressed the crowd who shouted, "Right On" and "Power to the People." He told the mostly young crowd, one-third of whom were white, how the United States had been conceived in liberty but was now "dedicated to death, oppression and the pursuit of profits." The *Chicago Tribune* continued, "Cheers echoed and reechoed as each spokesman presented his proposals, but the greatest cheers came when the spokesman for the Gay Liberation Front, a homosexual organization, said, 'You can't win this revolution without us. An army of lovers cannot lose.'"

A report on the 1970 Black Panther Revolutionary People's Constitutional Convention in Philadelphia appeared in the October 1970 *Chicago Gay Liberation Newsletter*, written by Victor, Joe, Peter, Art, Robbie and Michael. It begins with a quote from Angela Davis, who came out as a lesbian in *Out* magazine in 1997. "One of the most important things ... is to merge the personal with the political until they are no longer separate." The newsletter authors wrote:

> "Imagine 50 gays sitting as a bloc in a hall of 10,000 – holding hands, arms around each other, chanting 'Gay is Good' – and being warmly, respectfully received by the people; dig it, straight people! Gay Liberation had been invited by the Panthers to send as many sisters and brothers that wanted to go to the convention to help re-write this country's Constitution. This time we, as gay people, would have a chance to voice our needs and ensure that these needs would be protected as human rights."

On negative reactions to GLF, "Naturally some people acted according to the old society rather than the new one. At one point, someone insulted one of our sisters. She stood right up because he looked like he was going to get rough. Before anything could happen, the Panthers grabbed him and dragged him out of the hall."

On the camaraderie:

> "This new environment had a humanizing effect on us. At our meetings or at times when we were just being together, we acted in a new way toward each other. We weren't sex-subjects or sex objects, we were people who were beginning to love each other. We touched each other a lot, not because of someone being 'cute' or 'groovy' but to give warmth and support. ... It was not competitive or possessive."

Black Panther, Afeni Shakur, mother of rapper Tupac Shakur, attended one of the GLF workshops:

> "Afeni Shakur came to one of our workshops. She is one of the New York 21 Panthers now on trial for conspiracy to blow up the Botanical Gardens, Macy's, etc. She told us about how she had looked out of her prison cell window during a demonstration to free the New York 21. Seeing a Gay Liberation banner in the crowd made her think for the first time about gay people and Gay Liberation. She then began relating to the gay sisters in jail, beginning to understand their oppression, their anger and the strength in them and in all gay people."

## CHICAGO AFTER STONEWALL

Shakur mentions Huey Newton's letter of support to GLF. Newton, the Supreme Commander, Black Panther Party, supported women's and gay rights, unlike the other co-founder of the Black Panthers, Bobby Seale, who was homophobic, as was leading Panther Eldridge Cleaver, who once famously wrote, "Homosexuality is a sickness, just as are baby-rape or wanting to become head of General Motors."

On August 15, 1970, Newton gave this speech:

"During the past few years, strong movements have developed among women and homosexuals seeking their liberation. There has been some uncertainty about how to relate to these movements. Whatever your personal opinions and your insecurities about homosexuality and the various liberation movements among homosexuals and women (and I speak of homosexuals and women as oppressed groups), we should try to unite with them in revolutionary fashion.

"I say 'whatever your insecurities are' because, as we very well know, sometimes our first instinct is to want to hit a homosexual in the mouth, and want a woman to be quiet. We want to hit the homosexual in the mouth as soon as we see him because we're afraid we might be homosexual, and we want to hit the woman or shut her up because we're afraid she might castrate us, or take the nuts that we might not have to start with.

"We must gain security in ourselves and therefore have respect and feelings for all oppressed people. We must not use the racist-type attitudes that the white racists use against people because they are black and poor. Many times the poorest white person is the most racist because he's afraid he might lose something or discover something that he doesn't have. You're some kind of threat to him. This kind of psychology is in operation when we view oppressed people and we're angry with them because of their particular kind of behavior or their particular kind of deviation from the established norm.

"Remember, we haven't established a revolutionary value system; we're only in the process of establishing it. I don't remember us ever constituting any value that said that a revolutionary must say offensive things towards homosexuals, or that a revolutionary must make sure women don't speak out about their own particular kind of oppression. Matter of fact, it's just the opposite: we say that we recognize the women's right to be free. We haven't said much about the homosexual at all and we must relate to the homosexual movement because it is a real thing. And I know through reading and through my life experience, my observation, that homosexuals are not given freedom and liberty by anyone in this society. Maybe they might be the most oppressed people in the society.

"What made them homosexuals? Perhaps it's a whole phenomenon that I don't understand entirely. Some people say that it is the decadence of capitalism—I don't know whether this is the case, I rather doubt it. But whatever the case is, we know that homosexuality is a fact, that it exists, and we must understand it in its purest form; that is, a person should have the freedom to use his body in whatever way he wants.

"That is not endorsing things in homosexuality that we wouldn't view as revolutionary. But there is nothing to say that a homosexual cannot also be a revolutionary. And maybe I'm now injecting some of my prejudice by saying that 'even a homosexual cannot also be a revolutionary.' Quite the contrary; maybe a homosexual could be the most revolutionary.

"When we have revolutionary conferences, rallies, and demonstrations, there should be full participation of the Gay Liberation Movement and the Women's Liberation Movement. Some groups might be more revolutionary than others. We shouldn't use the actions of a few to say that they're all reactionary or counterrevolutionary, because they're not.

"We should deal with factions just as we deal with any other group or party that claims to be revolutionary. We should try to judge somehow whether they're operating sincerely in a revolutionary fashion from a really oppressed situation (and we'll grant that if they're women they're probably oppressed.) If they do things that are unrevolutionary or counterrevolutionary, then criticize that action. If we feel that the group in spirit means to be revolutionary in practice, but they make mistakes in interpretation of the revolutionary philosophy or they don't understand the dialectics of the social forces in operation, we should criticize that, and not criticize them because they are women trying to be free. And the same is true for homosexuals.

"We should never say a whole movement is dishonest when in fact they are trying to be honest; they're just making honest mistakes. Friends are allowed to make mistakes. The enemy is not allowed to make mistakes because his whole existence is a mistake and we suffer from it. But the Women's Liberation Front and Gay Liberation Front are our friends, they are our potential allies and we need as many allies as possible.

"We should be willing to discuss the insecurities that many people have about homosexuality. When I say 'insecurities,' I mean the fear that there is some kind of threat to our manhood. I can understand this fear. Because of the long conditioning process that builds insecurity in the American male, homosexuality might produce certain hang-ups in us. I have hang-ups myself about male homosexuality where on the other hand I have no hang-ups about female homosexuality. I think it's probably because male homosexuality may be a threat to me, and the females aren't. It's just another erotic sexual thing.

"We should be careful about using terms that might turn our friends off. The terms 'faggot' and 'punk' should be deleted from our vocabulary and especially we should not attach names normally designed for homosexuals to men who are enemies of the people, such as Nixon or Mitchell. Homosexuals are not enemies of the people.

"We should try to form a working coalition with the Gay Liberation and Women's Liberation groups. We must always handle social forces in an appropriate manner and this is really a significant part of the population—both women and the growing number of homosexuals that we have to deal with."

---

The GLF/Black Panthers alliance didn't go unnoticed in Chicago's black community. In the *Chicago Defender*, columnist Audrey Weaver wrote under the headline, "Gay guys movement in Midwest is going strong." "This is the age of liberation. We have Black Liberation, Women's Liberation, Girls Lib, and wouldn't you know, Gay Liberation. And like Women's Lib, the latter is not to be taken lightly." Weaver goes on to mention the October 1970 *Mattachine Midwest Newsletter* and its reference to Huey Newton's endorsement of gay rights. "The gay fellows of the nation feel that their oppression is inseparably tied to the oppression of other minorities and that discrimination and oppression must be fought on a broad front. Gay and proud is one of their slogans." She ends with a quote from Thomas Mann, "Opinions cannot survive if one has no chance to fight for them." Weaver's column coincided with Chicago's longest standing "underground" black gay event, the 35th annual Finnie's Club Female Impersonators Ball. In November, in the *Chicago Defender*, columnist Doug Akins wrote, "On Halloween night the Finnie's Club had the largest crowd of spectators and masqueraders than the organization has had in its 35 years history. Over 4,000 people packed the Coliseum to capacity, and then some."

Though cross-dressing was accepted onstage, on the streets it was a different story. One month after Finnie's Ball, a *Chicago Defender* headline read, "'Female Impersonator' killed by cop in W. side street brawl." The *Chicago Sun-Times* headline read, "Man slain fleeing police in bizarre W. Side clash." According to police, 24-year old James Clay was no angel, notching up 12 arrests for impersonating a person of the opposite sex, prostitution, battery, attempted murder and resisting arrest. This time, two patrolmen, James Finnelly and Thomas Bolling ("Bowling" in the *Chicago Sun-Times*), saw Clay waving down motorists in a "suggestive manner." When the cops questioned him, Clay hightailed it. Later the cops returned and Clay, now wearing a man's topcoat and slacks, was chased into a building where he allegedly pulled a knife on Finnelly. Clay then ran, but was gunned down, shot eight times in the head and abdomen.

New York's *Gay Flames: A Bulletin of the Homofire Movement* wrote:

> "Street Transvestite Murdered
>
> "The night before 'Thanksgiving,' the Chicago pigs showed us what we Gays have to be thankful for. 'James' Clay, a transvestite, was murdered in cold blood by James Finnelly and Thomas Bowling, two of Daley's 'finest' fascists.
>
> "Clay, 'in women's clothes,' was standing by the street early in the morning. The policemen say he was trying to flag down motorists. Finnelly knew Clay. He had arrested him before. The fact that our half-sister was back on the streets was a tremendous insult to his cock privilege. So he tried to arrest Clay. Supposedly, Clay ran.
>
> "According to the pigs, they tracked him down into an apartment house where he slashed out with a knife and got away. They 'shot to prevent his escape.'
>
> "Eight shots in the back killed James Clay. He can not tell his story. We can't either but we can say one thing. Clay was in 'men's' clothes when he was killed. When did he change?? During the chase???"

The *Chicago Gay Alliance Newsletter* noted, "We do not mean to impugn the officers and we lack knowledge of the actual substance of the charges against Clay. Nevertheless, being shot eight times in the back strikes us as more than just a simple police action involving the minimum required force." The CGA promised to urge the FBI to investigate the case. The article continued:

> "Readers who question our intercession in what well may be a dubious case, or who ask why we involve ourselves when we are not a transvestite organization, are referred to a quotation by Pastor Martin Niemoller killed by the Nazis.
>
> "They came after the Jews and I was not a Jew, so I did not object.
>
> "Then they came after the Catholics, and I was not a Catholic so I did not object.
>
> "Then they came after the Trade Unionists. I was not a Trade Unionist so I did not object.
>
> "Then they came after me, and there was no-one left to object."

In April 1971, CGA received a letter from the FBI:

> "This is in reply to your letter of February 16, 1971, concerning the killing of James Clay by two Chicago policemen.

## CHICAGO AFTER STONEWALL

"We received reports of the investigation into the circumstances surrounding his killing and after studying the reports, determined that the evidence did not warrant prosecution by the Civil Rights Division."

It was signed Jerris Leonard, Assistant Attorney General Civil Rights Division and Maceo Hubbard, Supervisory Trial Attorney Criminal Section.

The CGA insisted that, "the matter does not end there and further avenues are being explored to see what can be done." Nothing came of it.

The new wave of publicity around gay radicals led to homosexuality being debated in the African American community in Arletta Claire's "Arletta's Advice" column in the *Chicago Defender*. "Tony," a reader, wrote, "The reason for writing is not in hopes of getting advice. Instead I would like to talk about something which I feel very strongly about. I am a young black man, attending school, very interested in the life that surrounds me. I am also a homosexual. But I am not afraid, ashamed or embarrassed."

Readers responses to Tony's letter ranged from sympathetic to vicious. In the July 21, 1970, *Chicago Defender*, Miss Peaches, a 47-year old transsexual wrote, "There are many who know me and, of course, they feel I am, along with all the other homosexuals, abnormal. Of course, I know better than this for I am as normal as anyone."

A week later, "Teamster" wrote:

> "I keep reading letters in your columns from male homosexuals, and to tell you the truth I'm sick and tired of these damn perverts fouling up the world. I think they should be lined up against the wall and whipped to death by another fairy, possibly one dressed in high-heeled leather boots and a vinyl mini-skirt. Who do these fags think they are?"

A year earlier, an article with the headline "He's Missing" appeared in the *Chicago Defender*:

> "Reported missing from home is 13-year-old Ronald Hewitt of 210 S. Springfield ave. He is described as 5ft, 9 in., of medium build weighing 135lbs and has a medium brown complexion, brown eyes and black hair. The teenager is an alleged homosexual and may be seen wearing ladies clothing. He is known to frequent the vicinity of 43rd st. and S. Wabash ave. Any information about his whereabouts should be given to Area 4 of the Chicago Police department's Youth section."

# 9
# THE CHICAGO SEED GAY SUPPLEMENT AND BOYS IN THE BAND

In March 1970, the *Chicago Seed,* an underground newspaper, published an eight-page Gay Liberation Supplement. One article was "Duck and the Dragon Killer" by Michelle Brody, a founding member of UC-GLF. The article lamented the low numbers of women in GLF. Ads like the one in the March 6, 1970, *Maroon* that read, "GAY WOMEN: Gay Liberation is no bastion of male chauvinism. Come join us" did little to swell the numbers of lesbians in GLF.

In the *Seed,* Brody writes:

> "There aren't enough gay women in Gay Lib, for a lot of reasons. Probably mostly because Gay Lib, like everything else in Amerika, except Cold Power, Virginia Slims and living girdles, is considered to be for men. While many of the problems of gay women are closely allied with Women's Lib, I think it's important for gay women to become active in Gay Lib. First, because Gay Lib is the best place to work on erasing male chauvinism and creating an atmosphere of sexual equality, and consideration purely as a person. We've achieved it pretty damn well already, and we're really working on it. We (gay women and gay men) don't need to threaten each other. Secondly, as gay women, we've already hassled through a lot of things that Women's Lib is just now dealing with. I see the aims of Gay Lib and Women's Lib as very similar; we're working together somewhat now, and greater unity will come. But we have to get our individual shits together first.
>
> "Another reason that there are so few women in Gay Lib is the fact, for better or worse, there isn't the sense of community (ghetto) among gay women that there is among gay men. Many gay women have no one at all with whom they can relate in a homosexual context. In a sense we have it

better than gay guys because society merely dismisses us with a casual wave of its wrist. We're not angry enough to fight back, and since we're just women anyway, we know we're supposed to just be passive, be docile, sit still, shut up, and take it. But it's time to be angry."

Brody's article ends with the provocative question, "Don't you think it's about time you stopped hiding?"

The *Seed* Gay Liberation Supplement also mentioned GLF leafleting the Midwest premiere of the movie *Boys in the Band* at the Carnegie Theater on Rush and Oak Sts. on March 18, 1970. The film, the first major American movie about gay life, is based on an Off-Broadway play by Mart Crowley. Set in the late-1960s in the New York apartment of Michael, a recovering alcoholic. He is hosting a birthday party for his friend Harold. The plot unfolds as the drinks flow, party guests arrive, and their dirty laundry gets washed in public. At the time, the play was controversial in the gay community because it depicted homosexuals as tragic figures.

On the opening night, GLF handed out leaflets that read:

"Homosexuals in our society are consistently and cruelly oppressed by the myth that they are in some way less than their fellow men. Whether this characterization of homosexuality as inferior is expressed in terms of 'immorality,' 'perversion,' or 'maladjustment,' it places upon a valuable part of society a sometimes insupportable weight of guilt, anxiety, and self-hatred. The pain and cruelty typified by *Boys in the Band* should be understood as the expression of human lives damaged by an environment of condemnation, suspicion, job discrimination, and legal harassment.

"Gay Liberation refuses to apologize for the occasionally humorous but often tragically destructive lives of some Gay people – we condemn the society which is responsible for our oppression and call to all to join us in the struggle for a world in which human beings are free to love without fear or shame."

The original play opened in Chicago four months earlier at the Studebaker Theatre, and was reviewed by William Leonard in the *Chicago Tribune* under the headline, "Crowley's *Boys in the Band* Realistic Look at Homosexuality":

"The age of permissiveness has reached as far in the theater now as the world of the homosexual. No longer does he have to commit suicide at the end of the play, as some sort of expiation for his nonconformity. The Studebaker stage will be filled with players representing homos ... and all of them will be alive and healthy at the final curtain."

Leonard describes the play as being about "eight faggots and one square at a birthday party." He continued, "Some persons of the homosexual persuasion have told Crowley that his characters are too neurotic and self-destructive to reflect a realistic representation of that kind of life. Crowley retorts that this is a play about neurotic, self-destructive people, not about the sources of their present troubles."

In a review by Jerome Landfield in the *Chicago Daily News*, the writer asks, "Is Mart Crowley's play about homosexuals, *The Boys in the Band*, truly representative of the gay world?" Landfield consulted members of Mattachine Midwest. One suggested the characters were realistic but represented an older generation who hadn't accepted their homosexuality, while another said the play was important because "it lets the straight world see the results of its hostility – these people suffer." Landfield also points to a "generation gap" between older and younger homosexuals. One college student told him, "It isn't like that anymore. A lot of gay people don't like the play because it portrays homosexuals as neurotic, pathetic, and frustrated."

Landfield continued:

> "Another segment of the younger generation, the far out fringe, is probably even less representative of the gay world than the group in the play. They are part of the hard-hip movement, the new militants who are so alienated from the world we are bequeathing them that they reject conventional values.
>
> "Paradoxically, they are like the Nellies because they are compelled to get satisfaction by asserting themselves in ways designed to get us straights more uptight than we are. They take drugs, wear freaky clothes, play at group sex, work as little as possible, and generally defy society where society resents it the most. ... A leader of the Mattachine Society has about as much influence over these people as the Rev. Ralph Abernathy has over a group of Black Panthers."

Interestingly, *Playbill* for *The Boys in the Band* at the Studebaker Theatre contains a full-page ad for perfume depicting the back of two androgynous people's heads. The shoulder-length hair and sweaters are identical, the gender unknown. The ad reads:

> "Once upon a time, it was easy to tell the girls from the boys.
> Once upon a time, all you had to do was look.
> Today, it's not so easy.
> So today, more than ever, a feminine fragrance is almost essential.
> Toward this end,

# CHICAGO AFTER STONEWALL

we suggest My Sin.
It does what
dropping a handkerchief
used to do.
MY SIN by Lanvin."

Another advert in *Playbill* for H. Horowitz Co. Jewelers reads:

"In this day of
Yippies
and Hippies
and Tomato Soup Can art,
hardly anyone
believes in
old-fashioned
beauty
anymore.
We do."

# 10
# GAY PRIDE WEEK 1970

On May 24, 1970, Chicago's gay groups held a joint meeting for the first time at 2<sup>nd</sup> Unitarian Church, 656 W. Barry. The groups included GLF, Mattachine Midwest, the Daughters of Bilitis and the Women's Caucus of Gay Lib. In spite of differences, the meeting ended with all groups agreeing to work together on certain projects, separately on others. Their primary focus was the upcoming June 21-28th Gay Pride Week, the first annual celebration of the Stonewall Riots, known at the time as Christopher Street Liberation Day. It was mostly organized by GLF and endorsed by Mattachine Midwest.

However, cracks were appearing in the façade of GLF's "brotherly and sisterly love." Lesbians split off and held several women-only workshops, often joined by straight members of Women's Lib. Richard Larsen covered one mixed event in the *Chicago Seed*. His coverage appeared under the headline, "Ho-Ho-Homosexual." Larson described a workshop, where a gay man suggested, "homosexual men have more warmth and sensitivity [than straight men]." To which a woman in the group said, "Have you been in a gay bar lately?" Larsen goes on to say gays in bars are "cold and cutting," that homosexual liaisons are made on the basis of age, beauty, or as a cash transaction.

Even before the first Chicago celebration of the Stonewall Riots, Chicago GLF was splitting into factions over gender, ethnicity, ageism, sexism, pornography, and politics. Over the next two years, attempts were made to form one unified Chicago gay-rights group. On January 17 the following year, a second city-wide meeting of Chicago's gay organizations took place at the Lincoln Park Presbyterian Church, 600 W. Fullerton. This time, several hundred attended, including representatives from Mattachine Midwest, One of Chicago, Chicago Gay Alliance, Red Butterflies, Chicago Gay Liberation, Women Identified Women and several university groups. The outcome was the formation of the short-lived Gay Unity Council of Chicago, an umbrella group that dissolved soon afterwards. Unity met March 7 and again March 21 but that was the end of it. Given the political gulf between groups like Mattachine Midwest and the revolutionary socialist Red Butterflies, it wasn't surprising an alliance failed to materialize. In May/June 1971, there was another attempt at forming a unified political action group called Homosexuals Organized for Political Education (HOPE). It fell apart two years later.

According to *Chicago Seed*, who published the Schedule of Events, the 1970 Gay Pride Week festivities kicked off with an evening cruise on Lake Michigan aboard the Trinidad, a charter boat. On June 22, the Midwestern Gay Lib Conference opened at the UIC-CC. It was a week of consciousness-raising workshops. The conference opened with, "The Analysis of the Gay Manifesto," and the weeklong event included such workshops as "Women of Gay Lib," and "Building the Counter Culture." The conference workshops were, for the most part, unstructured with many of them conducted as "rap sessions." The conference ended June 26 with an all-day continuous workshop on "Gay Lib Organizing; Gay Lib and the Movement; Education and Social Change."

Little is known about Chicago's first Gay Pride march, except for a report by Richard Larsen in *Chicago Seed*:

> "Supporters of Gay Liberation came together at Bughouse (Washington) Square on Saturday, June 27, 1970, 12:00 Noon for a rally and march to celebrate the first year of Gay Liberation. The weather was super as one hundred fifty people gathered to hear Sunny King of Detroit Gay Lib; Jonathan Smith, ACLU attorney; Kitch Childs, Chicago Gay Lib, Michael Barta and Henry Weimhoff both of Chicago Gay Lib to rap about where Gay Lib has been and where we are going.
>
> "Bughouse Square, long infamous as a Chicago cruising and hustling park for gays, was a natural location for the rally marking the first anniversary of homosexuals renouncing the guilt, repression, fear and shame that that park represents. Sunny King told the group how she gave up her high paying job to work for Gay Lib because Freedom is more important than any job or security that living a lie might bring. All Gay Libbers are standing up and shouting: 'We're gay and we're proud!' and that was what the rally was all about.
>
> "After the rally, the group marched with its banners flying high over to Michigan and Chicago Avenues and then down Michigan Ave. to

Randolph St. and then over to the Civic Center [now Daley Plaza] shouting gay slogans and holding hands while being ourselves. By the time the group reached the Civic Center, the pig quota was up to five squads and two meat wagons, to protect us no doubt.

"In the middle of the bright sunny Civic Center Plaza we sang, rallied and celebrated the first gay circle dance around the famous Picasso. Chicago's rally may not have been as big as New York City's, but it was every bit as 'mind blowing.'"

The following day, the 1970 Gay Pride Week ended with a picnic in Lincoln Park at the Farm in the Zoo and an evening dance at the Aragon Ballroom.

In an interview with the author, Chicago LGBT Hall of Fame inductee, Richard Pfeiffer, remembers the first Pride March:

"The first Pride march, I just watched. I was still in the closet, in my late-teens, and I was awed by it. The first parade was actually a 'march' in 1970, then the second year it became a 'parade.' There were about 100 people at that first march. I wasn't involved with the community then, but I may have heard about it from a newsletter, or it might have been word of mouth. I was too young to go to bars in those days, but there was a group of folks that I knew that were gay. I worked in Old Town, and that was the hub of the city in those days, late '60s, the Democratic Convention and all that, and I had gay friends, but I wasn't gay identified. So I may have heard about the march from one of them.

"I remember at one point I was in Bug House Square. I know that because one of the speakers was Kitch Childs, who actually ended up in the Gay and Lesbian Hall of Fame. Kitch ended up being my teacher when I was at Harold Washington college years later. I remember being in Bug House, but I was just such a nervous wreck."

# 11
# GLF VS. THE PSYCHIATRISTS

On January 30, 1970, the *Maroon-Grey City Journal* published Henry Weimhoff's "The 'Problem' of Homosexuality." Weimhoff poses the question, "With the challenge to traditionally accepted mores and values of our society increasingly endemic, a new voice is heard, from the segment of the population labeled 'homosexual.' Who are they, these homosexuals, and what do they want?" He goes on to describe homosexuals as "human beings with the abilities and potentials of any other human beings, with a sexual orientation different from the majority, but in essence equally meaningful and valuable."

Weimhoff continues:

> "Homosexuality is neither an affliction to be cured, nor a weakness to be resisted. ... Why then does society persist in treating homosexuality as something less than acceptable? Currently the argument is that homosexuality is a 'sickness,' a symptom of a deeper personality disorder. However, previous to widespread public acceptance of psychoanalytic theory, homosexuals were seen as criminals, threats to the state and the established order of society, and before that as heretical sinners, blasphemers of the 'natural' order established by God and subject to appalling and barbarous persecution. What the designations of homosexuality as 'sinful,' 'criminal' or 'pathological' have in common is neither fact nor logic, but rather a subjective negative attitude – in short, prejudice."

Weimhoff blames the psychiatric profession, the virulently anti-gay Irving Bieber, MD, in particular, whom he refers to as "a renowned psychoanalytic 'authority' in the field." He quotes from Bieber's 1962 book *Homosexuality: A Psychoanalytic Study of Male Homosexuals*, that "all psychoanalytic theories assume that homosexuality is psychopathologic." Even after the American Psychiatric Association removed homosexuality from its list of illnesses in 1973, Bieber wrote, "A homosexual is a person whose heterosexual function is crippled, like the legs of a polio victim."

In "The 'Problem' of Homosexuality," Weimhoff argues that psychiatrists judged all homosexuals by those they saw as patients, and not by the majority, who enjoyed a happy, stable existence. Weimhoff suggests the problems of homosexuals aren't medical but sociological, due to "entrenched prejudice and discrimination." He writes, "The problems of the gay person are the direct result of a relentless barrage of assaults upon his self-esteem and his dignity, the results of which are manifested in damaged self-image, lack of self-confidence, and unwillingness to come forward as a homosexual in society."

The article ends, "The gay contribution to society at this point in time ... can take the form of a radical re-evaluation of the nature of human relations, freeing us from the restrictive cultural categories of 'masculine' and 'feminine,' and allowing deeper and more meaningful relationships between human beings regardless of sex."

During the 1970 Gay Pride Week, the American Medical Association (AMA) convention in Chicago was "zapped" when 18 GLF members infiltrated the convention to protest Dr. Charles Socarides, a physician who claimed homosexuality was a curable disease. He was not alone. In the 1950s and 1960s, homophobia was a moneymaker for doctors and snake-oil salesmen penning medical books, like: *Homosexuality: Disease or Way of Life* (1957) by Edmund Bergler, *Homosexuality* (1962) by Irving Biebler, *Homosexuality, Its Causes and Cures* (1964) by Albert Ellis, *Homosexuality and Pseudohomosexuality* (1969) by Lionel Ovesy, *Changing Homosexuality in the Male* (1970) by Lawrence J. Hatterer, MD. and *The Overt Homosexual* (1968) by Charles Socarides.

The AMA zap took place during "Family Medicine," a workshop where Socarides was due to speak. The previous month, in the *Journal of the American Medicine Association* (JAMA), Socarides wrote about the causes of homosexuality, "The pattern arises from faulty sexual identity, a product of the earliest years of life. Typically, we find a pathological family constellation in which there is a domineering crushing mother who will not allow the developing child to achieve autonomy from her, and an absent, weak, or rejecting father."

In June, the *Chicago Defender* quoted Socarides, that homosexuality was a medical disorder reaching epidemic proportions. "It's frequency of incidence

(2,500,000 to 400,000) surpasses that of the nation's four major illnesses from 1963 to 1965: heart disease, 3,619,000; arthritis and rheumatism, 3,481,000; impairment (except paralysis) of the back, 1,769,000; and mental and nervous disease, 1,767,000."

On the day of the AMA zap, the protestors were scattered throughout the hall. When Socarides said the word "homosexual," a GLF member shouted, "Homosexuals are beautiful." Others distributed a leaflet. Socarides continued but was interrupted again with calls of "you're making things up" and "do you cure your straight patients of heterosexuality?" A report by Step May in an undated New York *Gay Flames*, housed in the McCormick Library of Special Collections at Northwestern University, reads:

> "After Socarides finished, one furious doctor demanded to know by what authority we were attending the session. Another doctor suggested that the issue that the Gay Liberation people were raising should be given legitimacy, and that one homosexual should join Socarides and the other authorities on the panel. A gay guerilla raised the objection that there were women homosexuals and men homosexuals and that both groups would have to be represented. A gay woman and a gay man then took their places on the panel and explained that homosexuals are not inherently sick, but that society and psychiatrists force them to think of themselves as sick. Socarides reiterated his position about gender identity being confused by childhood trauma, which by now must have sounded pretty lame to just about everyone present. That evening a man called the number on the leaflet and said that he approved of the action we'd done. 'I'm a doctor,' he explained. 'I'm gay.'"

The GLF leaflet handed out read:

> "The establishment school of psychiatry is based on the premise that people who are hurting should solve their problems by 'adjusting' to the situation. For the homosexual, this means becoming adept at straight-fronting, learning how to survive in a hostile world, how to settle for housing in the gay ghetto, how to be satisfied with a profession in which homosexuals are tolerated, and how to live with low self-esteem.
>
> "The adjustment school places the burden on each individual homosexual to learn to bear his torment. But the 'problem' of homosexuality is never solved under this scheme; the anti-homosexualist attitude of society, which is the cause of the homosexual's trouble, goes unchallenged. And there's always another paying patient on the psychiatrist's couch.
>
> "Dr. Socarides claims, 'a human being is sick when he fails to function in his appropriate gender identity, which is appropriate to his anatomy.' Who determined 'appropriateness?' The psychiatrist as moralist?

Certainly there is no scientific basis for defining 'appropriate' sexual behavior. In a study of homosexuality in other species and other cultures, Ford and Beach in 'Sexual Patterns of Sexual Behavior' conclude 'human homosexuality is not a product of hormonal imbalance or 'perverted heredity.' It is the product of a fundamental mammalian heritage of general sexual responsiveness as modified under the impact of experience."

"Other than invoking moral standards, Dr. Socarides claims that homosexuality is an emotional illness because of the guilt and anxieties in homosexual life. Would he also consider Judaism an emotional illness because of the paranoia which Jews experienced in Nazi Germany?

"We homosexuals of Gay Liberation believe that the adjustment school of therapy is not a valid approach to society.

"We refuse to adjust to our oppression, and believe that the key to the mental health of all oppressed peoples in a racist, sexist, capitalist society, is a radical change in the structure and accompanying attitudes of the entire social system.

"Mental health for women does not mean therapy for women – it means the elimination of male supremacy. Not therapy for blacks, but an end to racism. The poor don't need psychiatrists (what a joke at 25 bucks a throw!) – they need democratic distribution of wealth. OFF THE COUCHES, INTO THE STREETS!

"We see political organizing and collective action as the strategy for affecting this social change. We declare that we are healthy homosexuals in a sexist society, and that homosexuality is at least on a par with heterosexuality as a way for people to relate to each other (know any men that don't dominate women?)

"Since the prevalent notion in society is that homosexuality is wrong, all those who recognize that this attitude is damaging to people. And that it must be corrected, have to raise their voices in opposition to anti-homosexualism. Not to do so is to permit the myth of homosexual pathology to continue and to comply in the homosexual's continued suffering from senseless stigmatization.

"A psychiatrist who allows a homosexual patient – who has been subject to a barrage of anti-homosexual sentiments his whole life – to continue in the belief that heterosexuality is superior to homosexuality, is the greatest obstacle to his patient's health and well-being.

"We furthermore urge psychiatrists to refer their homosexual patients to Gay Liberation (and other patients who are victims of oppression to relevant liberation movements). Once relieved of patients whose guilt is not deserved but imposed, psychiatrists will be able to devote all their effort to the rich – who do earn their guilt but not their wealth, and can best afford to pay psychiatrists' fees)

"We are convinced that a picket and a dance will do more for the vast majority of homosexuals than two years on the couch. We call on the medical profession to repudiate the adjustment approach as a solution by working in a variety of political ways (re-educating the public, supporting pickets, attending rallies, promoting social events, etc.) to change the situation of homosexuals in this society.

"Join us in the struggle for a world in which all human beings are free to love without fear or shame."

In June 1970, in the *Chicago Defender*, Faith Christmas reported on a meeting of the Chicago Mental Health Association. Brian O'Connell, the executive director, spoke of the high incidence of mental illness in "ghetto" areas and how poor blacks had inadequate health care. He also urged the medical profession to stop diagnosing "homosexuals, student activists, anti-war protestors and Black Panthers as being mentally ill." The debate on homosexuality continued within the medical profession. In August, the *New York Times* published Steven V. Roberts' "Homosexuals in Revolt," an article pitting the new gay militants against the older "in the closet" homosexuals afraid to "come out." On the subject of gay militants, Dr. Lionel Ovesy told the paper:

"Homosexuality is a psychiatric or emotional illness. I think it's a good thing if someone can be cured of it because it's so difficult for a homosexual to find happiness in our society. ... It's possible that this movement (Gay Lib) could consolidate the illness in some people, especially among young people who are still teetering on the brink."

In January 1971, GLF hit the headlines when a "bearded, heavy-set youth" ran onto the set of Howard Miller's Chicago TV show, to – according to the *Chicago Daily News* – "attack Miller and his guest," sex book author Dr. David Reuben. At the time, Reuben was riding high on the success of his sex manual *Everything You Always Wanted to Know About Sex (But Were Afraid to Ask)*. Reuben had a low opinion of homosexuals, writing that lesbians were "immature," while homosexual relationships were "mercifully short." He also harbored strange theories, like, "Food seems to have a mysterious fascination for homosexuals," because most chefs are gay, and "Some of the fattest people are homosexuals."

The "bearded, heavy-set youth" was UC-GLF member, Murray Edelman, who was restrained by the show's host, WLS-TV crewmen, and ushers. Ten members of GLF and the Red Butterflies, a gay revolutionary socialist organization, were invited to the show but were told Reuben wouldn't discuss homosexuality on air. Reuben warned producer Michael Fields he would walk off the set if the subject came up. Near the end of the taping, Edelman rushed the stage and demanded Reuben answer questions. The show aired in its entirety January 19 with Miller misidentifying Edelman as a Red Butterfly. Reuben kept his cool but accused the show's producer of planting gay people in the audience. He later canceled a scheduled appearance on another WLS-TV show.

Clarence Petersen in the *Chicago Tribune* played down the incident:

"I saw the fabled program Friday morning, the day after the taping, and it was considerably less sensational than, say, the televised murder of Lee Harvey Oswald.

"It was difficult to tell if the bearded member of Gay Alliance, a homosexual organization, who got up from his seat in the audience and stalked to the stage was actually bent on assault or if he was determined to get his face before the camera and his questions about Reuben's attitude toward homosexuals answered.

"Miller is seen rising from his chair, standing between the youth and Reuben, and asking ushers to remove him from the studio. They do, quickly, and efficiently (and practically in the dark), and there is some awful language (that will be bleeped out), and that's about all there is to it."

On April 19, 1970, an interview with Dr. David Reuben appeared in the *Miami Herald*:

"Can a homosexual be cured?

"The answer is emphatically yes. Homosexuality can be cured, given these requirements: If the homosexual wants to be cured, and if he's fortunate enough to find a psychiatrist who is able to cure homosexuals. I have many ex-homosexual patients whom I have cured. I think it's important to emphasize that, because there's so much written and said that is so disparaging about homosexuality. So many homosexuals have come to me and said: 'My God, I know there's no hope for me because I've read in this textbook …' Nothing could be further from the truth.

"Can only a few psychiatrists cure homosexuals?

"I would say not more than 10 per cent of the psychiatrists in the United States have success. It's not their fault. Dealing with the problems of a homosexual is an extremely delicate area. It's an area where it's not so much the training and experience of the psychiatrist as his own intuition. It's not something they can learn in schools, and that's the problem. A psychiatrist who can cure homosexuals is born, not educated."

## CHICAGO AFTER STONEWALL

In June 1971, the *Chicago Defender* reported on the theories of Dr. Lawrence J. Hatterer, author of *Changing Homosexuality in the Male*, writing in *McCall's* magazine. Hatterer wrote, "Homosexuals, according to the best evidence so far, are made, not born, and a complex of situations and influences throughout infancy, childhood, adolescence, and early adulthood are involved in the making."

Hatterer warns parents against overreacting when they discover their son (no mention of daughters) is gay:

> "The parent who learns that his child is 'homosexual' must not panic, or react with anger. It is important to show no disapproval, but to try to communicate with him.
>
> "First, determine the degree of involvement. Find out just what he means by 'homosexual.' Sometimes such a statement is rooted in fears and fantasies and not much in the fact of overt homosexual behavior. Other times there is only a small degree of commitment.
>
> "Try to determine his motivation in telling you this. Is he showing defiance, or asking for help? Most often, an open announcement of homosexuality to parents is the very first cry for help/Help him. He is not committed; much can be accomplished if he gets professional guidance."

Hatterer claims to have treated more than 800 homosexuals. "I have never known a family yet where love, acceptance and open communication prevailed that turned out a totally committed homosexual."

In the *New York Daily News*, Bob Lardine interviewed Dr. Lawrence J. Hatterer:

> "Lardine – You claim a good deal of success in curing or, as you put it, changing homosexuals. But have you ever given up on a homosexual? In other words, is there any hope for the committed homosexual?
>
> "Dr. Hatterer – Of course, I've given up on some people. They are the homosexuals who say they want help, but when I reviewed their history it was evident nothing could be done for them. I've never seen a total change in any homosexual past the age of 35. There are some past that age who become partially adapted to heterosexuality, but some homosexuality remains.
>
> "Lardine – Why is it apparently impossible to rehabilitate a man past 35?
>
> "Dr. Hatterer – If a man has been a homosexual for 15 or 20 years, you just can't take his brain out and remake it. Homosexuality has become a part of his psychic-organic nature. It's a question of conditioning. We're all like Pavlovian dogs. If a person does a thing for 15 or 20 years, he'll

continue to do it when the stimulus presents itself. Longtime alcoholics can be helped, however, through group action such as Alcoholics Anonymous. But there's no such thing as Homosexuals Anonymous. If there were, it might be beneficial."

In the November 5, 1973 *Dispatch*, a newspaper out of Moline, IL, Paul A. Hauck, Ph.D. writes, "Many adults are afraid to grow up" in his "The Human Scene" column. Here he shares his thoughts on homosexuality being a financial choice:

> "Some homosexual men also fear the financial burdens of raising a family. That's one of the reasons they may have for choosing men instead of women. Usually, of course, the homosexual is afraid of being rejected by women, so he chooses the safer male. Along with this logic is the argument that a family can drain a man for life and take away his pleasures which he would otherwise keep.
>
> "I don't want to appear to be belittling men with physical aches or homosexuals. Only in some cases do these conditions mean the person was afraid to become an emotional adult. There are numerous instances I have encountered where the fellow was quite mature, sincere, and unafraid of life even if he had a neurotic pain or practiced homosexuality."

Paul A. Hauck, Ph.D. was a clinical psychologist and marriage counselor in Rock Island, IL. According to the *Dispatch*, on March 10, 1969, Hauck sponsored a seminar for the Upper Mississippi Valley Psychological Association during which Dr. Leonard Hullman, a psychologist and professor at the University of Illinois, Champaign, claimed that "behavior modification" was 75% successful in making homosexual men heterosexual.

On December 15, 1973, the American Psychiatric Association (APA) voted to remove homosexuality from its list of mental disorders. The front-page headline in the January 1974 *Chicago Gay Crusader* read, "20,000,000 Gay People Cured!" The change of APA opinion came after the 1970 San Francisco APA zap, an action that resulted in a debate within the APA, leading to the formation of a committee in 1972 to study homosexuality. One member of that committee, Dr. Robert L. Spitzer, authored the resolution to remove homosexuality from the mental disorders list. Spitzer wrote that homosexuality did not fit the criteria for defining a psychiatric disorder. However, if a person was troubled by their homosexuality, a new classification was created called "sexual orientation disturbance." The criteria for this would be, "Individuals whose sexual interests are directed toward their own sex and who are either disturbed by, in conflict with, or wish to change their sexual orientation."

Heterosexuals did not have a similar category for their "sexual orientation disturbance" and APA President, Dr. Alfred M. Freedman, acknowledging the disparity, hinted that internal politics played a part in some of the language by pandering to the naysayers, e.g. "For a mental condition to be considered a psychiatric disorder, it should regularly be associated with generalized impairment of social functioning. Homosexuality does not meet this criteria. This is not to say that homosexuality is 'normal' or that it is as desirable as heterosexuality."

There were dissenting voices within the APA. Thirteen of the eighteen board members voted to declassify homosexuality, three were against, and two abstained. Among APA members who did not support the decision were Drs. Irving Bieber and Charles Socarides, two long-time foes of gay rights, who had built their careers on the shaky foundations of homophobia. Both Bieber and Socarides traveled to Washington DC to persuade the APA board of trustees to reject the resolutions. However, the board not only removed homosexuality from the list of disorders, they went one step further, issuing a statement supporting "the enactment of civil rights legislation at local, state, and Federal levels that would ensure homosexual citizens the same protections now guaranteed to others." They also urged the repeal of laws making "sexual acts performed by consenting adults in private" illegal. After the vote, Bieber and Socarides filed a joint petition requiring a referendum question be included in the February issue of *Psychiatric News* for all APA members to vote on.

In the introduction to his book, *Homosexuality and American Psychiatry: The Politics of Diagnosis*, Ronald Bayer writes:

> "In 1973, after several years of bitter dispute, the Board of Trustees of the American Psychiatric Association decided to remove homosexuality from the Diagnostic and Statistical Manual of Psychiatric Disorders, its official list of mental diseases. Infuriated by that action, dissident psychiatrists charged the leadership of their association with an unseemly capitulation to the threats and pressures of Gay Liberation groups, and forced the board to submit its decision to a referendum of the full APA membership
>
> "Bayer suggests the decision to remove homosexuality from the mental disorders list was reached by violating the usual methods by which questions of science are resolved, 'Instead of being engaged in a sober conversation of data, psychiatrists were swept away in a political controversy. The American Psychiatric Association had fallen victim to the disorder of a tumultuous era, when disruptive conflicts threatened to politicize every aspect of American social life.'"

Bayer notes:

> "A furious egalitarianism that challenged every instance of authority had compelled psychiatric experts to negotiate the pathological status of homosexuality with homosexuals themselves. The result was not a conclusion based on the approximation of the scientific truth as dictated by reason, but was instead an action demanded by the ideological temper of the times."

The National Gay Task Force hailed the APA decision as "the greatest gay victory," and that diagnosing homosexuality as a mental illness had been "the cornerstone of oppression" and that "it has been used as a tool of discrimination in the private sector, and in the civil service, military, adoption and child custody courts." In the *Chicago Sun-Times*, William Hines, the paper's Washington correspondent, wrote, "10 percent of the population were given what amounted to a 'clean bill of health.'" Hines also reported that Dr. Frank G. Kameny, a Gay Task Force leader, said he hoped the APA decision would change the minds of "opinion-molders," like *Chicago Sun-Times* columnist Ann Landers. Kameny told Hines, "If Ann Landers is intellectually honest – if she had any intellectual integrity, when this is called to her attention, she will publicly reverse her position that homosexuality is a sickness and that homosexuals are sick. If she does, the impact will be enormous."

Commentator and syndicated advice columnist, Ann Landers, had been a thorn in the side of the gay community throughout 1973. In the *Chicago Sun-Times* a FORMER READER responds to one of her anti-gay columns, "You are an empty-headed, ignorant, meddling fool. For years I have read your column and believed you were a friend of homosexuals. A few days ago, you turned on us like a jungle animal and exposed your hypocrisy and ignorance."

Landers had written that homosexuals were "sick" and "unnatural."

FORMER READER challenged Landers to read the latest papers by psychiatrists, "They have given us a clean bill of health. They say we are not sick. We are only different." Landers claimed that she had read the papers but sided with "psychiatrists who believe homosexuals are sick and that sex between two men or two women is unnatural." She then backed up her argument with a handful of letters, including one from an ex-gay in the British West Indies who "after six years of in-depth analysis" went straight. Another was a missive from Dr. Sara Charles, Assistant Professor of Psychiatry at the University of Illinois, "I have worked with many homosexuals and, in my opinion, they are individuals whose emotional development was arrested at a preadolescent level. When a massive lack of development in the maturation process occurs in any area, it can be referred to as an illness in psychiatric terms."

NATALIE SHAINESS, MD wrote FROM NEW YORK:

> "I would not call homosexuality a 'dysfunction' as you did in your column recently because this means the inability to use sex organs adequately, which many homosexuals are able to do. Homosexuality, however, is a distortion of the choice of sex partner from the natural to the unnatural. This distortion comes from severe and early development problems caused by an inability to relate to significant adults."

On April 24, 1973, the subject cropped up again in the *Chicago Sun-Times* with a letter from C.A.L. of the Miami Sexual Identity Crisis Center referring to Landers' column printed in the *Miami Herald*, "I am a member of Miami's gay population and I do not read the *Miami Herald* for the purpose of finding myself (and 20 millions of my sisters and brothers in the United States) referred to as 'unnatural, sick, or dysfunctional.' I feel you owe the gay community of Miami an apology."

Landers' reply threw gas onto the flames. "From the day that column appeared in print I've been swamped with letters the likes of which I haven't seen since I printed my Omaha sister's meatloaf recipe," she writes. She goes on to say that after much consideration, she still thought "homosexuality is unnatural" and "individuals who prefer members of their own gender as sex partners are sick." Her anti-gay stance remained entrenched over the years. On July 23, 1976, a gay man challenged her again: "Did you not read that the American Psychiatric Association removed homosexuality from its list of mental disorders?"

Landers replied:

> "The record will never be set straight until the story is told about the behind-the-scenes battling that went on when the American Psychiatric Association ran into that buzz saw.
>
> "Many psychiatrists refused to accept the decision. They made it abundantly clear that the American Psychiatric Association does not speak for all its members. My principal consultants disagreed with the decision. And that's where I stand."

Landers then insisted she had defended the civil rights of homosexuals for 20 years, "However, I do NOT believe homosexuality is 'just another lifestyle.' I believe these people suffer from a severe personality disorder. Granted, some are sicker than others, but sick they are, and all the fancy rhetoric by the American Psychiatric Association will not change it."

On May 26, 1973, the Gay Caucus Against War and Fascism organized a protest outside Ann Landers' "reported residence" in Chicago's Hancock Building. (She actually lived at 209 E. Lake St.) Larry Gulian, in the *Chicago Gay Crusader*, wrote that twenty-seven protestors marched up State St., then along the "Magnificent Mile" chanting: "Ann Landers, we won't take your slanders" and "homosexuality, we are fighting to be free."

One speaker at the Ann Landers protest was Margaret "Skeeter" Wilson, a coordinator for the Gay Teachers Association, who read a statement:

> "Ann Landers has set progress in this area back millenniums by her articles. This is the reason that we are here – to show that Gay people are in all areas of life and that we have more in common with than differences from the straight community and are just as skilled and capable as our colleagues. Ann Landers says that her articles are aimed at helping other people. We say her articles have resulted in needless suffering. If one straight person died for each Gay person who has been murdered by or sacrificed to Straight oppression and sexism, as the old testaments eye for an eye dictates, there would be very few straight women and men left. It is important for Gay people everywhere to stop repressing their sexual feelings and for straight people to stop oppressing us for making a choice that differs from theirs.
>
> "We would like to challenge Ann Landers to meet with and debate the Gay community at large, esp. those involved in helping professions – teachers, social workers, doctors, lawyers etc. If she is secure in <u>her</u> sexuality, she will meet this demand. Let her name the place and the time, WE WILL BE THERE."

A further sign that attitudes toward homosexuality were changing came in a September 1973. A Harris Survey, that polled 1,546 US households found homophobia was on the decline: "Let me ask you about different types of people in this country. For each, tell me if you feel they do more good than harm, more harm than good, or are neither helpful nor harmful?" The results of "Those who do more harm than good" showed a sharp turn away from cold war thinking. "Blacks who demonstrate for civil rights" were down from 65% (1965), 59% (1969), to 40% (1973); "Communists" were 89% (1965), 85% (1969), and 72% (1973); and homosexuals thought to be harmful to society fell from 70% (1965), 63% in (1969) to only 50% (1973). Homosexuals were still more harmful than "students who engage in protest activities," "people who don't believe in God" and "prostitutes," but not as harmful as "college presidents who are lenient with student protestors" and "vigilante groups such as the Minutemen, White Citizens Councils, and the Ku Klux Klan."

# CHICAGO AFTER STONEWALL

On June 10, 1974, an episode of *Advocates* debated the subject of gays vs. the psychiatrists, with Dr. Charles Socarides claiming the APA was unfairly pressured to declassify homosexuality by the National Gay Task Force. *Advocates* was a public television network show out of WGBH, Boston, that focused on current topics, presenting both sides of the argument and encouraging audience participation.

One opinion of the June 10 *Advocates* episode came from African American columnist Ethel L. Payne in the *Chicago Defender*. Payne starts by saying she is not writing about "the either for or against homosexual behavior" argument. She adds, "Life styles ought to be a matter of individual choice. I will not get into the bag of whether it is right or wrong. I leave that fight to the clergy, psychiatrists, psychologists, sociologists and the legal profession."

What angered Payne was how the show was presented:

"Frankly, I was appalled at the hostility shown by the audience which was overwhelmingly in favor of legal sanction of homosexual partnership. The bias was so strong that the opponents would be well within their rights to demand another hearing on the basis of equal time. They were booed, jeered and sneered at on every point. The Advocate for the pros, Dr. Franklin Kameny ... has been leading the fight for homosexual rights for several years. He is president of the [Washington D.C.] Matrichine [sic] Society, which is devoted to homosexual adherents."

The opposing "Advocate" was Miami lawyer Tobias Simon, who Payne described as "combative, to say to least." She continued:

"Dr. Kameny's star witness whose name I missed, was a woman from Emerson College. She was young, attractive, very intelligent, cool and deadly. She had [an] air of detached amusement bordering on contempt. Each time she let fly one of her shafts, the spectators cheered lustily. I had the sensation that she was spearing fish.

"On the other hand, Dr. Socarides, an opposition witness, was treated as though he were a prisoner in the stocks. It was impossible to listen clearly for the catcalls."

What riled Payne, even more, was that the moderator, Tom Atkins, "a well-known black Boston civic leader, and council member," did nothing to stop "the outrageous conduct of the proponents":

"It may well be that homosexuals are entitled to feel that they have been too long treated as moral lepers and social pariahs. It is the same attitude that many blacks adopt in venting years of anger and rejection in boisterous public behavior and riding pell mell over anyone who stands in their way, black, brown or white.

"However deep the wrongs, there is no justification for replacing one kind of tyranny with another."

Ann Landers wasn't the only homophobic "Advice Column." In the December 2, 1971 column "The Worry Clinic," in the *Dixon Evening Telegraph*, the conservative syndicated psychologist Dr. George W. Crane writes about "The Homosexual Revolution":

> "Thousands of homosexuals feel trapped in their abnormal erotic state and wish they could escape from their homosexual 'twilight zone' of the human race.
>
> "Others, however, like the scared boy whistling as he passed the darkened cemetery, now loudly publicize their juvenile attachments to their own sex.
>
> "But this is like boasting by leaders of the women's liberation front!
>
> "For those women who are trying to 'sell' themselves on their belief, for most of them know they'd gladly play second fiddle to any male who'd put a wedding ring on their third finger!
>
> "In fact, a recent poll showed that the women's liberation doctrine was popular chiefly with the unmarried and career women. (Sour grapes?)
>
> "The wives and widows were quite content to let the male sex remain dominant!
>
> "... Homosexuality is thus a bad habit, like alcoholism, drug addiction and even cigarettes."

Later that month, Dr. Crane wrote:

> "Are Men Sissy?
>
> "Do readers believe that American males are growing more effeminate? ... Alas, nowadays, many American males are boldly publicizing the fact they are homosexuals. They even try to marry other such half-females! And many of them appear so effeminate they not only can't wield a ping pong paddle. But they aren't even interested in watching robust competitive sports on TV or from the stadium seats! This suggests lack of normal male pugnacity! Meanwhile, they act like jittery infants who must have their 'pacifier' to keep them quiet and docile. The modern adult 'pacifier' is the cigarette, which emotionally disturbed adults now suck on frantically like the disturbed baby in its crib."

In July 1973, Dr. Crane turned his attention to lesbians:

> "Homosexual Techniques
>
> "The public often think of the male homosexual as being slender and effeminate.

"While that applies to many of them, there are big burly male homos who are over 6 feet tall and weighing 200 pounds.

"Similarly, female lesbians (homos) are not always the large masculine type of woman.

"Sometimes a very frail looking girl may be the aggressor in launching her roommate into a lesbian relationship.

"Like the older male who tries to molest children, such an aggressor may start making gifts to her intended victim.

"She may offer her roommate some of her clothing or cosmetic lotions and perfumes.

"And she soon likes to touch her victim's hair, either by stroking it or by offering to comb it and arrange a new hairdo.

"Girls normally greet each other with a quick kiss, so the lesbian merely carries this custim [sic] to greater extremes.

"And instead of a cheery little peck on the cheek, the lesbian soon begins to kiss her female roommate more often and with greater fervor.

"She prolongs the kiss in an erotic manner of a male sweetheart who is trying to inflame his girl friends' passion.

"If they should ever occupy a double bed, then the lesbian (ostensibly in her sleep) will place her arm around her companion's shoulders.

"Next she begins to stroke her roommate's skin and fondle her breasts.

"If the intended victim pushes the lesbian's hands away, the latter can always act as if she has been asleep while this sexual prelude has occurred.

"If the female homo and her prospective victim have taken a little wine or other alcoholic beverages (which lesbians often urge as a shortcut to their speedier conquest of the innocent girl), then liquor becomes a confenient [sic] 'smoke screen' for more aggressive erotic fondling.

" ... Once the lesbian has completed the conquest of her female partner, the latter begins to feel bewitched by the lesbian's erotic charisma.

"For whoever initiates an innocent victim into a complete sexual climax, there after holds almost a magic power!"

However, not all of Kameny's "opinion-molders" were homophobic. In the De Kalb, IL. *Daily Chronicle*, a letter to the "HELEN HELP US" column from GOING BY THE BIBLE reads:

"Dear Helen

"You recommend 'tolerance' for the homosexual 'who doesn't bother anybody.' No matter how secretive he is, he bothers us normal people! Read your Bible, Romans 1:27:32, among other chapters and then dare to say 'tolerance is on the way' for those depraved and loathsome creatures."

Helen answers, "Dear Going. In reading the passage you suggested, I came across another which I recommend to folks like you: Matthew 7:1 (Judge not that ye be not judged.)

Ann Landers may have been homophobic, but Abigail Van Buren, her twin sister, was not. In October 1973, in her "Dear Abby" column, a reader asks if homosexuals are sick:

> "DEAR ABBY: Another advice columnist keeps insisting that homosexuals are 'sick.' She says: 'Thousands of homosexuals have written asking me where they can get straightened out so they must consider themselves twisted, or they wouldn't be asking for help. Occasionally I hear from homosexuals who are at peace with themselves, but they are few and far between. I believe the majority of homosexuals would be straight if they were really free to choose.
> 
> "What say you, Dear Abby?"

Abby answers:

> "DEAR READER: I say if a heterosexual had been raised to believe that his preference for the opposite sex was 'sick,' twisted, abominable, sinful, and a disgrace to his family, he would ask for help on how to 'straighten himself out,' too.
> 
> "Homosexuality IS a problem because an unenlightened society has made it a problem, but I have received letters by the thousands [not just 'occasionally'] from gay people telling me that they wouldn't be straight if they had a choice. All they ask is to be allowed to love in their own way without facing the charge that they are 'sick and twisted.'
> 
> "I say, love and let love."

Again, in Bloomington's *Pantagraph,* in October 1975, "Dear Abby" received a letter from A PROUD GAY:

> "Dear Abby: My family name is 'Gay.' My ancestors have been traced back to France in the 1600s.
> 
> "I am writing this in hopes that the Gay Liberation Society will see it and realize how unfair they are being in using our name for their organization.
> 
> "The gay liberation group holds that they have the right to live and let live – a philosophy with which I am in complete agreement. But in so doing, they have infringed upon the rights of others.
> 
> "Since the homosexuals have organized and officially adopted our name for their group, we have been harassed with crank phone calls at all hours and subjected to insults and ridicule.

# CHICAGO AFTER STONEWALL

"Our name was 'Gay' long before they took that name, so I think in all fairness to us Gays, they should change the name of their society to one more befitting to their crusade.

"The last straw came when my father called me long distance after he saw a TV series on homosexuality and he seriously suggested that WE change OUR name."

Abby writes, "Dear Proud. I understand your plight and am most sympathetic, but I doubt if the Gay Liberation Society will consider changing its name. Although you were Gay first, I believe there are more of THEM than there are of YOU."

In the *Mt. Vernon Register-News*:

"Dear Abby: About four months ago, the house across the street was sold to a 'father and son' – or so we thought.

"We later learned it was an older man about 50 and a young fellow about 24.

"This was a respectable neighborhood before this 'odd couple' moved in. They have all sorts of strange looking company. Men who look like women and women who look like men, blacks, whites, Indians, and yesterday I even saw two nuns go in there.

"They must be running some sort of business, or a club. There are motorcycles, expensive sports cars, and even bicycles parked in front and on the lawn. They keep their shades drawn so you can't see what's going on inside, but they must be up to no good or why the secrecy?

"Abby, these weirdos are wrecking our property values! How can we improve the quality of this once-respectable neighborhood?

"UP IN ARMS."

Abby writes, "Dear UP. You could move."

# 12
# THE GLF SPLIT

Although several hundred people turned up for a GLF dance, only a handful showed up for a picket line. Not everyone agreed with the far-left politics of GLF. Some people were closeted and reluctant to rock the boat. On May 16, 1970, Chicago GLF picketed the Spanish Consulate offices at 11 E. Adams to protest Spain's systematic persecution of gays under the dictator Francisco Franco Bahamonde. Under Franco, LGBT's were incarcerated in special prisons called "galerías de invertidos" (galleries of deviants). The headline in the *Chicago Gay Liberation Newsletter* read, "picket spanish pigs."

Throughout the summer of 1970, GLF remained active. In August, the *Chicago Gay Liberation Newsletter* urged readers to attend the Cain Dance Troupe show at Northeast Community College. It was a benefit for the Venceremos Brigade, a group of young American volunteers working alongside Cuban workers to protest US policy toward that country. Then GLF turned their attention to the Astro, a Greek restaurant at Clark and Diversey, in the heart of the gay neighborhood, owned by brothers Gus and George. According to Ronnie Drantz, a lesbian waitress there, the brothers were oblivious to the fact that most of their customers were gay until a flamboyant couple came in and were refused service.

Ronnie tipped off the gay groups and GLF picketed, handing out leaflets urging a boycott. On August 7, thirty-five members of GLF stood on the picket line. Ronnie Drantz tells her story:

> "'Don't you know a queer when you see one? I can smell a queer a mile away!' The Astro restaurant was located on the southeast corner of Clark & Diversey, or Clark and Diversity, as we queers liked to say back then. This was in the heart of Chicago's gay neighborhood and the Astro was

frequented by gay people who lived and/or worked in the area. Gus and his brother George were from Greece and were co-owners of the Astro. Gus was the dapper one, always in a white business shirt and tie, stationed at the register to greet customers as they entered and take their money as they left. George was the sinewy, sweaty one who was the head cook. Many of Gus and George's favorite customers were gay but they didn't know this. One afternoon I glanced up to see two guys, one of whom immediately tripped my gaydar, enter the restaurant and sit in a small booth in my waitress section. As I took their order for coffee, Gus rushed over and commanded me: 'Charge them the higher price for the coffee.' A policy in the menu charged more for customers ordering only coffee when sitting in a booth as opposed to the counter, but I had never seen that policy enforced until now. Then he told the two guys to hurry up and leave. 'Don't come back. We don't want your kind in here!' he hissed at them. The hurt looks on these guys' faces were heart-breaking and I apologized to them profusely. 'It's okay, we know it's not your fault' they responded. After the two guys left, I passed by Gus at the register and he glared at me saying: 'What's the matter with you? Don't you know a queer when you see one? I can smell a queer a mile away!' I wanted to say: 'Do you smell anything Gus? I'm only a few feet away from you.' But I needed the job. Gus never guessed that his favorite new waitress was lesbian. I don't remember knowing about the Stonewall Riot in New York at that time, but I had just read that Barbara Gittings and Frank Kameny were picketing and disrupting meetings of the American Psychiatric Association to stop pathologizing homosexuality. This bravery inspired me to activism, and I visited the headquarters of Chicago Gay Liberation to tell the guys about this incident. Gary Chichester, passionate and good-looking, was clearly the leader. CGL already had heard a long list of complaints about the Astro Restaurant refusing to serve gays, but now they had a story from an employee who was instructed to discriminate against gay customers. CGL decided to picket the Astro. They met at my apartment to plan the picketing. Gary told the guys to not wave or smile at me through the windows of the restaurant while picketing because I needed my job and would be the 'undercover waitress.' On Friday, August 7th, 1970, I looked out the Astro windows and saw 35 CGL guys with signs striding down Clark Street toward the restaurant. They started picketing the Astro entrance and leafleting passersby, explaining why they were picketing and asking people to boycott the Astro. They showed no fear. My heart was pounding. I had never before seen gay people publicly protesting their mistreatment. The leaflet mentioned Gus's statement to me about smelling queers a mile away. I thought Gus would conclude I was part of the picketing, but he never did. Then I realized he had probably made statements like this to many people. My favorite sign was carried by a CGL picketer who was a friend. I had posed as his girlfriend for a dinner with his parents in order to placate the hyper-religious father who was desperate that his son gets married now that he had left the seminary and wasn't going to be a priest. This ex-seminarian friend's sign irritated Gus and George immensely. The sign read: UP YOUR ASTRO. On the second day of picketing, George became so irritated he ran out and shoved one of the picketers. George must have thought a gay guy would literally be a pushover, but this gay guy immediately and fiercely lunged back at George. George ran back into restaurant looking terrified and looked at the phone on the vestibule wall as if considering calling the police. I told him he couldn't because everyone saw him start the incident. He just stood there looking dazed for a moment and then walked back into kitchen, his shoulders drooping. The CGL picketers came back for a total of nine consecutive days, ending on Saturday, August 15th. The activism happened inside the restaurant as well as outside with the waitresses functioning as allies to the gay picketers and gay customers. Soon after the picketing started, I gathered the waitresses together to discuss Astro's gay customer treatment among ourselves. To my delight the waitresses immediately concluded that their best customers were the gay ones. Customers who crossed the picket line came in holding the leaflets and asked the waitresses lots of questions. The waitresses answered that they disagreed with Astro's policy because the gay customers treated them with respect and were the best tippers. The public reaction was largely sympathetic to the gay customers. I don't know if those two gay guys who came in for coffee ever found out about the picketing of the Astro or realized their role in this historic event. I'm sure they never thought that the waitress was also gay. I never heard another word from Gus or George about not serving gay customers after this. To my knowledge, this was the first picketing by gay people to protest discrimination by a public establishment in Chicago."

Of the Astro protest, the *Chicago Gay Liberation Newsletter* wrote:

"The turnout was good and included many gay people who were demonstrating for the first time. The pickets carried posters and signs and distributed more than 1,000 leaflets. Many straight people responded sympathetically, although there was some heckling.

"At 9:30 that night, as the picket line was disbanding, John Maybauer was arrested for 'assaulting' verbally a heckler who had consistently called him a 'fucking faggot.' John was immediately bailed out by other members of CGL [Chicago Gay Liberation]; a jury trial has been set for October 1st."

This wasn't the first time a restaurant was boycotted. In a letter to historian Gregory Sprague, activist Patrick Townson wrote:

# CHICAGO AFTER STONEWALL

"The first boycott I remember happened in 1960 at a local restaurant in the Clark/Division neighborhood. You may remember the old B/G restaurant chain. At one time, there were about 50 in the Chicago area. There used to be one on the southeast corner of Dearborn and Division. ... It sort of functioned as the place for the underage gay kids. B/G's policy was thirty-five cents for all the coffee you could drink. And sit there they did. The waitresses got good tips, so no-one complained. And the kids were allowed to dance (same sex yet!) to the juke box. All was well until one night when the manager came in and rudely cut off the jukebox, then to everyone present announced, 'I want all the faggots to get up and pay their checks; then get out, and stay out. Faggots are a goddamn offense to decent people ...'

"Well, I want to tell you that in a matter of minutes the restaurant was empty – save two or three old ladies sitting in a booth together. The place held almost a hundred customers, and it had been full. All of us went down to the A&P market on State and Division and purchased several dozen eggs. Tomatoes and what have you. We went back and trashed the restaurant. Never again did the place have any business. It was almost empty all the time. Finally, about six months later, they closed the location, blaming, of course, 'the queers who ruined our business.'"

On August 8, 1970, twenty members of GLF marched as a contingent in the annual Hiroshima Day March, sponsored by the Chicago Peace Council and the Student Mobilization Committee. The purpose of the march was to commemorate the bombings of Hiroshima and Nagasaki in World War II and to protest the Vietnam War. The march started at the Federal Building with a rally, where one of the speakers in the open mic section was Joe [Joel] Hall of the Black Caucus of GLF. He spoke of the arrest of Ortez Alderson and the Pontiac 4 and also the picket at the Astro restaurant.

Three weeks later, GLF held a fundraiser at Sparrows drag bar at 5214 N. Sheridan. The owner, gay businessman Charles "Chuck" Renslow, designated August 28 Gay Lib Night. Onstage that night was "Mr. Roxanne and his Fantasy Revue" and there was same-sex dancing, which thanks to GLF was no longer an arresting offense.

In the September 1970 *Chicago Gay Liberation Newsletter,* GLF was riding high on a wave of success. Well-attended citywide meetings were held every Sunday at 7:30 p.m. at the Arts and Architecture building, at the University of Illinois Circle Campus at Halsted and Harrison. Chicago GLF new members met at 1909 N. Mohawk every Thursday at 7:30 p.m. "COME OUT ... and come on over. Bring along a six-pack and maybe someone will love you." The editor of the newsletter, Tom Biscotto, was leaving his post but noted the improvements:

> "By now, readers have undoubtedly noted the new look to the Newsletter. A Gestetner machine replaces the former (and more expensive) offset press. The new process uses electronically imaged stencils, which may allow us to reproduce photographs in future issues. Since the machine accepts a maximum page size of 8 ½ by 11, the Newsletter will now consist of several pages stapled, rather than one sheet, folded, as in past issues."

However, in spite of GLF's success and growth, they soon followed New York GLF, when a split occurred between leftist radicals determined to fight for the rights of all oppressed minorities and one-issue Gay Libbers concerned only with gay rights. At a September 27 meeting, simmering tensions led to Chicago GLF splitting in two with a new group called the Chicago Gay Alliance (CGA) forming.

Trouble had been brewing for weeks. Not everyone supported the alliance with the Black Panthers and other far-left groups. According to the *Chicago Gay Liberation Newsletter*, the schism occurred on September 20 when the Black Caucus announced a change of name to Third World Gay Revolutionaries and presented GLF with a list of demands: (1) That political consciousness sessions be a regular function of GLF/Chicago; (2) That consciousness raising sessions on racism be a regular function of GLF/Chicago; (3) That self-defense lessons be made available for GLF members; and (4) That consciousness raising sessions in sexism be a regular function of GLF/Chicago.

The Third World Gay Revolutionaries added that they would "clarify, discuss and help in any capacity to see that the above-mentioned demands be met."

These "demands" grated on some. After the meeting some members formed the Chicago Gay Alliance (CGA), an organization that focused solely on gay issues. Article 1 of the CGA Constitution reads:

> "We seek to accomplish the following basic goals: 1) Personal Liberation – to integrate one's sexuality with the total being through a program of social interaction; 2) Gay Community – to instill an awareness of gay brotherhood through mutual respect; to recognize the diversity of lifestyles among ourselves and to unify them into a common culture; and to develop informational programs pertaining to homosexual problems; 3) Reformation – to change oppressive institutions, laws and policies

through educational and political activities, thereby initiating a parallel change in human attitudes."

The first issue of the *Chicago Gay Alliance Newsletter* listed the newly elected officers as Chairman – Gary (Chichester), Secretary – Nick (Kelly), Treasurer – Jerry (Cohen), Vice-Chairman – Tim, Deputy Secretary – Ed (Hart), and Deputy Treasurer – Henry.

In May 1971 the *Chicago Gay Alliance Newsletter* reported that UC-GLF had opened an office on campus at the Ida Noyes Hall. A "Gay Message" flyer read:

> "The office is just a place to meet and talk with other gay people – for whatever purpose you want. The important thing is that it's your office – not the 'leaders' or the 'doers.' If you want to come and answer the phone, answer some questions or ask them, or just talk to other people, this is your office to do it in. The office has no organization or leaders; it is operating only when people are there. Come for as long or as short a time as you want, but please come, otherwise there is no office."

The "Gay Message" was sent by "some gays who have just abdicated their leadership positions, nasty and subversive as it is to be leaders." In the same "Message":

> "After several weeks of inactivity, the Gay Coffee House will be open again Saturday nights at the Blue Gargoyle from 8:00 p.m. to 1:00 a.m. for the rest of the month. ... People who have been through Gay Lib in the last year and a half and no longer relate to it are asked to take part in its rebuilding. Although the beginning of the summer is perhaps not the best time to undertake new projects, it seems that with the new gay office at Ida Noyes, the Gay Coffee House in the Garg, and the second Gay Pride Week there are opportunities to participate in gay activities on many different levels from political action to celebration to dances. In the past cliquishness in Gay Lib has frightened people away. Please come to a gay activity and let each other know how you feel about what is happening or what could be happening."

Clearly UC-GLF was in disarray.

# 13
# THE GLF AROUND TOWN

After the split, both GLF and CGA forged ahead with GLF holding a dance October 9, 1970 in the Illinois Room of the Chicago Circle Center and weekly meetings at the home of David Thierry 667 W. Barry, while CGA met at a gay juice bar, the Big Basket at 436 N. Clark St. The Big Basket had dancing, live bands, a light show and a "coffee house" serving food. When the Big Basket closed through lack of support, the CGA held meetings on Sundays at 3:00 p.m. at Lincoln Park Presbyterian Church, 600 W. Fullerton, and rap sessions continued at 1909 N. Mohawk, Thursday evenings at 8:00 p.m. Meanwhile, Mattachine Midwest stepped up its media presence, when on October 2 Tom Erwin (Dr. Thomas Erwin Gertz) and Rev. Charles Lamont appeared on "Night Line," on WBBM in Chicago. The Rev. Lamont led weekly non-denominational Saturday night services at the Avondale United Methodist Church, 3246 W. George.

According to the November 1970 *Mattachine Midwest Newsletter*, "radio and television stations as well as school, church, and civic groups have been calling us for speakers." On October 20, Tom Erwin, Valerie Taylor, and GLF's Mike Barta were on Stan Dale's *Confrontation* WLS call-in show. On November 2, Tom Erwin, Mike Barta, Bill Way and attorney Renee Hanover, appeared on Dan Price's show *Extension 720* on WGN.

In March 1970, six members of GLF spoke to seniors in the sociology program at Elk Grove High School. Judy Covelli in the *Daily Herald* wrote:

> "Speakers from organizations have been invited to the class to acquaint the students with problems in society related to the class topics, dating, marriage, family and human sexuality.

## CHICAGO AFTER STONEWALL

"The speakers, members of the Gay Liberation and most of them university students in Chicago, are publicly acknowledged homosexuals."

The invitation to speak came from Joseph Wellman, team teacher. Wellman told the *Daily Herald* that he wanted "to provide the students the opportunity to ask questions of a segment of people upon whom the public looks strangely":

"'I wanted them to find out that they don't have three arms,' Wellman said. 'I want to dispel some of the myths around the idea of homosexuality.'

"Wellman explained that the topic arose when the classes began discussing attitudes toward the opposite sex.

"'Among other things, we discussed the 'Playboy Philosophy' and the growing feminist movement,' he said."

Other speakers invited were from the National Organization of Women (NOW) and members of a radical feminist group called Women's International Terrorist Conspiracy from Hell (WITCH). Wellman and Sue Kaineg, team-teachers of the sociology class, stressed that only senior students were present and that the speeches and speakers had been approved by the administration, cleared by division heads and the principal. Covelli continued:

"The members of the Gay Liberation, somewhat poised and at times quite humorous, explained how they lived, what they felt, and how they wish society would react toward them. In brief, this is what some of the members of the Gay Liberation had to say.

"Richard: a graduate at the University of Chicago, 'You don't know what it's like to walk around and know that society says that what you are feeling inside you is wrong. Because many homosexuals are oppressed, they develop a neurosis and can really become sick, although they weren't before.'

"Henry: 'I have to accept myself as a valid human being. If I want to hold another guy's hand, I am free to do it. I have to deal with a society, though, that doesn't accept that view.'"

The following month the *Daily Herald* quoted from an article in the *Seed* underground paper about GLF and the talk at Elk Grove High School. They quote a GLF member who was there:

"Wednesday six members of Gay Liberation, one Gay woman, four gay men, and Susan the Polyamorous Perverse traveled to the white middle-class suburban high school to talk to a succession of sociology classes.

> "The six of us sit facing the class, the kids sit quietly listening. What's going on inside their heads? Do they hate us, are they afraid of us? Do they view us as a curiosity?
>
> "It occurs to me that the most freaked-out person in the room may be one of the Gay high school kids in his closet struggling to control his emotions not to let it show. His face is calm he sits quietly while his guts are ripping apart, his mind is in a turmoil."

On April 3, the *Daily Herald* published Tom Wellman's article, "This Novice Is Determined" ... "Mrs. Sophia Basile of Elk Grove Village, one of eight candidates fighting to fill three open seats on the High School Dist. 214 board, is a novice board candidate."

Basile, who described herself as "an ordinary housewife' jumped on the homophobia bandwagon to leverage votes. Her other concerns were smoking, making clothing out of the flag, and drug use. Wellman continued:

> "Several weeks ago, representatives of women's liberation groups and several homosexuals spoke at Elk Grove High School. She [Basile] questions the need in the community for such speakers, and she will state, at a future candidate's night: 'I question the need of bringing homosexuals into the school as part of the research study of sociology. What would be the approach to the study of sex orgies? Representatives from NOW and WITCH (two feminist groups) who state the need to reproduce is a tradition that necessitated marriage and say this need is not necessary, do not express the ordinary average home in our district, which has religion and believes in the home, love and marriage.
>
> "She and her family ... have lived in Elk Grove for five years. And she has been active in the community for those five years.
>
> "She said she contributed her battered 1959 Oldsmobile to the industrial arts department at Elk Grove High School, and she has worked to get a walking bridge installed near the high school. So, for Mrs. Sophia Basile, public activities are not a new experience."

# 14
# THE ALDERMANIC CANDIDATES

A part of the CGA strategy included engaging politicians. In late 1970/early 1971, the CGA polled all 161 aldermanic candidates in an upcoming election, to state their views on gay rights. The *Chicago Gay Alliance Newsletter* published the answers of the twenty-one who filled out the questionnaire:

The questions were:
1) Would you support legislation providing for injunctive relief where a definite pattern of persistent harassment of homosexuals can be demonstrated?
2) Would you work for an end to police harassment of bars and other public facilities catering to homosexuals, if such were to arise?
3) Would you support a fair employment law which prohibits the refusal of hiring and the firing of employees solely on the basis of their homosexuality?
4) Would you work for an end to the income tax discrimination against single persons?
5) Would you support legislation removing penalties for public displays of affection between homosexuals – kissing, holding hands, embracing, dancing – such acts as are considered tasteful and proper for heterosexuals?
6) Would you work to oppose governmental collection of data on the sexual practices of individuals?
7) Would you work for immediate investigation of the insurance and bonding companies which practice discrimination against homosexuals?

A sample of the answers received:

4th Ward:

John Barber answered yes to all but 4 and 5. He explained his nays by saying, "My negative responses by no means are designed to derogate others for whatever sexual things they privately dig. Do your thang, gays! Right on! ... I need to kick Daley's ass and that of his policemen who fuck over y'all and my young black brothers ..."

22nd Ward:

James Gullatte answered yes to all the questions, adding "Power to all peoples ... We are looking forward to working with your organization."

35th Ward:

Stephen J. Telow answered yes to question 1 and 2, no with question marks to 3, yes with a question mark to 4, "absolutely no" to question 5 (which he called asinine and ridiculous), and yes to questions 6 and 7. He added: "Since the liberals have created a monster and find it hard to control – makes a conservative aldermanic candidate like me question where we are headed in this society with 'free love,' homo, more rape, promiscuity and expression of 4 letter words."

49th Ward:

Richard Davis answered yes to all the questions. He added: "If CGA has any suggestions that would help me further the cause of gay liberation, please contact me at (he includes phone number) or at my home address (He includes home address).

---

Within the heavily gay 43rd Ward, only Theodore Pearson and Naomi Allen answered the questionnaire. Pearson answered yes to all the questions but queried number four (Would you work for an end to the income tax discrimination against single persons?). After number seven (Would you work for immediate investigation of the insurance and bonding companies which practice discrimination against homosexuals?) he wrote, "But it is not the most important question facing the people."

Allen answered yes to all the questions, adding after six (Would you work to oppose governmental collection of data on the sexual practices of individuals?): "We are not opposed to the government collecting data voluntarily given, we are opposed to the government snooping into peoples' lives where it has no business and is not wanted."

Other candidates in the 43rd Ward were incumbent Ald. William Singer, Christopher Michas, Bernard Moschel, and Edward F. Boyle. At a public meeting of aldermanic candidates at St. Clement's Church, 642 W. Deming, CGA Chairman Gary Chichester asked why some candidates failed to fill out the questionnaire. There was laughter from the crowd, until Chichester said, "Homosexuality is not funny." After a twenty-minute discussion several candidates agreed to take the questionnaire; during coffee Boyle and Moschel volunteered to speak at a CGA meeting. However, it was Ald. William Singer who took the CGA up on their offer to come and speak to the group. On February 18 at the Lincoln Park Presbyterian Church, he became the first elected City of Chicago official to address a gay group. Singer was running for re-election in the 43rd Ward.

# 15
# MIDWEST REGIONAL GAY LIBERATION CONVENTION

In April 1971, Chicago's GLF groups attended the First Midwest Regional Gay Liberation Convention at Northern Illinois University in DeKalb. Albert of NIU-GLF wrote a report, housed in the McCormick Library of Special Collections at Northwestern University. It reads:

"Friday, April 16, 1971, 6 p.m. Six members of the University of Wisconsin Gay Liberation Front arrived at the University Center of Northern Illinois University. This event marked the beginning of the historic First Midwest Regional Gay Liberation Convention.

"Suggested by several NIU-Gay Liberation Front members in October, the Convention grew out of discontent over big city domination of other Gay Liberation conventions held in other cities around the country and a recognition of a need for some togetherness of Gay Brothers and Sisters on Midwest college campuses. For DeKalb, Illinois, and Northern Illinois University the Convention expressed a hope to reinforce the message that Gay is beautiful, that we are all together. We believe also that such a message is especially important for spreading claustrophobia among persons in the closet! Never before has NIU-Gay Liberation worked so long and hard on a project.

"With the arrival of a member of the University of Iowa (Ia. City) Gay Liberation Front the Convention began to take shape. The total picture included 110 persons from fourteen schools in six states. Other delegates were from University of Kansas, Lawrence; University of Louisville; Wisconsin State Univ., Platteville; University of Chicago; Oberlin College, Ohio; University of Illinois-Urbana and Chicago Circle; Southern Illinois University, Carbondale; Northwestern University, Evanston, IL; Roosevelt University, Chicago; and Illinois Institute of

Technology, Chicago. As for Northern Illinois University, we have never seen so many members of our Gay Liberation Front together in one weekend. Thirty-eight of us attended the Convention.

"On Friday evening, so as to not crowd the Gallery Lounge (scene of registration) and to provide our guests with coffee, congeniality, and conversation, we moved upstairs to the Heritage Room. There everyone had a chance to sit down and get acquainted. The Heritage Room also served as a departure point for a party in our sister city, Sycamore.

"There was a valid criticism from our Gay Sister, Phyllis (University of Chicago GLF), that the party should not be planned that night, since it preceded a long day of activity. We were inclined to agree with her because several cases of fatigue and tardiness were noted the next day. In fact, past evidence has shown that Gay parties in the DeKalb-Sycamore area have been known to go into the wee hours of the morning. But we only planned the party because there really isn't anything to do most weekends in DeKalb, anyway, whether you are Gay or straight. We also believed that a party would give the delegates a chance to communicate with one another. However, we did have rather broad definition of communication.

"Robert, our host for the evening, declared open house during Convention weekend for parties and housing. After the formalities of exchanging greetings, things got under way at the party with the Soul Sounds of Diana Ross, followed by the Jackson Five. This was the night of the All-Star Sheena-Debbie Revue, a display of great dancing led by Stephen, former NIU-GLF treasurer.

"For a change of pace, we slowed all the way down to Jeannette MacDonald; the mood was one of humor rather than nostalgia. The pace was quickened a bit by the Cruising series (don't let the title fool you, an anthology of the rock 'n' roll scene of the Fifties. At this point, this reporter left the party; all reports seem to indicate that everyone continued to have a good time.

"Saturday morning was similar to Friday night; we waited for new arrivals and for the past night's party set to arise. The first event to create a high level of excitement was the arrival of our most-traveled delegation. Despite a long night of interstate riding in a sea-green Volkswagen love bug, the four young men from the University of Kansas were able to greet us with cheerful smiles. Other arrivals were four Brothers from the University of Louisville; most of the Chicago area delegates and part two of the Southern Illinois University contingent, with the SIU delegation including beautiful Karen, noted for the Superwoman jersey.

"The main events of the Convention began when the delegates filed into a cozy fifth floor conference room for the General Session, which mainly consisted of one member of each group giving a summary [of] his group's experiences.

"Al from NIU-Gay Liberation (regrettably the only Black person attending the Convention) spoke for his group. Northern Illinois University Gay Liberation Front became an official student-government-approved organization on April 12, 1970. There have [been] no major hassles from anyone anywhere. We have spoken to classes in education, psychology, sociology, and home economics; have twice been on local radio; and have participated [in] various school activities. The membership fluctuates; there are about 40 members, eight of whom are women.

"The University of Kansas Gay Liberation Front, organized in August 1970, is still working for university recognition. Their fight for recognition may soon move into the legal system. Oberlin College GLF has been in existence less than a month and has 30 men and five women; they are still trying to get their thing together. The University of Wisconsin's development has been similar to that of NIU, except that their university has a well-known street and bar scene with people who are still uptight about Gay Liberation. Their consciousness-raising group, who was on a retreat during the Convention, appears to be a success.

"Besides having a problem with the bar crowd, University of Louisville Gay Liberation is also having a legal problem: two women in the group applied for a marriage license. Paul from Iowa told us that after speaking before a high school class his group became involved in [a] lawsuit concerning corruption of a minor. Iowa City has outside of the university a very together Gay Women's collective. Officially recognized by the University only two days before the Convention, Southern Illinois University GLF brought the largest out of town group. They also had the benefit of $100 traveling money allocated to them by their student government to attend the Convention.

"The inspiration for the many Gay Liberation groups now in existence in Chicago grew out of Chicago Gay Liberation, which started in December 1969, at the University of Chicago, according to Murray [Edelman], UCGLF. One of UCGLF's current projects is a weekly Saturday night coffeehouse in Hyde Park on the South Side. On the North Side, Chicago Gay Alliance has opened a Gay Community Center at 171 W. Elm, where meetings, dinners, and other activities are held. There have also been sever[al] Gay dances in the Chicago area at the University of Chicago, University of Illinois Chicago Circle, Northwestern University, and at the Chicago Coliseum.

"The first workshop was on Gay Civil Rights and was led by our Gay Sister, Renee Hanover, Chicago attorney and member of the National Lawyers Guild. Mrs. Hanover was the leading defense lawyer in the 'D.C. 12' case, which involved attacks on and discrimination against twelve Gay Brothers in a Washington restaurant during the November Plenary Session of the Revolutionary People's Convention.

"The first issue Renee stressed is that Gay Liberation should get away from the universities and into the surrounding communities. With the same level of emphasis, she asked, 'What are you young people going to do with your degrees? Are you going to use them in a way that will help fight sexism and promote Gay Liberation?' She stressed that especially the social sciences and law could be useful in this fight. Renee Hanover's last point was that Gay Liberation groups should take advantage of the National Lawyers' Guild; we should contact them and educate the members to our needs and use their services.

"After lunching in various places in and around the University Center we returned to a very busy schedule of workshops. During the lunch break two events took place: the filling out the questionnaires designed by a NIU-GLF psychology major to check the validity of Irving Bieber's highly questionable conclusions on male homosexuals; and the workshop, Introduction to Homosexuality, intended to help any straight people who might be attending the Convention clear their heads of misconceptions and popular myths concerning Gay people. Also, the Women's General Center, scheduled for 1:30 p.m., was canceled by the women because they felt that wherever they were together they were conducting a Women's General Center.

"At 2 p.m. Saturday a very together doctor from the University Health Center conducted a workshop on Venereal Disease. Those in attendance thought that he gave an excellent lecture on a topic of great importance. The workshop was scheduled so that our Gay Brothers and Sisters wouldn't be in the dark on this important subject.

"The weather that afternoon in DeKalb, as our Gay meteorologist predicted, was very beautiful. So our beautiful conventioneers took off for the Arboretum for a consciousness-raising rap group led by our brother Murray of University of Chicago GLF. We broke up into small groups and just talked for two hours. Later we walked around the Lagoon talking in the radiant sun.

"When we returned to the University Center we went to the Illinois Room for a workshop on Counseling the Young Homosexual. Stephen, one of the workshop's leaders, has had his telephone number published for people who have Gay-related questions or want someone to talk to. He asked us, 'What do you say when someone asks you over the telephone, 'Am I Gay?' Stephen and others talked to a counselor who gave them many helpful tips on how to give council over the telephone. He said usually the telephone councilor is more nervous than the caller. We should not be so afraid that the person on the other end is going to commit suicide because of what we say to him, since if he is determined to do it he will anyway. Volunteers from the workshop did some role-playing, with one person playing the caller and the other the telephone councilor.

"The last workshop on Saturday concerned the housing problems encountered by Gay People on college campuses. This group was co-chaired by Bob, a grad student in sociology, and Fred, chairman of the NIU-GLF Art Committee. Conflicts concerning living in university dorms was discussed as well as the search for alternatives to living in straight housing, including gay communes.

"The Convention's longest day was near an end. Now everyone was off to dinner in small groups. A group of delegates from the University of Louisville, University of Wisconsin, Illinois Institute of Technology, and NIU got together for an informal party at the home of Al of NIU-GLF. Even though it was a short, small party, it was the kind of party where the discussion ranged from, is it easier to drive a Chicago Transit Authority bus or a New York taxi, and how many of us liked our middle names. We danced, talked, and partook of refreshments. It was a small, quiet party before the big party in Sycamore.

"The second Sycamore party was larger and had a faster pace than the one Friday. Again it was kicked off by the Rocking Soul of Miss Ross and other Motown Heavies. The newly-formed Scarlet Revue took to the floor with the latest dances from New York and Miami. Small rap groups were formed. The guests were really turning it out and were dressed in fashions ranging from Farmer John overalls to hot pants. It was a party long to be remembered.

"At last the night was over and we awoke to the last day of the beautiful First Midwest Regional Gay Liberation Convention.

"Our first workshop of the day was on Gay Liberation Organizing, held in the Heritage Room. It was described by Gary and Guy, president and past president of NIU-GLF, as 'An open rap session where people from all the existing chapters and those who are organizing new chapters can get together and attack common problems and arrive at workable solutions.' The Universities of Wisconsin, Kansas, and Southern Illinois had a wide range of situations for discussion. In Madison, Wisconsin, our Brothers and Sisters made the best of a physical attack because it prompted two editorials on a popular local radio station. The Kansas delegation is having legal hassles in getting university recognition. A wonderful suggestion was made by a young man from University of Illinois, Urbana, that GLF groups arrange to speak to students in the dormitories.

"A discussion of how to get people to come out uncovered a variety of methods. In Madison, GLFers passed notes in the male johns. Sandra from NIU said that she sometimes left Gay Liberation literature in the women's lounges at the Union. Once in GLF, some GLF organizations offer their members a variety of smaller groups, such as Women's groups, Third World caucuses, radical or political groups, and consciousness-raising groups. We all learned a lot and shared a lot of important insights.

# CHICAGO AFTER STONEWALL

"At the closing session announcements were made about other Gay get-togethers. The University of Chicago is participating in the Chicago Gay Mayday Celebration and in Gay Pride week activities in June, including the Gay Pride March on June 27. It was generally agreed that another Convention of this type should be held in the Midwest soon.

"Before we all returned home we had a Wienie Roast in the Arboretum in the afternoon. We even had marshmallows, and it was fun for all. At the very end we all hugged and kissed each other goodbye; Parting was such sweet sorrow. It was a beautiful conclusion to a beautiful Convention. Bert from the University of Wisconsin Gay Liberation Front summed up the general feeling by declaring, 'It was my Woodstock!'"

"GAY PRIDE! GAY POWER! GAY UNITY!

Peace and love,

Albert

NORTHERN ILLINOIS UNIVERSITY GAY LIBERATION FRONT"

Gay activist groups were springing up around the Midwest and articles appearing in local mainstream newspapers. In May 1970, in *Capital Times*, out of Madison, WI, a headline read, "At U.W. Teach-In 'Gay Lib' Idea Comes Out from Underground." Charlotte Robinson begins:

"Add one more group to the list of oppressed minorities – the homosexuals. 'If black is beautiful, why not gay is golden,' queried one observer at the first-of-its-kind 'teach-in' held today by the Madison Alliance for Homosexual Equality (MAHE).

"The day-long teach-in, held at the U.W. Memorial Union, featured panel discussions on 'The Meaning of Gay Liberation,' homosexuality and religion, the sociology of homosexuality, and showings of an early classic movie dealing with lesbianism. The event will end with MAHE (pronounced like May) Day dance at 9 p.m. in the Union cafeteria."

Robinson goes on to write that MAHE's goals are the "repeal of antiquated, repressive sex laws," education of the public as to the true nature of homosexuality, and the realization 'dignity and respect' for homosexuals" She continues:

"At the entrance to the Memorial Union cafeteria, members of MAHE had set up a table from which they dispersed leaflets and sold copies of *Giovanni's Room* and bibliographies of books on homosexuality by James Baldwin, and an *Esquire* article entitled, 'This is an All-American, Red-Blooded Faggot You're Talking To – Show Some Respect."

In the *Quad City Times*, out of Davenport, IA, Marilyn Osweiler wrote, "The Gay in Iowa City":

> "'It isn't easy to be a homosexual. It's not pleasant for a man to live a double life of trying to play the role of a 'normal' male while trying to hide his real feelings,' said Gary Smith, 724 Bayard St, Iowa City. A bearded young man of slight stature, Smith freely admits he is 'gay'
>
> "Smith is a former University of Iowa student. He and Paul G. Hutson Jr., a university senior, last fall organized the Iowa City Gay Liberation Front, an organization that received national news coverage in October when members, chanting slogans, rode in open convertibles between fraternity and sorority floats in the U of I homecoming parade."

In the *Great Bend Tribune,* an article about the Lawrence Gay Liberation Front begins:

> "The University of Kansas announced Saturday it has again denied official recognition as a student organization at the school to the Lawrence Gay Liberation Front.
>
> "... Chancellor E. Laurence Chalmers Jr. said in a statement: 'Formal recognition of a proposed student organization confers only one significant advantage. A recognized student group may submit requests for funds to the student senate. Since we are not persuaded that student activity funds should be allocated either to support or to oppose the sexual proclivities of students, particularly when they might lead to violation of state law, the University of Kansas declines to formally recognize the Lawrence Gay Liberation Front.'"

Homosexuality in Kansas remained illegal until 2003.

# 16
# THE 2ND GAY PRIDE PARADE, THE KISS-IN, AND THE FIERY FLAMES COLLECTIVE

On May 4, 1971, the city of Chicago granted Permit #71-114 to the Chicago Gay Alliance for the Gay Pride parade on Sunday, June 27. The Gay Pride Week Committee published a one-off *Chicago Gay Pride*, a twenty-four-page high-quality newspaper containing news, a schedule of events, articles about the various gay groups involved in Pride, photographs of Pride 1970, and a list of resources and advertisements. Ads included clothing stores like Sirreal, 2204 N. Clark St. – "clothes to fuck around in" – and Don Juan, 2457 N. Clark – "mod fashions for men, jumpsuits, knit pants and shirts, bells, flares, tops, jackets, coats, jewelry. Also, smoking needs." There were also ads for the new Lincoln Park Baskin-Robbins, 2468 N. Clark St., and gay bars like the King's Ransom, 20 E. Chicago, Club Alameda, 5210 N. Sheridan, the Ritz, 937 N. State, and the Annex, 2865 N. Clark. Pride Week 1971 kicked off on Thursday, June 17 with the Gay Pride Week Committee discussing Pride Week on Chuck Collins' *Underground News* (11:30 p.m., WSNS-TV, Channel 44). Collins was a 22-year-old graduate in political science and the show was directed by Howie Samuelsohn and written by Linda Freedman. The show offered a radical take on political and cultural events. First broadcast July 1, 1970, it focused primarily on the anti-Vietnam war movement with guests like the Grateful Dead, John Lennon and the Chicago Seven. The Gay Pride discussion began after a showing of *Out and Proud* by Lilli Vincenz, a freelance filmmaker and activist with Washington DC Mattachine.

Among the scheduled events for the 1971 Chicago Gay Pride Week was a CGA film festival at the new Gay Center, 171 W. Elm St., with a showing of *King Kong, Son of Kong, Phantom of the Opera*, and *The Lost World*. Popcorn provided. Other events were a June Cruise on Lake Michigan aboard the Trinidad. Also workshops on "Toward a Gay Lifestyle," "Bisexuality," "Transsexuality," "The Positive Homosexual," "The Third World Gay Revolutionaries" and Jack Baker, the president of Minnesota Student Association, speaking on "Same Sex Marriage."

Another Chicago Gay Pride Week event was a GLF Chicago Committee on Gay People and the Law protest outside the Federal Building on June 28. The Alvin Golden case prompted it. Golden was a 31-year-old black man, a postal employee of twelve years and recipient of several awards for his work. On March 29, 1969, cops arrested him for prostitution and soliciting a police officer. Golden was never convicted, but on February 26, 1970, he was given a year's supervision. Soon after that, the Post Office fired Golden, charging him with "conduct unbecoming a postal employee." An internal investigation accepted the police report, as did the Regional Director of the Post Office. Golden received a pink slip on March 20, 1971. His attorney, Renee Hanover, took the case. She appealed it to the Civil Service Commission in Washington DC. Thirteen months later the Post Office were overruled and forced to reinstate Golden.

Harassment at work was commonplace. In the November 1971 *Chicago Gay Alliance Newsletter*, Capricorn writes about a "gay brother" hired by the department store, Carson, Pirie Scott & Co.:

> "After he had worked for two or three hours he was called to Security for a 'Security Check.' The interrogator started off by asking where he had gone to school. When he mentioned a far north suburb, the Security Officer said, 'I take it you don't live with your family now.' When the brother said no, he asked who his roommate was and whether he was married or not. When the brother told his roommate's name and confirmed the fact that neither were married, the interrogator asked whether they slept together and made love. When the brother hesitated to answer, the man said, 'Never mind, I know the answer. You're one of those queers. You're a security risk. We can't hire you.' The gay brother *was* hired, in spite of the efforts of the Security Officer, as there was no law in the State of Illinois saying it was illegal to be gay."

Also, in November 1971, a headline in the *Chicago Defender* read, "Gay Lib fights job bias":

> "In a formal proposal filed with the Illinois Fair Employment Practices Commission, the Chicago Gay Alliance, 171 W. Elm St., asked the Commission to prohibit discrimination by private employers against female and male homosexuals and against single persons. ... Discrimination against the unmarried 'becomes de facto discrimination

against homosexuals.' ... John Abney, CGA president, testified earlier in October at a public hearing held by the Commission on its proposed enforcement guidelines under the new Illinois law barring sex discrimination in employment."

Another 1971 Gay Pride Week protest took place at noon on Friday, June 25. This was a GLF picket and Kiss-In at the Civic Center protesting the April 30 arrest of two gay men, John Cantrell and Richard Chinn – two gay men charged for "a peck of a kiss that would have been overlooked had we been two men from the 'old country,'" wrote Chinn in *Chicago Gay Pride*:

> "To the plainclothes pigs who arrested us, the sight of two men kissing is indecent. They are not moved to anger by the death and mayhem this country is causing in Southeast Asia. They are not moved to anger by hundreds of years of racism and inequality for American minorities. They are not touched by hungry children whose lives are damned from the beginning by their poverty. ... But the sight of two men kissing they find 'indecent.'"

The GLF Kiss-In followed a protest outside the courthouse at 321 N. LaSalle, where John Cantrell and Richard Chinn were on trial. The indecent peck occurred after they alighted from a bus at State and Washington and parted ways. Only to be pounced on and charged with disorderly conduct, public indecency, and lewd fondling. They were released on $1,000 bond each.

"Virginia" wrote in the *Chicago Seed* that after the Kiss-In, protestors danced around the Civic Center, holding hands, waving signs and chanting, "Say it loud, gay is proud! 3, 5, 7, 9, lesbians are mighty fine! 2, 4, 6, 8, gay is just (twice) as good as straight. Ho-ho-homosexual, the ruling class is ineffectual!" She continued, "There were about ten pigs standing around looking uptight, but they weren't into hassling us. The vibes from the crowd surrounding us didn't feel particularly hostile. I think many of the people were interested in what we had to say – some seemed very sympathetic." The trial was continued until July 13, when the charges were dropped. In the July 30 issue, the *Seed* noted: "In the court of Judge Dunn, Branch 46, the state and the city both dropped their trumped-up charges to the surprise of the two pigs who arrested the Gay brothers. Before the judge dismissed them, he said that they would not use his courtroom to advance their cause and that now they 'wouldn't get the publicity.'"

Cantrell and Chinn were members of the Fiery Flames Collective based at 628 Buckingham Place #201. Their rhetoric was fiery indeed. One of their leaflets read:

"SMASH IMPERIALISM! ... We, Gay Women, Gay Men, Transvestites, and Transexuals in Amerikkka, who have been systematically and deliberately oppressed and exploited in this country through sexism, male supremacy, racism, and capitalism, feel that the war waged against the South-East Asian people by the government of the United States is a extension of our oppression.

"War, Amerikkkan style, is a male chauvinist's game, where to prove his masculinity, he must maim, or kill Women and Children, the very old and the very young, and his own brothers. War is an extension of our own Gay oppression because it reinforces the masculine image of hetero males and forces them into playing roles where the end result is the death of millions of people and their own spiritual self-obliteration.

"We, as Gays, are part of the struggle of the Vietnamese, Laotian, Thai, and Cambodian people and feel solidarity with them. In this spirit we sign this treaty of peace, love and struggle."

The Fiery Flames Collective wasn't the only revolutionary gay group in Chicago. The city was also home to the lesbian separatist group, The Flippies. In 1971 the following ad appeared regularly in the *Chicago Seed*:

"The Flippies (Feminist Lesbian Intergalactic Party) are a female nationalist, gay nationalist political party that works for the overthrow of everything in society that oppresses women and gay people (namely everything). We're publishing a paper called *Killer Dyke*. Contact us through our men's auxiliary by writing Flippies Men Auxiliary 2314 E. 70th Pl. Chicago 60649 We love you."

# 17

# THE BIJOU ADULT MOVIE THEATER, THE COPS AND THE MOB

In the summer of 1971, the Bijou Theater opened at 1349 N. Wells St. in Old Town. "It promises to be a welcome addition to the all-too-few theaters in Chicago showing really different films," initially enthused the *Chicago Seed* in August:

> "The theater itself is newly remodeled. The walls are streaked with bright vibrant colors and the ceiling done in dark, heavy texture. One could be in a cave where water has exposed colored limestone in layers. The cave floor is covered with a plush yellow carpet. The Bijou is small, intimate, with seats for only 75. For its premiere showing, the Bijou presented 3 films. First, the infamous 'Checkers' speech by the Hon. Senator from California, Richard M. Nixon. In 1952, Nixon, accused of accepting illegal funds from supporters, made a speech to the nation defending his actions. He melodramatically relates his life story and financial history and condemns the corruptness of a government that permitted the loss of American lives in an Asian war (Korea). Pat Nixon adds to the ludicrous situation, remaining immobile and stone-faced throughout her husband's speech.
>
> "The second feature at the Bijou consists of portions of Lenny Bruce's appearance on 2 Steve Allen television programs. Lenny satirizes films, fads of the day (airplane glue sniffing) and gets into some 'sick humor' with his sketch of a devoted son who blows up his mother and 40 other people in an airplane.
>
> "The third film *Pick My Daisy* was written and narrated by Jack Kerouac. It's about the afternoon when the bishop came to tea at the Lower East Side apartment of a railroad brakeman and his wife. There are the Catholic bishop, Allen Ginsberg, a saxophone player and a group of

original 'beatniks.' They discuss holiness amid 'cockroaches, peanut butter cockroaches, melted cheese cockroaches, spot cockroaches, ad infinitum. The beatnik life."

After the above review by "Janet" in the *Chicago Seed*, a postscript was added: "(NOTE: As we went to press, the next feature at the Bijou was announced – it's turning into a porn house – don't go there.)"

The issue of pornography split the gay community. Those who supported it were the "Silent Majority," too closeted to speak out in its favor. The voices of GLF dissent were not silent. Larry Larie wrote in the *Chicago Seed*:

"One of the best features of Women's Liberation is the more human way it has related to heterosexual physical sex. Women have told men that they will no longer tolerate being exploited as just a piece of ass. Unless men are open to the possibility of a total human encounter, forget it. It's about time gays started raising their consciousness too.

"In a recent issue, the *Seed* exposed the Aardvark, Festival and Bijou Theaters as oppressors of women. However, the Bijou oppresses men-all men, gay as well as heterosexual. Prior to its opening we heard it was to be Chicago's first gay theater. It's really bad. The Bijou at 1349 N. Wells does not actually cater to the 'gay' community. It's a social parasite that lives off the painfully alone, neurotically bored, and frustrated closet cases who simply have not as yet found the courage to come out into a potentially rewarding, guilt-free, happy gay life style. It's translated the conscious and unconscious suffering of thousands into good old Amerikan dollars and cents (What in this country can't be?)

"And what do you get for your $3?

"You get smirking condescension of the theater staff: a horribly tasteless porno flick utterly devoid of any gay talent (and very often a very sick and sad pseudo S & M film of human beings attempting to relate to each other by physical subjugation and mental contempt), and unlimited access to the john, where, if the stars are right, you may meet another closetty, un-liberated, guilt-laden homosexual for a strange interlude of superficial contact. Sounds icky? It is.

"People can only be liberated by other people. Love and caring is the only avenue of deliverance. Gay people can only be liberated by gay love. The oppressive pigs at the Bijou and the Newberry don't love us, they oppress us.

"Their psychological oppression is every bit as devastating as more tangible physical police oppression, economic corporate oppression, social and family oppression and religious church oppression. Oh yes, and as bad as bar oppression too.

## CHICAGO AFTER STONEWALL

"Along with anti-women theaters, the anti-gay Bijou, Newberry & Village theater should immediately close. Or at the very least, actions taken to let the patrons know how and by whom their minds are being fucked.

"This is not a call to censorship – all you liberals out there can continue your nap-or a threat to anyone's right to do exactly as they please. However, gays should realize exactly what's really involved here. Gay liberation isn't going to come about in Chicago until gays demand an end to anti-gay sexism and oppression. The sick porno movie industry – supported sadly enough by those people who can't or won't relate intimately to others – must stop and the patrons enlightened."

Two months later, in July 1972, Cook County authorities launched one of their periodic crackdowns on adult movie theaters, both gay and straight. The investigation, led by State's Atty. Edward V. Hanrahan, targeted fifteen theaters, the first two in court were the gay Bijou Theater, 1349 N. Wells, and the straight Admiral Theater, 3940 W. Lawrence. The Bijou was owned by Steven H. Toushin, Jeffrey S. Begun and Paul Gonsky. The Admiral was run by Chicago attorney Frank Oliver, and Patrick "Patsy" Ricciardi, a cousin of crime syndicate hoodlum, Felix "Milwaukee Phil" Alderisio. Two other gay theaters under scrutiny were the Capri Theater, 2424 N. Lincoln Ave., and the Newberry Theater, 856 N. Clark St. Harold E. Fordley, the manager of the Admiral, was held in contempt of court by Judge Joseph A. Power for refusing to produce for viewing by the grand jury a film entitled *Inga, the Animal Lover*. Obscene or not, the *Chicago Tribune* carried ads for this movie, as it did for the Bijou and other adult movie theaters. This sudden flurry of anti-porn activity prompted Tom Fitzpatrick of the *Chicago Sun-Times* to ask, "If pornographic films really turn men into depraved sex fiends, aren't we placing the members of the FBI under an extreme risk by having them spend all their time looking at this kind of thing."

Four films and several shorts were ordered seized from the Bijou and the Admiral. The Bijou complied and handed over *Ranch Slaves* and the shorts. However, the Admiral refused and hid *Deep Throat, Kiss This Miss* and *Vacation in Hot Pants* from the cops who searched the theater. They were finally handed over after Patrick Ricciardi spent a night in the County Jail. On October 16, Toushin, Begun, and Gonsky from the Bijou were indicted for shipping an obscene movie, *Ranch Slaves*, across state lines and showing it at the theater.

The problems didn't end there for the Bijou. In December 1973, the *Chicago Tribune* reported on bomb threats to Toushin, Begun, and Gonsky, and their five adult movie theaters: Festival, 3-Penny, Aardvark, Termite, and

Bijou. The article notes the three owners were in no way linked to organized crime syndicates. An assistant US attorney told the paper, "Those guys are straight, just entrepreneurs."

The *Chicago Tribune* continued:

> "It had been suggested that syndicate biggies might have been buying into the business so they could 'launder' gambling and narcotics profits by mixing them with box office receipts. In Chicago the suspicions revolved around Patrick (Patsy) Ricciardi, a partner in the Admiral Theater on the Northwest Side and reportedly a minor hoodlum. Ricciardi told the U.S. District Court in 1971 that his share of the theater's revenue came to $200,000 during nine months of that year. The figure sounded awfully high to anyone familiar with the skimpy audiences usually found in such places."

Though Toushin, Begun, and Gonsky were not involved in organized crime, they were victims of it. Toushin told the *Chicago Tribune* that he once found dynamite behind the Coke machine with a note that read "F--- you. Get out. Close your theater." Toushin considered posting, "Viet Nam veterans with M-16s" on the rooftops. He continued, "I guess it *could* have been the Outfit. Lord knows, we weren't about to be frightened. We opened the show right after each hassle as if nothing had happened. There was no way we could be frightened. I watch too much Eliot Ness for that."

In November 1974, the *Chicago Tribune* reported on a night of bombings in adult movie theaters, two of those targeted were gay: the Newberry, 854 N. Clark St., and the Bijou, 1349 N. Wells St. The three explosions, and a failed one, all occurred within twenty minutes of each other with one injury; a man at the Newberry had metal fragments removed from his chest, leg and face, after an explosion from three or four sticks of dynamite. Shortly before that, a bomb on a window ledge blew out the screen at the Rialto Theater, 546 N. State St. and another explosion started a fire in a shed adjacent to the Follies Theater, 450 S. State St. The Bijou bomb failed to go off. Keith Allison, the manager, heard a popping sound and smelled "exploded firecrackers." On investigation, he found a fuse, a blasting cap, three sticks of dynamite, and one pound of TNT left outside the back door.

According to the *Chicago Tribune*, the police suspected the bombings were connected to a dispute involving a projectionist's union, the mob-controlled Chicago Moving Picture Operators Union, Local 110. The theaters targeted for bombing all used non-union projectionists. Police also investigated links between the theater bombings and the bombings a month earlier of two nude manicurist and body painting salons and a nude dancing spot. On September

26, Tiffany's Manicure Parlor, 2512 N. Lincoln Ave., was shaken by an early morning bomb blast causing $1,500 to $2,000 damage. On October 18, police raided Tiffany's and arrested one woman, Drew Ferguson, and the manager, Michael Palumbo, for indecent exposure and operating without an amusement license. Eight days later, it was raided again, also two other nude manicure establishments. This time they made ten arrests. Yet another raid on four establishments netted seven customers. On October 22, the *Chicago Tribune* reported that police suspected the mob planted the Tiffany's bomb.

Things settled down for a while, until a headline on the front page of the September 22, 1976, *Chicago Tribune* read, "Sex film chain owner slain":

> "Paul M. Gonsky, 34, Chicago's major operator of X-rated movie theaters, was ambushed and shot Tuesday in a parking lot at 1317 N. Wells St.
>
> "He died in Henrotin Hospital of five gunshot wounds in the head and one in the right shoulder three hours after he was found at 11:50 a.m. by police in a passing squad car who were waved into a lot by two boys."

Gonsky's body was found near the Bijou Theater. Police suspected the crime syndicate after Gonsky refused their attempt to muscle in on the lucrative porn trade. He was shot with a 22-caliber automatic pistol, most likely with a homemade silencer, not the standard crime syndicate weapon. Although, as the *Chicago Tribune* notes, syndicate chief Sam "Momo" Giancana was fatally gunned down the year before with a similar weapon. The 38-caliber revolver Gonsky carried in a bag didn't protect him that night. Investigators also looked at a recent bombing of Gonsky's car, parked in the driveway of his home at 116 Eastwood Dr., Deerfield, a village 25 miles north of Chicago.

Philip Whattley reported in the *Chicago Tribune* that a few days earlier, on September 17, Gonsky met with a "middle-echelon" mobster in his office above the Bijou Theater, who tried to shake him down for $300 a week. Gonsky refused and sealed his fate.

On September 24, the *Chicago Tribune* reported that police questioned his business partners Begun and Toushin. Joseph Di Leonardi, citywide homicide commander, said Toushin was "totally uncooperative." At the time, Toushin was in a legal battle with Gonsky and Begun, who were suing him for allegedly skimming $30,000 from the profits of the adult movie theaters to open three massage parlors, Just Filmz, Venus, and Crazy Horse. Two years earlier, in the raids on nude manicure parlors, Toushin's wife Susan was arrested at Just Filmz and charged with keeping a house of ill fame.

The murder of Paul M. Gonsky remained unsolved for years. Over 400 people attended his funeral where Rabbi Harold Shusterman of B'nai Ruven Congregation said Gonsky had a duel personality, "His life contained a personal yearning and aspiration up there (pointing up), but at times he was there (pointing down) because the demands of society brought it on him."

Another theory for the murder appeared in the *Indianapolis Star*, in an article written by Harley R. Bierce and Donald K. Thrasher. Gonsky, Toushin, and Begun also owned adult theaters in Indianapolis. Bierce/Thrasher wrote:

> "Gonsky was part owner of the Festival Theater, 5507 East Washington Street, and purchased the Hamilton Theater, 2116 East 10th Street, two weeks ago.
>
> "The other owners of the Festival are Steven H. Toushin, 34, and Jeffrey S. Begun, 35, both of Chicago.
>
> "Police officials said yesterday they believe the murder might be an effort by mobsters to move in on the lucrative pornography business.
>
> "Other Chicago investigators, however, said the 'hit' most likely was the result of an internal feud.
>
> "'You can't tell me that the mob waited until now, after the pornography business had passed its peak, to muscle in,' one investigator said."

They go on to claim that one "Indianapolis investigator" believed that Gonsky was getting out of the business and was "stopped by underworld colleagues":

> "A Chicago source said Gonsky recently had planned to move his base of operation to California and concentrate on producing legitimate films.
>
> "Gonsky already had produced a successful legitimate movie, *Jackson County Jail*, and wanted to do more."

*Jackson County Jail* starred Yvette Mimieux, Tommy Lee Jones, Robert Carradine, and Howard Hesseman and was produced by Paul Gonsky, Jeffrey Begun, and Roger Corman. In 1962, Corman produced *The Intruder*, starring a young William Shatner, a film about racial integration in southern states.

After Paul Gonsky's assassination, trouble at adult movie theaters fell out of the headlines. That is, until July 26, 1985, when the *Chicago Tribune* reported that Patrick Ricciardi, owner of the Admiral Theater, disappeared a month after a business acquaintance, Helen Lawrence, a Chicago pornographer, was indicted in Cleveland by a federal grand jury. The authorities were investigating underworld infiltration of the adult movie business. Ricciardi's body was found the next day in the trunk of a stolen 1980 Oldsmobile under a viaduct at 1651 W. Webster. He had bullet wounds in his back and head.

Both the murders of Paul Gonsky and Patrick Ricciardi went unsolved until 1990. Or, at least, a suspect was identified. On February 17, a *Chicago Tribune* headline read, "Mob enforcer gets 13 years for threatening shop owner." ... "Mob enforcer Frank Schweihs was sentenced to 13 years in prison on Friday by a federal judge who said Schweihs used organized crime 'as a weapon' to extort $21,450 from an Old Town pornography store owner who cooperated with the FBI to videotape the crime."

The pornographer was William "Red" Wemette who ran the Peeping Tom at 1345 N. Wells St. During the trial, Prosecutor Thomas Knight asked for a 20-year sentence because Schweihs was a longtime enforcer for the crime syndicate and "remains a suspect in the slayings of Chicago porn movie distributors Paul Gonsky in 1976 and Patrick Ricciardi in 1985." Frank Schweihs owned the parking lot where Gonsky was gunned down.

The Bijou remained a gay adult movie theater until it closed in September 2015.

# 18
# THE GAY COMMUNITY CENTER ON ELM STREET

In February 1971, work began remodeling and opening Chicago's first Gay Community Center, a two-story red brick house at 171 W. Elm St., one block south of Division at the southeast corner of Wells and Elm. The Center included a lounge and library on the first floor and a meeting area and conference room on the second. In April 1971, the *Chicago Gay Alliance Newsletter* invited the gay community to attend the Grand Opening on May 1 from noon on Saturday until 6:00 a.m. Sunday morning – "18 hours of snacks, coffee and good vibes":

> "The festivities mark two occasions: a celebration of the end of three months of remodeling and, more importantly, the beginning of what we hope will be a valuable addition to the entire gay community.
>
> "In addition to housing the CGA business meetings and communal dinners Sunday evening at 7 p.m., the Center is open for a special rap session for prospective members, visitors, and regular members at 8 p.m. on Thursdays. Those meetings are open to all who wish to attend. On Monday evenings, the Women's Caucus is open to all interested women (at 8 p.m.); a sensitivity group is meeting on Wednesdays (note—this session is now closed but new groups will be formed as interest is expressed in doing so). While the building houses additional CGA activities such as committee meetings and Newsletter publishing, it should be noted that the general areas of the house are open to the people of our community every weekday evening from 7 to 12 and on weekends until 1:00."

Plans included installing a "telephone switchboard ... with an answering device" and offering legal referral and draft counseling. According to the May

*Gay Chicago Alliance Newsletter,* the opening went, "Without the pretense of formal speeches and typical Grand Opening fanfare":

> "Throughout the day, evening and early morning hours a steady flow of familiar faces and new friends passed through the attractively decorated rooms. Lively colors, the smell of fresh flowers and delicious food greeted everyone.
>
> "Upstairs could be heard the rumble of dancing feet, the breaking of balloons and the happy laughter of a simulated Chinese Snake dance.
>
> "Small groups of people rapping together and celebrating in a beautiful demonstration of love and support."

In the early afternoon of October 20, 1971, four police officers raided the Chicago Gay Alliance Community Center. The *Chicago Seed* reported that one man and one woman were in the building at the time. "The pigs flashed a warrant to search the house for drugs," wrote the *Seed*. "However, the person in charge of the house at the time was not permitted to inspect either the warrant (he found no names or organizational title on it) or the policemen's identification."

The woman was physically removed from the building. The *Seed* continued:

> "The person in charge of the house was manhandled while the pigs ransacked the house supposedly looking for narcotics. They also prowled through the desk and closet in search for important papers of which they took several. As they were getting ready to leave they ripped the phone off the wall. While exiting one turned and said, 'If you'll forget this, we will too.'"

No illegal substances were found, as there was a strict no-drugs, no-alcohol rule at the Center. Neither did the police find the CGA membership files as they were kept elsewhere. When CGA complained, the police initially denied a raid had taken place. However, after evidence was presented, they changed their tune, admitting a "communications vacuum" prevented information on the raid reaching the head of the department. The *Seed* wrote, "CGA is still following up the incident so all the details are not available at this time. But it looks as though the whole thing may be another royal screw to Gay People presented by our pig department."

The raid wasn't the only nightmare on Elm Street. Visitors to the Gay Center were sometimes questioned as they left the premises. Some had their cars and belongings searched, while others were photographed. "DO NOT FEEL INTIMIDATED!!!!!" continued the *Seed*:

"That is what the pigs want! They would like to diffuse C.G.A. because it is a threat to them now. It is a threat to their perverted code of ethics and an infringement on their 'masculinity' to have Gay sisters and brothers in THEIR district. To prevent this usurpation of all gay people's civil liberties from repeating we must unite against these Gestapo tactics."

On December 12, 1971, Terri Schultz wrote, "Homosexual Discusses Struggle for Legal Equality" about the CGA Gay Center in her column "Our Town" in the *Chicago Tribune*. It begins:

"The boy stared in wide-eyed fright at the room of silent men. With one hand, he pushed the front door closed behind him; the other hand nervously twisted the fringe on his leather jacket.

"He was a homosexual, he said. His psychiatrist had dropped him off here at the Chicago Gay Alliance center to show him the kind of life he could look forward to, he said. He was 17 years old.

"Disgust, embarrassment, and dismay registered on the faces of the dozen homosexuals lounging on living room couches and chairs. Their glances said: 'When will the straights ever learn we're not curable – because we're not diseased? The old Freudian psychologists with their electric shock treatments, the academic nit pickers, the Dr. David Reubens – when will they ever learn?'"

Schultz goes on to say that in Dr. Alfred Kinsey's report on *Sexual Behavior in the Human Male,* 80,000 of the men in Cook and Du Page counties were homosexual their entire lives. "But only a few show up here, in this rundown, $100 a month, red brick house at 171 W. Elm St., or at any of the 50 gay bars around the city. Most stay incognito for fear of economic reprisal."

Schultz spoke to John Abney, "the talker, soother," ... "Our battle would be half won if all gay people turned purple so straight society could identify us. That would force everyone out of hiding."

Events at the Gay Center were advertised in the *Chicago Tribune*. A typical ad appeared September 3, 1971. It read, "Understanding the Other Side: The Gay Community Center at 171 W. Elm St., will be the testing [sic] for a meeting for Gay Youth at 8 tonight. Radical lesbians will meet at the center at 2 p.m. tomorrow, and tomorrow night there will be a Chicago Gay Alliance meeting at 7 after a communal dinner."

In June 1972, *Chicago Today* reporter, Barbara Ettorre, visited the Gay Center, describing it as "a Near North ramshackle place which is a clearinghouse for several gay groups," and the décor as "a hodgepodge of casual furniture, boxes of printing supplies, a duplicating machine for pamphlets and newsletters, a communal kitchen, cluttered with bulletin boards and wall posters." By the end of the year, the Chicago Gay Alliance and the Gay Community Center were besieged with financial problems. The end of the year saw them $860 in debt. "DEAR FRIEND OF CGA" began the begging letter sent out in December, signed by William B. Kelley. "We've constantly been plagued by the lack of money and members. They are the red and white corpuscles in the lifeblood of an organization like ours. Without enough of either, we are limited in what we can do, and we've been troubled by our inability to do better jobs in many areas because of lack of people or funds."

The letter goes on to solicit a $3 donation from each member to keep the Community Center open. The donations kept the Center open for a while, but on September 15, 1973, it closed its doors for the last time, after two years of serving as the hub of political and social gay life in Chicago. According to the *Chicago Gay Crusader,* the Gay Community Center on Elm Street was over $1000 in debt. After-the-fact analysis concluded that one group operating a gay center was impractical, and plans were floated to open two new ones: one by local gay social workers William Gallimore and David Sindt (Lambda House), the other by some members of Chicago Gay Alliance (Gay Horizons). An editorial in the October *Chicago Gay Crusader* lambasted Chicago's gay community for its lack of support:

> "How much do gay people in this city have to lose before they'll wake up?
>
> "Chicago has finally lost its first and only gay community center. This was mainly because of a lack of financial as well as moral support. It's sad when people get so little support from the community that they cannot meet $100 a month rent for an entire house."

The paper was clear on who was to blame, "If you want to see the real fault, walk into the bathroom and look into the mirror. Chances are, it will be as plain as day."

# 19
# LAVENDER WOMAN AND THE DAUGHTERS OF BILITIS

November 1971 saw the first issue of *Lavender Woman*, a 25c eight-page lesbian monthly newspaper. In her book, *Are We There Yet? A continuing history of Lavender Woman, a Chicago lesbian newspaper 1971-1976*, Michal Brody writes:

> "[The Gay Women's Caucus] wasn't an organization that we had, it was a collection of events. And events they were. The meetings were chaos. Bedlam. Total free-for-all. We did try at times having chairwomen, we tried to operate in some order, but by then we knew that hierarchies and rules were militaristic tools of patriarchal oppression, and of course we opposed that. We wanted everyone to participate freely. They did, usually all at once.
>
> "Those meetings were frustrating, distressing, and also somehow exhilarating. There was so much trying to happen that nearly everyone could find a like-minded sister or two to share ideas or make plans.
>
> "Out of that swirling, molten mass of spirit, *Lavender Woman* was formed."

On the cover of Issue No. 1 is a drawing of the Red Queen and Alice from *Through the Looking Glass,* kissing each other while the white rabbit blows his trumpet. It was drawn by Susan Moore, a member of the collective of women who started the paper. Next to the drawing, there's a quote from the Lewis Carroll book:

> "'Well in our country,' said Alice, still panting a little, 'you'd generally get to somewhere else if you ran very fast for a long time as we've been doing.'

## CHICAGO AFTER STONEWALL

"'A slow sort of country!' said the Queen. 'Now <u>here</u>, you see, it takes all the running you can do, to keep in the same place. If you want to get somewhere else, you must run at least twice as fast as that!'"

The editorial on page 2 reads:

"We, of the *Lavender Woman*, feel that this newspaper, written by and for lesbians, is a powerful weapon against the society that tries, in vain, to keep us closeted and out of sight. More important, the paper will be a tool for growth. Through it, we can create a positive, viable Lesbian community; increase our political consciousness; communicate our feelings to one another; share with each other our knowledge and gifts and, above all, thank ourselves again and again for each other. We are not Lesbians in spite of ourselves, but because of ourselves. The paper will affirm that."

Page 3 of *Lavender Woman* is made up of letters written by the newspaper staff to their mothers. Writers like Merrilee Melvin, Susan Moore, Betty Peters, and an African American lesbian called Margaret Sloan. On page 4, Ruby Watkins writes about her drug addiction, and Sloan writes:

"When you are around us you talk black and we find ourselves talking white and you even come to our parties bringing a 1969 Aretha Franklin record and when we confront you, you say we're too powerful to deal with and you don't come to our neighborhood after dark except in groups when <u>your</u> men have raped us (you too) for over 300 years."

On page 5 is poetry, with two contributions from Chicago-born singer-songwriter Linda Shear. On page 6, Shear writes on the subject of lesbian women, "And are we not truly the nigger in our sexist society? At the expense of being accused of delivering a more oppressed than thou attitude to non-lesbians, I must continue." There follows an impassioned plea to cast off the chains of male oppression – and that includes subjugation by gay men:

"We have ridden a metaphoric journey through the centuries on the back of the bus to avoid confrontation. We have even allowed syndicate MEN to run our bars and tell us what is, and what is not, acceptable behavior. We have been co-opted by every other cause and every other struggle because of a lack of pride in our own. We have become everyone's nigger. Here in Chicago, we need to bond together and gain strength in our numbers and our love. We must throw the oppressor off of our backs. We have been on the bottom too long – let's struggle TOGETHER."

On page 7, Muffie Nobel writes about Radclyffe Hall's groundbreaking 1928 lesbian novel *The Well of Loneliness*, and Betty Peters talks about a self-help healing group. On page 8, Cathy Nelson writes about women and DIY in

"Lavender Handy Woman" ... "Most of us were taught to suppress our natural curiosity about how things work and to rely on either professional repairmen or fathers, or some other male, to fix things when they go on the blink. Well, sisters, not only is it time to come out of your closets, but on your way out, bring that tool box with you."

Also on page 8, Margaret Sloan writes "Lesbians and Abortion" about the "5,000 years of patriarchy and racism ... exemplified today in the country's obscene and archaic abortion laws – where old white men in the state legislature makes decisions affecting all women."

A headline in the *Daily Chronicle* out of DeKalb, IL, read "Gloria Steinem Coming to NIU":

> "Gloria Steinem, editor of New York's *Ms*. Magazine and national crusader for women's liberation, will speak at Northern Illinois University at 8:30 p.m. Wednesday in the University Center Ballroom.
>
> "Joining her will be Margaret Sloan, Chicago writer for *Lavender Woman*, who is affiliated with the Gay Liberation Caucus."

At the time of the Stonewall Riots, the Daughters of Bilitis (DOB) was on hiatus in Chicago.

The DOB was one of the first lesbian organizations. It was formed in 1955 in San Francisco and took its name from a book of poems by Pierre Louÿs called *Songs of Bilitis*. Bilitis was a female character in a romance with the Greek poet, Sappho. According to documents at the McCormick Library of Special Collections at Northwestern University, in August 1969, Helen Baldwin attempted to start a new DOB group from a P.O. Box in Brookfield, IL – the outcome of this attempt is unknown to the author. On November 2, Sharon James from a DOB P.O. Box in Northlake, IL, wrote to the president of the Chicago Women's Liberation Movement, 5336 S. Greenwood:

> "We are organizing a local chapter of the Daughter of Bilitis here in Chicago and we could certainly use any help which you might be able to give us.
>
> "It would seem that some members of your group might be interested in DOB just as some members of our group might be interested in the Women's Liberation Movement. Our causes, after all, are similar since we are all striving for greater women's rights."

The Daughters of Bilitis/Chicago Newsletter begins:

> "HI! CONTRARY TO POPULAR BELIEF, DOB IS ALIVE AND WELL IN CHICAGO. AFTER MORE THAN OUR SHARE OF

## CHICAGO AFTER STONEWALL

TRIALS AND TRIBULATIONS, WE CAN HAPPILY REPORT THAT ALL SYSTEMS ARE 'GO' AND YOU CAN NOW LOOK FORWARD TO A HAPPY AND ACTIVE NEW YEAR WITH YOUR SISTER MEMBERS.

"FOR THOSE OF YOU WHO ARE NOT YET AWARE, THE CHAPTER HAS BEEN TEMPORARILY TAKEN OVER BY SHARON JAMES AND KAY KELLY. AS SOON AS WE HAVE A COUPLE OF MEETINGS BEHIND US AND HAVE COME TO KNOW EACH OTHER A LITTLE BETTER, WE WILL HOLD A FORMAL ELECTION OF OFFICERS. THEN, WE'LL REALLY BE IN BUSINESS.

"WE ARE STILL IN NEED OF MORE NUMBERS, GALS. SURELY WE ALL HAVE AT LEAST ONE FRIEND WHO WOULD BE INTERESTED ... SO LET'S SEE WHAT WE CAN DO ABOUT GETTING A FEW OF THOSE SHY VIOLETS TO A MEETING ... SOON!"

The newsletter announced a visit from Rita LaPorte, DOB national president, on January 25, 1970. On October 10, 1969, while attending "Sex Week" activities at the University of Nevada, LaPorte is quoted in the *Reno Gazette-Journal*, "A man isn't necessary for making love – and because he realizes it, he's miserable ... men are merely necessary for impregnation and it bothers their egos." LaPorte goes on to suggest that men feel threatened by lesbians and attempt to seduce them, "They have to be big shots. It upsets them a great deal if a woman isn't interested in what they have. And they are also threatened on the intellectual level." LaPorte did not support same-sex marriage, but would "like to have the legal and tax advantages that go with marriage."

Though united in sisterhood, the discreet Chicago DOB with their plea to "shy violets" and the more strident "cast off the chains of male oppression" of the *Lavender Woman* collective were opposite ends of the lesbian political spectrum. Nothing else has so far emerged about this 1969-1970 incarnation of DOB. Still, it seems unlikely it lasted because it harkened back to the genteel Gab 'n' Java get-togethers of Chicago DOB groups in the early 1960s. In the DOB Chicago Area Provisional Charter minutes of March 9, 1962, the names of those present were Marge Heinz, Nellie Tumilty, Jean Stroud, Betsy Boyette and Del Shearer. At a time when lesbians could be fired from their jobs, lose their children, and be arrested for not wearing three items of female apparel, "discretion, loyalty and secrecy" were paramount. The screening procedure for new members was stringent and strictly adhered to. The Provisional Charter minutes read:

"A discussion of interviewing procedures for new members led to the passing of a motion that all members shall be questioned on the following topics in the following manner: at a meeting or outside interview, she shall be asked by a member whether or not she is homosexual, her reasons for joining D.O.B., her familiarity with D.O.B.'s purpose, how she feels the organization may benefit her, and how she may benefit the organization. At a second meeting or interview she shall be asked again what she feels the purpose of D.O.B is, whether or not she believes in that purpose, if she realizes the primary nature of the organization over the individual personality conflicts and feelings, and questions to determine whether she realizes the requirement of the group loyalty."

# 20
# THE TOM FORAN ZAP

In the fall of 1971, intense police activity resulted in many gay and lesbian arrests – at least one lesbian and two gay men's bars were raided. The situation was volatile, and GLF became more active and radical. A headline in the *Chicago Seed* read, "Gays Zap Foran." Tom Foran was the abrasive chief prosecutor in the Chicago 8 Conspiracy trial, when Abbie Hoffman, Jerry Rubin, David Dellinger, Tom Hayden, Rennie Davis, John Froines, Bobby Seale and Lee Weiner were charged with conspiracy and inciting to riot. It was during the trial that Tom Foran famously called beat poet Allen Ginsberg a "damn fag." In an interview with Ginsberg in the *Chicago Gay Crusader*, the beat poet recalled the incident:

> "I was giving testimony about our peaceable intentions in the assembly in the parks, and then, in order to discredit me as the so-called religious advisor or the religious ritual advisor for the Yippies and their organization, Foran and the Government prosecutors got out a couple of my books, especially early poems – *Empty Mirror* and, I think, *Reality Sandwiches*, which is the only thing they had around – and they found some dirty words in the poems, and they asked me to read them aloud to the jury, including a number of gay poems, thinking that this would discredit me as the supposed religious advisor to the political scene – I don't know if 'religious' was the right word, whatever it was, you know – meditation advisor. So I eagerly grabbed the texts and began reading them in the most charming manner possible, so that the jury saw the humor of it and saw the ridiculousness of what Foran was trying to do, and he went out of the court when it was adjourned, muttering 'freaking fag revolution' or 'fucking fag revolution – it's nothing but a fucking fag revolution.' ... The poems read were 'In Society' and 'Nightapple.' 'In Society,' which is like a cocktail party which mentions eating a sandwich with a dirty asshole,

and then 'Nightapple,' which is sort of an impressionistic description of a wet dream ..."

After the Chicago 8 trial, Foran continued his bigotry with a speech at the Rotary Club in Evanston, IL, where he questioned the masculinity of the Chicago 8 defendants. He said, "Our kids don't understand that we don't mean anything when we use the word 'nigger' ... they just look at us like we're a bunch of dinosaurs ... we've lost our kids to the freaking fag revolution."

The "Foran Zap" wasn't an organized zap but a zap of opportunity. On November 23, the Hyde Park GLF (née UC-GLF) held an open forum on coming out as gay in the straight "Movement." Allen Young, a former Students for a Democratic Society (SDS) member and Liberation News Service (LNS) editor, was speaking on the subject of "Gays and the Old Left" in the South Lounge of the Reynolds Club, 5706 S. University Ave. Partway through the forum, news arrived that Tom Foran, who aspired to be the Democratic candidate for governor, was across the street holding a city-wide fundraiser in the Quadrangle, a chic club for University of Chicago faculty only.

In the *Chicago Gay Alliance Newsletter*, an anonymous author writes:

> "Finding out about the farce across the street, Gay people listening to Young planned a spontaneous zap. About 30 of us marched across the street and started chanting, arm in arm. When a high school band was brought in to drown us out, we danced to the music and found ourselves joined by many other sisters and brothers. The general mood of the whole thing was a festive one – everyone seemed puzzled as to why Foran would want to come to Hyde Park, and how he managed to have this 'event' in the faculty club of the great liberal university.
> 
> "After marching, singing, and dancing for about an hour, and noticing the carloads of pigs that had been called to the scene, we found out that Foran's speech was really an open reception. Six of us managed to get inside before the pigs realized the mistake they made and started manhandling anyone who attempted to get to the door without straight drag on and short hair.
> 
> "Inside was a mindblower; the invasion of middle America into the staid, academic sterileness of Hyde Park. Foran was talking about the good old times (when men were men). His wife and daughter then spoke of the fun times they had with their husband and dad, respectively. They both said the same thing – they loved their man. As Gay people, we were tired of hearing about this <u>heavy</u> man. We wanted him to talk about some other men – those faggots he was so fond of beating. 'Hey Tom, what about the

faggots?' I found my arm twisted from behind my back almost simultaneously. A big butch number was telling me to shut up or we'd be asked to leave. We all decided that a little shouting was worth getting kicked out for, rather than listening to more boring lies. We all began to shout 'Gay Power' and 'Freaking Faggots are here to stay' on our way out. Then the shit came down. We were all pounced upon, pushed through closed doors head first, our hair pulled. About 30 Gay people formed a circle around the pig cars, but it was busted up by the pigs.

"We were charged with disorderly conduct. ... It's not by accident that the same charge is used against Gay people for getting busted in a Gay bar, holding hands in the Coop, or actively fighting against our oppression, as in the Foran Zap."

Four protesters were arrested. The zap led to a protest on December 18 that started with a rally in Bughouse Square, then a march to the 18th District Police Station where GLF demanded police stop harassing gays. The cops pacified the crowd by promising to meet with GLF at a later date. They backed out later.

# 21
# VENCEREMOS

Allen Young, the GLF speaker on the night of the Foran Zap, was also a brigadista in the Venceremos Brigade, a US political group formed in 1969 to show solidarity with the Cuban Revolution; brigadistas harvested sugar alongside Cuban workers, defying the US embargo. Young is the author of *Gays Under the Cuban Revolution*. Along with Young, Step May and Robbie Skeist, two members of UC-GLF, were also brigadistas who labored on Cuba's Isle of Youth in the late summer of 1970. On their return, several gay brigadistas spoke at a forum held at Alternative U in New York City. A transcript of a tape recorded at the forum was published in *Out of the Closets: Voices of Gay Liberation* edited by Karla Jay and Allen Young. Step May says:

> "The Communist Party rules Cuba, and I really disagree ... that there are no laws against homosexuals. There might not be laws in the sense that we know them, in the sense that they're legislated by a house of representatives or a senate, but there are policies that exist and are enforced. Like the way open homosexuals can't be teachers and can't be in the Communist Party. This is enforced right down the line, and if you want to call that a policy or a rule of law, the truth remains that it's made to work and it has an effect. As a part of the Communist Party's position, there's even a word for it; they call it peligrosidad, which means a dangerous thing, or a danger to society. And because of the way the Communist Party or government operates in Cuba, there is a policy that once the government takes a position on something, or determines that something is a peligrosidad, such as marijuana or homosexuality or whatever, then it's considered to be a closed matter, in the sense that people cannot propagandize or agitate for a position that's in opposition to the position that the Communist Party has taken."

# CHICAGO AFTER STONEWALL

May goes on to say that if gays organized in Cuba and tried to put out a leaflet, "the government ... would actively seek out the source of these leaflets and act in a really repressive way."

Open criticism of the Cuban Revolution led to the National Committee of the Venceremos Brigade issuing guidelines prohibiting homosexuals from joining future brigades. The "Venceremos Brigade on Gay Recruitment" was published in late 1971:

> "Through many discussions in the past few months by the National Committee and the Regionals, we have formulated a policy concerning recruitment to the BV (Brigada Venceremos) of gay North Americans. The BV is not pretending to analyze the potential or the validity of the gay liberation movement in the United States. (The potential or validity of any sector in the U.S. will be determined by their practice within the context of the struggle carried out inside the U.S.) Our policy is based on practical considerations of the Brigade in Cuba: Cuba's position toward homosexuality, the Political Objectives of the BV, our purpose in Cuba, thus our position toward Cuban policies, and the past practice of gay Americans on the Brigade.
>
> "The Cuban people, as a whole, do not accept homosexuality. There is no material base for the oppression of homosexuals in Cuba. They are not repressed in work camps or anything of the sort. But it should be clear that Cuba does not encourage homosexuality.
>
> "The First Congress of Education and Culture, a congress of three years of work and hundreds of thousands of participants, published a report of major importance in the creation of a Cuban culture, a culture which in the past had been robbed, denied, and infiltrated by U.S. imperialist domination.
>
> "Concerning homosexuality, this congress took the position that homosexuality is a social pathology which reflects left-over bourgeois decadence and has no place in the formation of the New Man which Cuba is building.
>
> "This position was formulated by the Cuban people for the Cuban people. It was not formulated for the U.S., or any other country. Cuba is for Cubans, and while progressive and revolutionary people are always welcome in Cuba, the Cuban culture is not created for them in particular.
>
> "'As to the BV, the past activities of gay North Americans have generally been destructive. A list of specific activities would include 're-educating the Cubans' (assuming that the situation in Cuba must be the same as in the U.S.), outright attacks and denunciations of the Cuban Revolution, imposing North American gay culture on the Cubans (for example, parading in drag in a Cuban town, acting in an overtly sexual manner at parties). Also, some gay North Americans have shown a greater

interest in finding out about Cuban homosexuals than in finding out about the Cuban people and their Revolution. This kind of activity has been a flagrant insult to Cuban culture. And it has demonstrated a lack of understanding of the position of the Brigadistas in Cuba as guests of the Cuban Revolution. One of the objectives of the BV is to show solidarity with the Cuban Revolution–to affirm the Cuban peoples right to self-determination. While this does not mean that we deny the importance of dialogue, we are not in Cuba to carry out confrontations over our disagreements. The BV involves activity within the Cuban setting. As guests of the Cuban Revolution, we must realize that internal questions concerning Cuba's development can only be answered by the Cuban people; answers cannot be imposed from the outside. Only the Cuban people have all of the essential elements to analyze and solve their problems correctly.

"The attitudes and actions described above are particularly dangerous at this time because they join a cultural imperialist offensive against the Cuban Revolution, carried out by U.S. imperialism in an attempt to discredit the Revolution and alienate North Americans from it.

"There are gay Americans who share the objectives of the BV. Our policy is not meant to exclude them. However, given the gay North American position, the Cuban position on homosexuality, and the problems that have arisen from this situation, we will require of gay North Americans a clear understanding of revolutionary anti-imperialist priorities and total identification with the Political Objectives of the BV. It must be understood that going to Cuba means respecting Cuban culture."

In response, the Gay Committee of Returned Brigadistas issued a statement:

"We, as gay North Americans who have identified with and supported the Cuban revolution and our gay sisters and gay brothers in Cuba through our participation in the Venceremos Brigade, denounce the anti-homosexual policy formulated at the recent Conference on Education and Culture and endorsed by the Cuban government. ... Gay people owe allegiance to no nation. The anti-homosexual policy of the Cuban government does not simply fail to include gay people in the revolutionary process–it specifically excludes them from participation in that process and the right to self-determination. We have been told that it is reactionary for us to criticize and condemn our oppressors when they call themselves 'revolutionary' or 'socialist.' A policy of ruthless and incessant persecution of gay people is contradictory to the needs of all people, and such a policy is reactionary and fascist. ... Also, we denounce the national committee of the Vinceremos Brigade as the agents of a sexist hierarchy.

They, in their liberalism, have not engaged in critical relationship with either the Cuban people or with revolutionaries here.

"We call upon all progressive people to join in our protests against this reactionary policy and to make their feelings known by writing to the Cuban Prime Minister and First Secretary of the Communist Party in Havana. Turn it out!"

On November 13 at the IWW Hall at a Brigade Dance, UC-GLF members and brigadistas Step May and Robbie Skeist circulated a petition protesting the anti-gay policy of the Venceremos Brigade. It read:

"The National Committee of the Venceremos Brigade prohibits gay people from going on future Brigades as open homosexuals, discussing gay liberation, and caucusing.

"WE PROTEST. We have to find ways to support the Cuban struggle against imperialism and not mess over gay people in the process.

"We demand that gay people have full participation in the Brigade."

They collected 110 signatures, including at least four from brigadistas and six members of the Chicago Regional Committee of the Brigade. May and Skeist vowed to continue their struggle, but to no avail. Fidel Castro's Cuba would never accept homosexuals. It was years later that a glimpse of behind-the-scenes Cuba was revealed. Published in 2005, *The World Was Going Our Way: The KGB and the Battle for the Third World*, by Christopher Andrew and Vasili Mitrokhin, shed light on the issue. The book was based on the thousands of documents Vasili Mitrokhin, a senior KGB archivist, smuggled out of the Soviet Union in 1992. The book notes that while Fidel Castro publicly supported the Venceremos Brigade, he "looked askance at the presence of gay and women's liberation movements among his American New Left supporters." The Dirección General de Inteligencia (DGI), Cuba's KGB, told Castro that "the New Left brigadistas were homosexuals and drug addicts" and that DGI was looking into using homosexuality "to bring about the physical degeneration of American imperialism."

# 22
# THE NATIONAL GAY CONVENTION IN CHICAGO

In February 1972 the New York Gay Activist Alliance and Chicago Gay Alliance jointly held a national convention to plan a strategy for dealing with the upcoming elections. Their plans included protests at the 1972 Democratic and Republican party conventions, both held in Miami. Bruce Voeller, Chairman of the State and Federal Government Committee of New York's Gay Activist's Alliance, sent this invitation to 495 gay organizations:

> "URGENT NOTICE ELECTIONS 72 STRATEGY MEETING. Because of the importance of the 1972 elections campaign to GAY LIBERATION efforts, CHICAGO GAY ALLIANCE and NEW YORK GAY ACTIVIST ALLIANCE are jointly sponsoring a work conference to plan strategies for our 1972 election year actions. PLEASE SEND TWO OF YOUR ABLEST PEOPLE TO HELP PLAN!!!"

The invitation said the conference was being held at the Chicago Gay Alliance community center at 171 W. Elm Street, but possibly because of the large numbers attending, it was moved to the Armitage Avenue United Methodist Church. Two hundred representatives of gay groups in eighteen states attended. The representatives voted to form the National Coalition for Gay Rights (NCGR) and drew up a 1972 Gay Rights Platform that included seventeen federal and state "demands." The most controversial of the proposals were two items at the state level. The first reads:

> 6) Repeal of all state laws prohibiting transvestism and cross-dressing.

Not all convention-goers saw trans-issues as gay issues. Many were angered by the presence of a group of Radical Drags i.e. gay men wearing women's clothing, make-up and beards. The Radical Drags were three men from Philadelphia, one from Minneapolis, one from New York, and three from

## CHICAGO AFTER STONEWALL

Chicago. After the convention, the Radical Drags of Chicago issued a statement, "Oppression and undue harassment has been displayed against gays by their own brothers and sisters because of the ignorance of these so-called 'together' people of 'what is Radical Drag.' Homosexuals are oppressing Homosexuals!"

The statement goes on to say the Radical Drags were the "truly together" people of the conference:

> "There were several reasons for the Radical Drag display. They were not in Radical Drag to make a scene or to rabble rouse or to disrupt the conference. Radical Drag is not stereotyping homosexuals. Radical Drag is a support of cross-dressing; it is a mild defiance of society's dress codes. It is a mild form of protest against the 'male' – 'female' roles in society. We cannot change society until we have gotten society used to the changes. Radical drag is a preparation of society for total abolition of the dressing standards. Radical drag has become a popular tactic of the Gay Movement. It is regrettably unfortunate that many candidates at the conference are unaware of certain very real aspects of the movement although they claim to have their heads together. We suggest people think about these things and get their heads together before the Minneapolis Convention so as to prevent another Homosexual oppressing Homosexual atmosphere."

The second of the contentious "demands" read:

> 7) Repeal of all laws governing the age of sexual consent.

Although passed by a majority, Chicago groups refused to ratify this "demand." Since then, fundamentalist Christians have held up this document to prove the existence of a Gay Agenda and make a link between homosexuality and pedophilia.

The 1972 Gay Rights Platform in full reads:

FEDERAL LEVEL:

1) Amend all federal Civil Rights Acts, other legislation, and government controls to prohibit discrimination in employment, housing, public accommodations, and public services.

2) Issuance by the President of an executive order prohibiting the military from excluding for reasons of their sexual orientation, persons who of their own volition desire entrance into the Armed Services; and from issuing less-than-fully-honorable discharges for homosexuality; and the upgrading to fully honorable all such discharges previously issued, with retroactive benefits.

3) Issuance by the President of an executive order prohibiting discrimination in the federal civil service because of sexual

orientation, in hiring and promoting; and prohibiting discrimination against homosexuals in security clearances.

4) Elimination of tax inequities victimizing single persons and same-sex couples.

5) Elimination of bars to the entry, immigration, and naturalization of homosexual aliens.

6) Federal encouragement and support for sex education courses, prepared and taught by gay women and men, presenting homosexuality as a valid, healthy preference and lifestyle as a viable alternative to heterosexuality.

7) Appropriate executive orders, regulations, and legislation banning the compiling, maintenance, and dissemination of information on an individual's sexual preferences, behavior, and social and political activities for dossiers and data banks.

8) Federal funding of aid programs for gay men's and women's organizations designed to alleviate the problems encountered by gay women and men who are engendered by an oppressive, sexist society.

9) Immediate release of all gay women and men now incarcerated in detention centers, prisons and mental institutions because of sexual offense charges relating to victimless crimes or sexual orientation; and that adequate compensation be made for the physical and mental duress encountered; and that all existing records relating to the incarceration be immediately expunged.

STATE LEVEL:

1) All federal legislation and programs enumerated in Demands 1, 6, 7, 8, and 9 above should be implemented at the state level where applicable.

2) Repeal of all state laws prohibiting private sexual acts involving consenting persons; equalization for homosexuals and heterosexuals for the enforcement of all laws.

3) Repeal all state laws prohibiting solicitation for private voluntary sexual liaisons; and laws prohibiting prostitution, both male and female.

4) Enactment of legislation prohibiting insurance companies and any other state-regulated enterprises from discriminating because of sexual orientation, in insurance and in bonding or any other prerequisite to employment or control of one's personal demesne.

5) Enactment of legislation so that child custody, adoption, visitation rights, foster parenting, and the like shall not be denied because of sexual orientation or marital status.

6) Repeal of all state laws prohibiting transvestism and cross-dressing.
7) Repeal of all laws governing the age of sexual consent.
8) Repeal of all legislative provisions that restrict the sex or number of persons entering into a marriage unit, and the extension of legal benefits to all persons who cohabit regardless of sex or numbers.

## 23
# MICHAEL BERGERON AND THE DEMOCRATIC CONVENTION

In early 1972 Michael Anthony Bergeron tried unsuccessfully to become an Illinois delegate to the Democratic Convention in Miami. It was the first time an out-gay ran for political office in Illinois. He was endorsed by the Gay Liberation Front, Fiery Flames, Feminist Lesbian Party, Transvestite Legal Committee, Advocates of Gay Action (Bergeron was president), HOPE (Homosexuals Organized for Political Education), and several university groups.

After graduating high school in Louisiana, where he was on the Student Council and president of the Speech and Debate Club, Bergeron turned down a debating scholarship to travel and see the country. With his shoulder-length blond hair and neatly-trimmed mustache, he arrived in Chicago in 1970 and joined the gay rights movement. In one of his campaign flyers, Bergeron explains that based on the percentage of gays in society the 170 Illinois delegates should include ten or fifteen gay people. The flyer reads:

> "The 160 already-elected delegates can start to recognize gay people's concerns for equal opportunity and full participation in American society by electing me as one of the 10 delegates at large. Cumulative voting by enough of you can assure representation of the gay minority in Illinois' delegation. I know I will faithfully represent my special constituency's concerns, and I earnestly ask your support.
>
> "Besides being gay, I have the additional advantage of youth (I am 20 years old) and would thereby help balance the Illinois delegation on the side of both young people and minority groups, two key segments of the population whom our party is bound to make affirmative efforts to

include. In addition, I know that by being gay, I can more easily support and relate to the women's struggle against sexism."

Later in the year, in an interview in the *Paper*, Bergeron explained that he ran because "Gay people were running in San Francisco, New York and Washington DC, but no-one was running in Chicago." Bergeron announced his candidacy after 160 of the 170 delegates had already been chosen. On June 2, those 160 delegates met at the St. Nicholas Hotel in Springfield, IL, to elect the remaining ten delegates at large. Bergeron's supporters plastered the hotel with posters reading "Equality for Homosexuals." On each door into the hotel two people wearing "Gay '72" buttons handed out gay rights literature. "When Mayor Daley came in, he was approached by one of our people but was promptly pushed aside by one of Daley's aides," said Bergeron. "When he got upstairs, I walked directly up to him and shook his hand and said, 'Hello, Mayor Daley, I'm Michael Bergeron, Gay Rights candidate for the Democratic National Convention and I would appreciate your support.' His mouth fell open and he mumbled something unintelligible and shuffled on."

"I got five votes – and I think that was very good," continued Bergeron. "You see, all the McGovern people voted for McGovern delegates, and the Daley men voted for other Daley men. My candidacy was to educate the 160 delegates on Gay Rights issues so they would be aware of them when they went to the convention in Miami; that was the whole purpose of the campaign. We knew we couldn't win."

Mission accomplished. However, Bergeron wasn't the only "radical" fighting for those few delegate seats. At the time, Mayor Richard J. Daley was under siege from a new generation of political activists. The Rev. Jesse Jackson and others demanded greater representation of minority groups like African Americans, women, youth, and Spanish speaking people. Daley had been Mayor since 1955 and, feeling the winds of change, was struggling to keep his position of power. He was the third consecutive mayor from Bridgeport, the heavily working-class Irish area of the city. Too entrenched and powerful to oust, Daley died in office of a heart attack in 1976. In his speech to the delegates, Daley claimed a conspiracy was afoot to eliminate his own delegates. "The same forces that framed the conspiracy of 1968 are at work today," he said, referring to that year's contentious Democratic National Convention. "If you don't think so, get out of bed."

# 24
# REV. CHARLES LAMONT

On October 20, 1970, a closeted Rev. Charles Lamont, a minister at Logan Square's Avondale United Methodist Church and Chicago Gay Alliance member, spoke openly about his support of gay rights on the WBBM TV program *Nightline*. Alongside him sat Mattachine Midwest's Tom Erwin (Dr. Thomas Erwin Gertz), hidden behind a frosted glass screen. Gertz deftly fielded questions like, "When did you discover you were gay?" and "What do your parents think of you being gay?" One year later, the Rev. Lamont was fighting to remain a Methodist minister after coming-out to Chicago Bishop Thomas M. Pryor.

On November 16, 1971, a headline in the *Chicago Sun-Times* read, "A special minister bids for a special ministry":

> "A Methodist minister has acknowledged that he is a practicing homosexual and has formally requested his church to assign him to a congregation.
>
> "The Rev. Charles A. Lamont, 29, made the request Nov. 2 in a letter to Bishop Thomas Pryor of the Northern Illinois Conference of the United Methodist Church."

At the time he wrote the letter, Lamont, a divorced father of two, had no assignment. He had left Avondale United Methodist Church to study social work at George Williams College. However, with limited finances, he ended up driving a cab.

In his letter to Bishop Pryor, Lamont wrote:

> "I offer no apologies for my lifestyle. It is one part of the complexity that is me. Being a liberated gay is not easy. It would be much better for me

> to hide in a closet and to pretend to be something I am not. This I cannot and will not do.
>
> "I realize that it will be difficult with a congregation that is made up of 99 per cent sexist people. However, Gay Liberation is here and now. We are in the world and in the church. Therefore, the difficulty must be faced, now. ... I would most sincerely consider a ministry that would help interpret the church to the gay community and the needs of the gay community to the church. Will the church deprive the ministry of God to a half-million people?"

Lamont claimed there was no Methodist church law prohibiting a homosexual from serving as a church minister. Bishop Pryor agreed with him on the technicality, but he was far from supportive. Pryor told the *Chicago Sun-Times*, "How many congregations are going to take a practicing homosexual and his queen into the parsonage?" He also described Lamont as a "misfit" and recommended he stop ministerial work but keep his status as a minister. Pryor said Lamont's case would be put to a vote at the United Methodist Church's annual Northern Illinois Conference in June. It wasn't voted on. However, on June 10, 1971, the *Chicago Tribune* reported that delegates at the Conference, held at Northern Illinois University, De Kalb, voted unanimously to study the feasibility of establishing a ministry to homosexuals, kicking the can down the road. The results of the study were to be submitted to the General Conference in Atlanta the following year.

In the March 1972 *Advocate*, an article begins, "The Methodist Church is about to suspend the ministerial credentials of the Rev. Charles Lamont ... who has formally sought to establish a special Methodist 'outreach' to the gay community":

> "The Northern Illinois Conference, the Methodist organizational jurisdiction for the greater Chicago area, formally advised Rev. Lamont that he *must* 'request voluntary location.' Under Methodist church law that means the Rev. Lamont is being forced to discontinue 'regular ministerial or evangelical work' (Section XVI, par. 366, *The Methodist Discipline*).
>
> "'If you are unable or unwilling to do this,' Paul O. Whittle, secretary to the cabinet of Bishop Thomas M. Pryor of Chicago, wrote Rev. Lamont Feb. 29, the cabinet will recommend that the Board of Ministry proceed to recommend that the Annual Conference vote 'Involuntary Location.'
>
> "In layman's language, that means the gay minister will be kicked out of the church in shame.
>
> "'I'm going to fight them,' Rev. Lamont told the *Advocate*. 'I cannot cop out.'"

Lamont listed the charges against him, approved unanimously by the seven district superintendents of the Northern Illinois Conference of the Methodist Church February 14:

1) There is a continuing longstanding personal financial irresponsibility;

2) Three immediate past Superintendents confirm his unacceptable administration of local churches;

3) His ineffective and unsatisfactory conduct of the pastoral office has put the influence of the Christian ministry in jeopardy;

4) He had not fulfilled the requirements of his appointment to attend school, granted at his request, prompted by his expressed desire to equip himself for another profession."

Lamont continued:

"I feel I've done nothing to justify these proceedings against me. ... Of course, there's merit in the charges, but they are the same merit that can be laid against practically any member of the annual conference if they dug far enough.

"I did agree in June of 1971 to attend school. Technically I'm in violation of my appointment because I'm not attending school. Pragmatically, it was just impossible. I could not get a grant, and tuition was impossible with no money coming in."

Lamont had the support of the Chicago Gay Alliance. The March 1972 *Chicago Gay Pride CGA Newsletter* reads:

"He [Lamont] has been working in the Gay community for some time and will continue to do so whatever the outcome of the June vote. But winning that fight can be a victory for Gay people as well as a healthy influence on the church. We must confront organized religion and demand at the very least its awareness of our existence. Our support should be with Chuck Lamont, who has decided to press such demands within the church's bigoted walls."

In June 1972, the *Advocate* reported that Lamont was in Miami protesting the presidential nominating conventions. Regarding his expulsion from the Methodist church, he shared his intention to force a "show trial" under church law (the Methodist Discipline). Another strategy was that since the General Conference ruled that homosexuality was "incompatible with Christian doctrine," some gays are already:

1) Refusing to stand for hymns;

2) Placing written notes demanding their religious rights, rather than money, in collection plates as they are passed;

3) Sitting in the pew in worshipful prayer portions of the liturgy calling for participation by the congregation.

The findings of the Northern Illinois Conference study on the feasibility of a gay ministry were presented at the 1972 General Conference in Atlanta, and a new language for the Social Principles was included:

> "Homosexuals no less than heterosexuals are persons of sacred worth, who need the ministry and guidance of the church in their struggles for human fulfillment, as well as the spiritual and emotional care of a fellowship which enables reconciling relationships with God, with others and with self. Further, we insist that all persons are entitled to have their human and civil rights ensured."

After the debate, the following phrase was added, "... although we do not condone the practice of homosexuality and consider this practice incompatible with Christian teaching."

Also added, "We do not recommend marriage between two persons of the same sex."

In an October 29, 2010 interview with the author, Lamont explains:

> "As quite often happens in disputes, a compromise was reached, and the case was never actually presented to the Annual Conference. I was offered the option of 'requesting' voluntary location status and retaining my orders, just not a job. I accepted the offer, eventually, when my 'advisors' called to my attention that possibly I could do more good remaining in semi-good standing than if I were out in the cold. It turns out that was the case. To this day I remain an ordained United Methodist minister without financial support of any organization."

## 25
# MARY HOULIHAN AND THE GAY CATHOLIC MASS

On April 2, 1972, Easter Sunday, the first "official" Catholic gay Mass took place at St. Sebastian's Church, 824 W. Wellington Ave., though "underground" Masses had been held there for several months. At the time, homosexuality and the Catholic Church was a hot topic; in June, a *Chicago Tribune* headline read, "End Celibacy Rule, Priest Group Asks." The National Federation of Priests' Councils, a liberal Catholic group meeting in Denver, passed a resolution calling for an end to the Vatican law of celibacy. Further, they called for a study of ways to provide a ministry to homosexuals. It was approved unanimously. Afterwards the Rev. Eugene Boyle said, "There are 60,000 homosexuals representing 10 per cent of the population in San Francisco. Society's attitude toward homosexuality is less than human. It is our duty to do something about that." However, this had no effect on entrenched and draconian doctrine. In 1973, the Roman Catholic Church published "Principles to Guide Confessors in Questions of Homosexuality," a committee report of the National Conference of Catholic Bishops. The report grants the right of homosexuals to live together, to be homosexual "in condition," but forbids any sexual contact. Also, the report states that a "committed homosexual" is "hopeless unless he seeks professional help, which can help him either to live with the compulsion without giving voluntary consent to its movements, or to rid himself of it by therapy."

The first notice of a Catholic Mass for Chicago's gay community appeared in the January 1971 *Chicago Gay Alliance Newsletter*, "A Roman Catholic Mass with a homily on the Christian homosexual will be held Wednesday, Feb. 17th, and also on Wednesday, March 17th, 8:00 p.m., in the apartment of

Wayne Evans, 642 Aldine." However, Evans, formerly a Benedictine monk, hosted the first "Gay Mass" on October 14, 1970. The idea for the Mass came earlier, when Denny Halan, a GLF member, was at a meeting at 1909 N. Mohawk and overheard Mary Houlihan, a member of the Legion of Mary, talking to an unnamed Dominican priest. Houlihan told the priest that the Legion of Mary held Masses on skid row for derelict men, and in Old Town for wayward youth. Denny Halen interrupted, saying: "Why not a mass for gays?"

The conservative Legion of Mary is a voluntary group of Catholic laity that directs Spiritual Works of Mercy to those on the fringes of society. In June 1970, Houlihan and the priest contacted GLF and called a meeting at Grace Lutheran Church, 555 W. Belden Ave. Attending were GLF activists John Maybauer, Jack Onge and Richard Larsen, among others. Soon after, the Dominican priest was transferred to Kansas, and a Franciscan, Fr. Robert "Father Max" Behnen, took his place. The "Gay Mass" was born. Behnen was the celebrant at the first gay Mass in Wayne Evans' apartment and twelve people attended. In September 1971 the Masses were moved to St. Sebastian's, where sixty-five people, including sixteen lesbians, attended the first anniversary Gay Mass in October 1971. Though the Mass was for gays, straight supporters were welcome. Both Houlihan and Behnen were heterosexual. A 1977 article by Grant Pick in the *Reader* describes Houlihan as "a matronly Rogers Park mother of five who looks like Martha Raye." The paper also wrote, "To this day, she [Houlihan] believes gays should remain celibate, so it is ironic that Mary began the Mass for gay Catholics in Chicago."

In April 1971, the "Gay Mass" received unofficial approval from Chicago's John Patrick Cardinal Cody, though permission was withdrawn briefly in February 1972. The 1977 *Reader* article reads:

> "Cardinal Cody's position on the gay question is see no evil, hear no evil. 'There is no official policy,' answers Monsignor Francis Brackin, vicar general of the Chicago Archdiocese, when asked about Dignity and the gay mass 'Certain priests think they can help these people. We said a priest can serve them, but we haven't asked them to; we haven't sent anybody to do it.'"

In June 1972 a split occurred, when the Chicago chapter of Dignity, the national gay Catholic group, was founded and took over the Gay Mass. In the March 1972 *Chicago Gay Alliance Newsletter*, the Rev. John E. Gilun DD., writes that after the Mass on March 21 at St. Sebastian's, there was a discussion about the founding of a local chapter of Dignity. Also, gays participation in the Catholic Church was discussed on April 8 and the 21st at 1917 W. Touhy. It was at these two meetings that Dignity/Chicago was formed. Houlihan and the young radicals who started the Mass preferred to continue under the wing of the Legion of Mary, while Dignity wanted the Gay Mass to be gay-run. In the *Reader* one congregant said, "She [Houlihan] wanted to control the mass." Houlihan lashed out and criticized Dignity as being made-up of older white males, most belonging to ONE Inc., a conservative gay social group. Houlihan's faction, now renamed Unity, suggested a compromise:

> "We have worked out a proposal for the 'Independent Gay Mass Council Board' that would have the responsibility of the Mass. It is as follows:
>
> "We, the undersigned, believe that the Mass for Homosexuals held weekly at Sebastian Church should have a broader representation of all Gays and Major Gay Organizations, instead of one organization [Dignity] in control of it. We find that the young people and lesbians are being ignored. They should have an equal voice in the governing of it. We propose that a Gay Mass Council Board be set up which will consist of three priests involved, two members of the Legion of Mary (the Catholic organization which started the Mass) as de facto members, two member delegates from Dignity, two from 'One,' two from Mattachine, two from Gay Alliance, two from Lesbian Liberation, two Youth delegates and two additional women delegates and with one member to be chosen to preside.
>
> "This will give greater scope and will be more representative of the gay community. Also, that four committees, Liturgy, Social, Promotion and Finance would be open to all gays interested. We believe that the Coffee Social Time afterwards should not be given to any one organization to hold meetings, but should continue to carry out the Eucharist celebration just held in the spirit of love and hope.
>
> "We have over two hundred names already on our petition and if you are in accord with this proposal we would appreciate you signing and returning."

Dignity refused the proposal. Unity continued as a "rap group" discussing gay issues in the Catholic Church. Dignity and Father Behnen continued with the Gay Mass at St. Sebastian's. In April 1973, Roy Larson, the Religion Editor in the *Chicago Sun-Times* wrote, "Unlike the weather, the ministry to homosexuals is something few are talking about, but many are doing something about." Larson quotes Behnen:

# CHICAGO AFTER STONEWALL

"'What we have to deal with ... is the whole natural law sex ethic we all were taught. This ethic leaves no room for homosexual activity. It says anyone who engages in it is wrong.

"In addition to this, we have to deal with the idea held by most people that gays become gay because they want to be gay and are not able to do anything about it.

"This being the case, we have to ask the question: Is it always and everywhere wrong for a homosexual person to express his love physically?

"What many are coming to now is a conviction that homosexual activity can be good or evil depending upon many things, including the quality of the interpersonal relationship."

Larson also quotes Mary Houlihan of Unity:

"We've heard horror stories at the rap sessions ... one young man ... after telling his priest-confessor that he was a homosexual was told by the priest, 'Go stick your head in a toilet.' Now, an attempt is being made to draw up a list of 'compassionate confessors.' ... In my Legion of Mary activities, I have worked in nursing homes, ghetto missions and on Skid Row. Nowhere have I seen the suffering that I have seen among the gays."

# 26
# WOMEN'S CAUCUS/MUSIC AND LINDA SHEAR

In a letter published in the April 1972 edition of the *Seed,* a Gay Women's Caucus member writes that the group has been "struggling for some time now with our organization and lack of organization." The two-year-old group had fifty members, meeting twice a week at the Lincoln Park Presbyterian Church, 600 W. Fullerton. "We have our differences, we have our similarities," the anonymous author writes:

> "Some of us have left, some have stayed. We have felt the need for new directions and we have taken some steps toward re-defining who we are and who we can become. We are focusing now on what we feel we need. For some that means political action; for others it means an increase in feminist consciousness; other sisters are tired of social isolation and we need to meet other lesbians on that level; some of us need to talk; all of us need to be heard."

The Gay Women's Caucus was a splinter group from the Chicago Gay Alliance. A headline in *Lavender Woman* reads, "Why We Left Chicago Gay Alliance":

> "The following statement was read to the *Chicago Gay Alliance* by a group of Lesbians from the Gay Women's Caucus. It expresses our final frustration with the men of C.G.A. It has become a 'position' paper for the Caucus, the result of a two year struggle among ourselves over the question of working with men. We will wait no longer for them to confront their own sexism and racism. We need only one another to validate ourselves and perpetuate the love and energy necessary for our Liberation."

The statement reads:

## CHICAGO AFTER STONEWALL

"We of the Gay Women's Caucus, like other oppressed people, have chosen to work on our liberation independently – in our case, independent of Gay men. We hesitate to call you brothers as long as you participate in our oppression. We had hoped that you would appreciate this need, analogous to that of blacks during the first stages of their liberation.

"As women, we are imbued with the slave mentality our sexist fathers, brothers and educators have passed off on us in order to perpetuate our oppression. We need the ABSOLUTE SAFETY AND FREE SPACE of an all-women's group to work out and recognize these trends, to get them out of our systems.

"We have appreciated the C.G.A.'s previous cooperation and apparent understanding of this need and for this reason have not hesitated to meet your request to make a financial contribution from our Monday night meetings. However, we have also felt that the major share of this money obtained from passing a bowl would go towards building our own group–recognizing that regardless of the parallel of sexual preference (i.e. our gayness) we, as women make substantially less money on the labor market than you as men.

"We were severely disappointed therefore at John Abney's performance at our meeting on Monday night November 15, where, under the pretext of reporting on the upcoming Madison Conference, he abused our hospitality (which was an exception to the rule of no men at our meetings) to harangue us about our lack of financial contribution to your group. We feel his tasteless and unfair attack was merely a cover for deeply held sexist and racist attitudes.

"We lesbians need to work apart from you, and have our own center. We are not putting down your work toward your own liberation. We simply feel that our Liberation, as women and Lesbians, must take an independent direction at this time and will not benefit from your support since you continue to evidence racist and sexist attitudes of the oppressor. There may be some day too when we can all work together with all people–female, male, black, brown, white, gay and straight. That time is not now. The seeming similarity of our sexual preferences clouds and covers the real and deep differences between us, which only time, hard work and critical self-examination can begin to resolve."

The article in *Lavender Woman* ends:

"Gay Women's Caucus is now meeting independently. We thanked the men for their past help and wished them well on their own liberation. Our time is now our own. We have transcended our hassles with the men and can now deal with our own needs. We are finally AUTONYMOUS! We urge all Lesbians to join us in our struggle for ourselves and the

Lesbian community at large. There is nothing we can't do with the total support of all our Gay Sisters. WE ARE OUR OWN REWARD!"

The ailing Gay Women's Caucus was given a boost on May 13, 1972, when Chicago-born lesbian singer, songwriter, and pianist Linda Shear, accompanied by percussionist Ella Szekeley, performed a benefit. It was held at the University of Illinois Chicago Circle Campus (UIC-CC) and is thought to be the first out-lesbian concert in the US.

In *Lavender Woman* Barbara Lightfoot wrote the only known review of Shear's performance:

> "As you sit listening for almost two hours, it becomes apparent that her voice is definitely distinctive. She doesn't sock you with Joplin-like hysteria, or surprise you as do [Laura] Nyro's inconsistencies, nor does she drag you down in sentimentality. Rather, her voice has almost a hypnotic quality. Part of the key to her style, to this hypnotic quality, is versatility. It is this that makes Linda original and dynamic.
>
> "As evidence of her versatility, Linda's selections ranged from soft sounds like *Until It's Time For You To Go* to the pulsating song about revolution from the play *Marat De Sade* [sic]. Linda's voice moved in and out of songs so smoothly and quickly that one found it difficult to hang on to every note as long as they might have wanted.
>
> "*Albatross*, a song sung by Judy Collins, was another example of the concert's promising demonstration of Linda's talents as a superb musician and vocalist. Her song for Susan, her lover, was sung so affectionately and tenderly that one became so engrossed in the performer's magnetic quality that it was easy to lose the lyrics of the song.
>
> "Musically speaking, the concert was a success. But most concert reviews are based wholly on the performer's talents (or lack of) as an entertainer, with little regard to the person behind the music. This review would be incomplete without considering Linda Shear as Linda Shear.
>
> "It definitely does something to you to sit and listen to someone singing when you know they've felt oppression at its worst–when you know that they have the courage to let the world know who they are and what they believe. Let's face it, it takes guts to admit you're gay and survive the penalties for being honest with the world and yourself.
>
> "For that reason, you admire Linda Shear for doing something you've never been able to do. Her songs have a special significance, and you can't help feeling that she's singing them to you personally. Linda sings affection and understanding–she touches you deeply inside because you know she feels empathy for your frustration, for your anger at a society that refuses to accept you.

## CHICAGO AFTER STONEWALL

"It's rare now-a-days to find performers who mean what they sing, but Linda's sincerity shines through in every song. Whether it was all those smiles, or the every once in a while wink, or maybe just a few of the lyrics like, 'baby it isn't easy,' that makes you believe in her, one can't be certain. But Linda Shear does, in fact, leave you feeling a little different–perhaps stronger, a little less afraid, and a little more optimistic.

" ... Linda Shear was accompanied on drums by Ella Szekely whose solo in *High Flying Bird* was a highlight of the evening ... "

On Shear's 1977 album *A Lesbian Portrait*, subtitled "lesbian music for lesbians only," the back cover explains her separatist philosophy:

"This album is a record of the music I wrote from 1972 to 1975. I was encouraged to produce and distribute the record on a national scale by my own needs as a lesbian musician and by the needs of lesbians who wanted and needed lesbian. My lover Tryna and I started out with a small distribution goal and only pressed 400 records. My concerts then, in 1975, were for wimmin only, and most of my audience was lesbians. I learned, however, that to passively 'allow' my concerts to be mostly lesbians was just not good enough. When I began to aggressively perform for lesbians ONLY I experienced just how true that was. The power and energy in the room were huge and uniquely beautiful. I began doing lesbian only concerts early in 1976. We continued the distribution to wimmin only. Now, Tryna and I can no longer distribute the album to straight women. All of the music and lyrics are for lesbians."

Also on the bill, at the same benefit, was the Chicago Women's Liberation Rock Band. In 1972, they released the album *Mountain Moving Day* featuring them and the New Haven Women's Liberation Rock Band. The liner notes read:

"Both the Chicago Women's Liberation Rock Band and the New Haven Women's Liberation Rock Band were begun about 2 1/2 years ago by women in and around the women's movement in our two cities. At that time some of us were already musicians who had gotten an education in sexism by playing in male bands. Some of us were fugitives of high school marching bands, folk music groups and Mrs. Porter's music recitals. Some of us had stashed unplayed instruments under our beds years ago. And some of us were would-be musicians, learning to play for the first time. All of us wanted to create a new kind of band and a new kind of music, though we had no clear idea how to do that.

"We knew what we didn't want: the whole male rock trip with its insulting lyrics, battering-ram style and contempt for the audience. We didn't want to write the female counterpart of songs like *Under My Thumb, Back-Street Girl, It's a Man's Man's Man's World* where men say to us 'you're beneath contempt and we will celebrate your degradation.' We had to think of some other way to make a hit besides bumping and grinding like Mick Jagger, raping and burning our guitars like Jimi Hendrix, or whacking off on stage like Jim Morrison. We didn't want to pulverize our audience's (and our own) eardrums with 1010 decibels. As performers we didn't want to get off by trashing the people we played for, and we didn't want to have a star backed up by a squad of secondary musicians.

"But what did we want anyway? We knew that we wanted to make music that would embody the radical, feminist, humanitarian vision we shared. And the lyrics were the obvious place to begin – the field was wide open. Most of the rock songs women have sung till now were about the pain men cause us – the pain that's supposed to define us as women. We didn't want to deny that tradition (women struggled hard for the right to sing even that much) but we wanted to sing about how the pain doesn't have to be there – how we fight and struggle and love to make it change. At first it was easiest to write new lyrics to old songs, but as time has gone on we have begun to write entirely new material (the record contains examples from both these phases).

"We also had to demystify the priesthood of the instrument and the amplifier – move and set up the equipment, find the fuses, fix the feedback, mike, monitor and control it all ourselves. We had to try to break down the barriers that usually exist between performers and audiences by rapping a lot between songs about who we are, what we're doing, and where our songs come from. Whenever possible we've played in places where people can dance, done some theatre and comedy, passed out lyrics so people could sing with us, and invited other women to come and jam with us.

"The hardest thing to deal with was the music itself – what could we make out of such a motley collection of tastes, backgrounds and instruments? We had started from scratch, not by fitting accomplished musicians into traditional slots. We had no leaders, arrangers, managers, agents, roadies – even equipment or instruments. We thought of the bands as collectives, so we wanted to learn together and work toward eliminating the inequalities of (musical) power that existed among us. Our progress has been slow and difficult – it has come out of thousands of hours spent practicing, teaching each other, taking lessons, listening to other bands, jamming, writing and working all kinds of things out with each other. Over the past 2 1/2 years each band has evolved its own material and style which is partly the result of the combination of instruments we happened to end up with and largely the result of our efforts to make collective, non-assaultive joyful rock music.

"WHAT WE DO: We are the 'agit-rock' arm of our respective women's movements. In Chicago this means we are a chapter of the

## CHICAGO AFTER STONEWALL

Chicago Women's Liberation Union (more about this later). In New Haven we are all members of New Haven Women's Liberation. We go places where leaflets can't go – college dances, women's conferences, rallies, benefits, festivals, prisons and miscellaneous events. And perhaps we say things that leaflets can't say because we have music and performance to help us generate for those few hours while we're playing some glimpse of the world we'd like to see happen. Some of our jobs have been more than just exciting – we and the audience have shared in a deeply-felt celebration of our vision. At others we've been met with bad vibes, hostile men, inadequate electricity, freezing weather.

"We charge for our performances according to what people can pay, and so far have spent our earnings on equipment, transportation, food, drink, rent for rehearsal space and donations to the women's movement. We don't see the bands as profit-making (all of us have other jobs which support us) but as part of what needs to be done to change the culture of this society.

"What we all want to do is use the power of rock to transform what the world is like into a vision of what the world could be like; create an atmosphere where women are free enough to struggle to be free, and make a new kind of culture that is an affirmation of ourselves and of all people.

"CWLU

"We in the Chicago band wanted to add just a little note about the organization that we're a part of because we feel that it has been important to us and to the women in Chicago. This is the Chicago Women's Liberation Union, which is the only on-going radical feminist organization of its type in the country. In its three years it has provided a political unity and sense of direction for much of the women's movement in Chicago. Some of the projects included in the Union are:

"Women's Graphics Collective (original feminist art & posters) Liberation School for Women (alternative education for and about women)

"Health Project (which fights to keep city maternity centers open and offers pregnancy testing and health referrals)

"Work Work Group (to equalize salary and job differentials for city employees)

"Womankind (a women's newspaper)

"Speakers Bureau

"Rape Crisis Center"

A portion of the proceeds from the Linda Shear/Chicago Women's Liberation Rock Band concert went into a fund to open a lesbian community center. In an interview with Marie Kuda in the *Paper*, Shear explained:

> "I think that once we get a Lesbian Women's Center that it's going to make a huge difference. With a center we can start to offer women something other than meeting two or three times a week.
>
> "We can offer women who are still in the bars a valid alternative. We hope to have a library, a kitchen, a coffeehouse, a game room. We'd like it to be a place where people can be, not pay a cover charge and hear a band. Just be, and meet other women and talk to other women. The whole atmosphere of a bar is alienating. We have already learned that you can't go in the bars and talk about the movement. But if we can offer something that's good then we can bring the women out of the bars. Right now, there's no alternative. There's the bars or you stay home with your friends. There's nowhere to go."

On January 30, 1972, Terri Schultz in her "Our Town" column in the *Chicago Tribune* writes:

> "When I first heard the Women's Liberation Rock Band two summers ago in Grant Park, only pity kept me from laughing out loud. The tunes hit the audience like cold flapjacks and settled uneasily in the pit of our collective stomachs. But never underestimate the persistence of women scorned. At long last the band, like the feminist movement, is getting itself together."

Schultz goes on to name the members of the band: Dr. Naomi Weisstein, a psychologist "bobs up and down on her organ bench like a cork in a whirlpool, her heavy hiking shoes bouncing spasmodically to the beat"; Drummer Suzanne Prescott, "a doctoral candidate in human development at the University of Chicago, puffs staunchly on a pipe she smokes to kick her cigaret [sic] habit"; Second drummer, Fanny Montalvo, "a bio-engineering student in the University of Illinois"; Kathy Rowley and Sherry Jenkins, "music majors in Loop Junior College, on vocals and lead guitar along with Susan Abod of De Paul music school; and Pat Miller, "a student in Carthage College in Kenosha, Wis." on tambourine.

Schultz continued, "By the final number, *Mountain Moving Day*, adapted from a 1913 poem by feminist Yosano Akiko, not one foot stayed still. *"The mountain moving day is coming ... oh, man, this alone believe. All sleeping women will now awake – and move."*

In July 1972, the Women's Caucus changed its name to Chicago Lesbian Liberation, the largest lesbian group in Chicago, with sub-groups like the

Artemis Players theater group, Lesbian Mothers, Lesbian Alcoholics, Motorcycle Mechanics, and a Sunday baseball team. According to *Lavender Woman*, the name change came after the group decided "the term Gay Woman is merely a weak way of saying Lesbian. We are strong women, proud and happy to be Lesbians struggling towards Liberation (Lesberation). Hence the name change."

On October 6, 1972, Chicago Lesbian Liberation and the Women's Center, 3322 N. Halsted, held a joint benefit at the UIC-CC, again featuring Linda Shear and Ella Szekeley, this time augmented by Sherry Jenkins on bass and Joan Capra on violin. The benefit, attended by approximately 600 people, mostly women, was named "The Family of Women." Guitarist Michelle "Michal" Brody later joined the group, singing and reciting her poetry. After the event, the group adopted the event name as their official band name and became, "The Family of Women." The warm-up act was Patricia Kerr, songwriter, singer, and multi-instrumentalist, who *Lavender Woman* described as "a poised, polished and vivacious performer." Next on the bill was a showing of *Lavender*, a thirteen-minute documentary by Chicago filmmakers Colleen Monahan and Elaine Jacobs about two women, one who wants to become a minister, the other a housewife. The November 1972 issue of *Lavender Woman*, described the film as portraying "two lesbians in their life together, playing, doing daily things, each at her job, caring for each other, and throughout, talking about coming out, being lesbians, and living together."

In the *Paper* Patricia Lumen reviewed another performance by Linda Shear at Aisle 5, 2936 N. Clark St., a popular venue for women folk singers like Loree Lynn, Patricia Rusk, and Cathy and Carolyn Ford. Lumen writes:

> "... the billing read: 'Linda Shear: Feminist – in the most radical sense.' Inside the dark coffeehouse a woman dressed in denims, blue shirt and brown suede vest took her place at the piano. Wavy brown hair reached to past shoulder-length, hugging a laughing/crying face. Her sound consisted of a collage of moods ranging from the soft acceptance of a futureless love in Buffy St. Marie's *Until It's Time for You to Go*, to the crashing explosion of revolution in a song from *Marat/Sade*."

Shear's set included a medley of Melanie songs, Bob Dylan's *Just Like A Woman*, and her self-penned *Ghosts*, with the lyrics, "She comes with cloak and dagger/To awake me with her spell/She brings to me black roses/she knows my mind so well."

Onstage Shear switched between guitar and piano. Ella Szekely accompanied her on drums, who Lumen describes as having "wire-rimmed glasses peeking through strands of shag."

On the other side of the women's liberation debate was Mrs. Harriet Pierce, the Midwest director of the Anti-Women's Liberation League, and wife of the minister of the Chicago Methodist Temple, 77 W. Washington Ave. In June 1972, the *Chicago Tribune* reported the anti-feminist group had chartered buses and were heading to Springfield, IL, to protest the House's ratification of the proposed Equal Rights Amendment. Pierce told the *Chicago Tribune*:

> "We see this amendment as a weapon by the women liberationists to destroy the family structure, like termites eating away at wood, or like Communists undermining democracy. Furthermore, we fear this amendment will lead to marriage among homosexuals, the drafting of women into the Army, and the crumbling of the American family as a way of life."

# 27
# GAY PRIDE 1972

In 1970, Chicago's first celebration of the Stonewall Riots had been a political march from Bughouse Square to Civic Center Plaza, but by the third parade in 1972, it was a mix of politics and social gatherings. The schedule of events for Pride Week 1972 was as follows:

Saturday June 24

AFTERNOON:

Workshops at University of Illinois Circle Campus. Noon to 4:00 p.m. TOPICS: National gay issues, women's problems, men-women problems, gay-straight issues, gays and the church.

EVENING: Dance. University of Illinois, 750 S. Halsted 9:00 p.m. $1.50. Featuring the Chicago Women's Liberation Rock Band.

Hawaiian Luau (Sponsored by ONE of Chicago, Inc.) 4221 W. Irving Park (100F Hall) 9:00 p.m. $5.00

Cruise: Midnight cruise on Lake Michigan aboard the Trinidad (Sponsored by OO-Us Social Club, a new South Side group) Food – Music– Drinks. $12.00. Midnight to 4:00 a.m.

Sunday June 25

"Celebration of Life" at Belmont Rocks, beginning at 10:00 a.m. and lasting until late afternoon.

GAY PRIDE PARADE assembles at Belmont Rocks at 4:00 p.m. Parade begins at 5:00 p.m. proceeding along Belmont to Broadway to Clark, and ending at Lincoln Park. Gay Pride Rally at Lincoln Park.

Monday June 26

Workshop on Gay Unity.

Chicago Lesbian Liberation presents a FILM Festival at Lincoln Park Presbyterian Church, 600 W. Fullerton at 8:00 p.m.

Tuesday June 27

GAY PRIDE WEEK DANCE at the American Legion Post, 1750 N. Cleveland 9:00 p.m. to 1:00 a.m. for the benefit of the Gay Liberation Task Force of the American Library Association (which will be holding its annual convention in Chicago at that time)

Gay Conference: "Psychology, Religion and the Homosexual" at St. James' Cathedral, Wabash and Huron. 7:30 p.m.

Wednesday June 28

Candlelight vigil outside Cook County Jail at 8:00 p.m. in protest against individuals arrested and jailed solely for homosexuality, and against the way homosexuals are treated in jail.

Thursday June 29

Dance. 2442 N. Lincoln. 9:00 p.m. to 1:00 a.m. at I.W.W. (Wobbly) Hall. (Sponsored by the Transvestite Legal Committee).

Friday June 30

Chicago Lesbian Liberation Coffee House. Lincoln Park Presbyterian Church, 600 W. Fullerton. 8:00 p.m.

Saturday July 1

Gay Pride Week Picnic at Wilson Shelter, Indiana Dunes State Park, at 10:00 a.m.

---

In July 1972, the first issue of the *Paper* hit the newsstands, describing itself as a "community paper of the arts, of alternative lifestyles, of what's happening on the Chicago scene." It cost 35¢ and was short-lived – perhaps three issues; it was certainly defunct by January 1973. One notable gay writer who co-founded the *Paper* was Chicago-born Frank M. Robinson. Robinson co-wrote the novel, *The Glass Inferno*, with Thomas N. Scortia. It, and another novel, *The Tower,* inspired the 1974 film *The Towering Inferno*. Robinson later wrote speeches for Harvey Milk, the first openly gay man to be elected to public office in California. On November 14, 2010, in an interview with the author of this book, Robinson said of the *Paper*:

> "My name doesn't appear [in the *Paper*] for a very good reason. I was working for *Playboy* at the time as the 'Playboy Advisor' and I was 'in the closet' at the company. If they'd known I was gay, I would have lost my job – *Playboy* was a very open organization but to have a gay man handing out advice to young heterosexuals would never have worked. The *Paper* was sort of a sequel to *Gay Pride*, which I'd put out a year earlier – also while at *Playboy*."

An editorial in the *Paper* pleads the case for a gay press:

> "Despite the existence of four dailies and the various weeklies, bi-weeklies etc. there are vast areas of the city scene that never get reported at all. A case in point is the Gay community's recent Gay Pride Week, an annual celebration complete with speakers, parades etc. The *San Francisco Chronicle* and the *New York Times* covered the parades in their cities, but no Chicago paper covered the local one."

If it hadn't been for coverage in the *Paper* and the *Mattachine Midwest Newsletter*, no written account of Chicago's 1972 Pride Parade would exist.

In the early afternoon of June 25, crowds gathered at Belmont Rocks beach, a well-known gay men's cruising area, for a "Gay Pride Birthday Picnic." Around 5:00 p.m., the parade assembled in Belmont Harbor parking lot with an estimated 1,000 people, some traveling from St. Louis, Iowa City, Minneapolis, South Bend (Indiana), Indianapolis, Madison, Springfield (Illinois), Bloomington (Indiana), Champaign, and Milwaukee. The largest single group in the parade was Chicago Lesbian Liberation. Dick Galliette in the *Mattachine Midwest Newsletter* noted, "The parade bulldozed and swished through the most notorious avenues of Chicago's 'Gay Ghetto.'"

The route was west on Belmont, south on Broadway, continuing south on Clark Street, east on La Salle Extension Drive, then north to Lincoln Park Free Forum for a mass rally. The *Paper* wrote:

> "At several points along the parade route there was an obvious anti-Gay sentiment expressed by onlookers. More than once, high school aged hoods threw rocks and eggs at the paraders. However, these incidents were limited to specific parts of the parade and the majority of the marchers were not aware of the violence.

The police dispersed the troublemakers. One man commented, 'I've never seen so many fairies in all my life,' and a young woman remarked, 'You wouldn't mind so much if so many of the guys weren't so good-looking.' An older woman waved excitedly for a while, then asked a marcher what it was all about. When told it was 'Gay people marching for Gay Pride Week,' her face dropped, then she smiled and began waving again, 'It's a lovely parade anyway.' At the Free Forum, several speakers took the stage: Gay Lib's Murray Edelman; Marge Wilson from the Feminist Lesbian Intergalactic Party (Flippies) recited a Christopher Street commemorative poem she wrote; Tony Johnson of the Transvestites Legal Committee; Richard Chinn of the Fiery Flames Collective – Chinn and his lover, John Cantrell, had been arrested a year earlier for kissing in public; Michael McConnell of Gay House in Minnesota also spoke. McConnell, a librarian, was refused a job at the University of Minnesota after applying for a license to marry his lover, Jack Baker. He was in Chicago for the American Library Association convention, as was veteran activist Barbara Gittings who led the crowd in a rousing chant of Gay Power and Gay Love.

Dick Galliette summed up the festivities in the *Mattachine Midwest Newsletter*, 'The Gay Pride 1972 Parade was a minor success, even though it was poorly organized and coordinated and actively supported by only a small fraction of Chicago's gay community.'

Gay Pride Week ended with the third annual rally at Civic Center Plaza on June 27. Gay rights campaigner William B. Kelley served as moderator, introducing the speakers: Jim Bradford, past president of Mattachine Midwest, urged the audience to be open with themselves; Barbara Gittings spoke about her work with the Task Force on Gay Liberation and the American Library Convention; John Maybauer, vice president of Chicago Gay Alliance, spoke of worldwide gay oppression, giving emphasis to prisoners in Cuba and the US; Mary Richardson urged the audience to keep Gay Pride alive after the rally was over; Michael Bergeron and William B. Kelley also spoke, then Rev. David Sindt talked about his ordination as an openly gay minister in the Presbyterian Church. The rally ended with the customary standing in a circle, holding hands and chanting gay slogans.

The following day, the second annual Gay Book of the Year award was presented by the Task Force on Gay Liberation (TFGL) at the American Library Association (ALA) convention in Chicago. The TFGL was founded in 1970 to educate the ALA about the need for gay resources in libraries and to defend employees' rights. The TFGL set up a hospitality suite in the Palmer House Hotel, and after keynote speeches by Barbara Gittings and Israel Fishman, local gay activists discussed and read the works of gay and lesbian writers: Vernita Gray of the Third World Gay Revolutionaries and Chicago Lesbian Liberation, talked about Sappho of Lesbos; Israel Fishman read from

Walt Whitman; and Muffie Nobel of Chicago Lesbian Liberation read Gertrude Stein. Gittings' lover, Kay Tobin, co-author with Randy Wicker of *The Gay Crusaders*, was also there. The 1972 TFGL Gay Book of the Year award went to Del Martin and Phyllis Lyon, co-authors of *Lesbian/Woman*, and Peter Fisher, author of *The Gay Mystique*.

*Chicago Gay Pride* reported on a spontaneous zap:

> "The laugh of the week occurred when it was decided that after the Gay Book Awards we would liberate the Charade, a discotheque in the basement of the Palmer House. About thirty of us ordered drinks and waited for the bellydancer to appear. Those of us who expected a go-go-boy to do his thing were sadly disappointed when a woman named Inklas appeared – not even the lesbians in the party enjoyed watching her. When her belly finally stopped shaking, the band came in. It was a three-piece female combo whose eyes became large when the tiny dance floor started filling up with same-sex couples. There were no problems. The manager of the club was laughing his head off."

# 28
# GAY BARS AND DISCOS IN THE EARLY 1970s

To celebrate Gay Pride 1972, *Chicago Today* published a series on the gay community written by Barbara Ettorre. The June 27 headline read, "Gay men discuss their lives, parents, images." Ettorre describes a gay bar for the straight readers:

> "The music from the latest records was blaring as bodies, half caught in the dizzying strobe lights bounced around the dance floor. Mirrors picked up reflections of the people huddled around the bar. The atmosphere was noisy, contemporary, jostling. It might have been any number of Chicago's singles bars, except this North Side establishment catered almost exclusively to gays."

Though not mentioned in the article, the bar was the Trip, 27 E. Ohio St., and Ettorre spoke to the unnamed owner – either Dean T. Kolberg or Ralf L. Johnston. On another floor in the bar, over the sounds of a folk-rock quartet singing a Carol King song, the owner spoke of the bar's legal troubles:

> "We were open a year and got busted twice in 1968. The Liquor Commission handed down an emergency closing order. The first time, in January, thirteen were arrested for prostitution, solicitation and public indecency. The second time, in May, two were arrested. Last May 19, the Illinois Supreme Court awarded us a complete reversal.
>
> "We used to have a huge straight luncheon crowd with a women's fashion show. The bad publicity has ruined our luncheon business. We had one arrest last November for public indecency, but the case was dismissed."

Ettorre describes the bar as "semi-crowded with gay men of all ages, some older, in suits and ties, some very contemporary with body-shirts and longer hair, some in tee-shirts, workshirts – generally impossible to categorize the group as being from a certain segment." The bar owner continued, "Things have changed a little. We aren't hassled legally much anymore. Maybe it's a combination of favorable court cases, a certain liberation and some measure of tolerance by the public.'"

Several gays aired their grievances. One told Ettorre, "I know a gay couple who invested several hundred dollars in fixing up an apartment. The lease was not renewed. No explanation. After they moved out, the landlord upped the rent to $50 a month and rented the place to straights. It's the old stereotype: Bring in a fag and let him fix up the place. After all, they're all good interior decorators, aren't they?"

The *Chicago Today* series coincided with the 3rd Gay Pride Week celebrations. Just before Pride, Chicago got its first taste of live DJ disco. PQ's opened and featured a live DJ. The Grand Opening was August 30, 1972, of which the *Mattachine Midwest Newsletter* wrote:

> "The bar has been in existence since 1917 – 'Only the customers have changed over the years.' Tiffany lampshades and acres of real varnished wood add to the atmosphere of this very popular spot. Crowds estimated at up to 500 persons gathered, consuming gallons of free champagne provided by the management, with disco dancing and socializing enjoyed until the early morning hours."

PQ's wasn't without its problems. In February 1973, The *Maroon* reported on an "allegedly racist incident when a black University of Chicago student was refused entry to PQ's after the bouncer told him it was "because his black brothers had spoiled it for him":

> "Evidently, the bouncer had earlier had a fight with some black people. The student left, but later saw four blacks enter the bar and leave almost immediately.
>
> "As a result of the incident, University Gay Lib organized a 'Boycott PQ's' picket line on February 16th. Despite the snow and near zero temperatures, about 30 people showed up. ... A group of demonstrators negotiated with the proprietor of PQ's, demanding obedience to the civil rights law governing the bar, a reduction of the requirement of 5 IDs to 2 IDs (the student who had been thrown out claimed that only blacks were required to present 5 IDs, while whites were served after showing only 2), and the hiring of more black people. The source said that the bar agreed to two of the demands but refused to lower the number of required IDs from 5 to 2."

Within a year, PQ's was Ms, a lesbian bar run by Marge Summit and Chee Chee, then Saturdays and later O'Banion's, a gay punk rock club. In the premiere issue of the short-lived magazine *Tuffy*, the Chicago Gay Bar Listings read:

> "Sparrows, 5224 N. Sheridan; Togetherness, 61 E. Hubbard; Up North, 6244 N. Western; Shari's, 2901 N. Clark St; Twenty One Club, 3042 W. Irving Park Rd.; King's Ransom, 20 E. Chicago Ave.; Kitty Sheons, 745 N. Rush St.; New Jamie's, 1112 N. Clark St.; Blue Pub, 3059 W. Irving Park Rd.; Broadway Sam's, 5249 N. Broadway; Checkmate, 2546 N. Clark St.; Gold Coast, 501 N. Clark St.; the Haig, 800 N. Dearborn; Alameda, 5210 N. Sheridan; Annex, 2865 N. Clark; Bentley's, 640 N. State St.; Office, 4636 N. Broadway; Peppers, 1502 W. Jarvis; Queen's Surf, 436 N. Clark St.; Ritz, 937 N. Clark St.; Ruthie's, 3231 N. Clark St.; and the Trip, 27 E. Ohio."

There were at least three dozen other gay bars in Chicago. Those listed were the most "out," while some like Punchinello's, 936 N. Rush St., and the Nite Life, 933 N. State St., were mixed gay/straight; the former attracted a theatre crowd, the latter was a drag bar dating back to the mid-1940s.

August 1972 saw the launch of another short-lived bar rag. *Michael's Thing/Chicago* was published and edited by Ron Thomas, with Mike Karlin as advertising manager. The ad in the *Mattachine Midwest Newsletter* read, "Exploding onto the scene. Chicago's own ENTERTAINMENT GUIDE. Get to Know the Scene! ... A Gay Publication for the Benefit of all the Gay Community." It didn't last long.

In the *Paper*, an article about Punchinello's by Bob Fish gives a glimpse into "the life" in 1972. He writes that the bar is in "an English basement" and was sometimes "hot, fetid and smoky":

> "Framed antique covers of *Theatre* magazine encircle the dimly-lit room, attesting to an intense passion for the performing arts common to all the regular clientele. Otherwise, the patrons are a mixed crowd in every conceivable sense of the word. Small cocktail tables squeezed tightly together, bare wooden chairs and the absence of a dress code contribute to an informal mood generated by what the menu calls 'spontaneous entertainment.' Bob Moreen takes to the piano about 10:30 p.m. ... Where the show goes from there depends on who shows up on a particular evening, for the policy at Punchy's is to let the audience entertain itself. In theory the stage is open to anyone who wishes to perform, but in actuality there is a large pool of highly talented regulars from which to draw. It might be Emily with her haunting ballad or Tim with a sadly-neglected show tune. Jerry may let out with some impromptu blues usually reserved for the south side spots where he performs. Even Barry, the bartender,

graces the stool on occasion, and if Bob can induce Lynn, the hostess, to perform, you might hear the most poignant version of *Little Girl Blue* imaginable. Punchy's is often a post-performance haven for touring company cast members and noted celebrities, many of whom are more than willing to vocalize just for the hell of it, and consequently the early morning hours are often the brightest. The menu is an adequate offering of small steaks and sandwiches, all palatable and moderately priced. An order of French-fried mushrooms is a bargain at $1.00. Drinks are reasonable and well-made."

In an interview with the author, Nancy Reiff talked about working at Punchinello's:

"The first bar I worked in was in 1973 and that was Punchinello's. I started working there over the Gold Coast Art Fair weekend 1973, and it was on a fluke. I was in there, and they were so busy it was unbelievable. So they said to me, 'Have you ever waited on tables?' I said, 'No.' And they said, 'Well, you're going to now. We need help.' I said, 'Fine.' I made a ton of money that day, for 1973, like $100 dollars was a lot of money. So I started working there.

"That was owned by an Austrian by the name of Pierre. He didn't bill it as a gay bar, he said it was a theater bar. All the entertainers who were appearing at the different theaters would come into Punchinello's. They had entertainment in the bar, a gentleman by the name of Bruce Robbins was the piano player. It was spontaneous; if Carol Channing was there, she'd get up and do a song, if Della Reese was there, she would get up and do a song. Barry Manilow would come in, Bette Midler would come in. It was a wonderful, wonderful time."

"Punchinello's finally closed and I don't remember what year it was, but I wasn't there at the end. The owner was always on the premises, he was a screaming queen and an entertainer beyond belief. He was extremely flamboyant, very entertaining, loved the whole social scene. Zsa Zsa Gabor would come in, and one day I served her a blue cheeseburger, and she just looked at me and said, 'Darling, French fries are not chic.'"

Punchinello's closed in 1979.

The same issue of the *Paper* took a behind-the-scenes look at the female impersonators in "Roby Landers' Hot Pants Revue" at Sparrows, 5224 N. Sheridan Rd., a gay-owned drag bar that opened August 28, 1970. The show's creator, San Francisco-born African American Roby Landers had been a registered nurse in the Army Medical Corps before turning to female impersonation. As early as February 1963, Landers was performing as a "femme mimic" at the Colony Club in Kansas City. In November 1969, an ad appeared in the *Chicago Tribune* for "The Jewel Box presents Roby Landers and show at the Artists & Models Costume Ball at the Aragon Ballroom." At Sparrows, Landers ruled over a bevy of drag queens, including Tanya Terrell, Audrey Bryant, Ebony Carr, Wanda Lust, Artesia Welles, and Ricky, a "near naked" male dancer. In the "Hot Pants Revue," Landers walked onstage wearing a blond wig. He fired off zingers, like when he pointed to his glamorous dress and said, "You know how many tricks I had to hustle at 35 cents a throw for this." The manager, David Cardwell, told the *Paper*, "We've done something like 75 productions at Sparrows, including *Mame* and *Hair*, where we used the music but wrote our own lines."

In September 1973, Michael Bergeron wrote an article for the *Reader* called "Reader's Guide to the Gay Scene: Gay City":

> "Chicago boasts 76 gay bars. Most of them on the North Side but a scattering is found elsewhere in the city and even a few suburbs. Just as there are many types of gay people, gay bars come in different varieties. Whether you want to boogie at the Bistro, 420 N. Dearborn, Broadway Sam's, 5246 N. Broadway, and the Annex, 2865 N. Clark St., or enjoy the quiet atmosphere of a tavern like the Wooden Barrell (their spelling), 2326 N. Clark St., you don't have to go far. Gay bars are spotted throughout Old Town, the Glory Hole, 1343 N. Wells.; the Devil's Den, 163 W. Burton Place; Finochio's, Burton Pl. & Wells St. and the Near North Side, the King's Ransom, 20 E. Chicago Ave; Jamie's, 1110 N. Clark St.; the Haig, 800 N. Dearborn, as well as the area around Clark St. and Diversey Ave., the Knight Out, 2936 N. Clark St.; the Checkmate, 2546 N. Clark St.; La Noche de Ronda, 2626 N. Halsted St.; the Coming Out Pub, 2519 N. Halsted; Shari's, 2901 N. Clark St. They're found as far north as Jarvis Ave., Pepper's at 1502 W. Jarvis, and south as far as the Chain, 7860 S. Cottage Grove Ave., not to mention suburbs.
>
> "Coats and ties are di rigueur at Kitty Sheon's, 745 N. Rush St. It's grubbily casual – and a little tough – at the Office, 4636 N. Broadway. A long established and well-known leather bar is the Gold Coast, 501 N. Clark St. Downstairs is the Pit, home of the Leather Toy Store (chains, whips, leather clothing, and some more exotic items). One of the oldest Chicago gay bars is the 12 year old Twenty-One Club, 3042 W. Irving Park Rd. while the newest is Ms, 661 N. Clark St., which opened Sept. 8. If you like drag shows, Chicago offers several, the most popular being those of the House of Landers, 936 W. Diversey, the Baton, 436 N. Clark St., and David's Place 5232 N. Sheridan Rd. The latter seems to have invested more in lights and equipment than Mr. Kelly's. The dazzling drags and handsome male entertainers often boggle the minds of straight observers; a common exclamation is 'I can't believe that's a guy!'"

# CHICAGO AFTER STONEWALL

Chicago's gay bar and club scene in 1973 was thriving. Raids were at a minimum – Chicago Police Department members, including Police Capt. Clarence E. Braasch, were paraded before the courts charged with shaking down taverns, many of them gay." Another factor was GAY POWER, as gays got "uppity," organized crime lost their monopoly on gay bars. One notable example was the closing of Chez Ron, a mafia-controlled lesbian bar. The bar had a troubled history with the gay community. In November 1970, an ad for Chez Ron appeared in the *Mattachine Midwest Newsletter*: "THE GAY PLACE TO GO. WITH AD 1 DRINK FREE."

In the following issue, an apology read, "We regret to learn that customers have been refused admission to Chez Ron, 4210 N. Lincoln Ave. That was altogether contrary to our understanding when accepting their ad. We apologize on our behalf as well as theirs."

An obituary for Chez Ron appeared in *Lavender Woman*, reprinted in the 1985 book *Are We There Yet? A Continuing History of Lavender Woman, a Chicago Lesbian Newspaper 1971-1976*, edited by Michal Brody:

> "Chez Ron Obitz
>
> "What can you say about a 18 month old lesbian bar that died?
>
> "That it was Mafia run. And male dominated. That it loved bad bands, no windows, cheap drinks, and not 'us.'
>
> "Where was the love? And why did 'we' go?
>
> "It can be said that this bar rated lowest in almost every area on the now infamous CLL [Chicago Lesbian Liberation] Bar Survey: that the pictures of 1930 chorus girl types passed off as gay women should have been hung around necks instead of on walls: that – thanks be to lesbian power – the bar was forced 'under' by the addition of new and better social gathering spots; and that it is no longer.
>
> "Tsk. Sigh
>
> "Goodbye."

Another lesbian bar was the Bradberry, 7101 N. Clark St., possibly owned by the same "outfit." It came onto the scene just prior to the Chez Ron closing and at least one Chez Ron employee, Chris, a woman, worked there. The Bradberry flourished for a while, but Bobby Barker in *Chicago Gay Crusader* writes, "News is that Bradberry is bad news for our sisters. Strike it from your list. They don't want our business."

In the summer of 1973, several bars were run by politically active and community-minded gays, including Jim "Felicia" Flint at the Baton, 436 N. Clark St.; Charles "Chuck" Renslow at the Gold Coast, 501 N. Clark St.;

Woodrow "Woody" I. Moser at the Legacy/Twenty-One Club, 3042 W. Irving Park; Jack David at the Up North, 6244 N. Western; and in October 1973 Marge Summit and Chee Chee opened Ms., 661 N. Clark St.

In August 1973, Fred Alexson wrote a rundown of Chicago gay bars and restaurants in *David*:

> "If you didn't care for the old Jamie you might like the new Jamies, now that Patrick Renslow of Kris Studios and the Club Baths and David Cardwell, former manager of Sparrows, have taken it over and spruced it up. Jamies opens at 7 a.m. in the morning for you early birds till 2 a.m. at night and is a daytime gathering place for many of this town's pretty bartenders. Why not catch them on their time off. Located above Jamies is the new Crystal Hotel; only minutes from all the action spots."

In the November 29, 1975 *Gay Life*, Patrick Townson wrote, "Jamies raided by cops":

> "Jamie's bar, 1110 N. Clark St., sometimes known as New Jamies, was the scene of a bar raid last Saturday night, by uniformed and plainclothes officers of the Chicago Police Department. The raid was reminiscent of the old time bar raids in Chicago (re: fifties and sixties for the younger readers) complete with a large number of squad cars and an appropriate number of paddy wagons to escort the patrons and employees of the bar to the Police Station. As one uniformed officer at the scene stated to a patron, 'Come on lady, we're going for a ride downtown.' Police blocked off the 1100 block of Clark, from Division to Maple, while the raid was in progress, when curious passers by began to gawk from car windows, and slow traffic to a stand-still.
>
> "Officers on the scene alleged that an officer had been solicited to participate in an act of prostitution, thus precipitating the hostile action of the boys in blue. (Blue jeans in the case of the one plainclothes officer spotted inside during the raid.). In an unusual, but reoccurent move in recent days, the police elected to arrest all patrons of the bar, and employees, rather than just the patrons allegedly committing an offense. Thus, some forty or more people were arrested in the raid which took almost an hour to complete. Officers arrived on the scene shortly before midnight, and the last wagon and squad cars pulled away about 12:45 AM. Shortly before 2:00 AM the bar reopened, when substitute bartenders had been located to operate the establishment.
>
> "Although the raid was a serious offense to the freedom of association and freedom of action in sexual matters demanded by gay rights groups nationwide, the raid had a less serious aspect as many of the uniformed officers laughed and kidded each other, creating an impression that they were not terribly offended by the alleged criminal transaction which had

occurred. Many of the patrons also joked with each other and police as they entered the paddy wagon.

"In recent months, the management of New Jamies has feuded with automobile dealers in the block in which they are located. The operator of Jamies told this reporter he was convinced the harassment of the bar stemmed from nearby business places, including the automobile dealers. Whether or not the raid on October 25-26 was part of a harassment technique is open to debate."

In an interview with the author, Chicago LGBT Hall of Fame inductee, Richard Pfeiffer remembers the first time he went into a gay bar:

"It was a bar called Jamie's and it was on Clark Street. It was a little bit of everything, probably like the Stonewall. You had street queens in there, you had transgendered people, you had leather people, you had everybody that could be anything ... it was a street type of bar. I had just turned 21.

"I was never really a hippie boy, but I had my hair real long, almost to my waist; I hadn't cut it in seven years. I remember walking in there about ten minutes before it closed. I walked in and was surrounded by a number of transgendered people who said, 'We love your hair, girlfriend.' It was my first experience and it was real positive. The next night I went back. It was the day after I turned 21. For a 21 year old kid that had been in the closet, it was a neat thing."

In *David*, Fred Alexson writes about the rise of gay restaurants in 1974:

"Although the Trip has always had a fine restaurant as part of their offering, it wasn't until Jack of the Up North proved a gay restaurant by itself would be supported if the purpose, service and price were right that the doubters took notice. Now there are three more fine restaurants in Chicago, the Belfry, Burton Place, and the Grubstake. ... The Belfry, upstairs at 111 West Hubbard Street, is the place to go for quiet intimate dining to the most nostalgic music in town. Delly, the owner, prepares the superb menu himself with all the style and finesse of a first class chef.

"Across the street from the Gold Coast, Bill Swank has opened the newest restaurant with a casual atmosphere, the Grubstake, which promises to be the place to go anytime (24 hours). It will have counter service and an upstairs area for dining with a birds-eye view for cruising. Now we don't have to go where they just tolerate us after hours."

The Chicago Gay Directory 1974-1975 researched and written by Michael Bergeron and financed by the Up North bar and restaurant, 6244 N. Western Ave., listed over sixty bars in the Chicago area. In 1974 four new bars opened: On May 8, 1974, Le Pub, 1936 N. Clark St., was the latest straight bar/restaurant to go-gay; May 28 saw the Grand Opening of Our Den, 1355 N. Wells St., another bar/restaurant; May also saw the opening of the Closet, 3325 N. Broadway; and in October, Marge Summit from Ms., opened His 'n' Hers at 2316 N. Lincoln Ave.

Other bars in the Chicago Gay Directory 1974-1975 were:

"Adron's, 41 S. Harlem, Forest Park; Alameda, 5210 N. Sheridan; Augie's, 3729 N. Halsted; Annex, 2865 N. Clark; Another Place, 7300 S. Cottage Grove; Baton, 436 N. Clark; Bistro, 420 N. Dearborn; Blue Pub, 3059 W. Irving Park; Boys At Sea, 642 W. Diversey; Bradberry, 7101 N. Clark; Broadway Sam's, 5246 N. Broadway; Carol's Coming Out Pub, 2519 N. Halsted; Chain, 7860 S. Cottage Grove; Checkmate, 2546 N. Clark; Chez Ron, 4210 N. Lincoln; Club Yoyo, 3909 N. Ashland; Episode, E. 77th and Cottage Grove; Gate, 650 N. Dearborn; Glory Hole, 1343 N. Wells; Gold Coast, 501 N. Clark; Haig, 800 N. Dearborn; Hideaway II, 7301 W. Roosevelt; Hitching Post, 13101 S. Cicero, Crestwood; In Between, W. 63rd and S. Harlem; Jamie's, 1110 N. Clark; Jeffrey's Pub, E. 73rd St. & S. Jeffrey; Jesse's, 1012 W. Lawrence; King's Ransom, 20 E. Chicago; Kitty Sheon's, 745 N. Rush; Knight Out, 2936 N. Clark; Levin's Inn, 3526 N. Lincoln; Lost & Found, 2959 W. Irving Park; Mike's Terrace Lounge, 1137 W. Granville; Mike's Aragon, 1113 W. Lawrence; The Mark III, E. 73rd St and S. Cottage Grove Ave.; Mr. B's, 606 State Line Rd., Calumet City; My Brother's Place, 111 W. Hubbard; Name Of The Game, 2616 E. 75th St.; Nite Life, 955 N. State St.; Office, 4636 N. Broadway; Our Place, 1655 S. Throop St.; Our Place, 706 Stateline Rd, Calumet City; Parkside, E. 51st and Cottage Grove; Patch, 201 155th St., Calumet City; Peanut Butter and Jelly, 659 W. Diversey; Penguin, E. 74th & S. Yates; Pepper's, 1502 W. Jarvis; Pour House, 103 155th Pl., Calumet City; Ritz, 937 N. State St.; Shirley's Set Lounge, 6539 W. Roosevelt Road, Berwyn; Shari's, 2901 N. Clark; Shoreline, 7650 S. South Shore Drive; Snake Pit, 2626 N. Halsted; Sue & Nan's, 3920 N. Lincoln; Sunday's, 430 N. Clark; Trip, 27 E. Ohio; Twenty-One Club, 3042 W. Irving Park; Willoughby's, 1608 N. Wells.

"Semi gay bars: Blue Dahlia, 5640 W. North; Finochio's, 1400 N. Wells St.; High Chaparral, 7740 S. Stoney Island Avenue; Isle of Capri, 14511 S. Western, Dixmoor, IL; Machine Juice Bar, 4363 N. Sheridan; Punchinello's, 936 N. Rush; Tenement Square, 247 E. Ontario."

One gay nightclub that opened with much fanfare and then burned out – literally – was the Inner Circle, 233 W. Erie. At the opening week of February 14-23, Holly Woodlawn, Andy Warhol Superstar and star of the 1970 movie *Trash*, was the guest. Another performer at the Inner Circle was singer/comedienne Marilyn Sokol, who the *Chicago Gay Crusader* called a

## CHICAGO AFTER STONEWALL

"new sensation." Bruce Vilanch, in the *Chicago Tribune* wrote, "The girl has been leaving lots of clouds of dust around the town. But the biggest cloud she's leaving is the one directly behind her as she soars from the chorus line to the very brightest star." Most often compared to Bette Midler, Sokol went on to an illustrious career on Broadway and in films, but also had the dubious honor of being nominated for a Golden Raspberry Award for Worst Supporting Actress in the Village People movie *Can't Stop the Music*. Also appearing at the Inner Circle was female impersonator Arthur Blake, who played Dolly Carney in Yul Brynner's 1949 movie *Port of New York*. However, three months after the bar opened, the *Chicago Tribune* reported that on May 10 the Inner Circle was the victim of an arson attack. "Firemen found four five-gallon plastic bags filled with gasoline ... " Charles Rojek, the owner of the Inner Circle, was in Florida at the time. It never reopened.

Another gay bar that opened and burned down was Le Pub. The opening was reported in the *Chicago Gay Crusader* headlined "Le Pub 'Comes Out' as Gay":

> "Latest entrant – and a plush one it is – in the Chicago gay bar sweepstakes is Le Pub, 1936 N. Clark St.
>
> "The bar, which has operated for years as a non-gay dating bar and dining spot, made the switch at the beginning of May and is now bidding for its share of the local gay crowd. Rusty Rhodes directs the dining room.
>
> "Andy Cahill and The Four of Us will kick off the new entertainment policy at a private grand opening party May 8.
>
> "The bar has a lower level (pizzas available) and a main floor, with subdued "library" and fireplace off the main room. It has a 4:00 AM license."

Early on Christmas morning 1977, *Gay Life* reported that Le Pub was "Gutted by Fire":

> "'If it takes two weeks or two months, however long it takes, Le Pub will open, bigger and better than ever.' Those were the words of Danny Reilly, Le Pub's owner, shortly after the disastrous fire which gutted much of the very popular bar at 1944 N. Clark Street early on the morning of Christmas Day.
>
> "Smoke was first noticed coming up from the basement about 12:45AM and Le Pub employees calmly ushered the customers out into the wintry night, confident that they would be able to resume the evening's pleasures as soon as the fire department found the source of the smoke.

"However, when firemen arrived they had difficulty finding the fire because of the dense smoke. The blaze had reportedly started in mattresses in a storage area used by the North Park Apartments which occupy the largest part of the building. After several hours as the heat became more intense, the flames spread through the clay pipes leading up from the basement through the 18 inch thick cement floors of Le Pub. From that point it spread quickly, gutting the main lounge.

"One fireman was reportedly injured slightly. Some 200 residents of the North Park Apartments were forced to leave their homes and one Le Pub employee commented that the sight of frightened pajama-clad children spending part of Christmas morning in the cold was the saddest part of the scene."

Le Pub never reopened.

# 29
# TROUBLE AT DUGAN'S BISTRO

On June 1, 1973, Eddie Dugan (aka Edward Davison) opened Dugan's Bistro at 420 N. Dearborn, a high-tech gay and "hip crowd" disco inspired by New York discos like Le Jardin. Dugan's Bistro opened at the dawn of disco music and rode its wave until disco died. The club closed nine years to the day after it opened, a victim of the wrecking ball and Chicago's North loop redevelopment project. Within three weeks of its opening, Dugan's Bistro's license was revoked. The bar opened the following night.

This was the first of many problems.

In the *Chicago Gay Crusader*, Eddie Dugan described the revocation of his license as "a purely political move on the part of the city." He called the city's treatment of gay bars "totally disgusting." The paper also mentions an unconfirmed report that two other gay bars lost their licenses on the same day, though both opened the following night. They were not named.

In DUGAN'S BISTRO, INC. and Edward Davison v. Richard J. Daley, Mayor of the City of Chicago (56 Ill. App.3d 463 14 Ill.Dec. 63) the charges brought were:

1) On June 17, 1973 the licensee corporation, by and through its agent, Edward Davison, knowingly permitted a violation of the laws of the State of Illinois and/or Rules and Regulations of the Illinois Liquor Control Commission to be committed on the licensed premises, to-wit: lewd fondling by patrons, contrary to chapter 38, section 11-9(a)(4), Ill.Rev.Stat.1973.

2) On January 5, 1974, the licensee corporation, by and through its agent, James Hough, doorman, knowingly committed a battery upon Gerald Britt,

a person on the licensed premises, contrary to chapter 38, section 12-3(a)(1), Ill.Rev.Stat.1973.

3) On February 13, 1974, the licensee corporation, by and through its agent, Michael O'Callaghan, doorman, knowingly and without lawful reason denied Linda Deleonard entry into the licensed premises, contrary to chapter 43, section 133, Ill.Rev.Stat.1973.

The *Chicago Gay Crusader* reported that on November 6, 1975, all license revocation charges against Dugan's Bistro were dismissed. Cook County Circuit Judge Edward F. Healy, "spoke favorably in his ruling of gay people's right to associate with each other in bars and elsewhere. He also lambasted the City of Chicago's Law Department for bringing the charges against the Bistro."

DUGAN'S BISTRO, INC. and Edward Davison v. Richard J. Daley, Mayor of the City of Chicago (56 Ill. App.3d 463 14 Ill.Dec. 63) provided a more detailed account of the incidents leading up to the three charges:

> "The first of the three charges before the commissioner and now before the court is that the Bistro knowingly permitted certain lewd conduct to occur on its premises. The gist of this charge is knowledge. It is immaterial whether such conduct at the time of the occurrence and by its inaction permitted it. ... The licensee cannot be charged with conduct over which it has no control.
>
> "The city's only witness was police officer Thomas Fuller. Fuller testified that he and his partner entered the Bistro at about 1:30 A.M. on June 17, 1973. At that time the Bistro was filled to maximum capacity. The police officers went up to the bar, and ordered a drink. The room they were in, including the whole length of the bar, was about 85' by 40'. There were about 100 people in that room and it was crowded at the bar. While the police officers were standing at the bar, they saw two men sitting in a booth kissing each other and fondling each other in and around the groin. The conduct continued off and on for approximately ten or fifteen minutes.
>
> "Officer Fuller noticed several of the Bistro's employees in the room. When he first entered, he had seen one employee at the door checking identification. This is how Fuller determined he was an employee. He later saw him in an area around the bar. He also observed a man with a bar cloth on one occasion approach the table where the acts were taking place. This man, whom he assumed was a waiter, spent approximately one-half minute at the table – about the time it takes to pick up five or six glasses – and wiped the table with a wet towel. Fuller also observed persons whom he believed to be employees, because they

were carrying trays and bar towels, passing within five or six feet of the table on two other occasions.

"After about fifteen minutes, the two men in the booth and the manager of the Bistro, Edward Davison, were arrested. The charges were later dismissed at a hearing.

"The two men testified for the Bistro, denying that they had engaged in any lewd conduct. Mr. Davison also testified for the Bistro. He said that at the time of the arrest the Bistro had been open for seventeen days and had no waiters at the time. It did have one waitress, Barry Carol, who was very obviously female and always wore dresses or skirts. If a customer wanted a table cleared it was customary for them to clear the table and pick up drinks. There were rags lying on the bar for customers to use. Doormen did not clear tables. He did not observe the two men in the Bistro before he was arrested.

"The general policy of the Bistro was not to allow any necking or petting."

Second charge:

"The second charge was that the Bistro through its employee, James Hough, committed a battery on Lloyd Britt. Britt, a 33 year old salesman, testified that he and three of his friends, Mike Miller, Jennie Anderson and another girl named Mary went to the Bistro about 11:00 P.M. on January 25, 1974. They had been together since about 7:30 P.M. They had gone to the London House for dinner, having an 8:00 P.M. reservation for its first show. He had a scotch on the rocks before dinner and wine before and with dinner, possibly also a cocktail with dinner and a Straga after dinner.

"When they arrived at the Bistro, they got in line and waited for several minutes. After a few minutes, his date went on to the lavatory without being checked. The others waited in line for about ten minutes. They were asked for identification. One of the ladies (presumably Mike Miller's date) was asked for five pieces of identification. She did not have it. They asked why she needed it since she was obviously of age. The employees then asked the group to step away and continue their conversation on the side, and they were then asked to leave. Mike and his date went outside; Britt, however, remained standing on the side. When told to leave by Mr. Hough, he responded that he was waiting for his date, and would not leave until she appeared. Mr. Hough then struck him twice. He hit Britt on the cheek and dislocated his left shoulder. It happened quickly and at no time did Britt defend or protect himself. He did not recall striking anyone. Britt was not sure whether the first blow was struck when he was standing inside or outside the door. Hough was forcing him out the door and Britt believed the first blow was struck on the way out the door. Britt was then taken to the hospital by his friends.

"Patrick Moran, a police officer, was not an eyewitness, but investigated after the occurrence was over. He testified as follows: He spoke to Britt's friends at the hospital and saw Britt. Mr. Miller and one of the young women were intoxicated. All of the three were under the influence of alcohol. Officer Moran concluded they were under the influence because they had an odor of alcohol on their persons and they had been at the London House and then at some other place before going to the Bistro in order to dance. Anyone would have concluded that Miller had been drinking since his clothes were a little bit messed and there was an odor of alcohol on his breath; however, he was steady in his moves. Officer Moran did not give any opinion as to whether Britt had been drinking. He saw him at the hospital in the emergency room but was only able to get his name. Britt was covered with sheets and there was an amount of blood on his lower face, mouth and nose area.

"After talking to the four at the hospital, Officer Moran and his partner went to the Bistro. Hough told him he had struck Britt in self-defense; that the problem arose out of a conflict over identification cards. Someone else, not Hough, told Moran that Britt had threatened to 'blow that nigger's head off if he did not let him in and stop bothering him for identification.

"It appears from Officer Moran's testimony that while the police officers originally responded because of a telephone call from Wesley Hospital, a call was also made at the time of the incident by someone in the Bistro who identified himself on the telephone as a bartender.

"All the Bistro's witnesses had been employed by it at the time of the incident. Michael Anderson, the assistant manager, testified that he was checking the identification cards of persons waiting in line to enter when he first saw Britt. Britt was staggering and was either drunk or too high. Anderson told Britt he could not serve him in that condition. Britt became argumentative and started calling Anderson names. Anderson felt he could not handle it so Jim Hough, another I.D. checker, came over. Anderson continued to check identification cards of others trying to enter; however, he did notice Britt grab Hough by the collar; then they went out the door together. He did not see anything else of a physical nature. Mr. Anderson testified that during the time he was trying to handle Britt, Britt's companions were trying to calm him down.

"James Hough, who no longer works at the Bistro (he left voluntarily), testified that he went over to Anderson when he heard Britt say, 'I am going to blow that nigger's head off.' He then said to Britt that he believed Britt should not have made that remark and would Britt please remove himself from the premises. Britt then called him some abusive names. Hough then told Britt that he believed Britt was drunk. Britt grabbed him by the collar and Hough continued to say 'Sir, would you please remove your hands and remove yourself from the premises, because I do not feel you have the ability to come into the business.' Britt continued to use abusive language. Britt pulled Hough out of the door, then pushed him back against a brick wall. Hough was hit in the jaw. Hough did not grab or shove Britt or shove him out of the door. After Hough was shoved against the brick wall he grabbed Britt but he did not swing at him. Davison and an off-duty policeman separated them. The policeman did not remain on the scene but did make a report. However, the report was never introduced as evidence.

"According to Hough, Britt's friends apologized to Hough for Britt's actions and said Britt was too high. He had taken some M.D.A.'s. [A controlled substance under the Controlled Substances Act] Miller was not however called to testify. Robert Smith, who also had been acting as a doorman that night, testified he heard Britt say, 'I am going to get my gun and blow that nigger's head of.' He saw Hough go over to Britt. He did not notice anything else.

"Michael O'Callahan, another employee, testified that he saw the very end of the altercation outside. He saw Britt and Hough fall to the ground. Those nearby asked an off-duty policeman who was passing by to stop the fight. O'Callahan called the police and they came over and told everyone to stop it. They did. Miller put Britt into a taxi once the fight stopped and declined to wait for the police, saying Britt was too high on a drug called M.D.A. (this although O'Callahan had just testified that it was the police he had called who broke up the fight).

"Davison testified that he first noticed Britt when he heard him say something about shooting a nigger. Davison followed the others outside the door. He told O'Callahan to call the police and O'Callahan told one of the bartenders to call them and then come back outside. Hough was against the wall and Britt was swinging at him. Then Britt and Hough tussled and fell to the ground; Davison stopped the off-duty policeman but he did not get his name. Britt's friends took him in a taxi and declined to wait for the police although Davison asked them to. Miller told Davison Britt was too high and apologized.

"Florence Levine, an employee and wife of one of the owners of the Bistro, testified that she had noticed Britt because of the bit of confusion at the door. He was staggering and leaning against the door and the wall. His eyes were kind of blurring, blood shot, and he made quite a spectacle of himself, a lot of very loud talking and unruly behavior. She heard some profanity and she heard the word 'nigger' used. A young man with him tried to get him to leave and Britt said that 'no punk son-of-a-bitch is going to tell me whether I can come in or whether I have had enough to drink.' She did not know what happened after that since there was a car waiting for her and she left."

Third charge:

"The third charge was that the Bistro, in violation of section 12b of Article VI of the Liquor Control Act (Ill.Rv.Stat.1973, ch. 43, par. 133), knowingly and without lawful reason denied Linda Deleonardis entry into the premises. There is little serious dispute as to the facts involved as to this charge. Deleonardis, who was 25 years of age, went to the Bistro at about 11:30 P.M. on February 13, 1974 with two friends intending to have a nightcap. Upon attempting to enter they were asked for five pieces of identification. Deleonardis had only three, a driver's license, a student I.D. from Triton Junior College and a voter's registration card. She was told that was not enough. Indeed, the doorman would not even look at her driver's license, simply insisting she must have five pieces of identification. Likewise when Davison, the manager, came over he did not look at her identification. According to Deleonardis, other people were walking right in at this time. She also testified that Davison said "we do not want any 'cunts' in here.' Mr. Davison denied making this statement and both the doorman Smith and O'Callahan, another doorman, denied hearing Davison make any such statements.

"There was a sign in the vestibule stating that patrons must carry five I.D.'s. There had also been stories in the Chicago *Maroon* and the Chicago *Reader* which indicated that five pieces of identification are required. The Bistro required nearly everyone to carry two pieces of identification with their age on it and at least one with a physical description on it. The other pieces are generally corroborative. It required five pieces because many people divided their identification documents allowing others to use some of them.

"In fact, however, if a person has a passport no other identification is required because everything one needs is on it. Also, regular customers may be let in without checking; so, too, persons who are known and obviously of age. According to the testimony, most people coming to the Bistro are aware that identification is required. They usually hand the checker a wallet or a piece of identification to look at. He checks them and if he does not feel that it is enough he asks for more.

"Mr. Davison testified that they do not exclude females or blacks. About 20 percent of the business is female. They do, of course, exclude minors."

In late-1974 Gloria Gaynor released her album *Never Can Say Goodbye*, which on one side contained a 19-minute "Disco Suite," the first Disco megamix. On February 5, 1975 Gaynor performed at Dugan's Bistro. A year earlier in April 1974 the *Chicago Tribune* music reviewer, Lynn Van Matre, wrote about the club. In the article, Eddie Dugan said, "For the last two years, there's been a very cool atmosphere as far as the law goes. The police even told me not to try to handle problems myself – if a fight starts, call them, and let them handle it. Not that we have much trouble, anyway. When we do, it's usually with a couple of drunk straights. And I've never made a payoff."

Payoffs or not, it didn't take long for the authorities to set their sights on the Bistro. An alleged discriminatory door policy had already angered some in the gay community. In the November 1973 *Chicago Gay Crusader*, Bobby Barker, in his debut "Bobby Barfly" column, wrote, "Passports are the 'in' thing this year – or at least that's what the BISTRO would have you believe when they say you can produce a passport to help satisfy their requirement of five 'official' IDs. One wonders how long the community will put up with this crap."

In the *Chicago Tribune* article Van Matre described the Bistro:

"Lighted neon lips glow on the walls, the music starts at 10, and the dancing doesn't stop 'til 4 – either on the discotheque floor or above, where a couple of male dancers, including a Bearded Lady decked out in dowdy drag for comic relief, ply their trade by turns.

"The Bistro, or Dugan's Bistro as the bar and disco answers to these days, is unabashedly gay. It is also the essence of hipness. And in case you haven't noticed, the two have become synonymous to a certain degree.

"Attribute it to changing sexual consciousness, the rise in gay pride, the bisexuality espoused by certain of the members of the gay liberation movement, the androgynous sexuality of rock's tastemakers à la David Bowie or Mick Jagger, the unisex look in fashion, or the opening up of contemporary culture to alternative lifestyles. Or just call it a fad. Whatever the reasons, gay – or at least the semblance of a little good bisexuality for straights unable to really be anything but straight – has become the latest thing in hip circles, and the gay places have become the most *au courant* of all."

Van Matre adds, "If you're a woman, you'd better have five ID's handy. The Bistro isn't nasty to females, and on busy nights, you can find half a dozen or more on the crowded floor, dancing to Barry White or Bette Midler records. Nobody bothers women, but nobody exactly encourages them either."

Dugan told Van Matre, "The trouble with girls is they draw guys looking for them. ... Gay girls I don't mind, and I don't really mind straight couples all that much, but I don't like that Rush Street greaser group or the convention crowd."

In the *Chicago Gay Crusader*, William B. Kelley reported on a complaint of racial discrimination against the Bistro, filed with the Illinois Liquor Control Commission. Racial bias in bars and clubs was the hot topic at the time, the subject of a series of *Chicago Sun-Times* articles. Eddie Dugan denied any racial bias. He told the *Chicago Gay Crusader*, "I'm nowhere near prejudiced and I can prove it – I'm a homosexual and I've got a black lover, and 30% to 40% of my business is black."

Roosevelt Alexander, an investigator for the liquor commission, claimed he and a twenty year-old-woman were refused entry to the Bistro on May 4, 1974. Alexander said he was turned away because of alleged intoxication and his companion for being underage, even though she produced an ID. (At the time the legal drinking age was nineteen). Both Alexander and his friend were black. Dugan told a different version. He told the *Chicago Gay Crusader* that the woman only produced "one piece" of ID. The doorman, who was also black, told her it wasn't enough. Dugan then claimed Alexander said, "That's all she needs," then started "ranting and raving." The doorman refused both persons entry "as he would anyone else who appears to be a troublemaker or intoxicated."

Three months later, in the *Chicago Gay Crusader*, a short item in William B. Kelley's "Eye on the News" column reads, "THE BISTRO ... will not lose its license because of recent charges of discrimination against black patrons. The Illinois Liquor Control Commission settled the case with a promise by the Bistro not to engage in such discrimination, though it did not admit ever having done so."

## CHICAGO AFTER STONEWALL

Dugan's Bistro finally closed its doors on May 31, 1982, with a Final Celebration 9th anniversary "Black and/or White Party." In *Gay Chicago*, Nancy Reiff and Ralph Paul wrote:

> "'A Living Legend,' well, maybe not quite, but Monday night – nine years to the day that Dugan's Bistro opened, Dugan's Bistro closed with a party to end all parties. 'A Living Legend' was the theme last year for the Bistro's eighth anniversary party – one of many annual events the community has come to enjoy throughout the years. Besides regular holiday parties, Ed Dugan specialized in bringing in top entertainment and made famous his own birthday celebration. ... Most of the Bistro patrons agree that 'there's no place like Bistro' and with the closing of the Bistro there never again will be a place like the Bistro."

The music played in that final month of Dugan's Bistro was listed in *Gay Chicago* by resident DJ Lou DiVito:

> 1) "Don't You Want Me" – Human League; 2) "The Visitors" – Abba; 3) "Stormy Weather" – Viola Wills; 4) "Give Me Just a Little More Tim" – Angela Clemmons; 5) "The Best Part of Breaking Up" – Ronnie Griffith; 6) "Don't Come Crying to Me" – Linda Gifford; 7) "Native Love (Step by Step)" – Divine; 8) "We Got the Beat/Our Lips Are Sealed" – Go-Go's; 9) "Jump Shout" – Lisa; 10) "I Specialize in Love" – Sharon Brown; 11) "Rhythm of the Jungle" – The Quick; 12) "Don't Stop Your Love" – Booker T; 13) "Shake it Up" – Cars; 14) "Designer Music" – Lipps Inc.; 15) "The Two of Us (Remix)" – Ronnie Jones/Claudja Barry.

In interviews with the author, Chicagoans remember Dugan's Bistro and the Bearded Lady who performed there:

> "He was standing on a pedestal in the corner as you walked into the dancefloor. He was dressed in platform shoes, which in the '70s were hot, a white prom dress, lots of tulle, lots of satin. On his head was a full five branch candelabra, and all the seams had Italian lights and they pulsated to the beat. It was really quite spectacular. That was the same day that one of Mayor [Richard M.] Daley's brothers was there. The thing is that the Bistro in those days was like Studio 54. It had the best dancefloor, and everybody went there. It was a gay bar, but it was a 'dancebar,' so if you were a dance fanatic you would go because it had the best DJ's and there were all sorts of people. Gay people, straight people, it didn't make any difference. If you liked to dance and party ... cool!" – R.D.

"At Bistro all the time, especially when she did *Honey Bee* in her bee costume ... She came out in the bee costume doing *You're My Honey Bee, Come On And Sting Me*. It was fabulous." – Ray Thomas

---

"I did a dance contest at the old Bistro. When the Bistro was at Dearborn and Hubbard and they had dance contests and you would win records or whatever. That was at the time when Tommy Drag Queen, otherwise known as Tommy Noble, he's still alive ... and the Bearded Lady. They had dance contests there, it was fun ... when they remodeled the Bistro it was great, but before that you'd walk in the front bar and they had, off to one side, they had like bleacher seats covered with shag carpeting and the reason, I think, Eddie Dugan remodeled it was that the wood got so moldy and deteriorated from people spilling drinks and the drinks seeped into the wood and you had to watch where you sat because the wood was caving in. But when he remodeled it was gorgeous. They had dance contests there and they would give out drink tickets and they had to be used the following Wednesday or Thursday. Of course, my friend, cheap bastard that he was, would not only get his but pick up the ones the suburbanites would discard, and so he would have a handful of drink tickets." – David Plomin

---

"The Bearded Lady was at the Bistro, which was a wonderful bar. Again, it was a part of that whole near-Northside bar scene. She was absolutely fantastic. I remember one time I was there, and she was wearing Lucite shoes with goldfish in the heels ... fantastic!" – Mark Palermo

---

"The Bistro, the original Bistro, on Kinsey and Dearborn, in 1973. It was the ultimate discotheque. On the weekends, the Bearded Lady was a major attraction. His real name was Robby, I don't remember his last name. He had a full beard, and he would show up looking very much like a bearded lady out of a carnival, with maybe a big Mamie Eisenhower hat, or a big feathered hat, and a dress or a sequined lamé jump suit. His real aspiration, though, was to be an opera singer. He could really sing, but he lip synched." – David Honegger

---

"I used to go to a little bar called PQ's and that was kind of the first club, a real popular dance club. I loved that bar, real tiny, sleazy. I remember getting kicked out of that bar for taking my shirt off... I'm such a rascal. There we are on this dancefloor, sweating it up, and I took my shirt off, and they said, 'We're sorry, you have to put your shirt on.' I said, 'I'm dancing and I'm hot'... I said, 'Oh well, I'll leave.' So I left. Then one night I remember going to the Bistro and being asked to leave... now, I'm not a rabble rouser... we were asked to leave the Bistro one night because we came from a LaBelle concert, and I was with a Black guy and some other people, and we had hats on and they asked us to leave. No hats, you weren't supposed to wear hats at the Bistro. It was really a way of discriminating against Blacks. It was an excuse." – Nick Kelly

---

"It was about 1972. When I moved up to Chicago some of my pals told me about it and I went with them. But when I got inside, I ran, because I was in the closet. I ran. I didn't know it was going to be a gay bar, then all of a sudden, I see all these guys. I said, 'Oh my god, this is a fucking queer bar.' I was thinking, 'I'm queer but I can't let anybody know because I'm closeted.' So, I ran and got lost somewhere around Hubbard and Dearborn." – Frankie Da Kat

---

"The Bistro to me was like being unleashed into the most decadent thing I could ever imagine. And, of course, with me being a professional dancer and being at dance class all the time, it was the best thing for releasing all my tensions, because I had so much energy. After a job, just going to the Bistro and dancing for hours non-stop, I just thought it was the most remarkable thing and I just loved to dance. If anybody was looking for me, they could find me on the dance floor of the Bistro.

"I enjoyed every aspect of the Bistro; even after its popularization among the suburban community who came on Saturday nights. That was fine with me too. I just enjoyed going out to dance." – David Aaron

---

"I was a DJ at the Bistro and that was my one and only DJ job. I was only there six months. It was too physically taxing to be up from 10 at night to five or six in the morning. My body couldn't adapt to those hours. The big songs back then were *Money, Money, Money* by the Ojays, First Choice was one of the popular groups, and Barry White had a lot of stuff then.

"Eddie Dugan was always very professional and pleasant with me. He was a nice guy with me. The Bearded Lady was there, and he was wild. I had never really done any DJ work and I heard they were looking for another DJ and I thought, 'I'll just go and try it.' I had always loved music and putting it together on tapes, and so I went in and interviewed. They knew I'd never done any DJ work before, but the current DJ trained me. His name was Ronnie Bero. I think he moved to California, but I'm not sure. Actually, Ron and I had an affair.

"You'll hear people who went to the Bistro say that they liked it best when it first opened. Later on, they renovated it and made it into this big fancy club. It had been an old French restaurant in the front room and the room upstairs, which had been the banquet room, they made into the Disco. It was just black, just dark, with only the lighting effects, and they were very simple back then. Of course, there was so much drugs going on, and in a big black room like that, everyone got off even more.

"That one experience as a DJ put me off. I knew that if I was going to do it, I'd have to do those late night hours, and I couldn't take it; but that's what got me started into putting together music for other things, like production companies, industrials, magicians, fashion shows, theater companies, and also putting together sound effects and voiceovers and that type of thing.

"I really did have fun that six months I was working there, but there was too much drinking, and I gave it up. I was 25 at the time."

"Lou DeVito was the famous DJ at the Bistro and he was there the longest." – Johnny Bash

---

"B.L. who could forget B.L.? In fact, my roommate at the time, Gordon, worked with B.L. way up north at a club called Coconuts. At Coconuts they were all go-go people. B.L. was one of my favorite drag characters because he really did look like a bearded lady. He looked like that all the time, of course every now and then we'd see him walking down the street during the daytime and people would yell out 'B.L. B.L.!!' He just couldn't go anywhere without being recognized.

"On stage he was like the most flirtatious go-go boy stripper ever, but he was this round man with a beard and a dress. And he was afraid of no-one. He would go up to tease people and flirt with everybody. He'd wear costumes, huge costumes, or little costumes … even if he was wearing a little costume you couldn't miss him. He's not a small fella. He could change the atmosphere of a room just by walking in. I don't ever remember him lifting up his skirt, but I'm sure he did.

"Sometimes straight people would wander in and he had a nose for sniffing that out. It was great to see him embarrass them. Studio 54 had Rollerina, the drag queen who would roller skate, and we had B.L." – Joan Jett-Blakk

# 30
# A HANDFUL OF ARTISTIC DELIGHTS

Before the publication of *Gay Life*, "straight" and "closeted gay" writers in the mainstream press were wary of covering the gay lifestyle. Even in the arts, where one would expect a liberal slant, reviews of gay books, films and plays, were often tentative, awkward, embarrassed, offensive or they tiptoed around the subject of homosexuality.

One year to the day after the Stonewall Riots, Richard Freedman wrote a surprisingly positive review of H. Montgomery Hyde's *The Love That Dared Not Speak Its Name: A Candid History of Homosexuality in Britain* in the *Chicago Tribune*:

> "Considering the disproportionate contribution homosexuals have made to our founding civilization – Socrates, Da Vinci, Michelangelo, Shakespeare (probably), Proust, Tchaikovsky, to name but a few – and the invaluable role even the less talented ones play in stemming the Population Explosion, one would think a grateful society would give them medals rather than hound them with blackmail, disgrace and jail, and often drive them to suicide.
>
> "But society doesn't operate rationally, as this woeful history of British homosexuality repeatedly demonstrates."

It was a different story the following year when Anthony Storr reviewed William Aaron's *Straight: A Heterosexual Talks About His Homosexual Past* in the *Chicago Tribune*:

> "In recent years many of us have become rather tired of the flood of homosexual revelations which have saturated the world of books. We are all too familiar with the jargon, the squalid world of 'tearooms,' 'cruising,' 'rent boys,' 'closet queens,' and the like – that sad, sad, world which is

misappropriately named 'gay.' However, although 'William Aaron's' pseudonymous reminiscences of his homosexual past contain all too much of what is already to be found in other books, *Straight* is remarkable in that the author, after being an active, promiscuous homosexual for 20 years, abandoned his life at the age of 33, and married, apparently successfully."

Other highlights from the review:

"His family background to Aaron's homosexuality is pretty typical. His mother was warm, dominating, over-protective, and 'wore the trousers.' His father was comparatively ineffective, detached or absent, inept and diffident."

" ... Now that Gay Liberation is trying so hard to persuade us that there is nothing about homosexuality which is aberrant or immature, a glance at Aaron's account of the 'gay' world is salutary. It is not only a world in which sex is very largely divorced from affection or any continuing human relationship, but it is one in which every other kind of perversion flourishes alongside homosexuality."

Dr. Anthony Storr was an eccentric British psychoanalyst, the author of a book called *Sexual Deviation*. Storr was fixated on sex, especially sadomasochism and the sexuality of gurus, like Jesus.

In 1971, in the *Chicago Tribune*, Claudia Cassidy reviewed Luchino Visconti's movie *Death in Venice*. She wrote, "I do not think this a homosexual film. It is the ravished pursuit of beauty by that most vulnerable of men, the artist." It's hard to believe that a movie about an aging man with rouged lips obsessing over a Polish youth's beauty on a beach is not a homosexual movie. If more evidence was needed, Luchino Visconti was gay, it stars gay actor Dirk Bogarde, and the film was based on a novella written by Thomas Mann, a gay writer.

Also, in the *Chicago Tribune*, Carol Kramer wrote, "Is it a homosexual film? (After a screening, one cynic was heard to say it was the last great fag film. 'It's so boring they'll never make another')" Kramer goes on to say that Visconti himself said it was not a homosexual film. He said, "It is much more than that. It is about an artist searching for a perfection he can never attain. It is about the following of an ideal. The only physical contact you see in the film is when Aschenbach (Dirk Bogarde) caresses the boy's hair and this is fantasy."

Rex Reed in the *Chicago Tribune* writes about a press conference for *Death in Venice* at the Cannes Film Festival:

"Several hostile members of the press who were admirers of the Thomas Mann book grilled Visconti on the additional touches of perversion that were not in the book. 'How dare you ask me such a thing?' he snapped. 'It's not a homosexual movie, just a homophile movie.' Yeah, that's what I thought too. 'The boy represents beauty.' So why does Visconti show close-ups of the boy being kissed by another boy on the beach to taunt the old man? Why does the boy give him long, lingering come-hither looks that are quite lascivious? And why does the man tell the boy, 'I love you,' in a moment of fantasy, then make up his face in a hideous parody of a drag queen to attract the boy on a level of youth? Nobody was buying it at the press conference."

A year earlier, the *Chicago Tribune* published an anonymous review of John Rechy's novel, *This Day's Death* inexplicably under the headline, "Mommy's Boys." The reviewer writes, "John Rechy isn't writing faggot porn, but on the other hand, he isn't writing *Death in Venice* either; crippled from the outset by the narrowness of its viewpoint, it is finished off by the clumsiness of its execution."

The *Reader*, aimed at a younger, more-enlightened audience, even when trouncing a gay play, were never homophobic. The first issue was published on October 1, 1971. On October 27, 1972, Ron Offen reviewed David Gaard's *& Puppy Dog Tails* produced by The Company at the Drama Shelter, 2020 N. Halsted. Gaard, a young gay writer who finished the play in the fall of 1968, first saw it on stage after the Stonewall Riots in New York, then in San Francisco. When it opened in Chicago, Bill Murray was in the cast. At the time he was with the improvisational comedy troupe, Second City, before joining *Saturday Night Live* and starring in movies like *Ghostbusters* and *Groundhog Day*. Offen titled his review of *& Puppy Dog Tails* ... "Nay Love for Gay Love."

Offen describes The Company as having "struck on the magic formula of transforming two hours of theater into four":

> "Largely responsible for the alchemy is a hokey script, a cast that stumbles through its lines with all the élan of a pack of stoned sloths, and direction that seems mainly concerned with keeping the actors on their feet and milling about lest the audience drift into a catatonic trance. ... Though there were a few scattered titters out front on the night I attended over the mannerisms of a drag-queen character, the small, all-male audience stumbled out of the theater like a group of somnambulists with nary a cheer or handclap. Perhaps they shared my feelings of being slapped repeatedly in the medula oblongata with a wet noodle. At any rate not even the fact that this audience was obviously and predominantly gay seemed to affect their response to a work that reportedly shows a side of the coin ignored by *Boys in the Band*. I would have thought that the sight of two of the actors flouncing about in the altogether would have

generated some excitement – after all, it's the only gay skin-show in town. But I see now that my presumptions were the result of heterosexual chauvinism. Evidently, not even the swishest in attendance were fooled by Gaard's pastiche of insider jokes, references to Judy Garland, and turgid soap-opera dialogue. ... Leading the cast as the gay blade who welcomes a long-lost straight friend into the world of homophilia was Tom Davy. He has a nice lean bod and little else to recommend him for the role. His energy level suggests he is suffering from low blood sugar, his timing is way off, and he is tentative with his lines. In this last respect he does better than Bill Murray who can't remember his. The drag queen who eventually spills the beans about the sexuality of Davy (thus eliciting an unbelievable response of horror and hostility on the part of Murray) is played high and heavy by Ortez. He should tone down the portrayal about a million percent before he goes flying off some night."

Ortez was Ortez E. Alderson, the gay liberationist and Third World Gay Revolutionary who was arrested July 29, 1970 and jailed for stealing and destroying Selective Services records from the draft board office at Pontiac, IL. Alderson died of complications from AIDS in 1990 and a year later was inducted into the Gay and Lesbian Hall of Fame.

Sylvie Drake in the *Los Angeles Times* wrote about a production of *& Puppy Dog Tails* at the After Dark Cabaret, 8471 Beverly Blvd.:

"What the audience is faced with then is a gay situation comedy which bares a little skin (always in good taste) and long, often dull stretches of underlying seriousness sustained by one-line zingers rat-tat-tatting chiefly out of Tommy's incessant Tallulah Bankhead mouth. ('I know I'm smart; just tell me I'm pretty. It's the only truth I can handle').

"John (Bill Leonard) is a homosexual out of Fort Wayne, who lives in domestic comfort with Carey-Lee (John Barrett) in big bad New York City. Enter a childhood buddy, Bud Kelcorn (Peter Brandon), with whom John had had a couple of carefully glossed-over homosexual encounters back in Fort Wayne. Bud is good-looking and mixed-up. He's unsure of his direction and yearns for a real, female-type wife, but is simultaneously drawn to the gay world."

On February 1, 1975, a headline in the *Atlanta Constitution* read, "Director and Cast of Play Are Arrested Here":

"The director and the entire cast of a play about homosexuality were arrested by Atlanta police officers Friday night minutes after the conclusion of the play.

"Officers watched a performance of *And Puppy Dog Tails* at the Metropolitan Community Theater on North Highland Avenue and then arrested five members of the traveling company that brought the play to Atlanta.

"Director and coproducer Michael Devereaux, 33, was charged with allowing an indecent show. Charges of public indecency were filed against John Michael Barritt, 21; Jon Christian Erickson, 26; Billy Rollin Casper, 29; and Peter Vincent Grimes, 23.

"The play's author, David Gaard, was at the theater at the time of the arrests. Gaard said the play contains nudity but 'no explicit sex.'"

In April 1974, Will Leonard reviewed A.J. Kronengold's play *Tubstrip* in the *Chicago Tribune*. It was playing at the Gill Community Arts Center on Wells Street:

"ONE NUDE HOMOSEXUAL says to another nude homosexual: 'I was just thinking...'"

"And the second homosexual quips: 'You'll try anything once, won't you?'"

"And the gay lads in the audience break up in laughter.

"That's about the way it goes in *Tubstrip*, in which nine actors, almost every one of them parading around in the buff at one point or another, cavort about a tiny swimming pool in a steambath. ... They pose and prance and wave their genitals at one another, and pronounce their lines like characters in a kiddies' cartoon on TV."

In 1973 it was announced in *Lavender Woman* that the Lesbian/Feminist Theatre of Chicago, later renamed Artemis Players, would present J.M. Barrie's first all-female production of *Peter Pan* for Gay Pride Week. The production was canceled after the company received a letter from Samuel French, Inc. informing them that due to an impending Broadway revival the amateur rights were unavailable. Instead, they produced *Trevor*, a one-act gay comedy by John Bowen about two lesbians coming out to their parents. In August, in *Lavender Woman*, producer and director, Jody Lynch, relates the story of how the production came about. The Artemis Players began when a small group of women interested in various aspects of theater met during preparations for Gay Pride Week and called themselves the Lesbian/Feminist Theatre of Chicago. After deciding on *Trevor*, the first problem was finding a suitable theater, eventually settling on a space at 1032 W. Barry, the home of the Chicago Project of Columbia College. Lynch writes:

"It was located in an old church building and consisted of a huge hall with a small stage at one end and balcony seating space (which, in the end, we didn't use anyway). Unfortunately, the hall had a terrible echo (which the audience soaked up somewhat) and was rather expensive ($35 a rehearsal and/or performance). However, we were desperate. It was already June 19, and we were scheduled to open on June 23; so we decided to take it.

"The theater space was a mess and Beverley, the scene designer, and Carol, the head carpenter, set about building a thrust stage. Claudia and I scrounged the lumber from construction and demolition sites, taking it back to the theatre in Carol's house-on-wheels. I remember one time climbing over a fence where a new high-rise was going up and finding an especially nice piece of plywood, only to be told by a cop to 'put it back.' The problems of producing a low budget show!"

The opening was postponed until July 14. The play was a success, artistically, but not financially. However, one positive thing that came out of it was that the Artemis Players were invited to bring *Trevor* to the Women's Center in Madison, WI, for two evening performances on September 8.

The Lesbian/Feminist Theatre of Chicago was the first out-gay theater group in the city.

John Stark begins his review of the local production of *Trevor* in the *San Francisco Examiner*:

"John Bowen's *Trevor*, a 90 minute British comedy about two lesbians, is as worthless as a rejected *Love American Style* TV script.

"The painfully contrived work, now being performed by a troupe called City Theater at the Intersection, takes place in the London flat of Jane (Cheryl Jensen) and Sara (Gita Isak)."

Stark goes on to reveal the plot:

"The women, in their late twenties, are lovers, and lead quiet, stay-at-home lives. It's no wonder. A duller, more uninteresting couple would be hard to find.

"Afraid of being 'found out' by their parents, Jane and Sarah invent a boyfriend named Trevor to write home about. When Jane's mother and father (Susan Chapman and Harry Snyder) come to visit her and the fictional fiancé, the two women hire an out-of-work actor (Stafford Buckley) to play the part of Trevor.

"The very same afternoon, Sarah's parents (Kitty Newman and Cliff watts) unexpectedly drop in. Both sets of parents are shoved into different rooms, while Trevor, wearing a Superman T-shirt, hops back and forth pretending to be the lover of both women.

"Somewhere in this coincidental mess the landlord (Gary Schnell) enters the flat to put the telephone back on the hook. You see, he's an obscene phone caller, and, oh well ... never mind the rest.

" ... The play's forced attempts at humor are dreadful. The moments of coyness are embarrassing ... And its preachy ending, after Jane and Sarah come out of the closet, is unforgiveable."

# 31
# THREE DICKS: NIXON, OGILVIE, AND DALEY

Chicago gay and lesbian activists began 1972 by resolving to Lick 3 Dicks: M. Nixon (Federal), B. Ogilvie (State), and J. Daley (City). But, by the end of the year, they had only licked one; Gov. Richard B. Ogilvie lost his governorship to Daniel Walker by a narrow margin of 51% to 49%. Ogilvie was despised in the gay community since 1964 when he raided and closed down Louis Gage's bar, destroying the lives of those arrested.

Early in 1972, the Advocates of Gay Action published a leaflet that read:

"WE HAVE NOT FORGOTTEN ... The year was 1964.

"Richard Ogilvie, then Sheriff of Cook County, led one of the most vicious attacks on Chicago's gay community.

"Under direction of Sheriff Ogilvie, the police descended upon a gay lounge in the western suburb run by Louis Gage. Hundreds were arrested ... among them teachers, clergymen, prominent businessmen, and others. The *Chicago Tribune* in co-operation with Sheriff maintained their oppressive policies and published the names, addresses, and places of employment of those arrested!

"As a result, people were disgraced, reputations were ruined, jobs were lost, lives were destroyed, and even suicides were committed!

"This is the man who holds office of Governor of Illinois; a man who openly breeds contempt and hatred for homosexuals; a man who is responsible for gay lives.

"This man must not be re-elected. He must be thrashed out of office ... preferably out of existence.

"VOTE GAY! SMASH OGILVIE!"

Of the other two Dicks: President Richard M. Nixon was reelected in a landslide – he resigned on August 9, 1974, to avoid impeachment in the Watergate scandal. Richard J. Daley was also reelected and died in office on December 20, 1976 – only death could pry Daley out of the Mayor's office, where he ruled with an iron fist for twenty-one years. After Ogilvie lost, the Illinois Gays for Legislative Action (IGLA) wrote to Governor-elect Daniel Walker, a letter published in the December 1972 issue of *Chicago Gay Pride*:

> "You as Governor will be in a position to alleviate a serious injustice faced by homosexual women and men in seeking or retaining state employment. By using your executive authority, you can prohibit such discrimination based on sexual orientation.
>
> "At Dekalb, Normal, and elsewhere during your campaign, you publicly expressed support for such a nondiscrimination policy. We applaud this stand on basic human rights, and now call upon you to implement it by issuing appropriate executive orders following your inauguration as Governor. ... Employment discrimination against Gay people in state government can be ended by a variety of techniques, but most immediately through strong, progressive, meaningful executive action.
>
> "We would appreciate an opportunity to meet with you and your staff to discuss your issuing such an order, and look forward to your early response."

It was signed by:

> Larry Gulian, Illinois Gays for Legislative Action
>
> Leslie A. Trotter, Chicago Gay Alliance
>
> John R. Keller, Illinois State University Gay People's Alliance
>
> Eileen Wicker, Chicago Lesbian Liberation
>
> Michael P. Burk, Springfield Gay Liberation
>
> Margaret Wilson, Feminist Lesbian Party
>
> Rev. David B. Sindt, Chicago Gay Social Work Association
>
> George Alexander, Chicago Gay Youth
>
> Peter Wilson, Northern Illinois University Gay Liberation
>
> Step May, Chicago Gay People's Legal Committee

On January 8, 1973, Daniel Walker became the Governor of Illinois after defeating wounded World War II veteran Richard B. Ogilvie. *Chicago Gay Pride* notes that an answer was received from Governor-elect Walker's office, offering his support and cooperation. It didn't take long for Walker to renege on his promise. At his first accountability meeting in February he was booed when he refused a gay activist's request for him to issue an executive order banning discrimination against gays in hiring state employees. The *Mattachine Midwest Newsletter* reads:

> "He justified his stand by stating that the new Illinois constitution bans discrimination.
>
> "Walker went on to contradict himself by saying that he planned to issue an executive order banning discrimination against blacks and women.
>
> "On other issues, Walker proved to be a real people's governor. He stated that he favors aid to the CTA, American Indians, the poor, children, and the old. He has actively worked to remove political favoritism from State government.
>
> "The Governor's one blind spot seems to be Gay Rights."

It didn't end there. In the *Chicago Gay Crusader*, William B. Kelley wrote under the headline, "SIX CONFRONTATIONS: When Will Walker Get the Message?":

> "At six 'accountability sessions' he has held around the State – most recently April 24 in Lockport and April 26 in East St. Louis – members of Illinois Gays for Legislative Action (IGLA) have asked him [Walker] why he has failed to issue an executive order that would establish a formal policy of nondiscrimination against homosexuals in hiring by State agencies under his control and by firms doing business with those agencies."

Walker was consistent. His answer always the same: the Illinois constitution banning discrimination covered homosexuals and that "the proper place" to resolve "the question" of gay rights was in the courts. In the *Reader*, Nancy Banks names the gay activist who challenged Gov. Walker at that first February accountability session as Margaret Wilson. Ironically, when her boss saw her on TV, he fired her the next day. "Taking Walker at his word," writes Banks, "she [Wilson] then took her case to the Illinois Fair Employment Practices Commission, only to be told that discrimination against gays isn't one of the things that agency is empowered to investigate. If she'd been fired because she was a woman or black, it would have been a different story."

Margaret Wilson proved her point.

## 32
# HIPPIES, YIPPIES AND GAYS

After the violent clashes between police and anti-Vietnam war protestors at the 1968 Democratic National Convention, city councils nationwide were wary of hosting the 1972 conventions. The Republicans settled on San Diego, but a political scandal there led to a venue change to Miami, the same city as the Democratic National Convention. On June 23, in anticipation of thousands of protestors, the Miami Beach City Council voted to ban campsites. When the decision was announced, Patrick Small, a Zippie, slapped a pumpkin pie into a councilman's face. This resulted in other protest groups, including gay activists, to distance themselves from the Zippies. The Zippies were a splinter group from the Yippies. Earlier in the month, the Yippies, led by Abbie Hoffman and Jerry Rubin, announced they would attend the Democratic Convention, not to protest, but to be a non-violent presence. In July, the *Chicago Tribune* reported:

> "A small group of radicals are threatening to oust from power the old guard of street protestors 'ageing' Abbie Hoffman and Jerry Rubin. They rose to fame shouting under the banner of the Youth International Party, called Yippies. Now, four years later, the Zippies say Hoffman and Rubin are just wild publicity seekers and over the hill. ... Underground newspaper editor Thomas Forcade says Hoffman and Rubin have sold out to establishment politicians and are 'ego freaks.'"

The Yippies' reluctance to protest was, in part, due to having achieved at least one of their 1968 objectives, i.e., the 1972 Democratic Convention included minority representation. After the tumult of 1968, the twenty-eight-member Commission on Party Structure and Delegate Selection, aka the McGovern/Fraser Commission, was set up. It was so named because Sen. George McGovern chaired the Commission before resigning to run for

President. US Rep. Donald Fraser replaced him. The McGovern/Fraser Commission laid out guidelines ordering state parties to "adopt explicit written Party rules governing delegate selection." The most significant changes were new quotas to ensure the voices of women, minority groups, and youth (defined as under 30) would be heard. At the 1972 Democratic Convention taboo subjects like abortion and gay rights were openly discussed for the first time.

The idea that Chicago gays protest the Democratic Convention in Miami dated back to before the February 1972 meeting in Chicago, where the National Coalition for Gay Rights was formed. The Rev. Charles Lamont, under investigation by the Northern Illinois Methodist Conference, was one of the plan's instigators. While pastor at Avondale United Methodist Church, Lamont provided a meeting space for Mattachine Midwest – at the time, he was vice president of the group, later president. The idea originated at a meeting between John Thomas Abney, president of Chicago Gay Alliance, activists Bill Gilmore, Virgil Spangler and Lamont. "One evening we were all in John's 'apartment' in the upstairs back of the CGA Community Center," recalls Lamont, in an October 29, 2010 interview with the author of this book:

> "John suggested there ought to be a gay presence at the Democratic National Convention. ... We all agreed and started brainstorming about how such a thing might come about. We called the Fire House, operated by New York Gay Activist Alliance, and they thought it was a great idea and asked if CGA would take the lead since we had a printing press and they did not."

Lamont, Abney, Spangler and Gilmore then met with GLF at the University of Wisconsin (UW), Madison. There were parallels between GLF groups at the University of Wisconsin and the University of Chicago; both formed soon after Stonewall. In Madison on November 5, 1969, a group of men met in St. Francis House, the Episcopal student center, and founded the Madison Alliance for Homosexual Equality (MAHE). On March 13, 1970, MAHE organized Madison's first public gay "Coming Out Dance." They soon adopted the more radical name Gay Liberation Front.

The Madison GLF meeting with Lamont, Abney, Spangler and Gilmore, planted the seed that sprouted at the Chicago conference in February 1972. Lamont explains:

> "Since I had the eye of the media at that moment because of my fight with the Northern Illinois Conference, I volunteered to go to Miami and work with Miami GAA to create publicity to attract 'non-delegates' to

help protest at the convention. Things were going slowly until some female impersonators applied for a parade permit to put on a show on Lincoln Road Mall in Miami Beach and were told that it was illegal for a man to appear in public in clothing unbecoming of their sex and if they did it they would see 'the inside of our courts and the inside of our jails.' Bob Barry, president of Miami GAA and I, representing the National Coalition of Gay Rights, contacted the ACLU and jointly sued the City of Miami Beach and Rocky Ponwrance, Chief of Police, in U.S. District Court challenging the constitutionality of the ordinance. WE WON and cross-dressing became legal in the 5th District!"

The publicity from legalizing cross-dressing in Miami put a spotlight on gay rights and the upcoming Democratic Convention. Overturning the anti-drag law was even broadcast on the *CBS Evening News* by Walter Cronkite. An article in the *Asheville Citizen-Times* begins, "Two Miami Beach ordinances outlawing female impersonation struck down ... prompting cheers of 'bring out the gowns' from gay activist leaders who feared arrest at national political conventions in Miami Beach." US District Court Judge William O. Mehrtens ruled the two laws invalid on grounds they were vague, overbroad and discriminated against men. He urged police from basing any arrests upon them:

"Mehrtens hearing featured testimony by Miami Beach Police Chief Rocky Ponwrance, a 250 pounder who was given a 'male or female' quiz on various items of wearing apparel by Bruce Rogow of Miami, attorney for the American Civil Liberties Union. Rogow filed the suit, which led to the ruling for the ACLU in behalf of Lamont (Charles A. Lamont, 30, spokesperson for the National Coalition of Gay Organizations) and Barry (Robert Barry, 26, president of the Gay Activists Alliance of Miami). One law stricken by the judge made it illegal for a man to impersonate a woman; the second outlaws a man 'wearing a dress not becoming to his sex.'

"Rogow said gay liberationists had already been threatened with arrest by Ponwrance's men. Barry said a June 5 pre-convention demonstration was called off because Maj. Calvin Schuler told him. 'We're ready for you.'

"Lamont testified he expected 6,000 'gay brothers and sisters' in Miami Beach for the July 10-14 Democratic Convention and the Aug. 21-23 Republican gathering. Later, however, he said Mehrtens' ruling 'is going to have a big effect' on the crowd size. He said homosexuals planned to attend to demonstrate for rights for homosexuals, to contact delegates and to urge inclusion of prohomosexual planks in party platforms.

"Pomerance found himself coached by Mehrtens as he attempted to answer Rogow's quiz as to the gender of certain clothing and whether a man's wearing it would violate the two ordinances.

"'That's a purse,' said the chief.

"The judge interrupted: 'I would have said shoulder bag.'

"...When the chief faltered on identifying the sex of various blouses, the judge offered, 'Your answer might depend on who wears it.'"

The *Miami News* reported:

"NATIONAL COALITION OF GAY ORGANIZATIONS – a consortium of more than 500 gay liberation groups, which was formed in February primarily to organize protests at the Democratic and Republican Conventions.

"The group, which represents homosexual males, homosexual females, transvestites, transsexuals and bi-sexuals, has been formed to 'work for an end to legal, social, economic, psychological and physiological oppression of gay people.

"The NCGO, which describes itself as a 'one-issue group which works within the system for change,' is planning a 'kiss-in' on Tuesday and a 'drag and bizarre fashion show.' On Wednesday.

"In addition, the group is planning to lobby for a plank in the Democratic Party Platform calling for an end to all laws discrimination [sic] against gay people."

At the 1972 Democratic Convention, "Gay Rights" stepped out of the twilight and into the glare of mainstream politics. In the early hours of July 12, Jim Foster of San Francisco's Society for Individual Rights and Madeline Davis of Buffalo, NY Mattachine Society, stood at the rostrum and, according to the *Advocate*, "spoke seriously for nearly half an hour about gay rights" ... "We come to you affirming our rights to participate in the life of this country on an equal basis with every other citizen,' Foster began, while Davis drew attention to the potential '20 million (gay) Americans who would vote in November.'"

Throughout his campaign, the future Democratic Presidential Candidate George McGovern backed gay rights. He even took out ads in the *Advocate* supporting equality in federal employment, housing, and military. In June 1972, *Chicago Gay Pride* published McGovern's "six-point program" on Gay Rights:

1) Sexual orientation or preference should cease to be a criterion for employment by all public and government agencies, in work under Federal contract, for service in the United States armed forces, and for licensing in government-regulated occupations and professions;

2) Sexual orientation should cease to be a criterion for immigration into the United States;

3) Government and private investigatory agencies should cease to collect data on the sexual preferences of individuals;

4) Sexual orientation should cease to be a criterion for obtaining housing, insurance, or bonding;

5) Individuals previously given less-than-honorable military discharges solely for sexual relations between consenting adults or for allegations relating to sexual orientation should have the character of those discharged changed to honorable;

6) Federal sponsorship of educational programs which will foster further understanding of both professional people and the general public on these issues.

However, on July 25, McGovern issued a statement backing away from his pro-gay stance, leading gay activist Bruce Voeller to protest by chaining himself to phones in McGovern's campaign headquarters in New York.

Rob Cole wrote an article, "McGovern Denial," for the *Advocate*. It begins:

> "Presidential nominee George McGovern, speaking directly to a gay media reporter Oct. 13 for the first time since the start of his campaign, capped a month-long controversy and confounded his gay supporters with what seemed to be a clear personal repudiation of all the gay rights pledges issued in his name over the past 10 months.
>
> "Then he went on to tell George Nicola, a reporter for the Portland, Ore., *Fountain* that 'I don't believe in discrimination against people on the grounds of sex, and that's as far as I'm going to carry the issue.' He did not explain what he meant by 'sex.'"

According to Cole, Nicola continued:

> "Sen. McGovern, early in your presidential campaign, your local offices in New York and California released in your name a comprehensive statement on homosexual civil rights. I have here a copy being distributed here in Oregon by your Lane County headquarters. Among other things, it pledges in your name that you will work toward guaranteeing first-class citizenship for homosexually orientated individuals. This statement has at various times been denied or affirmed by your staff. Does this statement in fact represent your position?"

McGovern answered:

> "We've never put out any statement from either our New York or San Francisco office that was cleared by me, and I'm not to take responsibility for either of these statements.
>
> "Now, we have volunteer committees that are working on behalf of me all over the country that have issued statements. But I can tell you that I don't believe in discrimination against people on grounds of sex and that's as far as I'm going to carry this issue."

The DNC overwhelmingly rejected the gay minority plank. The *Chicago Tribune* reported:

> "Another plank proposal shouted down was that advanced on behalf of the 'millions of gay women and men in this country' allegedly subject to 'severe social, economic and legal oppression' because of their homosexuality. They sought a Democratic commitment to repeal all federal, state and local laws dealing with homosexuals, and the release of all persons now in prison or mental institutions 'for victimless sex acts.' The homosexuals waged a more intensive campaign for their platform plan than almost any other group."

The Miami News reported:

> "With respect to homosexuals, the platform writers turned down, after 45 minutes debate, a gay rights plank that would have endorsed full rights for homosexuals.
>
> "They adopted a milder platform declaration that 'Americans should be free to make their own choice of life-styles and private habits without being subject to discrimination or prosecution."

On July 16, Yippies Allen Ginsberg and Jerry Rubin predicted massive demonstrations at the Republican National Convention but no violence. On August 20, an alliance of groups called a press conference to announce plans for disrupting the Republican Convention. Groups within the Miami Conventions Coalition included Vietnam Veterans Against the War, the Miami Women's Coalition, and the Gay Liberation Alliance. One plan was to prevent delegates from entering the Convention Hall by surrounding it, and to disrupt traffic in the hotel district where many of them were staying. Four days later, the streets around the Convention Hall were filled with tear gas, as thousands of protestors blocked traffic. Almost 1,000 were arrested.

On August 21, 1972, in the Streator, IL *Times* it was noted that, "Some 200 members of the Miami Gay Activist Alliance, a group supporting equal rights for homosexuals, conducted the most peaceful protest of the day.

Carrying candles, they walked on the sidewalks to Convention Hall, sat briefly in a demonstration area in front of it, then returned without incident to the campsite."

## 33
# LEGISLATIVE ACTION

While some Chicago activists focused on the Conventions in Miami, others worked on gay rights at home. In July 1972, the *Chicago Tribune* reported that, at a hearing, William C. Ives, chairman of the Illinois Fair Employment Practices Commission (FEPC), predicted problems enforcing proposed job discrimination rules on employers. The new rules prohibited discrimination based on religion, race, national origin, or sex and applied to most contracts with local and state governments. Ives claimed there were too many contracts with too many companies, and the FEPC didn't have the manpower to enforce the policy. Speaking on behalf of the Chicago Gay Alliance, William B. Kelley asked the FEPC to also prohibit discrimination against homosexuals. Ives acknowledged a problem existed, but state law did not give the FEPC authority to act on behalf of homosexuals. Chicago wasn't the only city tackling gay discrimination in the workplace. On January 27, 1972, the New York City Council general welfare committee shot down Intro 475, a proposal that would have banned discrimination against homosexuals in employment, housing, and public accommodations. But the tide was turning, because within the next three months East Lansing, MI, followed by San Francisco both passed anti-discrimination laws that included protections for homosexuals.

In *Chicago Gay Pride*, under the headline "Legislative Action," it reads, "The Chicago Gay Alliance is in the process of introducing a bill into the City Council calling for the same equal protection under the law that other minority groups presently enjoy." The article goes on to request help from other gay groups and individuals in the city, "It is out of the question that any one committee of CGA would be able to handle this. Nor, for that matter, CGA itself." What emerged from this was the Legislative Action Project, later renamed Illinois Gays for Legislative Action (IGLA), a group founded by William B. Kelley and Larry Gulian, whose stated goals were:

"To work for the passage of fair employment, fair housing, and other types of equal-opportunity legislation for gay people in both the Chicago City Council (and suburban city councils) and the Illinois General Assembly; and

"To work for endorsement of such legislation by the Chicago Commission of Human Relations (and other human relations commissions), the Illinois Fair Employment Practices Commission, and other official and private bodies and opinion leaders; and

"To work in a consciousness-raising capacity: to politicize and organize gay people and to help gay people perceive themselves as members of an oppressed minority; and to serve as a consciousness-raising vehicle to lawmakers and mainstream society through media coverage, lobbying, etc."

Illinois Gays for Legislative Action (IGLA) lobbied for gay rights until the baton was passed to the Illinois Gay Rights Task Force of the Alliance to End Repression in 1977.

After Pride Week 1973, the *Chicago Gay Crusader* reported that on July 6, 20th Ward alderman Clifford P. Kelley and IGLA introduced two proposals to Chicago's City Council: (1) To enact comprehensive protection for homosexuals in jobs, housing and public accommodations, (2) To repeal the city's prohibition against cross-dressing. Besides Kelley, ten other aldermen co-sponsored the proposals: Ald. Eugene Sawyer (6th), Ald. William Cousins, Jr. (8th), Ald. Robert Wilinski (7th), Ald. Anna R. Langford (16th), Ald. Jimmy L. Washington (28th), Ald. Seymour Simon (40th), Ald. William S. Singer (43rd), Ald. Marilou Hedlund (48th), Ald. William H. Shannon (17th), and Ald. Leon M. Depres (5th); Depres co-sponsored the anti-cross-dressing law but not the equal-opportunity measure. According to Ald. Clifford P. Kelley, Ald. Depres objected to the term "sexual orientation." Of these ten co-sponsors, five were among the Council's Democratic majority and the others (Langford, Cousins, Despres, Simon, and Singer) were independents; six of the ten co-sponsors, including Ald. Kelley were African American.

The equal-rights proposal was modeled on Intro 475. The bill first introduced in the New York City Council by Council Members Carter Burden and Eldon Clingan on January 6, 1971. In November, the *Chicago Gay Crusader* reported that on November 6, the Washington DC city council voted unanimously to approve a measure prohibiting discrimination on the grounds of "sexual orientation" in jobs, housing and public accommodations. In Chicago, the two proposals introduced by Ald. Clifford P. Kelley went before the Council's Judiciary Committee on October 10. At the hearing, twenty-three people spoke in favor of the bills, and the committee took them "under advisement" and announced it would vote at the next meeting. In the *Reader,* Nancy Banks noted the odd-couple aspect of Ald. Clifford P. Kelley, "a straight black alderman from a machine ward on the South Side," working with Illinois Gays for Legislative Action. They were strange bedfellows. IGLA member Larry Gulian told Banks, "As far as we can tell, Kelley has no political advantage to gain by sponsoring gay rights." This straight/gay union formed after the 1970 Constitutional Convention (Con-Con) when Kelley, then president of the Illinois Young Democrats, responded favorably to a questionnaire sent out by Chicago Gay Alliance.

Banks noted the atmosphere at the Judiciary Committee meeting turned sour when the second speaker testified. Dr. Kitch Childs, a black lesbian, "gave a vague but militant sounding rap in defense of gay rights." This irritated Ald. Burton Natarus (42nd Ward), who "subjected her to a barrage of hostile questions." Alderman Natarus suggested lawmakers, before passing such measures, should first decide if homosexuality is "abnormal and deviant behavior that would harm the public." More witnesses followed – Judy Lonnquist of the National Organization of Women (NOW) ended her testimony with a rousing, "So long as one individual in our society is oppressed, we are all oppressed." Ald. William Barnett asked each witness if they were homosexual "by choice," until one stopped his parroting by asking if he was heterosexual "by choice." The proceedings were then interrupted by Ald. Edward Burke, who Banks described as "a nattily dressed young alderman (and son of a former alderman) from a heavily Catholic ward on the Southwest Side." Alderman Burke challenged the testimony of Rev. Don Shaw, speaking for the Midwest Association for the Study of Human Sexuality. Alderman Burke asked, "I mean, what do you study, what do you teach technique? Maybe some members of the City Council would like to attend."

There were a few schoolboy sniggers.

When a Catholic priest, Father Robert Behnen, (mistakenly called Dehmen in the *Reader*), talked about ministering to "the homophile community in Chicago." Burke asked, "Who appointed you?" Behnen replied, "Cardinal Cody." He was referring to John Patrick Cardinal Cody, Archbishop of Chicago. Burke was taken aback, and asked Behnen what other church doctrine had changed since he was taught by the nuns, like fellatio, cunnilingus, adultery and abortion? Behnen was visibly shaken by the verbal back and forth, which didn't let up until the chairman halted the two from "running amok in the thickets of Catholic theology." Both Ald. Kelley and IGLA appeared confident the measures would pass, but Ald. Leon Despres was skeptical, "The anti-transvestite ordinance is almost sure to be repealed, since it has been declared unconstitutional, but I don't know if the anti-discrimination one will ever be reported out of committee ... You have to remember that the dominant outlook in City Council is puritanical and Catholic."

Excerpts from Dr. Kitch Childs' "vague but militant sounding rap in defense of gay rights" were published in the November 1973 *Lavender Woman*:

> "Let me begin my remarks by pointing out that sexual love is a human experience, not a disease process ... Freudian theoretical assumptions have equated sexual preference for one's own sex as immature, as a 'fixation,' arrested development, or sexual identity malfunction. Conclusions based upon these descriptions serve to equate such behavior then with sickness. ... Under this rubric, the homosexual is described as a 'sick person whose behavior is predicated upon irrational impulsivity'; as a consequence, the homosexual is considered dangerous, if not criminal. There is no way in which females or males with primary homosexual identities can be differentiated from those individuals with heterosexual preferences using their responses to psychological tests of the kind used to get at personality abnormality. There are no researches which indicate that either group can be differentiated at all. ... The evidence from which Freud made his conclusions were drawn from a group of troubled, willing, patients. That is to say, upper-class Viennese ... Most of the human population is neither upper-class, nor Viennese. ... We cannot provide evidence for psychological damage in family experience to account for individual's sexual preferences or life style. ... There are however, profound social effects which follow the naive acceptance of these assumptions. In a recent Public Opinion Poll, about 80% of Americans still think that homosexuals are criminals. More important, that the only jobs that should be available to such people are the marginal, menial, personal service positions like: hairdresser, dress designer, librarian, or clerical labor. These limited service occupations and choices do much to persuade the homosexual individual and group to curtail their own creativity and contributions to the social community. They are forced to choose between constant vigilance, a double-life, and hiding for fear of loss of their economic income. Such forced choices create an incredible drain on the human spirit. ... It is impossible to legislate human respect, but your action can provide the beginnings of equal justice under the law. Difference cannot continue to be equated to criminality or to evil. Inclusion of the change in the ordinance will obviate one important issue–Blackmail. On the pages of

## CHICAGO AFTER STONEWALL

last month's *New York Times*, one of New York's City Councilmen described his efforts to conceal his life style from the city administration—he concluded his story with the information that about 50% of the other Councilmen were also homosexuals in hiding. ... Changes in the ordinance will expand the possibility of the involvement and active contribution in terms of creative energy and political investment in the community of a large segment of the population."

In the spring of 1974, organized opposition to gay rights legislation emerged, as the Roman Catholic Church flexed its muscles. In May, the *Chicago Tribune* reported that the New York gay rights bill was doomed after a concerted effort from the Roman Catholic Archdiocese of New York and the Uniformed Fire Officers Association. The Catholic Archdiocese published an editorial on the front page of the *Catholic News* headlined, "A Menace to Family Life," which many priests read verbatim from their pulpits. The editorial claimed that granting gay rights would "damage the true civil rights cause in this city and will endanger the freedom of every citizen to protect his family from a serious immoral influence":

> "There will be no effective way to decline the welcome into two-family dwellings of homosexual couples nor to decline to employ homosexuals in positions of sensitive personal influence such as elementary and high school teachers, counselors and persons on the staff of organizations that provide services to children and young boys and girls."

The Uniformed Fire Officers Association (UFOA) spent $10,000 to rally opposition among its members. However, a protest against the bill attracted only forty-five firemen rather than the expected 5,000. Clearly, union leaders were against the gay rights bill, not the rank and file membership. Deputy Fire Chief David McCormack predicted, "The admittance of self-proclaimed sexual deviates will be counterproductive to the efficient operation of the department and the best interests of millions of New Yorkers." McCormack was worried firemen would be reluctant to share sleeping quarters with homosexuals. To which Morty Manford, president of the Gay Activists Alliance, countered, "If firemen are so easily seducable ... it tells you something about their own sexuality. We pose no threat to any person who is secure in his or her heterosexuality."

This did not bode well for Chicago's two pending gay rights ordinances. On May 28, 1974, the Chicago City Council's Judiciary Committee voted 5-4 to refer the gay rights ordinances to a sub-committee, effectively a burial ground. Two committee members expected to support the bill had been absent. Ald. Clifford P. Kelley (20th Ward), the bill's primary sponsor, suggested if the full Judiciary Committee had been present, the bills would have passed. However, Kelley couldn't explain why Ald. William Shannon (17th Ward) and Ald. Seymour Simon (40th Ward), both supporters of the bill, voted to refer to the subcommittee. Although, with one-eye on New York, the daunting prospect of taking on the politically powerful Roman Catholic Archdiocese of Chicago may have factored into their thinking. On August 6, 1974, after a Judiciary subcommittee hearing in the Chicago City Council on gay rights, Ald. Edward Burke (14th Ward) announced in the City Hall pressroom that he had sent a "blistering" letter to John Cardinal Cody about his tacit approval of a gay mass. According to the August 1974 *Chicago Gay Crusader*, "He [Burke] said he had conferred with Queens (N.Y.) Democratic leader Matthew Troy, an arch-foe of New York City's Intro 2 gay rights measure. He told reporters that since the gay movement was organized nationally, he feels its opponents should organize similarly."

The Roman Catholic Church proved to be a formidable enemy of gay rights in both New York and Chicago. Leslie A. Trotter, an African American gay activist, wrote to the editor of the *Chicago Defender* on the subject of how black aldermen voted on the two pending gay rights ordinances:

> "I wish to express my support for and faith in Ald. Timothy C. Evans (4th) and Ald. Anna R. Langford (16th) for having the courage to stand up for the rights of gay people and not send the so-called Gay Rights Bill back in the Chicago City Council.
>
> "However, I was appalled by the actions of Pro Tempore Wilson Frost (34th) and William H. Shannon (17th) who did not support the bill. ... I am not trying to argue the merits of gay liberation or gay people but since the persons named are black it does seem they would give support to this other oppressed minority group.
>
> "Homosexuality is not a white or black thing. [However] it is a people's thing. Therefore, we must act with courage to end this vestige of oppression."

The setback in passing the two gay rights bills caused a rift among Chicago's gay groups, primarily between the Chicago Gay Alliance and Illinois Gays for Legislative Action. In the *Chicago Gay Crusader*, William B. Kelley, co-convener of IGLA and vice president of CGA, wrote, "At a stormy meeting June 2, charges and countercharges were aired between factions supporting and opposing techniques used in the campaign."

Most of those at the meeting were CGA and IGLA members. CGA member Jeffrey Graubert accused IGLA co-convener Larry Gulian of several transgressions, including failure to tell him and others about the May 28 City Council Committee meeting. Others also criticized IGLA's 'elitist' strategies.

Gulian admitted news of the meeting had been purposely withheld from those IGLA considered "counterproductive," "undependable" or "committed to protest activities." Graubert and other supporters, including CGA president Nancy Davis, responded by forming a group to engage in "mass action." Former CGA president Les Trotter defused the situation by calling for another meeting on June 6, where it was decided to implement a petition project. Petitions were a way of getting support from non-gays and showing City Council members that they had gays and gay supporters, in their wards. The first petitions were circulated at the Old Town Arts Fair on June 8 and 9. At the June 6 meeting it was also decided to focus the June 27 Gay Pride Week rally in the Civic Center Plaza on the need for gay rights legislation.

However, it wasn't until December 1988, fifteen years after alderman Ald. Clifford P. Kelley's first effort, that the "Human Rights Ordinance" passed the Chicago City Council.

# 34
# CRUISING

Typical of newspaper articles at the time was this one in the *Indianapolis News* headlined, "34 Seized in Drive on Homosexuals":

> "Thirty-four persons, including four high school teachers and a college professor, have been arrested in the last month in a crackdown on homosexuality, Sheriff's Maj. Ronald F. Bryant said today.
>
> "Bryant said city police and sheriff's deputies have stopped homosexual meetings in three locations, in an area known as 'the jungle' at 38$^{th}$ and White River, in Holland Park, and at 56$^{th}$ and Fall Creek.
>
> "...Municipal court judges have been levying a flat $10 fine for first offenders but recently have increased the fines to $50 and $75 and ordered suspended sentences of 60-180 days provided the offenders seek psychiatric treatment."

All over the country, gay men were arrested. In the *Tampa Times*:

> "MIAMI – Metro police said yesterday more than 30 arrests had been made in restrooms at Miami International Airport on charges of homosexual acts performed in a public lavatory during the past five weeks.
>
> "Police emphasized that the suspects were not arrested for being homosexuals but only for allegedly making a public exhibition of their acts. Metro police said they have received repeated complaints from male travelers who were propositioned and sometimes assaulted by the homosexuals."

In the *Akron Beacon Journal*:

# CHICAGO AFTER STONEWALL

"Pensacola, Fla. – Nineteen persons attending a homosexual convention to name a 'Mr. Gay America' were arrested and charged with lewd and lascivious behavior.

"Police Sgt. Jack Odom said City police began what he called a major crackdown on homosexual activities after learning of an influx of 3,000 delegates to the convention."

In the *Corsicana Daily Sun*:

"Dallas – Undercover police arrested 14 men Thursday night at a bath house where officers said they observed homosexual acts.

"Among those taken into custody were a Dallas lawyer, a college professor, a school counselor, a hair dresser, and a building contractor, police said.

"Officers said the men will be charged with indecent exposure and public lewdness."

In the *Chicago Daily Herald*:

"Police stakeouts to prevent homosexual activities in washrooms of Illinois Tollway oases have resulted in the arrests of about 30 men since January.

"Lt. William Burt of Illinois State police said Monday that investigators began patrolling washrooms at the oases because of complaints by patrons.

"Burt said he has been told that a newspaper for homosexuals lists the oases as places to pick up 'dates' but said he has not seen the publication."

The January 1973 quarterly *Chicago Gay Listings*, published by Townson Remailing Service, informs on "Outdoor Cruising in Chicago":

"A rule of thumb for outdoor cruising in Chicago is that caution and discretion are a must! Chicago police lurk everywhere, and will bust you in a minute if you even look guilty. Cruise outdoors if you wish, but try to avoid consummating your activity in the bushes at Grant Park. If at all possible, go to his place, or your place, or the Y.

"NORTHSIDE AREAS

"Along Lake Michigan is good anywhere in Chicago. From Ohio Avenue going north to Diversey Harbor encompasses Lincoln Park, the Zoo, and the Oak Street, North Avenue, and Fullerton Avenue beaches. The Zoo, and the sections of Lincoln Park immediately to the north or south are good, especially on weekends and evenings in the summer. I recommend you tend strictly to business if you must use the john facilities in the immediate area of the Zoo. Particularly, the one in the basement of the Greenhouse is filled with cops. All the time. North of the Zoo, the area called the 'Lagoon' is good at night but watch out for the occasional young thugs.

"At Belmont and Lake Michigan is an area called the 'Belmont Rocks.' It swings. For many years, the U.S. Army maintained a small base out there, and my correspondents say a good time was had by all.

"The neighborhood called 'Clark and Diversey' (which refers to an intersection of streets) is well known for its large gay population. ... From downtown, the best way to get there is on a #22 Clark bus or a #36 Broadway bus, and alight when either of them reach Diversey Avenue.

"Another gay northside neighborhood is the area around Bryn Mawr & Broadway. This is considerably further north, but the best approach by public transportation would be the Northbound State Street subway from downtown. Ride north to Bryn Mawr Avenue, which is about a 15 minute ride.

"Bryn Mawr is fast becoming the gay neighborhood in Chicago. A couple of nice restaurants are within a block of the train you will ride up on.

"CRUISING DOWNTOWN

"Civic Center Plaza, across from Greyhound and the Sherman Hotel is filled with hustlers. The four corners of Clark and Randolph are a special point in your visit, because if you look hard, you may see Mayor Daley in his City Hall office on the southwest corner. One thing is certain; you won't have to look hard to see a gaggle of queens on the northeast corner, loitering around Greyhound.

"Randolph Street from Michigan Avenue to LaSalle is good any evening or weekend. The USO is located on Randolph east of Wabash, as is the Illinois Central Suburban Electric Train. But, the ICRR toilet is better off left alone, as are almost all public toilets in Chicago, because of the police.

"Northwestern Railroad, at Canal & Madison, serves Great Lakes Naval Base. Friday is a big day for seafood in Chicago, usually after 6:00 p.m., anywhere between Randolph Street to Roosevelt Road (12 blocks). It may be OK, but I have always found it a little depressing there, even though I have scored successfully on several occasions. The area around 8th Street is good on Grant Park Concert nights in the summer. And, Buckingham Fountain generally draws a crowd.

"DOWNTOWN WASHROOMS

# CHICAGO AFTER STONEWALL

"Not generally recommended, unless you have business in the office building in which you are in. I would recommend a cautious visit to these, if you want quick action, fun and games; but have a care!

| | |
|---|---|
| Marshall Fields Store<br>State and Randolph<br>3rd Floor Men's Room | Chicago Public Library<br>Michigan & Randolph<br>3rd or 4th Floor Men's Room |
| Field Annex Building<br>Wabash & Washington<br>12th Floor Men's Room<br>(Room 1234, to be exact) | Willoughby Towers Building<br>8 South Michigan<br>various floors |
| Board of Trade Building<br>LaSalle & Jackson<br>Basement Men's Room | Lyon & Healy Building<br>Wabash & Jackson<br>9th Floor Men's Room |
| Roosevelt University<br>Michigan & Congress<br>12th Floor Lounge | Art Institute of Chicago<br>Michigan & Jackson<br>Basement Lounge & Men's Room |

"AND, SOUTH OF THE CITY, IN HAMMOND, INDIANA, TRY:

| | |
|---|---|
| Greyhound Terminal<br>52 State Street<br>Mezzanine Level Men's Room | Woodmar Shopping Center<br>Carson, Pirie, Scott Store<br>2nd Floor Men's Room |

Whiting Park

117th Street at Lake Michigan (men's room is outrageous!!!)

## "SOUTHSIDE CRUISING

"The Hyde Park neighborhood is good. It's not considered gay, but lots of gay people do live there. In the guide was mentioned House of Tiki and Hyde Park Coffee Shop. In addition, I suggest a trip to the Museum of Science and Industry, 57th Street & Lake Shore Drive. It is very easy to cruise and pick up there, especially on Sunday afternoons when it is literally jammed with humanity. Check out also the East End Park, at 53rd & Hyde Park Blvd. across from the aforementioned coffee shop. After dark is best, in the area just north of the playground. This is about 4 blocks due north of the Museum. Best transportation would be (from downtown), either the #1 Jeffrey or #5 South Shore bus, or the Illinois Central train from Randolph Street. (Buy a ticket to Hyde Park for 60¢. Get off at 57th Street. Walk a block east). If on the subway, transfer at 55th to the #55 Museum Bus bound eastbound."

# 35
# THE GAY TEACHERS ASSOCIATION

The first meeting of Chicago's Gay Teachers' Association took place on February 10, 1973, at an unknown location. It wasn't advertised, as members had to be discreet. The contact address was a PO Box.

At the first meeting a Statement of Purpose was drawn up. It read:

> "Recognizing the inherent right of every human being to be productive, to work in the area of their choice, training and competence, to make their contribution to the community at large, and in so doing earn their livelihood, we therefore join together as professionals in education to secure this right for ourselves and our colleagues. In so doing, we recognize that as professional educators our first commitment is to the children we serve. Under no circumstance can, nor will, we condone any sexual orientation directed towards children. We further undertake the task of reeducating the community at large that in fact homosexuality is a viable, healthy alternative lifestyle, which is in no way related to child molestation; that homosexuality is unrelated to classroom competence, and that Gay Women and Gay Men are as responsible for separation of their private and professional lives as are their heterosexual colleagues."

By the second meeting April 28, incorporation papers had already been submitted to the state for not-for-profit corporate status. That night, they held elections for two coordinators and a treasurer: Coordinators were Margaret "Skeeter" Wilson and John Keller, treasurer John Whalen. The guest speaker at the meeting was Penn. State student Joe Acanfora III, who was profiled by Howard S. Shapiro in the *Chicago Tribune* under the headline, "Homosexuals: Should They Teach?" ... "Three months ago, Penn State student Joe Acanfora III wrote Pennsylvania's education secretary asking the commonwealth's policy on hiring teachers who are homosexuals," wrote the

*Chicago Tribune*. "An aide to Education Secretary John Pittenger replied that Pennsylvania has no firm policy."

Acanfora then asked if he, a homosexual, could be certified as a teacher in Pennsylvania. Several Penn State deans, who made the recommendations on teacher certification, discussed the matter but could not reach a consensus. They deadlocked on the question of Acanfora's fitness to teach. The problematic question was, "Can a homosexual be 'known as a person of good moral character,' as the regulations stipulated. Another complication was that, at the time, sodomy between two men was illegal in Pennsylvania and gays were considered an "anti-social aberration." If Pittenger signed Acanfora's application for certification, he would, in effect, be redefining homosexuality as an acceptable lifestyle.

Homosexuality in the teaching profession wasn't a new issue. In 1970, the American Federation of Teachers decided gays be "judged on the basis of professional and personal criteria." Yet, the National Education Association later voted down a similar resolution. Adding to the patchwork of acceptance and condemnation, in early 1972 the District of Columbia decided homosexuality didn't impair a teacher's skills. Meanwhile, in Pennsylvania, Dr. Abram VanderMeer, dean of Penn State's College of Education and five decision-making deans, held a meeting with Acanfora and his lawyers. Acanfora told the *Chicago Tribune*, "They asked me, at that meeting, whether it was true I was a homosexual. I said that was true, to the extent I defined homosexuality. I told them I have emotional, physical and psychological feelings toward men and women, but those toward my male friends were more important to me right now." They then asked Acanfora which sexual acts he preferred to engage in. He told the deans it was irrelevant and to respect his privacy. Acanfora was then asked if he would be an advocate for homosexuality. He told the *Chicago Tribune*, "I said I was interested in the repeal of discriminatory laws. But no-one was trying to convert anyone. That's ridiculous. The types of questions they asked me indicated that homosexuals had no value, as far as they were concerned."

Dr. VanderMeer voted against Acanfora's certification, stating:

> "It is pretty clear that certain acts that are defined as homosexual acts are also acts that can be defined as felonies in the criminal code. Also, the teacher's influence extends beyond the confines of the classroom. In the case of sexual morality – particularly where the teacher is involved with the adolescent age child – there is a certain crucial quality. The adolescent typically, is developing his or her own self-image, and, I think, needs strong and helpful models in the people he tends to look up to."

"Influencing" children was a typical argument used against employing gay teachers. This "Letter to the Editor" appeared in the *Tucson Daily Citizen*:

> "Since homosexualism is more of a psychopathic condition than a physical medical problem, and the young mind is especially plastic, how can anyone avoid realizing that a homosexual teacher can condition the minds of his students without any physical overt act taking place?
>
> "It's called inductive-psychology. A homosexual teacher would have no problem in conditioning a young mind to accepting an ideology of this nature, without any physical molestation.

"Signed CURTIS LINDERMUTH"

## 36
# THE CASE OF REV. DAVID SINDT

A battle erupted in the United Presbyterian Church, when it refused to allow Rev. David Sindt the pastorship of Lincoln Park Presbyterian Church because he was gay. The church wrote:

> "The Committee on Ministerial Relations (of the Presbytery of Chicago) does not recommend that final clearance be given to the Rev. David Sindt so that he may accept a call to the Lincoln Park Presbyterian Church for a specialized ministry to the Gay Community. ... It is important that the minister not be himself an advocate of homosexuality, as then homosexuality would simply be another form of idolatry. Our conversation with Mr. Sindt indicated that he was a committed advocate of homosexuality."

In the *Chicago Gay Crusader*, Sindt wrote:

> "Thus began the five-paragraph motion, adopted March 10, 1973, by the Committee on Ministerial Relations (MR) of the Presbytery of Chicago, signaling the end of an attempt to establish in Chicago an officially-recognized ministry between the United Presbyterian Church and the gay community. Chicago Presbyterians have now taken their first public step down the anti-gay-clergy trail blazed by the United Methodists in both Dallas and Chicago, and away from the more positive approaches of Unitarian-Universalists nationally and the United Church of Christ in San Francisco."

The Dallas United Methodist case was that of Gene Leggett, a 36-year-old gay clergyman, suspended from the ministry June 1, 1971. Leggett, described in the *Chicago Tribune* as "a tall bearded man with mod clothes and a pink lapel button reading 'Gay!'" had served the Church for ten years and operated a home called "House of the Covenant" for people, including homosexuals, who he felt were ignored by the church. After pleading his case before the Southwest Texas United Methodist Annual Conference in San Antonio, where he said he wanted to continue his ministry as a Christian and hopefully a Methodist, Leggett was suspended by a vote of 144 to 117.

The "anti-gay-clergy trail" in Sindt's *Chicago Gay Crusader* article refers to the case of the Rev. Charles Lamont (see chapter 24). The "more positive approach" Sindt mentions relates to the United Church of Christ in San Francisco. The *Chicago Tribune* reported in 1972 that delegates from 19 San Francisco Bay area churches belonging to the United Church of Christ, approved the ordination of an affirmed homosexual.

In December 1969, the *Bensenville Register* published an article headlined "Book on Homosexuality Issued by Church Press":

> "A major Protestant denomination has for the first time opened up the long ignored discussion of homosexuality with publication of *The Same Sex* a new book by the United Church of Christ's Pilgrim Press.
>
> "The book provides new religious perspectives to the issues by presenting the views of clergymen, sex researchers and homosexuals themselves.
>
> "'The time has come,' writes Rev. Ralph W. Weltge, editor of the book, 'to move public discussion of homosexuality out from under the clouds of mythology that surrounds it into the light of modern knowledge.'"

*The Same Sex* is remarkable insomuch as it consults homosexuals on the subject. The article, though it does not include the opinions of out-homosexuals, goes on:

> "Asking for understanding of the homosexual, Rev. Dr. Roger L. Shinn, professor of applied Christianity and dean of instruction at Union Theological Seminary, New York writes: 'Whatever our final judgement about homosexuality, there is something peculiarly unhealthy in the zeal of its persecutors. Church and society owe to human beings a concern for justice and a respect for dignity and privacy.'"

David Sindt also commended the Unitarian Universalists for their pro-gay stance. At the 1970 General Assembly of the Unitarian Universalist Association, the following resolution passed:

> "A significant minority in this country are either homosexual or bisexual in their feelings and/or behavior;
>
> "Homosexuality has been the target of severe discrimination by society and in particular by the police and other arms of government;

"A growing number of authorities on the subject now see homosexuality as an inevitable sociological phenomenon and not as a mental illness;

"There are Unitarian Universalists, clergy and laity, who are homosexuals or bisexuals;

"THEREFORE BE IT RESOLVED: That the 1970 General Assembly of the Unitarian Universalist Association:

"Urges all peoples immediately to bring an end to all discrimination against homosexuals, homosexuality, bisexuals, and bisexuality, with specific immediate attention to the following issues:

"Private consensual behavior between persons over the age of consent shall be the business only of those persons and not subject to legal regulations;

"A person's sexual orientation or practice shall not be a factor in the granting or renewing of federal security clearance, visas, and the granting of citizenship or employment;

"Calls upon the UUA and its member churches, fellowships, and organizations immediately to end all discrimination against homosexuals in employment practices, expending special effort to assist homosexuals to find employment in our midst consistent with their abilities and desires;

"Urges all churches and fellowships, in keeping with changing social patterns, to initiate meaningful programs of sex education aimed at providing more open and healthier understanding of sexuality in all parts of the United States and Canada, and with the particular aim to end all discrimination against homosexuals and bisexuals."

Three years before Sindt was denied the pastorship of Lincoln Park Presbyterian Church, homosexuality had been discussed at the 182nd Assembly of Presbyterians at Chicago's Conrad Hilton hotel. Steven Pratt in the *Chicago Tribune* wrote, "The ruling body of the United Presbyterian church voted ... to accept and disseminate to its members a controversial report which recommends legalized abortion and says that in some cases adultery may be acceptable." The three-year study also recommended more sex education in schools and ordered further research into homosexuality. The study found that homosexuality was not an "irresolvable conflict" with membership in the Christian fellowship. Church officials were quick to stress that acceptance of the report didn't mean the church endorsed the recommendations, but that it would be published and available to church members for "study and appropriate action."

David Bailey Sindt was born on December 8, 1940, in Minneapolis, MN. After obtaining his Master of Divinity degree in 1966, at McCormick

Theological Seminary, he became assistant pastor at Erie Chapel Presbyterian Church of Chicago. In the late-1960s–early-1970s Sindt became aware of his sexuality, joined the Chicago Gay Alliance and began attending services at the gay-friendly Lincoln Park Presbyterian Church, 600 W. Fullerton. Sindt soon recognized a need for a ministry to the gay community. To that purpose Lincoln Park Church issued a call for him to serve, an action blocked by the Presbytery of Chicago's Ministerial Relations Committee (MR). In his *Chicago Gay Crusader* article, Sindt continues:

> "Having served churches in Chicago and St. Paul, I am currently a member of the Presbytery of the Twin Cities, despite my Chicago residence. MR in Chicago thus sent a copy of its motion to a member of the MR in the Twin Cities, the Rev. Stuart Cameron, who responded, in a letter to me: 'In their rationale, such as it was, it seemed to me that mostly they were unable to accept the possibility of a Christian homosexual. And they seemed unaware of the possibility that 'advocacy of a ministry to homosexuals' might well include a minister who advocates homosexuality ... And their reference to 'idolatry' was a plain cop-out.'"

Sindt first proposed a gay ministry in April 1972, "after a year of personal contemplation and struggle." On the subject of a suitable minister, his proposal read:

> "As with any other ministry, the suitability of the minister for the ministry is an important key to its success or failure. For a ministry of advocacy and reconciliation between the church and the Gay community, it is essential that the minister be not only a minister but also Gay, and secure as a Gay person. The reasons for this reflect the two-fold nature of this ministry between the church and the Gay community:

> "1. Because the minister would be Gay he would be able to relate freely within the Gay community and be trusted by other Gay people in a way that would be impossible in the 1970s for one who was not Gay.

> "2. Because the minister would be an ordained clergyman he would be able to relate with congregations and pastors and with the Presbytery and other judicult for a layman or non-churchman, even in the 1970s.'

> "Had MR taken this seriously, it would have recognized the hypocrisy of ending with a recommendation that while MR 'does not recommend that clearance be given to Mr. Sindt ... (it would) affirm the Lincoln Park Session (church board) as to the validity of a ministry to homosexuals.' MR denied the call on the grounds that I am openly and securely gay ('an advocate of homosexuality'). To then affirm the validity of a ministry to gay people is like saying that only a white minister could properly lead a ministry to blacks because a black minister might too closely identify with other blacks. 'Idolatry,' to use MR's word."

Sindt writes that MR suggested his "defensiveness of the Gay Liberation Movement would tend to lead to a ministry exclusive of heterosexuals." When, in reality, the basic tenet of Sindt's proposal was to bring heterosexual and homosexual congregants together. Sindt ended his *Chicago Gay Crusader* article, "The gay ministry at Lincoln Park Church, which has been at least a partial reality for nearly a year, will continue. I will work with it, at the session's request and invitation, in the role of an outside consultant ... "

The following year Sindt founded the Presbyterian Gay Caucus, later renamed Presbyterians for Lesbian/Gay Concerns (PLGC), and later still More Light Presbyterians.

David Sindt died on December 3, 1986.

# 37
# PROTEST AT THE ATHENAEUM THEATER

The Athenaeum Theater was built in 1911 as part of St. Alphonsus Catholic Church, to stage German operettas. Since the early-1990s, the Athenaeum has been the venue for Chicago Gay Men's Chorus concerts, but back in 1973, the clergy were not gay-friendly. In the *Chicago Gay Crusader,* the headline read, "We're Not Good Enough. Gays Shut Out, Picket Ward Fair." The problem arose when the clergy of St. Alphonsus refused to rent out the theater for the 44th Ward Fair unless "groups contrary to church policy" were kept out. The Church claimed there had been complaints about the Chicago Gay Alliance booth the previous year, even though it was just an information exhibit. The Illinois Gays for Legislative Action (IGLA), the only group holding membership in Ald. Dick Simpson's advisory assembly, organized the picket and "over 30 gay sisters and brothers protested their exclusion."

William B. Kelley, the spokesperson for IGLA, told the *Chicago Gay Crusader* they had met several times with church officials. Still, neither IGLA nor Alderman Simpson's 44th Ward Assembly could change their mind. In the end, the Ward Assembly reluctantly signed the contract but resolved to ban the same discrimination from occurring at the 1974 Fair. On May 20, protestors picketed the Fair, chanted, handed out leaflets, and waved signs reading "Simpson Allows the Church To Oppress Gay People," and "Inquisition." One protester with shoulder-length hair and a Frank Zappa mustache carried a sign that read, "St. Alphonsus Won't Let Me Have A Booth Because I'm Gay." David Shane, attorney for the Ward Assembly, told the paper that the church also banned other groups, including "people who want to overthrow the government and abortion advocates."

One fairgoer was author, historian and broadcaster Studs Terkel, who, after asking a protestor what was going on, was so outraged that he went inside, and took the stage. He voiced a fiery denunciation of the gays' exclusion to resounding applause.

The *Chicago Sun-Times* reported on the protest, with one misguided gay activist telling the paper, "no church policy against homosexuals exists. In fact, a weekly mass for gay people is conducted each week in another Catholic Church in the 44th Ward."

The second part was correct. The activist was referring to the Chicago chapter of Dignity meeting at St. Sebastian's, 810 W. Wellington. St Sebastian's became the venue for the 44th Ward Fair the following year. In April 17, 1974, John Chester, the Fair's coordinator, wrote to Illinois Gays for Legislative Action, inviting them to staff a booth or exhibit. The Fair took place on May 19, 1974.

## 38
# STATE REP. WEBBER BORCHERS VS. ISU-GPA

One attempt to halt the progress of gay rights came on April 26, 1973, when State Rep. A. Webber Borchers (R-Decatur) introduced a resolution in the Illinois State of Representatives, criticizing Illinois State University for funding a campus gay group. Borchers claimed the university's Gay People's Alliance was "immoral" and promoted "sexual perversions." *Vidette*, the ISU student newspaper, on May 1, wrote:

> "The purpose of the resolution, Borchers said, is 'to alert the people of Illinois that student fees at ISU are being used to promote perversion.'
>
> "'Perversion,' according to Borchers, is 'an unnatural act between consenting individuals of the same sex.' He added, 'If you think it's normal for one man to 'have oral sex with another man, that's ok. But I don't.'"

Even if passed, the resolution had no teeth legally, but that didn't stop twenty-seven other representatives signing on, seventeen from Downstate, eleven from Chicago. (Twenty-three Republicans and five Democrats, in all).

The Illinois State University, located at Normal, IL, allotted $1,400, out of a total $1,157,367 student fees, to the Gay People's Alliance (GPA) for the 1972–1973 school year, for its program of lectures, films, and a newsletter. *Vidette* published several articles condemning the use of student fees for groups with "limited appeal."

In November 1972 in *Vidette*, Mike Waters, Campus Editor, wrote:

> "If Columbus had been a fruit he could have probably got funded by student fees at ISU. It seems that the all-mighty dispensers of student fees

place a higher premium on gay liberation than they do on educational significance, as evidenced by the fact that the history club, as well as all other departmental clubs and honoraries are currently without funding."

The Gay People's Alliance complained to the paper:

"If Columbus had been a nigger, he could have probably been funded by student fees at ISU. Or if he had been a spic. Or a kike. Or a mick. Or a wop. ... Mike Waters would never dream of using any of these terms in public, much less in print. But by referring to Gays as "fruit" (Nov. 16) he has proven just how incorrect his feature article is.

" ... dispensers of student fees place a higher premium on gay liberation than they do one educational significance, ... " An organization or activity need not be academic to be educational. Complete education is a combination of academic and non-academic experiences.

"As a funded student organization, one of the main purposes of Gay People's Alliance is to present non-academic learning experiences to the University community. Gay organizations across the country, including G.P.A., are such as women's rights, taxation, employment discrimination, and civil liberties.

"The prejudice exposed by Waters' ignorance only serves to more greatly illustrate the tremendous task of education facing gay liberation.

"Homosexuals and lesbians are NOT second-class citizens and no longer will we stand to be treated as such. An apology from Waters is in order."

Waters replied:

"Looking into my mailbag, I find that the Gay People's Alliance has demanded that I apologize to them for some rather vague offense I rendered in my column on student fees.

"They allege that the use of the word 'fruit' is somehow derogatory in a quasi-ethnic sense (or something).

"In the first place, I did not equivocate being "gay" with being fruity. When I wrote, "if Columbus had been a fruit he could have got funded by Student Fees at ISU," I was exaggerating (not much) to make a point. True, I worked off the premise that Gay Lib is currently funded to the tune of $1,400, while many educational clubs are still scratching around trying to find funds, but I did not label gay people as fruits.

"Aside from the semantical implications of the issue, however, there is one point which must be emphasized. When Gay Liberation is funded at an over $1,000 level and educational clubs play hell trying to get a $200 budget approved, something is wrong."

"I do not deny that Gay Liberation has some educational effect. The question I raise is whether or not Gay Liberation is really worth $1,400 to the students of ISU.

"When one considers that the 'educating' that is done is primarily self-serving (gaining acceptance from the straights) it is doubtful if the students who fund Gay Lib are really getting their money's worth."

"Name Withheld" responded, "Mike Waters' disingenuous attempt to defend his slur against the Gay People's Alliance and against homosexuals in general is even more insulting than the original column. On the basis of the evidence he presents in his Dec. 1 remarks, I'd suggest he be replaced with a monkey who can type."

On December 6, 1972, Gregg Durham and Rick Olsen wrote to Vidette:

"While glancing through the *Vidette* of Dec. 1, we noticed the letter submitted by the Gay People's Alliance concerning the funding of the organization to the tune of $1,400. This fund goes to a group consisting of around 2 per cent [sic] of the campus population.

"We hereby submit the proposal for originating a local chapter of the Hetero-Sexual People's Alliance. Seeing as 2 per cent of the campus population gets $1,400, the other 98 per cent should be entitled to a proportionate amount. Therefore, we feel we deserve $68,600."

There were rumors that at least one staff member encouraged State Rep. Borchers to introduce the anti-gay resolution. After its introduction, resolution H.R. 221 went to the House Committee on Higher Education, which held a hearing on May 18. The *Chicago Gay Crusader* reported that, according to Terry Farrelly, three GPA members had been ready to testify. However, it was decided that Judy Boyer, the associate secretary of the university, would instead, speak on the group's behalf.

Farrelly continued, "After reading of the resolution, there was an immediate motion for killing it." The motion came from Rep. James Houlihan, a Democrat, from Chicago's heavily gay Near North Side. He said, "The only thing perverted in this resolution is the resolution itself." During a question and answer period, another detractor, Rep. Victor Arrigo (D. Chicago), whose district includes the University of Illinois' Chicago Circle Campus, called the resolution "witch hunting of the most offensive type."

H.R. 221 failed to pass, with the committee vote of 2 in favor and 9 against. The following year Borchers made another attempt to stop Illinois State University from funding the Gay People's Alliance and for the legislature to "go on record that 'the Gay People's Alliance' and similar groups and organizations are immoral and should not be encouraged or supported by the officials at Illinois State University.'" Again, the proposed resolution died in committee.

Borchers' resolutions often died, like his sponsorship of a March 1971 bill making it mandatory for certain women on welfare to be sterilized to continue receiving public aid. The *Chicago Tribune* reported the bill stated:

> "A woman who has received public aid for at least six of the nine months prior to birth of each of three children is to have a tubal ligation or similar operation if she is to continue receiving welfare checks. The same conditions would apply to a man on the public aid rolls, who would be required to have a vasectomy or other measures taken to prevent him from fathering additional children."

Borchers, who lived in a palatial house near the Sangfamon River, filled with Nazi memorabilia he looted during World War II, was indicted November 18, 1974, for fraud. He was found guilty, though his conviction was overturned on a technicality by the Illinois Supreme Court three years later. His enduring legacy was to introduce the bill that made the Monarch butterfly the state insect of Illinois.

---

The Gay People's Alliance formed as the Gay Liberation Front at Illinois State University in early 1970. The first meeting was held on March 8. A notice appeared in the *Vidette*, "The Gay Liberation Front will hold a meeting at 2:30 p.m. this Sunday in Centennial East in room 284."

An article on the cover of *Vidette* in April 1970 is headlined "GLF organizes at Illinois State":

> "Gay Liberation Front has come to ISU.
>
> "What is GLF? Jeremy, a Wisconsin member, defined the group in a recent issue of Milwaukee's *Kaleidoscope*.
>
> "'What it's all about is simply that homosexuals are beginning to get together ... and we are now ready to take our place as homosexuals beside other oppressed minorities ... and demand the right to define our own communities, to determine our own destinies, and to live our lives in a manner befitting free human beings without harassment or interference.'"
>
> "ISU's Gay Lib leader stated, 'GLF would benefit gay (homosexuals and bisexuals) people and others. There is nothing social for gay people on our campus and they're a big population.'

"HE WENT ON to say that the organization is basically left-wing, but not necessarily a political organization. We do 'want a certain amount of power; to have dances, to walk the streets; to be real.'"

" ... WEEKLY MEETINGS and dances will be sponsored by the GLF. Their first dance was held last Sunday. Gay Lib's leader commented, 'The dance is the most educational experience. Anybody who is straight (heterosexual) will learn something and those who are gay will learn something about themselves. Everyone is welcome.'

"One straight person in attendance said, 'It was a great dance. There was an atmosphere of freedom; you did what you liked.'

"Something that can be learned by going to the dance, according to the head of the organization, is how to face up to the pressures placed on such an activity by America's taboo attitudes regarding sex."

According to *Vidette*, Allen Ginsberg attended the dance and "danced with everybody and talked to everybody." Ginsberg was appearing at Illinois Wesleyan University that weekend as part of their fine arts festival. He promised to write the Gay Liberation Front (Gay People's Alliance) a poem. He kept his word. *Police State Blues* was published in *Vidette* on October 26, 1971. It begins:

> *Night meat lights*
>    *hypnotizing hungry autos. Iron bridges*
>       *crossing down Main*
> *"Get a goddamned haircut!"*
>
>   *front window cry, Whose face drunk dark*
> *beautiful-chiseled mouth kist by whiskey?*
>
>   *to Gay Liberation Front Dance Normal, Illinois*
> *—black, guitar, soul-mate drum & mustached hairy organ*
>    *pounding majestic repetition*

It ends:

> *(Illinois State University Solarium, first G.L.F. dance, S.D.S. attending ticket door, Women's Liberation & boyfriends, babies naked underfoot toddling where Black Coalition provided circle rock dance ritual.)*

# 39
# GAY PRIDE PARADE 1973

In May 1973, the Gay Pride Planning Committee issued a press release announcing, "Chicago gays plan festive Gay Pride Week." The Committee, representing forty gay groups, had been meeting since January. Early on, it decided the parade would be a celebration *for* gay people, rather than an exhibition for straight bystanders. There were suggestions that the parade should be downtown on State Street, but, in the end, they decided to keep it in the "gay ghetto." Michael Bergeron, coordinator of the Committee, explained, "It's 'our' celebration: by us and for us. It's time to come together in Gay Love, Gay Unity, Gay Power and Gay Pride."

The schedule for the 4th Annual Gay Pride Week was as follows:

Friday, June 22.

8:30 p.m.-1:00 a.m. GAY PRIDE DANCE: The American Legion Post, 1720 N. Cleveland, Chicago. Tickets $2 advance, $2.50 at door. Featuring the release of 1,000 Gay Pride Balloons to kick off Gay Pride Week.

Saturday, June 23.

11:30 a.m. GAY PRIDE PICNIC: Lincoln Park, south of lagoon (at Armitage, 2000 N.) Bring a picnic lunch.

8:00 p.m. *Trevor*: Performance with all lesbian cast. Sponsored by Lesbian Feminist Theatre Group.

Sunday, June 24

Afternoon: GAY PRIDE PARADE: Assemble 1:00 p.m. setoff 2:00 p.m. from Belmont Harbor. West on Belmont to Broadway, South on Broadway and Clark to Lincoln Park Forum (about 1800 North) for park rally. Speakers and Music.

8:00 p.m. *Trevor*: Performance with all lesbian cast. Sponsored by Lesbian Feminist Theatre Group.

Monday, June 25

8:00 p.m. CANDLELIGHT VIGIL at Cook County Jail, 2600 S. California. Sponsored by Gay Caucus of Youth Against War and Fascism.

Tuesday, June 26

7:00 p.m. GAY SOCIAL WORK ASSN. AND GAY TEACHERS ASSN. Workshops and Social. Grace Lutheran Church, 555 W. Belden.

[*AUTHOR'S NOTE: Some accounts say this event took place at Lincoln Park Presbyterian Church, 600 W. Fullerton*]

Wednesday, June 27

7:00 p.m. FILM: *Some of Your Best Friends Are* (UCLA documentary, not to be confused with *Some of My Best Friends Are*) and discussion, led by Rev. David Sindt, Asst. Pastor, Lincoln Park Presbyterian Church, 600 W. Fullerton.

9:00 p.m. BUFFET AND OPEN HOUSE: Left Bank, 2140 N. Lincoln Park W. Sponsored by Chicago Nites and the Left Bank. Entertainment.

Thursday, June 28

Noon. RALLY AND KISS IN: Chicago Civic Center Plaza, Clark at Washington. To catch the Loop lunch crowds. Sponsored by Chicago Gay Alliance.

7:00 p.m. GAY LAW FORUM: Panel and discussion, legal topics of gay interest. De Paul University, 25 E. Jackson. Sponsored by Gay Law Students Association.

# CHICAGO AFTER STONEWALL

7:30 p.m. BISEXUALITY RAP: Blue Gargoyle, 5655 S. University. Sponsored by University of Chicago Gay Liberation.

7:30-10:00 p.m. WORKSHOP on relationship between Women's Liberation and Lesbian Liberation. Sponsored by Chicago Liberation Union.

Friday, June 29

8:00 p.m. "FAMILY OF WOMAN" CONCERT. Columbia Dance Center, 4730 N. Sheridan. Presented by the "Family of Woman," lesbian feminist musicians.

8:30 p.m. CLERGY GAY RAP. 7070 N. Ridge. Sponsored by Unity.

Saturday, June 30

9:00 a.m.-12:30 p.m. LESBIAN COUNSELING INFORMATION EXCHANGE. Lincoln Park Presbyterian Church, 600 W. Fullerton. Sponsored by Lesbian Counseling Group. Donation.

1:00-5:00 p.m. WORKSHOPS on Lesbian Publications Writers. Sponsored by Chicago Lesbian Liberation.

Evening. TALK by JILL JOHNSTON of the *Village Voice*. Sponsored by Chicago Lesbian Liberation.

8:00 p.m. *Trevor*: Performance with all lesbian cast. Sponsored by Lesbian Feminist Theatre Group. [Postponed until July 14]

Sunday, July 1

Afternoon. GAY ART FAIR and FLEA MARKET. Sponsored by Chicago Lesbian Liberation.

2:00 p.m. *Trevor*: Performance with all lesbian cast. Sponsored by Lesbian Feminist Theatre Group. [Canceled]

In July, the *Chicago Gay Crusader* reported that the Gay Pride Dance was a huge success with 350 people packing into the American Legion Post. Several members of the Gay Pride Planning Committee formed an all-Chicano rock band called Just Us, who "wowed their sisters and brothers" upstairs. At the same time, other partygoers packed the downstairs bar. The lobby was turned into a flea market where groups set up booths selling buttons, flags, books, albums, newspapers, and handed out pamphlets. The following day 100 brave souls held a picnic in the rain by Lake Michigan, but the inclement weather didn't dampen their spirits as they "laughed, danced, ate Kentucky Fried Chicken, and drank bottle after bottle of wine."

The Sunday Gay Pride Parade set off from Belmont Harbor, where 1,500–2,000 people gathered, including visitors from as far away as Minneapolis, Milwaukee, Ohio, Indiana, San Francisco, New York, Philadelphia, downstate Illinois, St. Louis, and elsewhere. Although the parade stepped off on time at 2:00 p.m., Tom Fitzgerald in his "Fitz" column in the *Chicago Sun-Times* wrote, "A multitude of mini-snits among the gays prevented the parade from stepping off until more than an hour after it was scheduled to begin." Fitzgerald claims the delay was exacerbated by the larger than expected turnout of gays who answered the "exhortation to 'come out of the closet.'" The unexpectedly high numbers required last minute negotiations with the police and soothing the irate motorists' frayed nerves. A banner reading CHICAGO'S 4TH ANNUAL GAY PRIDE PARADE led the procession, followed by the Gay Pride Planning Committee car and then floats, marching groups, and assorted decorated vehicles.

The Gold Coast leather and Levi bar sponsored an S &M-themed float with the banner, "Being Gay Is a Kick." In an attempt at humor, Fitzgerald described the "half dozen sado-masochists" … "They were all done up in black leather and carried chains and whips. They demanded to lead the parade but were turned down." Among other notable marchers was drag queen and gay activist Wanda Lust wearing her "Chiquita Banana outfit." Fitzgerald wrote, "A 6ft 3 inch transvestite came dressed like a Mexican dancer and refused to allow anyone to march next to him … or her."

Among the multitude of banners were WELCOME SISTERS AND BROTHERS, SISTERHOOD IS POWERFUL, GAY UNITY, and LESBIAN LOVE. Gay groups marching included the Women's Liberation Union, Chicago Gay Alliance, Chicago Lesbian Liberation, Transvestite Legal Committee, Gay Social Work Association, Gay Teachers Association, Gay People's Legal Committee, Metropolitan Community Church, and the *Chicago Gay Crusader*. There were also cars and floats representing gay bars like the Knight Out, Dugan's Bistro, Trip, Noche de Ronda, Up North, In Between, Wooden Barrell [sic] Pub and the Glory Hole. In the *Chicago Sun-Times* Fitzgerald wrote: "One young man in a car with a sign that said Dugan's Bistro kept up a running commentary with straights who stood on the sidewalks watching the parade. 'Get those bodies good and tan darlings,' he said at one point, 'Then you can come over and join us tonight.'"

The parade proceeded west on Belmont Ave., south on Broadway and then Clark Street, with very little hassle from the "straights" lined up to watch. There were chants of "Two, four, six, eight, is your husband really straight?" … "Two, four, six, eight, is your wife really straight?" … "Two, four, six, eight, we don't overpopulate!" and "Hey, hey, what do you say. Try it once the other way." The only problem came when the parade approached Fullerton Ave., the street dividing the 19$^{th}$ Police District and the notoriously anti-gay 18$^{th}$ Police District. At Fullerton, the police set up a blockade. The *Chicago Gay Crusader* noted that Michael Bergeron, coordinator of Gay Pride, jumped out of the Committee car and got into "a screaming match" with the 18$^{th}$ District Police. "We've got a permit!" he insisted, to which the police said, "You either go east or west but not directly south." There were a few tense minutes when neither the police nor the parade would budge. With only a few blocks left on the route, the spectators south of Fullerton moved north and began to congregate at the crossroads. The crowd shouted, "Let them through," but rather than spoil the party atmosphere, it was decided to re-route the parade going east, then through Lincoln Park, past the Zoo and the children's playgrounds, ending up at the original destination at the Lincoln Park Free Forum.

As the parade filed into the park, organizers set up the sound equipment on a gold truck that served as a stage. The first speaker was the Rev. Iberus Hacker, a heterosexual street preacher and folk singer, who told the story of how he led the first Gay Pride Parade in Chattanooga, TN. Hacker then strummed his guitar and, accompanied by another guitarist and a banjo-player, led the crowd in a sing-a-long of civil rights songs. Hacker was a known "character" in the Uptown neighborhood, just north of the "gay ghetto," a neighborhood inhabited by white Appalachian migrants from the poverty-stricken mountains of West Virginia. An ordained minister, Hacker was immediately recognizable on the street; a heavy-set bearded man with a shock of wild long hair, he easily suited his role of Santa Claus at Uptown's Christmas parties for the poor. Hacker was born in Chattanooga, TN, the son of a lawyer, the grandson of a Choctaw chief. In the *Chicago Tribune,* Hacker said, "I worked in the coal mines, bootlegged whisky, and ran a small newspaper – the *Grundy County Herald*." In Uptown, Hacker ran another paper called *Plain Talk*, was head of the Uptown Community Organization (UCO), and had a connection with Liberty Hall at 2440 N. Lincoln, a large auditorium where the Sons and Daughters of Liberty met. The UCO ran food pantries, free legal and medical clinics, and campaigned to have derelict buildings pulled down.

Following Hacker were a dozen speakers, including Michael Bergeron, Richard Pfeiffer (Chicago Gay Alliance), Judy Brabeck (Chicago Lesbian Liberation), the Rev. William Johnson (San Francisco gay minister and executive director of the Council on Religion and the Homosexual), Larry Gulian (Illinois Gays for Legislative Action), Margaret "Skeeter" Wilson

(Feminist Lesbian Intergalactic Party (Flippies) and Killer Dyke Collective), Michael Goldberger (Gay People's Legal Committee), Michael Brown (Gay Caucus of Youth Against War and Fascism), Tony Johnson (Transvestite Legal Committee), and representatives from the Family of Women lesbian feminist musicians, the Milwaukee Gay Pride Planning Committee, and the Gay People's Union of Milwaukee.

Another report on the 1973 Gay Pride Parade appeared in the August 1973 issue of *David*, written by Fred Alexson:

> "Gay Pride Week has become a yearly event across the country, commemorating the 'Great Stonewall Battle' on June 29, 1969 when gays stood their ground against harassment on the basis of their sexual identity and since then gays have continued to fight together for their 'birth rights' and are proud of it. Gay Pride Week events in Chicago were fun, well-attended and sensible this year. After last year's fiasco, no one expected 1,500 to turn out for this year's parade with cars, costumes, and imaginative floats representing the Gold Coast, Knight Out, Glory Hole, Up North and other gay establishments. Bucky of the Gold Coast in just his attractive leather harness, Wanda Lust of the Baton in her Chiquota Banana outfit, gangsters from the '20s, clowns and Rolls Royces driven by members of Bistro lead the parade to its final destination at Lincoln Park where speeches brought it to a successful end."

The day after the parade, an estimated 40 people marched on Cook County Jail to protest prison conditions of their "sisters and brothers in penal institutions." One banner read, "STOP BRUTALITY AGAINST GAYS – TEAR DOWN THE JAILS." Prior to the protest, the Gay Caucus of Youth Against War and Fascism, who organized the event, issued the following statement:

> Support Gay Prisoners
>
> Of all the institutions in this society that oppress Gay people, prisons are the most oppressive. Inhuman prison conditions, which affect all prisoners, are made even harsher for gay prisoners. Shock treatments, psychosurgery, brutal beatings and solitary confinement are some of the most barbaric methods used against gay people by prison officials.
>
> PRISONS ARE CONCENTRATION CAMPS
>
> Prisons are concentration camps for the poor and working people (which make up 99.9% of prisoners) and oppressed people (85% are Black, Latin, and other oppressed nationalities). Just as racism is used to divide white and Black workers, prejudice against gays is used to divide gay and straight prisoners. This makes it all the easier for the oppressors–the guards, wardens, and other prison officials–to maintain control. Fighting

each other makes it impossible for prisoners to join together to fight back against their common oppressor–the rich businessmen and crooked politicians who never go to prison.

GAY PRIDE MEANS FIGHT BACK

But gays in prison are getting together. From Washington State Prison, to Leavenworth, to Walpole Prison in Massachusetts, Gays are fighting back against the racism and sexism that is used to keep all prisoners from uniting and fighting for their basic human rights, which are denied them in prison.

We feel that a very real expression of Gay Pride is to show our solidarity with our gay sisters and brothers who are struggling for survival within the prisons and have voiced the necessity for outside support.

In response to that appeal, the Gay Caucus of Youth Against War & Fascism is calling for a demonstration at Cook County Jail (as a symbol of every prison in this country) ... "The demonstration will be held at 8:00 p.m. on Monday, June 25. Cook County Jail is located at 26th Street & California Ave."

During Gay Pride Week, one popular event was a workshop and social sponsored by the Chicago Gay Social Work Association and the Gay Teachers Association with fifty teachers and social workers attending. Another was the Chicago Lesbian Liberation film night, which drew an overflow crowd of more than 200. Among the films shown were *Lavender, Some of Your Best Friends, A Position of Faith, Holding, Narcissia,* and *Meshes of the Afternoon. A Position of Faith* is a documentary relating the story of Rev. William Johnson, the first openly gay person to be ordained to the Christian ministry, the United Church of Christ. Johnson was in town to be a Guest Speaker at the Pride Rally and Kiss-In. *A Position of Faith* was first screened at the United Church of Christ synod in St. Louis the previous weekend. During Johnson's speech after the Pride Rally and Kiss-In, he quoted from Radclyffe Hall's *The Well of Loneliness,* "We are coming, we are still coming on, and our name is legion you dare not disown us. We have asked for bread. Will you give us a stone? You God in whom we the outcast, believe. Give us also the right to our existence."

The June 28 Pride Rally and Kiss-In, sponsored by Chicago Gay Alliance, had three stated goals: (1) To Prove We're Proud, (2) Memorial for the Dead in New Orleans, (3) To Let the Outside World Know We're Angry. The second goal referred to a recent arson attack on a gay bar in New Orleans. On June 25, 1973, the *Chicago Tribune* reported that the previous night a flash fire had swept through the Upstairs bar in New Orleans' French Quarter, killing twenty-nine people (the final tally was thirty-three). The bar had been crowded because on Sunday they offered all the beer and food you can drink/eat for $2. Chicago's gay community rallied, raising $5,000 to help pay for funeral services and hospitalization, blood, counseling, and plastic surgery. A memorial service was held on July 1 at Chicago's Good Shepherd Parish of the Metropolitan Community Church (MCC). The minister of the New Orleans MCC had died in the fire, along with one-third of the congregation. The *Advocate* agreed to be the custodian of the fund. New York gay activist Morty Manford visited Chicago on July 18 to mobilize the local community to raise funds for the National New Orleans Memorial Fund. Manford was known for having been in the Stonewall Inn the night it was raided. One Chicago benefit took place at Jack David's Up North bar and restaurant, 6244 N. Western Ave., and raised $3,000. Two hundred and fifty attended at $2 a head. Half the price of each drink was donated, as well as the salaries and tips of the staff. There were raffles and an auction, where African American drag queen Roby Landers sold her falsies to the highest bidder. Among the performers were singer Dina Jacobs and dancer Tony Lewis, both from the cocktail lounge/restaurant David's Place, 5232 N. Sheridan. From the House of Landers drag bar, 936 W. Diversey, came the dance team Laura Merrill and Jeff Cooper, also performer Jennie Lee.

The suspected arsonist, a drifter named Raymond Wallender, was arrested in November. He confessed to pouring gasoline on the stairs and setting it on fire because a patron of the Upstairs bar had reneged on a $200 deal offered to one of Wallender's friends for a sex act. Wallender was released without charge when police found inconsistencies in his story. He later killed himself. There has never been an official determination of the cause and culprit of the fire.

The Pride Rally and Kiss-In at Civic Center Plaza drew a crowd of almost 100 and, aside from the Rev. Johnson, the speakers were William B. Kelley (Vice president of the CGA); Valerie Taylor (Gay Grandmothers of America); Richard Pfeiffer (CGA President); Mary Himmel (Chicago Lesbian Liberation); Ted Hays (An Indiana teen who told of his arrest experiences); and Jim Bradford (Past president of Mattachine Midwest). The Killer Dyke Collective performed street theater, a play showing how Killer Dyke defeated Super Pig and his secret weapon, a faux penis. Speeches over, *Chicago Gay Crusader* publisher Michael Bergeron urged the crowd to form a circle, which they did, then danced counterclockwise while chanting.

"All right," cried Bergeron after a while, "After this chant we're gonna all run to the center of the circle and kiss our sisters and brothers." The crowd responded by rushing forward and embracing each other, in a blatant defiance of Chicago's obscenity laws.

That evening, thirty-five people attended another Pride event at De Paul University's Loop campus, a panel and discussion on "Gay Law Reform" sponsored by the Chicago Gay Law Students Association. The topics included job discrimination, lesbian mothers' child custody rights, gay political progress in Illinois and Madison, WI, and criminal arrests. According to *Lavender Woman*, the Chicago Gay Law Students Association held its first meeting on March 2, 1973, at the Up North restaurant/bar. The meeting, advertised only at DePaul, discussed initiating a gay arbitration board, based on Talmudic courts currently functioning in New York. The board would deal with property squabbles between roommates and collectives breaking up. Other suggested research projects included a study of police arrests and a survey of discrimination in employment.

Four months after the 1973 Pride Parade, a letter from "Freaked Out" appeared in the Ann Landers syndicated column that begins:

> "There seems to be quite a heated argument between Ann Landers, who says homosexuals are sick, and certain psychiatrists and gays who say they are NOT sick. Your opponents say you are ill-informed, stupid or nuts.
>
> "Anyone who witnessed the Gay Pride Parade from Belmont Harbor to Lincoln Park in Chicago has got to go with you, Ann. In my life I never saw anything to top it. Over 1,500 gays came out of the closet ... Some of the costumes were out of this world – sequins, feathers, tights, black leather coats, whips and chains. ... One fellow (I think) had a live snake wrapped around his neck. ... If those people are normal and healthy, then I wanna be sick."
>
> Landers answered, "I hope you don't think all homosexuals look and act like that. What you describe sounds like the lunatic fringe. Many homosexuals are dignified, soft-spoken people. They do not wear high-heels or wigs."

# 40
# GAY PRIDE WEEK 1973 WOMEN-ONLY

There were several women-only events during the 1973 Pride Week festivities. They included a sold-out dance at the Columbia College Dance Center, 4730 N. Sheridan Road, featuring the Family of Women lesbian feminist musicians. There were also workshops, on subjects like the relationship between Women's Liberation and Lesbian Liberation (sponsored by the Chicago Women's Union), on lesbian publications (sponsored by Chicago Lesbian Liberation), and a Lesbian Counseling Information Exchange (sponsored by the Lesbian Counseling Group).

One speaker at Gay Pride 1973 was columnist Jill Johnston of the *Village Voice*. Johnson was a rising star in the feminist movement, having recently published a new book, *Lesbian Nation*. Her talk was at a women-only event, though it wasn't advertised as such, raising the ire of at least one gay man. In the *Chicago Gay Crusader*, William B. Kelley writes:

> "When I arrived at the Jill Johnston talk during Gay Pride Week and found it closed to men, I told the women on the door that while I respected their or Johnston's position, I did not respect their lack of planning. By this, I meant that there was no announcement that only women were welcome until one arrived at the door (and that, after trekking two blocks from the scheduled location, where a sign directed people to the new location but even then didn't state that men would be excluded)."

Kelley goes on to urge "non-lesbian groups next year to stop worrying so much about schedule competition when planning their Gay Pride Week activities on the same nights with lesbian-sponsored events. Where it does not detract from either, let there be different events at the same times, so that people have a choice."

Clearly, there was tension between separatist lesbian groups and other gay community organizations. In the *Chicago Reader*, Sally Banes shares details on Jill Johnston's speech under the headline "Grande Dame of Dykes." Banes says of Johnston's previous book *Marmalade Me*, a collection of *Village Voice* columns published between 1960-1970, that it "charts [Johnston's] transition in that decade from a lively and sensitive critic of dance, various plastic arts and Happenings to an incisive critics' critic to a dreamy visionary surrealistic streamofconsciousness exploding chronicler of the endless performance of her own life from day to day." Banes describes Johnston's book *Lesbian Nation,* as "radical, ultrafeminist, a delicious stew of dogma and gossip."

Banes, who eschews uppercase lettering – (mrs, english, amerika, etc.) – writes that Johnston was "startling and persuasive enough, with an apparently impeccable political analysis coupled with an outrageously elegant style." In her speech, Johnston said:

> "Lesbian identity in truth is political identity. All identity is in fact political identity. There was, as I've stressed no lesbian identity, only lesbian activity. One could describe the activity but it had no name, for traditionally homosexuality has been the crime without a name. Names are political. As a miss or a mrs. We were all heterosexually identified and as such further classified under the aegis of the man whose names we were all required to assume. I never met my father and my mother never married him but I had his name anyway and if I didn't have his I would've had my grandfather's or my mother's father and in fact I was born in england with that very name although later in amerika my mother assumed the name of my english father so in a sense I still have both names which are her father's and mine and so far as I'm concerned neither of them ever existed. Who was my father? It's a political question. And who is my mother, the other political question."

She also said:

> "*Until all women are lesbians there will be no true political revolution* until in other words we are woman I am a woman who loves herself naturally who is other women is a lesbian a woman who loves women loves herself naturally this is the case that a woman is herself is all women is a natural born lesbian so we don't mind using the names it naturally I am a woman and whatever I am we are we affirm being what we are saying therefore *Until all women are lesbians there will be no true political revolution* meaning the terminus of the heterosexual institution through

the recollection by woman of her womanhood her own grace and eminence by the intense identities of our ancestors ... "

Presumably, Jill Johnston's "dreamy visionary surrealistic streamofconsciousness" was at work, or perhaps you just had to be there. In the *Chicago Daily News*, interviewer Betty Flynn describes Johnson as wearing "a blue denim shirt and pants, topped by a lumberman style plaid jacket and rolled up sleeves." Among her quotable remarks are that a woman's "first great sexual experience was with a woman, through birth." She goes on to describe orgasms as a "reenactment of the birth-death experience" and straight sex as "an attempt to re-enter the womb."

More conflict between radical lesbians and other gay organizations emerged in the March 1973 *Lavender Woman* with an article by Sara Thompson headlined, "The Politics of Drag":

> "Gay Pride Week, specifically the Gay Pride Parade, is supposed to be a call for solidarity, a call for unity between gay men and lesbians. But unity can only exist between people who have a common purpose, between those who have a love and a respect for each other that will help keep them strong and that will work to help them eliminate the exploitation of each other. This cannot exist, now or in the near future, between gay men and lesbians. Those who have the level of consciousness that will allow them to publicly mock and display their hatred of women, such as drag queens and those who are entertained by them, cannot be the allies of lesbians. And we cannot continue to participate in our own degradation."

Thompson argues that men "in the costume of high heels, wigs, falsies, and make-up" are saying, "This is a woman – that is all she is."

She adds:

> "This psychology is analogous to that used by white people in blackface comedy: painting their faces black, leaving big, white spaces for the eyes and lips, and then shuffling/tap-dancing across the stage. This was hardly the essence of a black person, but it was the white man's image and often the way the white man made he/she act in his presence. ... I will not align myself with men who show such contempt for me, my sisters, and the sisters that went before us. I will not align myself with men who are playing with themselves, with us, with straight society in the image straights want to see them. They are playing, not dealing, with their oppression and with our oppression. They take those dresses off and go back to work having money and power over us. Our liberation, the liberation of lesbians is not a game or an attempt to make this world 'happy.' Our liberation is in the destruction of this system and in the creation of our own."

However, Pride month saw the publication of the radical paper, *Cries from Cassandra,* produced by Amazon Nation. The masthead reads, "We are: betty peters, barbara lightfoot, nancy boothe, d.a. kelley, carla hilary dolinka, I pok, hummingfly, laurie mcdade, barbara doe, robbie and mona, greta bridgeway."

Barbara Lightfoot accuses *Lavender Woman* of "selling out":

> "Aside from consistently using the term lesbian, the LW could pass for a straight newspaper. To many women, a good newspaper must mean that it should have a little of this and a little of that but not too much of either, and, of course, be careful not to include anything of controversial importance because it might offend someone. However, the end result of such an attitude was a wishy-washy potpourri of a newspaper highly imitative of straight society and definitely lacking in any strong political feminist statement.
>
> "In fact, the LW reminded me gastrically [sic] of Monday night meetings and CLL [Chicago Lesbian Liberation] in general. When someone is lost, they automatically have been trained to take the well-traveled road to be found instead of forging through a hitherto unexplored jungle. Women at CLL constantly adopt straight patterns of behavior, and meetings usually bore on and on in the following enlightening fashion:
>
> "First we figure out what bar to go to, then we get a charter that says we're legal, then we hassle about dues, take time out to listen to a woman rant and rave about how we're all racist pigs and we should DEAL with it. Sometimes, if everybody's good and no one disrupts, we get cookies and can play in the basement. The final scene of this horror flick was to devote a meeting discussing men. My lord, the amazon queen must be rolling over in the sky!"

Lightfoot, and Amazon Nation, rejected the idea that the lesbian community had to "disintegrate into a cheap imitation of the world outside, and that setting a goal like legalizing gayness by picketing city hall or ann landers is the result of a straight myth that says that's the way to get anywhere. All it does is keep women's minds from exploring life in an original creative manner."

Lightfoot ends:

> "With such sad plagiarism among us, it becomes increasingly difficult for many of us ... to move past this idiocy and begin to build a Lesbian Nation ... a nation of mighty dykes who have discovered the worth and strength and power in each other, and who, instead of succumbing to imitations, are all off to see the wizard, goddammit."

# 41
# THE ANTI-DRAG LAW

In April 1972, the *Chicago Tribune* published an article by Robert Davis headlined, "Teacher Challenges 'Drag Law'":

> "A Chicago transvestite who works as a woman school teacher filed a federal suit yesterday challenging the city's 'drag law,' which forbids men to wear women's clothing.
>
> "Joy, or Anthony, Polley, 27, a Southwest Side resident, contends the law violates his right to privacy and also discriminates against women only in that they possess portions of the male rather than female anatomy."

Ronald J. Clark, Polley's attorney, refused to say where his client taught but said he was teaching under an assumed name and as a woman. The problems started when Polley was arrested on July 17, 1971, in a tavern at 311 E. 51$^{st}$ St. by Sgt. Sanford Neal. Polley was charged with resisting arrest, battery and a "discrepancy of sex," by wearing clothes of the opposite gender. On March 17, 1972, the case was stricken by Judge Lawrence Genesen with leave to reinstate. The suit was dropped when Polley said he wanted to fight the case on the grounds that the law was unconstitutional. According to Davis in the *Chicago Tribune*, the state's attorney's office routinely dropped drag law cases whenever the defendant brings up the constitutional question:

> "The suit states that state's attorney's office is attempting to evade a constitutional challenge, but arrests are still being made to harass transvestites.
>
> "The law is unconstitutional, the suit charges, because the city is punishing persons only because of their mode of dress.
>
> "Polley is asking the law be declared unconstitutional and the police be ordered to stop attempting to enforce it.

"Altho the law forbids members of both sexes from wearing clothing of the other sex for purpose of concealing their sex, the law is only being used to harass persons who are 'anatomically male,' Clark said."

Three months later a *Chicago Tribune* headline read, "Transvestite Suit Dismissed" ... "Federal Judge Abraham L. Marovitz yesterday dismissed a suit challenging a city ordinance forbidding a person to appear in a public place in clothing of the opposite sex. ... In dismissing the case, Judge Marovitz said it more properly belonged in Circuit Court because a city ordinance is involved."

Nothing more came of it.

On September 19, 1973, North Youth Court Judge Jack Sperling struck down the city ordinance banning a person from cross-dressing, saying it violated equal protection under the law guaranteed by the US Constitution. The case resulted from an incident in a South Side bar when four young men of Mexican descent were charged with underage drinking and wearing female attire. The drinking charge was deferred for later consideration. The arrest took place in Chicago's Pilsen neighborhood, after the four men had gone to the 10th. District Police Station to complain about being attacked in El Jalisciense, a tavern at 2200 W. 21st Place. They had gone in to buy a pack of cigarettes and the bar's customers had locked the door and beaten them. Instead of arresting the attackers, the police arrested the four young men and charged them with cross-dressing. According to the *Chicago Tribune*, Sperling noted that, "while the city could pass laws to protect the city's morals, the laws had to be 'reasonably related' to some danger. The only thing these defendants caused was laughter and derision,' Sperling said. 'They weren't even mistaken for women.'" The defendants appeared in court wearing female attire. Sperling noted the youths had caused no trouble and, underage drinking aside, were arrested solely for their choice of clothing.

The 1943 city ordinance banning the wearing of opposite gender attire "with the intent to conceal his, or her, own sex" resulted in a fine of $20 to $200. Ironically, this ordinance came at a time when women openly wore men's clothes for munitions factory work during World War II. In the July 17, 1943, *Chicago Tribune* a reader writes on the arrest of a cross-dresser:

"Chicago, July 15. – "Man arrested for his appearance on street in female garb." – Why all this fuss about one man dressed up as a woman when the streets are full of women dressed up like men? Men's clothes, men's shirts, men's hats, men's cigarets [sic], men's profanity, and men's bar room actions – what has become of our sweet, refined, delicate ladies."

Six months earlier, also in 1943, the *Chicago Tribune* hailed the arrival to the Civic Opera House of Irving Berlin's hit show *This Is the Army*, a wartime production with a cast of military personnel and a chorus line of female impersonators.

The original Chicago Anti-Transvestite Law read:

> "*Reports of the Committees* (January 25, 1943):
> January 8, 1943
>
> Amendment of Ordinance Provisions In Reference to Wearing of Apparel of Opposite Sex
>
> Section 192-8 of the Municipal Code of Chicago was amended to add the phrase "with intent to conceal his or her sex."
>
> Voting for the amendment:
>
> Yeas – Alderman Dickerson, Grant, Cohen, Smith, Olin, Lindell, Connelly, Hartnett, Hogan, Kovarik, Murphy, O'Hallaren, Duffy, Ropa, Kacena, Fischman, Bowler, Kells. Gillespie, Upton, Keane, Rostenkowski, Porten, Cowhey, Crowe, Bauler, Grealis, Meyer, Young, Hilburn, Quirk. Keenan and Quinn.
>
> Nays – None."

The 1943 law was impractical at best, absurd at worst, even more so when applied in the gender-bending 1970s. In 1973, Larry Weintraub in the *Chicago Sun-Times* took an ironic tongue-in-cheek look at the Judge Jack Sperling court case. He said the four defendants preferred to be known as Melinda Balderas, Mona Garcia, Tanya Williams and Tammie. Also, that "their faces and lips were made up with lipstick and rouge and they wore female wigs in addition to being attired in miniskirts and blouses and wearing ladies handbags":

> "Asst. Corporation Counsel Arthur Mooradian argued that the crux of the law was the prohibition of tranvestism "with the intent to deceive." He said one of the defendants was seen using the women's washroom in the tavern where they were arrested, but he also admitted there were times when the cross-dressing law did not apply e.g. Halloween costumes."

Weintraub continued:

"What the city is concerned about, he [Mooradian] said, is a person who would wear clothing of the opposite sex to get into a place for peeping or luring a victim for sexual molestation or robbery, or to get someone to agree to a sex act that he would not have had had he realized his partner was not a member of the opposite sex."

Defense lawyer, Renee Hanover, suggested modern fashions were often unisexual. It was impossible to say which garments were designed for men and which for women. "It's very difficult even on the street to tell the difference between men and women, especially for your generation and mine," Hanover told the judge:

"'Oh, I can tell,'" the judge replied with a smile.

"'From the front or from behind, sir?'" Ms. Hanover inquired.

"Sperling assured her that he could tell from any angle."

The *Chicago Sun-Times* noted, "Ms. Hanover was clad in a blouse and a knit, striped slack suit. Mooradian was attired in a striped sports jacket and slacks. The judge wore a floor length black robe."

Though not binding until the City Council repealed the ordinance, the judge's decision was bittersweet for the four cross-dressers. The day before the court hearing the home of defendant Mona Garcia was burned, the day afterwards Tanya Williams was fired from her job. The following day Melinda Balderos was evicted from her apartment, with no recourse to the law. All this resulted from trying to buy a pack of cigarettes.

The problem of Chicago's unresolved anti-drag law surfaced again on September 14, 1974, when two more trans-persons were convicted of "wearing the clothes of another sex with intent to conceal their own sex." The law still hung in legal limbo after Cook Judge Jack I. Sperling ruled it unconstitutional. City lawyers refused to appeal his decision, and other Cook County judges were still intent on upholding the law. In this latest case, Judge David Shields handed down a guilty verdict to Kim Kimberley and Wallace Wilson. The *Chicago Gay Crusader* reported that the two were arrested on February 17, 1974, at Mammy's Pancake House, 20 E. Randolph St. after seeing a matinee of *The Exorcist*. They were picked up by police officers Anthony LoBue and Marc Davilo, the most vicious and homophobic double-act in the Chicago police force. In court, Davilo testified that he knew Kimberley and Wilson were men, and that after their arrest, the defendants were photographed naked to determine their gender – these pictures were never produced in court. The city was represented by Assistant Corporation Counsel Arthur Mooradian, who the previous year had prosecuted the case where Judge Sperling ruled the law unconstitutional. Mooradian had argued then that the "crux of the law was the prohibition of tranvestism 'with the intent to deceive.'" The question now was, had Kimberley and Wilson intended to deceive?

Defense counsel Dan Swartzman, a senior law student, and Mark Schoenfield, a lawyer, both from Northwestern University Legal Assistance Clinic, argued the city had failed to prove its case by not showing probable cause, by not clearly defining what did/or did not constitute "female clothing," or whether the defendants were wearing it. It was difficult defining "female clothing" in the long hair unisex world of 1974. When arrested, Wilson was wearing palazzo trousers and Kimberly a skirt.

Wilson claimed to be a transsexual, defining that as "a person with the mind of a female but the body of a male." She said she was wearing those particular clothes "because I had to see how the world would accept me as a female." Wilson was in transsexual counseling at Cook County hospital, in preparation for "sex change" surgery. Swartzman tried to highlight the nebulous nature of modern dress styles by pointing out Wilson's attire in court, which consisted of a pants suit.

Judge Shields was unsympathetic, saying, "You might as well describe what the officer has on, too." Swartzman did so, pointing out that Davilo was wearing "slightly flared" trousers. At that point, Mooradian lost his patience and burst out, "Let the record reflect, officer, that you haven't got your balls and penis strapped on." This was an oblique reference to earlier testimony that the defendants wore brassieres when arrested.

Kim Kimberley and Wallace Wilson were both fined $100 and $5 costs. They were given until October 24 to file their formal notice of appeal.

After Judge Sperling ruled the law unconstitutional in 1973, it was finally repealed and appears in *Reports of the Committees* (January 17, 1978).

> "Section 192 of Municipal Code Amended Concerning Public Morals
>
> Yeas – Alderman Roti, Kenner, Sawyer, Wilinski, Humes, Adduci, Vrdolyak, Huels, Kwak, Madrzyk, Burke, Barden, Shannon, Kellam, Joyce, Stewart, Lipinski, Rhodes, Marzullo, Zydlo, Ray, Washington, Cross, Hagopian, Keane, Gabinski, Mell, Frost, Laskowski, Aiello, Casey, Gutstein, Schulter, Saperstein, Stone.
>
> Nays – Alderman Barnett, Lathrop, Natarus, Oberman, Simpson."

The amended ordinance reads:

# CHICAGO AFTER STONEWALL

"Be It Ordained by the City Council of the City of Chicago:

Section 1. The Municipal Code of the City of Chicago, Chapter 192, Section 192-8 is hereby amended by deleting the language in brackets below and adding the language in Italics as follows:

192-8. Any person who shall appear, [in a public place in a state of nudity], bathe, sunbathe, walk or be in any public park, playground, beach or the waters adjacent thereto, or any school facility and the area adjacent to, or any municipal building and the areas adjacent thereto, or any public way within the City of Chicago in such a manner that the genitals, vulva, pubic, pubic hair, buttocks, perineum, anus, anal region, or pubic hair region of any person, or any portion of the breast at or below the upper edge of the areola thereof of any female person, is exposed to public view or is not covered by an opaque covering, [or is in a dress not belonging to his or her sex, with the intent to conceal his or her sex, or in an indecent or lewd dress, or who shall make indecent exposure of his or her person] shall be fined not less than twenty dollars nor more than two hundred dollars for each offense.

Section 2. This ordinance shall be in full force and effect from and after its passage."

Officers Mark Davilo and Anthony LoBue were notorious in the gay community. In February 1969, the *Mattachine Midwest Newsletter* printed their names under the headline, "BEWARE: Enticement":

"Mark Davilo, tall with a plaid checked jacket and a goatee, is enticing homosexuals at the Monroe Theater and the Palmer House. Anthony LoBue (Tony the Bull) has been given the Prudential Building for his assignment ... but he works the first-floor men's room by Stouffer's. He apparently 'acts' like a homosexual, giving the impression he wants to perform. He gets his prey to make the first move, money comes into the picture and so does an arrest."

Seven years later, Officer LoBue was still working the men's restrooms. On July 25, 1976, he was featured in a *Chicago Tribune* article headlined, "'Vice Versa' Squad Fights Male Hookers." Police officials estimated 5-10 percent of their prostitution arrests were male and LoBue, a tactical officer with the Central District, wearing "a T-shirt and pants, both tight fitting" was the bait. He and his partner had just raided a Loop movie theater after skulking in the basement restrooms. Fifteen men and one woman were arrested as "inmates of a disorderly house":

"The 'house' was the Monroe Theater, 57 W. Monroe St., where LoBue said he observed homosexual sex acts throughout the theater, and all he had to do was loiter in the washroom to be mistaken for a prostitute. 'A man tried to solicit me to perform a sexual act for $15,' LoBue said. 'While my partner detained several men in the washroom, I went to the ticket taker and complained, as a citizen, about what was going on. He shrugged and said, 'So?' LoBue arrested the ticket taker as 'keeper.'"

LoBue told the paper, "I've arrested thousands of guys for indecency or prostitution charges, and 90 percent of them are married men with families. They haven't come out in the open. They go to these washrooms, looking for a brief encounter. No introductions. He doesn't want to know the guy he solicits."

Lt. George Bicek, head of the vice control division prostitution section, said, "Homosexual prostitution has been present here for a long time. Homosexuals have come out of the closet these days, and male prostitutes are more visible. But I still believe most male prostitutes we arrest are female impersonators."

In September 1974, a headline in *The Argus*, a newspaper out of Moline, IL, read, "Impersonator is jailed for prostitution":

"A 32-year-old man, dressed as a female, was sentenced to 10 days in county jail in Rock Island Division of Circuit Court today on a charge of prostitution.

"Ronald K. Parr, 1809 9 ½ St., Rock Island, was arrested on the charge early this morning in a downtown Rock Island hotel room after he allegedly propositioned a man in a nearby night club."

Police said that Parr was with another man, also dressed as a female. They left the Mardi Gras Night Club and went to the hotel – "a man followed several steps behind the pair." ... "Police stated they found one of the female impersonators in one room and Parr and the man in another room of the hotel. The second impersonator was released on police authority."

# 42
# GAYS FOSTERING TEENS

Another contentious issue was gay couples fostering children. In the May 7, 1974, *New York Times*, an article by Lucinda Franks summed up the problem. It began:

> "In a new and informal experiment, homeless adolescent boys who describe themselves as homosexuals and who are unwanted by or unable to adjust to youth homes, have been placed under the foster care of adult homosexuals.
>
> "Some psychotherapists call the program, which is sponsored by the National Gay Task Force, 'a spectacular advance' in understanding homosexuality as a sexual preference rather than a disease.
>
> "Other doctors and child-welfare experts, however, say the program is fraught with danger, open to legal challenges by the state and the children's parents, and could start of a deleterious social trend."

A year earlier, *Chicago Today* published an article by Warren Shore and Dianne Banis suggesting the Illinois Department of Children and Family Services (DFCS) were considering placing gay teens "in a home with two male or two female 'parents.'" In an exclusive interview, DCFS Director Dr. Jerome Miller told the paper:

> "I want to emphasize that such a placement plan would be used only as a last alternative – when all other placement efforts have failed.
>
> "I believe that the social pressure exerted on a youngster that we label as a homosexual, by virtue of such a placement, would be too great to risk unless we are quite sure of a lifelong pattern of such behavior.
>
> "This is far from an ideal situation ... and not one which I endorse personally. As far as I know, there are no homosexual households now

approved for placement. What arrangements already have been made have probably been handled informally with specific directive."

Thomas Jeffers, DCFS administrator and assistant to Miller, added, "Of the few such placement plans that have come to my attention, I have said only that if the caseworker and supervisor find this (a homosexual household) to be a viable solution, then the state can live with it. That is, we will back them up."

Apparently, at the time, the only submissions to place teens with gay parents came from the DCFS's Northern District Office. The director, Tom Kmetko, told the paper, "I don't have to tell you that this is a situation full of problems. But so is the plight of the young homosexual who is virtually barred from a normal placement situation and has been the object of scorn all his life."

Kmetko said the agency's lawyers found no legal obstacle to gays fostering children. However, one problem was finding gay couples willing to go public about their homosexuality, which would happen if they registered as foster parents.

A few days later, a follow-up piece in *Chicago Today* claimed that after the first article was published, DCFS Director Miller issued a ban on gays fostering. His directive stated, "No child under the care of the Department of Children and Family Services will be placed in the home of known homosexuals. We can conceive of no circumstances in which this would be in the best interests of any minor."

This statement was repeated two days later in the *Chicago Defender* under the headline "No sissies."

Miller told *Chicago Today*, "There has never been any plan for homosexual placement under consideration at any time. Your story created a false impression."

Miller's directive proved controversial within DCFS, with one anonymous social worker telling the paper, "The new policy is designed more to take the heat off the director than it is to help us put children in stable homes. It seems to make homosexuality a crime."

Miller's claim that there had been no plan to place gay teens in gay homes was false. In fact, he himself was quoted as saying that in the last four months social workers had approached several gay couples enquiring if they were willing to become foster parents.

Another DCFS social worker told *Chicago Today*:

"I have approached several stable, professional homosexual households since the first of the year. I had been led to believe that this was an acceptable solution for the child who had failed in previous placements because of his homosexual behavior. Now, I guess the heat has gotten to Miller on this issue. Still, I don't think this kills the program. It certainly wouldn't be the first time we had one policy for the public's consumption and one for our own use."

Chicago attorney Paul R. Goldman, author of the *Chicago Gay Crusader* column "The Law and the Homosexual," announced plans to sue the department for discrimination. "The ruling is an obvious slur," he told *Chicago Today*, "It says no matter how stable or loving or willing a particular household is, the mere fact of homosexuality would act as a complete bar to status as a foster parent."

The Illinois Foster Parents' Association (IFPA) also opposed the ruling. IFPA president Larry Levine said:

"The confirmed homosexual teenager faces insurmountable problems when it comes to placement opportunities. He almost always fails in heterosexual households.

"The homosexual foster parent can not only offer this youngster an understanding environment but can himself get a sense of contributing to his community which our society rarely allows."

Not everyone agreed. Local Jungian analyst Dr. June Singer said, "The possibilities for outright disaster are much too great. Even if we could accurately determine, at age 14 or 15, who are the confirmed lifelong homosexuals, we have no right to place these children in situations which could be exploitative to them."

Evanston psychiatrist Dr. Kenneth Denenberg disagreed:

"Where a person, even as young as 15, has been having consistently homosexual fantasies for five years, it is fairly safe to conclude that he has chosen his lifestyle.

"Since the practice of psychiatry offers these people no real alternative, why not at least provide a home life that substitutes understanding for rejection."

"The homosexual household which has remained stable for 10 years or so says a lot for the ability of its members to deal with difficult problems. They should be given a chance."

In the August 1973 *Chicago Gay Crusader*, William B. Kelley writes that according to "department sources," Miller's "directive" was more a press statement than a formal policy decision that DCFS had no firm ruling either way on gay teens in gay homes. Kelley also refers to a burgeoning scandal about emotionally disturbed Illinois children being placed in substandard, often unlicensed, Texas institutions. Although not mentioned in the mainstream press, many of these troubled youngsters were gay. It involved hundreds of Illinois wards of court sent to private institutions in Texas where they were abused. One thirteen-year-old black girl was given a hysterectomy at the Meridell Achievement Center in Austin without her father's, or her own, consent. In the *Chicago Tribune,* an article by Peter Gorner asks, "Are the Illinois Department of Children and Family Services and its controversial new director, Dr. Jerome Miller, doing a good job of caring for the 28,000 dependent and neglected children in their custody?"

Clearly, Miller and the DCFS had more on their plate than the question of gay foster parents.

In July 1974, in the *Dixon Evening Telegraph,* in Joanne and Lew Koch's column, "Family Lib," Lew writes about gays and fostering:

> "In a previous column I stated my opposition to lesbian mothers being allowed to have custody of their children.
>
> "I based that opposition on the idea that a young child should not be forced into a homosexual home environment purely on the basis of a parent's choice.
>
> "But an issue of even more subtle distinction has arisen; should young boys who describe themselves as homosexuals be placed in the care of homosexual foster parents?"

Koch agrees that "young boys who believe they are homosexuals are rejected by their families and treated like criminals by a heterosexual society," and that "heterosexual foster parents and youth shelter programs reject and abuse these youths":

> "At first glance, the idea [of gays fostering] appears to have merit. But on closer inspection, the concept is actually counter-productive to the needs of both the boy and society.
>
> "First, society should not be prepared to accept the sexual judgements of a 12-year-old boy as something final and irreversible. A 15-year-old car thief may brag that he is a gang leader and a hardened criminal, but society does not place him in the same environment with truly hardened adult criminals."

Koch ends his argument with:

"I have read the confessions, the demands, the manifestos of the homosexual community and I am not unsympathetic to the humiliation they have suffered. They call upon others to 'come out of the closets' and admit they're homosexuality so that the pain and isolation can be shared and perhaps lessened. But the unrelenting theme which runs through these writings is the incredible sadness and loneliness they feel.

"To acquiesce, in fact, even to aid a young boy in choosing this path is unwittingly to condemn him to a sexual lifestyle which will be filled with the same sadness and loneliness."

# 43
# THE HOUSTON MURDERS

On August 10, the *Chicago Tribune* reported the arrest of two Houston youths. They, along with "a homosexual friend," had tortured and murdered at least 28 teens over the course of three years. Those accused were eighteen-year-old David Owen Brooks, who had a pregnant wife, seventeen-year-old junior high school dropout Elmer Wayne Henley, and their "homosexual friend," thirty-three-year-old Dean Allen Corll. The murders came to light after Henley fatally shot Corll at a paint-sniffing sex party and called the police. Henley admitted to the killing, and then confessed that he and Brooks helped Corll in his murder spree. Henley lead police to Corll's rented boat shed in Houston where they had buried the bodies, then to two other gravesites in Texas.

Three days later, a *Chicago Tribune* editorial read:

"First, how is it possible that with a death toll that may reach 30 the Houston police did not track down the murderer and apparently did not even deduce that this homosexual murder machine existed?

"Police files everywhere, including Chicago, are bulging with the names and photographs of runaways and with the pleas of anguished parents that something be done – they can't suggest precisely what. How many of these may have met with foul play?"

The irony of that question became clear years later when on December 21, 1978, Chicago serial killer John Wayne Gacy was arrested and charged with killing 33 young men. His first admitted murder was of fifteen-year-old Timothy Jack McCoy on January 2, 1972, over a year before the Houston killings came to light. When the above *Chicago Tribune* editorial was published, McCoy was already cold under a concrete slab in Gacy's crawl space. As the story of the Houston murders unfolded, the details of the heinous crime turned ever more grisly. Inflammatory phrases appeared daily in the press. Whereas Richard Speck murdering eight student nurses in Chicago on July 14, 1966, was not described as a "heterosexual" mass murder, the *Chicago Tribune* wrote about "a homosexual ring that preyed on young boys" and a "homosexual murder ring."

Under the headline "'GAY' ANGLE IN HOUSTON MURDER STORY EXPLOITED," the *Chicago Gay Crusader* charted the progression of the "homosexual angle" press references on the day the story broke. The first AP and UPI reports referred to the killings as being the work of "sex perverts." Later in the day, reports referred to Dean Corll as "homosexual." In a noon broadcast, the "fine arts" radio station WFMT used the phrase "homosexual procurement ring." That evening Chicago TV coverage downplayed the "homosexual" angle, making reference to "sex torture deaths." Chicago Gay Alliance vice-president William B. Kelley contacted WFMT program director Norman Pellegrini, who defended the use of the term "homosexual procurement ring." He told Kelley, "You've seen how the story has been developing – it's clear that this particular murder case does involve homosexuality." Kelley pointed out the charges against Corll "were not inherently the product of homosexuality." Pellegrini answered, "I would think the day had long passed when it would be necessary to say, 'These murders involved homosexuality, but, of course, not all homosexuals are murderers,' especially considering WFMT's audience." Their audience were the artsy, folkie, jazz, classical music crowd. However, the *Chicago Gay Crusader* noted that in a broadcast later that night all reference to "homosexuality" was dropped.

In the *Chicago Tribune* a letter to the editor from lawyer Paul R. Goldman reads:

> "In my more than 44 years of legal practice, I have represented a substantial number of the homosexual community in both civil and criminal matters. All of the homosexuals I know are shaken by the unprecedented Texas murders and condemn the occurrences as perpetrated by madmen.
>
> "In no way can one equate homosexuality per se with sadism or masochism. It is hoped that the public will not generalize and equate homosexuality with homicidal psychosis; this is without basis."

While some activists winced and feared the Houston murders would set back gay rights for years, others confronted the slanders head-on. In the September *Chicago Gay Crusader,* the Chicago Gay Alliance (CGA) with the

National News Council (NNC), a recently formed watchdog organization for investigating news media bias, drafted a complaint. It concerned an August 15 commentary by Jeffrey St. John, which aired on the CBS Radio Network as part of its *Spectrum* series; the program later became the *Point/Counterpoint* feature on the TV network's *60 Minutes*.

Among St. John's statements were:

> "One cannot regard it as a coincidence that the Houston murders began at the time the gay militants took to the streets in 1970.
>
> "What the gay liberation groups want is to legitimize a revolt from male biology and reality itself."
>
> "We seem to have forgotten that it was the Nazi SA gangs, many of them sadistic homosexuals, who brought Hitler to power."

The CGA/NNC joint complaint read, "Air time seemingly is too precious to admit of anything more than superficial, oversimplified news coverage of the sexual factors involved in the murders, yet it then appears to become ample enough to allow 'commentaries' like St. John's capitalizing upon those factors to be broadcast." Although "commentary" didn't fall under the jurisdiction of the NNC, CGA wanted to emphasize that St. John's remarks made the already biased CBS news coverage even worse. Though CBS were not legally bound to provide rebuttal time, Murray Kempton, another *Spectrum* commentator, did a counter-commentary on August 25, but only after cajoling from New York's Gay Activist Alliance.

The *Chicago Gay Crusader* also notes that on the day the story broke, CGA called upon Associated Press (AP) and United Press International (UPI) to avoid "prejudicial terminology" when covering the Houston story. Only UPI editor and vice president H.L. Stevenson replied, "I agree with you about the dangers of oversimplification in news coverage. We are constantly vigilant in this area. Thank you for conveying your thoughts."

## 44
# GAY ANTHROPOLOGISTS AND "HOMOPHOBIA"

In the week of September 1–8, 1973, Chicago hosted the 9th International Congress of Anthropological and Ethnological Sciences at the Conrad Hilton Hotel, attended by 3,000 scientists from 100 countries. The theme was "Many Species, Many Cultures." Chairing the Congress was Dr. Margaret Mead, a closeted bisexual, who once shared a romantic relationship with anthropologist, folklorist and author Ruth Benedict. In August 1973, the *Chicago Tribune* wrote that 2,000 scientific papers were submitted for consideration dealing with topics ranging from blood-typing Peruvian mummies, the roots of the Ku Klux Klan, and Ojibwa cannibalism. The "situation and plight of gay anthropologists" was not on the agenda, but Chicago GLF founding member, Henry Weimhoff, made a statement on the matter at a Congress meeting. In October 1973, the *Chicago Gay Crusader* reported that Weimhoff's plea for tolerance received "a mixed and not-too-satisfying reception."

Weimhoff took another route. He placed a notice in the Congress's daily bulletin announcing a meeting for gay delegates. Many turned up, including one from South America and others from Western and Eastern Europe. On a later "field trip" to the gay bars, the Eastern Europeans were surprised to see same-sex dancing at the Bistro disco and, at the Baton, were "fascinated" by the drag show, something they had never seen behind the "Iron Curtain."

The Gay Anthropologists' first action was to issue the draft of a Position Statement, defining its goals and outlining ways to raise their profile within the anthropological profession. The Statement begins, "Anthropology, in spite of its broad tradition of scientific humanism, is permeated by Western societies attitudes of homophobia, that is, the fear, anxiety, and antipathy occasioned by homosexuality." The term "homophobia" was fairly new. Coined by George Weinberg, a New York psychotherapist and author, it first appeared in an article in porn magazine *Screw*. It was used by Weinberg's friends, gay activists Jack Nichols and Lige Clarke, who wrote a weekly gay column in *Screw* called, "He-Man Horse Shit." Nichols and Clarke used the word "homophobia" to refer to heterosexuals' fears that others might think they are homosexual. The column suggests men's "homophobia" excluded them from "sissified" things like poetry, art, dance and touching. Prior to "homophobia," the word "Homoerotophobia" was used briefly, coined by Wainwright Churchill in his 1967 book *Homosexual Behavior Among Males*. The word "homophobia" entered the mainstream when Clarence Petersen reviewed Weinberg's book *Society and the Healthy Homosexual* in the *Chicago Tribune*. In the review, headlined "Homophobia: fear and self-loathing on the sexual trail," Petersen defines "homophobia":

> "Homophobia is the dread of close contact with homosexuals or, when it afflicts homosexuals themselves, self loathing. There is no rational basis for it, but it is epidemic, especially among heterosexual men, some of whom are put to no end of trouble asserting their masculinity lest anyone, including them selves, suspect their fears.
>
> "Homophobia is what encourages the use of such terms as 'faggot' and 'fairy' among otherwise fair-minded men who would never speak of 'niggers' or 'kikes.' And the racial comparison is apt. Just as white society taught blacks to despise themselves, many homosexuals have been taught self-loathing and fear, certainly fear of discovery."

# 45
# TRANS-ISSUES AND "GENDER-BENDING"

In December 1969, in "The Worry Clinic," a syndicated column by Dr. George W. Crane attempted to explain "transvestites" to a wife with a "problem husband." The wife says:

> "'Dr. Crane, my husband seems to have an uncontrollable desire to dress in women's clothing. I was shocked the first time it occurred, for I was to be away from home all day but arrived earlier than I had expected.
>
> "And there was my husband, arrayed in my lingerie and dress and even painting his fingernails. He was embarrassed and tried to pass it off as a prank.'"

Dr. Crane answered:

> "Such males are not necessarily effeminate or homosexuals, for they often abhor erotic contacts with their own sex. ... But their yen to dress up in women's garb is much like the chronic alcoholic's desire to consume whiskey.
>
> "They often try to explain their compulsion by saying they crave the feel of silks and satins against their skin.
>
> "But that is not the correct explanation, for they could easily acquire men's shirts, pajamas and underwear made out of silk and get the same tactual feel, without adopting feminine lingerie!
>
> "... The explanation usually goes far back into childhood."

Dr. Crane goes on to compare transvestism to "a man's delight in the dinner table viands that his mother cooked":

> "For our gastric appetite at the table is usually determined largely by what our mothers fed us from the time we sat in our high-chair at the family table.
>
> "Infants can thus be 'conditioned' or brainwashed emotionally not only regarding food tastes, music, perfumes and religion, but also to their mother's clothing.
>
> "A transvestite thus has been 'marked' by his mother, albeit without her realizing that fact.
>
> "For when she held him to her breast, he subconsciously became 'conditioned' to the silky feel of her slip and other soft fabrics.
>
> "A transvestite's desire to put on feminine clothing thus is an indirect evidence of his desire to flee back to mamma and thus escape from the problems, tensions and responsibilities of the adult male world.
>
> " ... Some men flee from their adult duties via alcohol and dope. Others become rolling stones.
>
> "Another group escape via insanity or even by suicide. So tranvestism is merely a first cousin to these other escape mechanisms."

In February 1971, Terri Schultz in her "Our Town" column in the *Chicago Tribune* wrote about "Virginia Prince":

> "Virginia's real name is Charles. Despite his masculine legs, he wears women's dresses, nylons and heels. He also sports bright red lipstick with matching nail polish, a touch of eye makeup and pearl-trimmed glasses.
>
> "When we first met, he had just had his hair done at Marshall Field & Company.
>
> "Virginia Prince is a transvestite – a man who dresses in women's clothing."

Schultz writes that Prince, who had been married twice to women and treated by six psychiatrists, considered himself "to be a byproduct of a sick society." Prince explains:

> "'The natural femininity in a man has always been suppressed in this culture. I call it the 'pink-and-blue blanket syndrome.' We are taught masculine and feminine roles. A man cannot cry or be gentle or be graceful. He has a contract with society. He can be superior provided he never becomes feminine,' he [Prince] says as he delicately crosses his legs. For our chat, he wore a red pants suit with pale pink scarf."

Prince earned a doctorate in biochemistry from the University of California at Berkeley and for 18 years was president of a chemical manufacturing company in Los Angeles. Schultz writes that, "Today his greatest pleasure is keeping his kitchen clean." Prince insists he is not a homosexual, "We transvestites like females sexually. We also like to dress like them. If a man tries to flirt with me, that's his problem, not mine":

> "'Lack of paternal affection was one reason I became a transvestite. I could never get affection from my dad like my sister did. All I got was a handshake and a pat on the back. By the age of 18, I was dressing up in my mother's clothes. My guilt was overwhelming. ... When my wife found out, the whole thing was dragged thru the newspapers. I figured since I lost everything already, I might as well come out in the open and try to help others.'"

Prince was visiting Chicago to publicize her Foundation for Full Personality Expression and her book *The Transvestite and His Wife*. Prince also published a magazine, *Transvestia* – a magazine published bi-monthly from 1960 to 1980. Prince died in Los Angeles on May 2, 2009.

In August 1972, a column appeared in the *Elk Grove Herald*, entitled "Electric Shoek [sic] Used In Behavioral Therapy." The column was presented by "Forest Hospital in Des Plaines." It begins, "A transvestite is a person – usually male – who compulsively engages in dressing up as a woman yet usually feels humiliated and demeaned by this experience which he is unable to control."

The article goes on to quote Dr. Lee Birk of the Massachusetts Mental Health Center in Boston:

> "One patient I treated several years ago with this problem was so ashamed of his behavior he made heroic attempts to rid himself of it.
>
> "Although he didn't have very much money he'd go out and spend $75 to $90 for an outfit of women's clothes which he'd dress up in. Afterward he'd be so revulsed with what he'd done that he would throw away or burn what he bought and then like an addict looking for his next fix in a few days he'd have to find the money to buy a new outfit. All this is terribly destructive to his own sense of self and self-esteem."

Dr. Birk explained his "cure":

> "We brought him into our laboratory ... with all his outfits. We were in an adjacent room with a one-way mirror and we got him to engage in the same behavior he wanted to get rid of. At different crucial sequences he'd get one or two seconds of shock and after a while – that is 10 to 12 sessions – this habit was brought under control. He was no longer under the mercy of the habit and his self-esteem was helped considerably."

The November 1973 issue of the *Chicago Gay Crusader* was the "James Clay Memorial Issue," dedicated to Chicago's trans-community. An editorial begins:

> "Three years ago, on Thanksgiving, the Chicago Police department showed us what we had to be thankful for. James Clay, a black transvestite, was shot dead by Officers James Finnelly and Thomas Bowling, two of Mayor Daley's finest.
>
> "Transvestites are the most upfront part of our community. Some police take out on transvestites their hatred for those of us they can't reach so easily. James Clay was one such victim."

The editorial retells the story of James Clay, an unarmed man who ran from the police and was shot down in a hail of bullets (See Chapter 7). In the same issue of *Chicago Gay Crusader*, another cross-dresser, this one female to male, was shot dead by police, under vastly different circumstances. The cop was returning fire. The victim was 31-year-old Joanne Popiwchak, a legal secretary and divorced mother of two sons, who accused John Staley, a bartender at the Baton drag bar, of short-changing her. She was described as wearing men's clothing – a denim jacket, jeans and a flowered shirt. On October 23, Popiwchak left the bar, returned several hours later and shot the now off-duty bartender in the lower back, saying, "You won't do that again." Popiwchak ran from the bar pursued by six customers. Patrolman Robert Murphy, standing nearby, joined the chase. Catching up to her, Murphy told her to drop the weapon. Instead, Popiwchak pointed her gun at him and fired. Murphy fired back, and Popiwchak fell dead in the doorway at 505 N. LaSalle St. As she carried no ID, Chicago Lesbian Liberation (CLL) were asked to identify the body, on the assumption she was a lesbian. No one knew her, but CLL members noticed Popiwchak had scars on her wrists from previous suicide attempts. John Staley, the bartender, made a full recovery.

Her death notice in the *Chicago Tribune* reads:

> "POPIWCHAK
>
> "Joanne Popichak, nee Litwitz, loving mother of Chris and Scott; beloved daughter of Duke and Justine; dear granddaughter of Emily Litwitz; fond sister of Sandra Singer. Funeral Wednesday, 9:30 a.m., 4117 W. Armitage Av., to St. Philomena Church. Mass 10 a.m. Interment Maryhill Cemetery. Visitation Monday after 7 p.m."

Trans-issues and "gender-bending" were hot topics in the fall of 1973. The *Chicago Tribune* published a report by Science Editor, Ronald Kotulak, headlined, "Surgeon claims 95-98% success rate in sex change." Given the paper's squeamishness on the subject of sexual variants, the piece is surprisingly sympathetic on the subject of "females entrapped in a male's body," and their psychological turmoil. Dr. Robert C. Granato, a urologist at New York's Columbia University Medical School, gave a speech at the 59th annual Clinical Convention of the American College of Surgeons at Chicago's McCormick Place. He had performed 118 operations to "convert male sex organs into vaginas." In his speech, Granato explained how patients must be thoroughly evaluated by psychiatrists to identify and weed-out transvestites – those who merely wish to dress as women – and homosexuals – men who want to stay male but prefer relations with men. Granato goes on to say that some "sex changes" have taken place in Chicago, "More than 500 of these sex change operations have been performed in this country at about 12 medical centers, including Cook County Hospital."

Granato adds that transforming females into males has not, so far, been successful.

Popular culture was also embracing trans-images. A year earlier, gender-bender glam rocker David Bowie arrived in Chicago with his Ziggy Stardust persona and played the Auditorium Theater. November 16, 1973, marked his US TV debut. The *Chicago Tribune* in "ROUNDUP television" wrote:

> "Britain's David Bowie is considered a conglomerate superstar in rock music.
> 
> "Bowie, who flashes across the concert stage in glittering jump suits and satin gowns, will headline next Friday's *Midnight Special* on WOC-TV.
> 
> "... Bowie is noted for his stage appearance in a tight shiny jump suit, high boots and much facial makeup. He piles on the mascara until his eyes seem to sink into his head; lipstick enhances his thin lips, and his dyed hair sticks out like straw. He more often resembles a character from the defunct television series, Munsters. This is what makes glit (glitter) rock or glam (glamour) rock!"

Rock musician Alice Cooper launched his own mascara brand called "Whiplash." The ads read, "Whiplash Mascara WHIP YOUR EYES INTO SHAPE" and "Liberate your eyes with Alice's own unisex mascara." But nobody, not even the most cynical Cassandra of Middle-American values could foresee the trashy-drag of the New York Dolls cutting a swathe through the archetypal Adam and Eve gender roles. One Doll told an interviewer, "People have the wrong idea about us. They think we're a bunch of transsexual junkies or something." In September 1973 the *Chicago Tribune* wrote, "New

York Dolls prance into the Corporation in Elmhurst Friday for two nights of rock and rouge style rock 'n roll." That show was canceled, but the Dolls finally arrived in October to play with Mott the Hoople. In the *Chicago Tribune*, Lynn Van Matre wrote, "It can't be easy for David Johansen, lead singer and limp-wristed twitchy twerp, to find high heeled pumps to fit his male-sized feet. And to stand pigeon-toed and knock-kneed on stage, singing and swishing away, while the band plays abominably behind him – that takes real talent." Two days later, Aaron Gold wrote in the paper's "Tower Ticker" column that the New York Dolls "all-male glitter band" had dinner at the Pinnacle Restaurant in the Lake Shore Drive Holiday Inn and, "The patrons weren't ready for men in hot pants, satin pedal-pushers, teased hair and heavy make-up." Bruce Vilanch, in *Chicago Today,* interviewed Johansen about a recent arrest:

> "You know, they were waiting for us in Memphis. They heard we were all drag queens and that is illegal, apparently. So we played a very quiet set. At the end, this boy jumped on stage and kissed me and five cops dragged him down and started beating on him. So I told them to stop and Johnny Thunder broke his guitar in protest. That's when they shut us down and arrested me for rioting. I blew kisses as they dragged me off stage."

Another cultural phenomenon that kicked down the door of traditional gender roles was *The Rocky Horror Show*, the British comedy stage musical, that opened in London on June 19, 1973, and was an instant hit. The movie *The Rocky Horror Picture Show* followed two years later. It became *de rigueur* for young males in some of Chicago's clubs to wear lipstick and eye shadow. The first glimpse Chicagoans got into the strange sci-fi "sweet transvestite" world of *The Rocky Horror Show* was in the January 24, 1974, *Chicago Tribune* when Rex Reed reviewed the London production:

> "The show is a horror, all right, but any resemblance between this trash and anything resembling talent, freshness, and originality is purely coincidental. As you enter the gloomy theater, a hackneyed plot arises from the grave like a corpse: two kids have a flat tire on a stormy night. Following a lonely road, they reach a nearby castle for help. The inhabitants pour forth like a toilet in need of repair. An evil villain lurks over the couple in the form of a tattooed drag queen in Cuban heels, fox furs, and a leather jockstrap, singing 'I'm Just a Sweet Transvestite Transsexual Transylvanian.' There are assorted delivery boys frozen in refrigerators, tap-dancing Lesbian maids, a hunchback, a naked Frankenstein monster beach boy, electronic gadgets called 'sonic transducers,' deaths by laser beam, and simulated nudity and sex that is enough to make you gag. The rock score is beneath contempt, the acting is a disgrace, and the entire evening gave me a headache for which suicide

seemed the only possible relief. Wiping the whole rotten experience out of your mind forever, seems, on second thought, a safer solution."

Glitter rock, glam and *The Rocky Horror Show* gave the young trans-inclined male an excuse to cross-dress without the stigma of being labeled "homosexual." It was just a rock 'n' roll fashion, fun and harmless. However, the more male-to-female drag came out of the closet, the more some lesbians and feminists objected to it. In her *Chicago Gay Crusader* column "Lesbian Lore" Margaret Wilson commented on an upcoming Miss Gay Chicago contest at the Baton. She writes:

> "The Miss America contest has been used for many years to oppress Women and as such has been open to much scrutiny by the Women's Liberation Movement. This Miss Gay Chicago contest can be, and should be, subjected to the same objections.
>
> "... The contest being talked about by our Gay brothers (a contest where drag queens will compete for the title of Miss Gay Chicago) is solely a beauty contest and is just another form of the oppression that keeps alive the stereotypes that a Woman lives with every day.
>
> "There is a somewhat valid argument that a man has the right to dress and act as he pleases. I believe that this is true on an individual level, but as a Woman and as a Gay person I see many similarities between our struggle and that of the Black Liberation Movement. Not too many years ago, it was argued that an artist had the right to blacken his/her face and play the stereotype of a 'nigger' on stage, but few would stand for this in our 'enlightened' age."

Wilson goes on to say she hopes her "Gay brothers" will reconsider and, if not, that women boycott the contest and "use any methods necessary to protest its being held."

Trans-persons were not always welcome in gay bars either. In July 1974, a letter appeared in the *Chicago Gay Crusader*:

> "Dear Sirs:
>
> "My name is Jane Fitzgerald. I am a male transvestite or transsexual. Sometimes I am gay. I love to be in the gay community. I do not go out dressed very often. I do go to most of the gay bars and clubs dressed with men's clothes on, except sometimes I wear a blouse and feminine underwear. I do not go out to entice or tease. I go out to make new friends or visit others. ... We used to go to David's Place a lot, two or three times a week. I felt bad because they closed. It was one of the nicest places in Chicago where people like me could go 'dressed if I so wished' and no one

ever bothered us. ... Since David's, however, my TV friend and I have been searching for another nice place to go dressed.

"We started to go to the 'Le Pub' near Old Town. It seemed like a straight neighborhood but a nice gay bar. I enjoyed many nights there. We danced, met people and just relaxed. For, you see, people like me are also outcasts from society and find solace and peace of mind where people don't care what you are. So I asked a waiter one evening if we could come in drag or dressed in women's clothes. He went away and came back saying yes. We – my friend and I – were looking forward to Gay Pride Week.

"So, June 29, a Saturday night, friend and I prepared to go to the 'Le Pub.' It took about two hours to get ready. I wore my best dress and wig, applied my makeup carefully. In short, we wanted to look our best, but not overly done.

"Now, parking a car in that area is tough. We finally parked two and a half blocks away. So the three of us – two dressed and one not – started walking to 'Le Pub.' I was hoping the police would not bother me, because I am tall and therefore would be noticed.

"Well, we made it to the door. What relief, a joy of excitement. Also, knowing this is our week and tomorrow the big parade. But ... a doorman told us we were not welcome.

"I felt lower than a rug. Everyone was looking as we tried to explain we are gay and not straight, that we come here often. I'm afraid I was in tears and felt as though it was the end for Jane. Nowhere to go. Even the gay people I love rejected me.

"I kept saying to my friends on the way back home, I can't believe it, especially during Gay Pride Week.

"Once my friends and I were guests of the Gay Liberation Front at an out-of-State University. They paid all the expenses, treated us very nice. Met many new friends, helped some people with problems like ours, as we had a workshop and many people attended.

"We felt so good about going. We were very happy. Now, this bad situation that happened Saturday evening. Why can't one group and another get along? We are not bad. We are all God's children. We do not fit in the straight world."

In the *Chicago Daily News* in March 1974, reporter Sandra Pesmen spent a day at "Chicago's only sex-change clinic," the Fantus Health Center at Cook County Hospital. She sat in on a pre surgical and postsurgical group session, reputedly the first of its kind in the US.

Leading the group was psychologist Wanda Sadoughi; Dr. Irving M. Bush, chairman of the urology division and director of the sex clinic; Dr. Bangalore Jayaram, deputy chairman of the hospital's department of plastic surgery; and social worker Fay Litman. Pesmen reports that the "sex clinic" opened in 1969, and the first procedures were carried out in 1971. Jayaram explains:

> "At that time a few people came to our emergency room or trauma unit each year after mutilating themselves because they were so unhappy and confused about their sex. The surgeon then in charge of this unit began doing transsexual operations on those patients and the departments of urology and plastic surgery became aware of a great need to provide these people with more care."

It is interesting to note that the price of a "sex change" at the Fantus Health Center in 1974 meant hospital costs of $191 a day with an average stay of ten days, and patients were asked to put $400 down and the rest was to be paid in installments. This means that it was a very expensive procedure. In today's dollars, as of this writing, $191 dollars a day equates to $1,233 in current dollars, and the $400 deposit equates to $2,500. The entire procedure costing $2,310 in 1971 dollars equates to approximately $14,915, a fortune at that time.

# 46
# LADY BARONESSA AND SHAUN LUIS WIN MISS GAY AMERICA 1974 & 1975

In Nashville, TN, the Watch Your Hat & Coat Saloon, owned by Jerry Peek and Ray Cogdill, opened in 1971. In an article in the *Tennessean*, Peek says the bar opened as a country & western bar, "but it didn't work":

> "Saloon club co-owner Jerry Peek, 29, ... admits that his nightclub – which presently is featuring a cast of five female impersonators – is a meeting place for homosexuals.
>
> "However, he points out. 'We run a good business and our place is much different from other bars in town where they (homosexuals) go to 'pick up' or 'get picked up.'
>
> "ACCORDING to Peek, men and women are allowed to dance with their own sex when fast music is playing. But, he said, the club does not allow members of the same sex to slow-dance together."

The Watch Your Hat & Coat Saloon was the venue of the first Miss Gay America contest on June 25, 1972. That first year, the winner of Miss Gay America 1973 was Norman Jones, performing as Norma Kristie. He represented Arkansas. Two years later, Jones took over ownership of the pageant.

The following year's pageant did not go without incident. In May 1973, an article in the *Daily News-Journal*, out of Murfreesboro, TN, began:

> "The chairman of the Miss Gay America Pageant said Friday he would like to give away proceeds from a benefit program, but charities apparently don't want the money.

> "Jerry Peek said he had approached both the United Givers Fund and the Kidney Foundation about donating funds he expects to raise with a benefit May 13 in connection with the Miss Gay America."

The Kidney Foundation said if they accepted the money, they would lose half of the organizations who supported them. The United Givers Fund said they would have to have a meeting of their executive board which was a month away. Too late. They then offered the money to the Police Widows and Orphans Fund, who also turned them down.

The following day the *Johnson City Press-Chronicle* reported that a recipient for the estimated $5,000 had been found, "Jerry Peek said ... that he has been contacted by the Nashville Rescue Squad, the Vanderbilt University Medical Center, the local Rape Crisis Center, the father of a hospitalized child and the doctor for a man awaiting a heart transplant. Peek quoted all of them as saying they would be glad to accept the proceeds."

The *Times Standard* wrote:

> "More than 40 young men vying for the title of Miss Gay America arrive in this music city for a two day pageant in which they will be judged on poise, talent, makeup and other factors.
>
> "The female impersonators, ranging from 18 to 25 are winners of preliminary contests in 31 states, will appear in evening gowns and sportswear during the second Miss Gay America at a local nightclub May 10-12.
>
> "... The man chosen Miss Gay America will receive a 1973 car and $1,000 in cash."

Kathleen Gallagher in the *Tennessean* wrote, "Female impersonators from across the country danced and pranced and strutted their stuff last night at the Glass Menagerie in the first round of the Miss Gay American contest." On the subject of the money from the charity ball, Gallagher writes:

> "Previously, both the United Givers Fund and the Kidney Foundation refused to accept donations from the contest charity fund.
>
> "'To me, they hurt themselves more than they hurt us,' Peek said, adding that the charities' attitudes were 20 or 30 years out of step with the times.
>
> "THE NEXT time around here a man dies without a kidney machine, there will be people wondering why they didn't get down off their high horse,' Peek said.

"'They have to realize that gay people are here. They have to realize their existence. They've been here almost as long as straight society, and they will continue to be here as long."

On May 15, 1973, the *Jacksonville Daily Journal* wrote:

"Lady Baronessa, a Chicago female impersonator who is hoping to eventually undergo sex change surgery, assumed the crown of Miss Gay America Saturday with a pledge to work toward uniting gay people and 'straights.'

"The 24-year-old Puerto Rican native, born Carmelo Santiago, succeeded Norma Kristie of Hot Springs, Ark., following three nights of competition involving 27 contestants from across the nation."

The following year the competition took place in Atlanta, GA, at the Atlanta Americana Hotel Ballroom. On May 7, 1974 the *Chicago Tribune* wrote:

"Shawn Luis, a female impersonator who appears at the Baton Show Lounge, 436 N. Clark St., has just been crowned the new Miss Gay America in Atlantic City [sic]. Louis won over 53 other female impersonators for the title. The winner was judged on looks, talent and personality, according to Ed Zubbrick, a spokesman for the Near North bar."

In October 1975, Alice Alexander wrote "The Rebirth of Shawn Luis" in the *Tennessean*. Luis remembered the time she worked at the Baton:

"The owner, Felicia, like Shawn was a man living as a woman. With her striking Oriental looks, Shawn became popular with the customers at the club, accustomed as they were to pale redheads and blonds.

"One day in the early spring of the year, Felicia announced a plan. Thinking it would be good publicity for the club, she had decided to enter Shawn and one of the other 'girls' in the second Miss Gay America pageant coming up in May.

"... Hesitating at first, Shawn decided to go through with it. In Atlanta she met the 55 other contestants in the pageant, and was amazed to find the rules required she dress as a man unless told to do otherwise. She went shopping for men's T-shirts, jeans and tennis shoes. With her long hair and womanly figure, Shawn found to her amusement and dismay that many other contestants could not believe she was really male.

"Shawn was chosen Miss Gay America of 1974. She reacted in a manner that would befit a Shirley Cothran – she promptly fainted."

# 47
# TV STEREOTYPES

In the early 1970s, unwelcome stereotypical images of gay men and their lives appeared on television. The most egregious offender was an episode of NBC's popular *Sanford & Son*, sponsored by Gillette. The show starred Redd Foxx as Fred G. Sanford, a sixty-five-year-old junk dealer in the Watts neighborhood of South Central Los Angeles. Demond Wilson played his thirty-year-old son, Lamont. The episode that aired October 19, 1973 showed Sanford Sr. suspecting Sanford Jr. was visiting a gay bar containing a group of limp-wristed men. At the same time, Sanford Jr. hears his father has been seen in the same bar. Each fear "the worst," that the other is secretly gay. Sanford Sr. calls a doctor to examine his son for "illness."

Of course, everything gets ironed out in the end. It's just a misunderstanding, and normality returns. The response to the episode was a nationwide protest from the gay community. In Chicago, there was a "Smear In" at the Merchandise Mart, where both Gillette and NBC's WMAQ-TV (Channel 5) had their headquarters. Donald Kasper of the *Chicago Gay Crusader* and Richard Pfieffer of the Gay Speakers Bureau wore signs saying "NBC" and they sprayed a dozen cans of Gillette Foamy shaving cream on Michael Bergeron, who held a sign reading, "NBC is Smearing Gay People ... Sanford & Son ... Sponsored by Gillette." William B. Kelley of Chicago Gay Alliance and Larry Gulian of Illinois Gays for Legislative Action delivered a letter of protest to WMAQ-TV.

Throughout November, the National Gay Task Force (NGTF) and the Los Angeles Gay Community Services Center (GCSC) held meetings with media representatives in New York and Hollywood. The GCSC also met *Sanford & Son* producer Norman Lear, who said he personally found the gay bar episode storyline in "bad taste" and regretted there were no guidelines for writers. Lear suggested gays remain vigilant and inform the media when they were offended.

Another protest against TV depictions of gay men took place on December 11, 1973, when two members of Philadelphia's Gay Raiders posed as students and disrupted a live broadcast of the *CBS News* with Walter Cronkite. Mark Segal, one of the men, held up a sign that read, "Gays protest CBS bigotry." Harry Linghorn was the other Gay Raider.

In the *Chicago Daily News,* James Kloss profiled Segal when the activist was in Chicago continuing the Gay Raiders campaign to eliminate gay stereotypes from television. "Why not gay couples on *The Dating Game*? I don't see anything wrong with that," Segal told Kloss.

Prior to the Walter Cronkite zap, Segal was thrown off a Philadelphia teen show for dancing on camera with another man. He later turned up at Johnny Carson show tapings. "I was furious after seeing a Marcus Welby show about a 'sick' homosexual on ABC," said Segal. After threatening to protest other ABC shows, officials for the station agreed to stop misrepresenting homosexuals. "We won agreements with NBC and ABC – only CBS refuses to meet with us," said Segal. Kloss describes Segal as "a short man with a pixie face and long, parted curly hair who looks like the late Janis Joplin, but with a mustache." Kloss also writes that Segal is now a celebrity in his own right and appearing before the television cameras – "by invitation, that is" – on local talk shows. In Chicago, Segal made an appearance with the Rev. Troy Perry and feminist lawyer Florynce Kennedy on Channel 5's Kup's Show.

The August 1974 issue of *Chicago Gay Crusader* predicted "a major battle" was imminent, pitting the National Gay Task Force (NGTF) against the American Broadcasting Company (ABC) and producers of *Marcus Welby, M.D.*, a TV medical drama. The dispute was over an upcoming episode entitled "The Outrage," about a fourteen-year-old boy raped by his male science teacher. The script exploited the image of an out-of-control homosexual preying on children. Ron Gold, the NGTF communications director, wrote in a press release, "This is a time for gay people around the country to show that they will act in a unified manner to oppose anti-gay bigotry on television and elsewhere."

The Chicago Gay Alliance acting president William B. Kelley called a meeting on August 25 at Liberty Hall, 2440 N. Lincoln Ave. It was not the first clash between NGTF and the producers of *Marcus Welby, M.D.* Another episode, "The Other Martin Loring," broadcast February 20, 1973, had

Welby telling the character Martin Loring that he was not homosexual, but the fear of being homosexual was the cause of his depression. After an attempted suicide, Loring agrees to see a psychiatrist. That episode led to between thirty and forty members of the Gay Activists Alliance zapping ABC's New York City headquarters and occupying the office of ABC president Elton Rule.

In Frank S. Swertlow's "Television in Review" column in Chicago's *Daily Herald*, he writes, "What is the brouhaha about?":

> "... ABC should have the right to air a show about male rape, child molesters or homosexuality. They are facts of life, and it is time we faced them.
>
> "WHAT IS UNFORTUNATE about this show is that a sensitive subject is wrapped in a can of garbage, and this garbage can has been raised to a level it does not deserve.
>
> "Marcus Welby, 'superdoc,' is not the proper forum for a discussion about child molesters, or perhaps anything with intellectual merit.
>
> "The Welby image is fraudulent. There is no physician alive like Welby, just like there was no father alive like 'Father Knows Best,' also starring Robert Young.
>
> "In 'The Outrage,' everything is hinted at. The real subject seemed to be homosexuality, but it was a phantom cloaked in garb of child molestation, Marcus Welby, by these standards, is exploitative trash – a rating getter.
>
> "If ABC is going to present a program about child molestation or homosexuality, another forum, perhaps some sort of film or documentary, should be used, especially since the network is well aware that homosexual groups will object. In that case, it would have something worthwhile to defend."

After ABC refused to modify or cancel "The Outrage" episode, NGTF and other gay groups, focused on advertisers and affiliates. As a result, at least four ABC affiliates refused to screen the episode. It was the first time that affiliates refused a network's episode because of a gay protest. Sponsors also pulled their ads, including Bayer, Gallo Wine, Listerine, Ralston-Purina, Colgate-Palmolive, Shell Oil, Lipton, American Home Products, Breck, Sterling Drug and Gillette. Because of the controversy and lost revenue, ABC chose not to rerun "The Outrage." What came out of the Chicago Gay Alliance meeting August 25, at Liberty Hall, 2440 N. Lincoln is unclear. On July 28, 2011, William B. Kelley, answered the author in a Facebook message, "Since I was 'acting president,' it sounds as if this was in the days when CGA was on its very last legs, having lost its 171 W. Elm St. headquarters as well as its president. It may well be that almost no one came [to the meeting] and nothing happened. I recall no organized Welby activity here."

On October 8, 1974, Bruce Vilanch wrote in the *Chicago Tribune:*

> "The real issue is that homosexuals have never been portrayed on network TV as anything BUT child molesters. Or mincing queens. Or tired, theatrical fruits. Or handsome young men coping with identity crises.
>
> "...To my knowledge there has never been a decently-adjusted, fairly stable homosexual on a TV series or movie, although untold dozens of them turn up playing the pathetically stereotyped roles mentioned above. And dozens more appear on talk shows every night.
>
> "...Why is this? Certainly not because there are no homosexuals working behind the scenes. There are many. Rather, it's because anything even faintly gritty or off the Ozzie and Harriet mark of American normality is guaranteed to lure viewers, and the networks know this."

# 48
# MORE GOD AND GAYS

After the Stonewall Riots and the Gay Liberation Front formation, many Christian denominations began discussing homosexuality and the Bible. In July 1970 "Religion, Law, Homosexuality" was published in the Moline, IL, *Dispatch*:

> "Homosexual acts in private by consenting adults have not for several years been a violation of the law in the State of Illinois. Such relationships were removed entirely from the purview of the law when the General Assembly in 1961 enacted major revisions in the state criminal code.
>
> "At the time this was an unprecedented step for a state to take, and it aroused considerable criticism.
>
> "It is noteworthy that since then a number of churches have adopted positions on homosexuality that in effect lend religious sanction to what Illinois did by law.
>
> "The most recent instance is to be found in the statement on 'sex, marriage and family' drafted at the biennial convention of the Lutheran Church in America. In one passage this statement declares:
>
> "'Scientific research has not been able to provide conclusive evidence regarding the causes of homosexuality. Nevertheless, homosexuality is viewed biblically as a departure from the heterosexual structure of God's creation. Persons who engage in homosexual sexual behavior are sinners only as are all other persons – alienated from God and neighbor. However, they are often the special and undeserving victims of prejudice and discrimination in law, law enforcement cultural mores, and congregational life. In relation to this area of concern, the sexual behavior of freely consenting adults in private is not an appropriate subject for legislation or police action. It is essential to see such persons as entitled to understanding and justice in church and community.'

"In the light of this and other evidence of a changing attitude toward homosexuality in American society, the 1961 revision of Illinois' law on the subject stands out as a remarkable exercise in foresight."

Five months later, an article appeared in the *Sacramento Bee* headlined, "Homosexuals Have Own Church in South State":

"While music played in the background, a layman started the service by reading from the 37$^{th}$ psalm.

"... Cease from anger and forsake wrath; fret not thyself in any wise to do evil. For evildoers shall be cut off ...

"The meek shall inherit the earth ...

"... The churchgoers who filled the 385-seat Encore Theater on Sunday morning were nearly all males, most of them young.

"The church in Hollywood is believed to be the first in the country to have a homosexual pastor and a predominantly homosexual congregation and to identify itself unabashedly as a church for homosexuals.

"Formed a little more than a year ago, it is called the Metropolitan Community Church and has grown to more than 255 members. ... The pastor is 29-year-old Troy Perry."

Bill Kosman in the Long Beach *Independent* wrote, "They crowd into an art movie house with a purple and white marquee out front and red-draped walls inside to sing hymns and hear their pastor's voice." Kosman goes on to describe the congregation, "Churchgoers – outside of a handful of women – are all men. A few wear dark suits and ties, but most wear sweaters or mod shirts and scarfs and trousers. Most have their hair long and carefully fashioned. And a few wear lace shirts and earrings."

The Encore Theater showed movies like *Katarina Izmailova*, Dmitri Shostakovich's opera with Bolshoi soprano Galina Vishnevskaya, Luis Bunuel's *The Exterminating Angel* and a Japanese double feature of *Fires of the Plain* and *Ashes and Diamonds*.

Another description of those early services appeared in July 1970 in *Time*:

"On Sunday morning, the movie theater on Melrose Avenue in Hollywood is packed. The front rows are filled with a red-robed choir of men and women. Hymnals are distributed; an organ plays. By Hollywood standards, the congregation is run-of-the-mill: middle-aged businessmen, a few boys in rainbow-hued bellbottoms, muscular types in T shirts, women in assorted styles of pants or skirts, a few motorcycle boys in mustaches and black leather. Whites, blacks, Orientals, Chicanos. Prayers are read. From a chair at the side, a husky 30-year-old man in vestments abruptly rises, steps swiftly out in front of the makeshift altar, and, flashing a beguiling, boyish smile, booms out: 'If you love the Lord this morning, say 'Amen!' 'Amen!' roar the 700 worshipers – nearly all of whom are homosexuals. Another service of the Metropolitan Community Church is under way.

"The founder and inspiration of the M.C.C. is the Rev. Troy Perry, a homosexual who admits it without embarrassment or shame. Perry preached his first sermon when he was 13, and became a licensed Baptist minister at 15 (a year later he switched to Pentecostalism because he found its kinetic services more to his liking). Though he had his first homosexual experience at nine, he did not accept his sexual orientation until he was 23. By then he was married, the father of two sons and pastor of the Church of God of Prophecy in Santa Ana, Calif. When he finally faced his problem, the district elder to whom he spoke pronounced him demon-possessed and advised him to pray. 'I told him I'd prayed till I was blue in the face, but it didn't do any good,' says Perry.

"Finding a calling. Separated from both his wife and his church, he moved to Hollywood after a hitch in the Army. There, one summer night in 1968, Perry bailed a fellow homosexual out of jail and tried to calm him. 'It's no use,' sobbed the young man. 'No one cares for us homosexuals.'

"'God cares,' said Perry.

"'No, not even God cares,' came the answer. At that moment, Perry found his calling."

Prior to Chicago's 1st Gay Pride celebrations in 1970, a *Chicago Tribune* headline read, "A Church for Homosexuals." The article begins:

"The Rev. Troy D. Perry of Los Angeles found it possible to turn the stigma of being a homosexual to his advantage by being outspoken about it thru religion. After he was forced to step down as minister of the Church of God of Prophecy, a Pentecostal sect, because of his homosexuality, the Rev. Mr. Perry started a nondenominational church of his own for male and female homosexuals.

"He held the first services in his home with nine friends and three persons who responded to an ad he placed in a local homosexual newspaper. In successive weeks, the number of worshippers increased, and the group, named the Metropolitan Community church, began holding Sunday services in a Los Angeles movie house, the Encore theater."

Perry talks about being forced to resign from the Pentecostal Church of God of Prophecy because of his homosexuality. He said the forced resignation had prompted him to start the Metropolitan Community Church (MCC), ministering to the gay community. At the time of the article, there were MCC churches in San Francisco, San Diego, and Phoenix. What seems to have escaped the reporter's attention is that Good Parish MCC had already formed in Chicago. Two months earlier they held their first service at Broadway United Methodist Church. This was before MCC Phoenix, making Good Shepherd Parish MCC the first MCC outside California and the first gay religious group to form in Chicago.

The *Chicago Tribune* continued:

> "'I guess I always had homosexual impulses, but in 1963, when I was minister of a Pentecostal church in Santa Ana, Cal., I had a homosexual affair. I told my wife about it, and at first she thought maybe we could work things out by letting me have a night out with the boys, so to say. I decided it wasn't what I wanted. I didn't want to live a double existence, so we got divorced,' he said."

Sally Jardine, a *Chicago Tribune* reader from Tinley Park, wrote to the editor:

> "Altho I may be but one voice against many, I want to thank the author of the recent article on homosexuality ['A Church for Homosexuals,' June 7]. He brought us a little insight in understanding people who are different from most of us. We all want to be accepted for what we are, including the people of the church for homosexuals."

In the early 1970s, the fastest growing, most active and influential, gay organizations in Chicago were religious groups. Denied spiritual sustenance by the religious establishment, LGBT's formed their own congregations, or took refuge in gay-friendly churches, like the Rev. Clarence H. Cobbs' closeted African American First Church of Deliverance, embracing homosexuals since its founding in the 1920s.

On their third anniversary, on October 20, 1973, the Good Shepherd Parish MCC's launched a $100,000 fundraising drive. They held the launch at the Villa Sweden Restaurant, 5207 N. Clark Street. Two hundred and five people attended the meeting, representing thirty-seven gay organizations and businesses, including several gay bars. Representing the bars were: Ben Allen, House of Landers, 936 W. Diversey; John Britt, Boys at Sea, 642 W. Diversey; Jack David, Up North, 6244 N. Western Ave; Richard Farnham, Carol's Coming Out Pub, 2519 N. Halsted St.; Bob Hugel, Glory Hole, 1343 N. Wells St.; Sue Hughes, Sue and Nan's, 3920 N. Lincoln; Robert Levey, Broadway Sam's, 5346 N. Broadway; and Woodrow Moser, Legacy/21 Club, 3042 W. Irving Park.

## CHICAGO AFTER STONEWALL

The Rev. Arthur Green, the pastor of Good Shepherd Parish, announced that Bruce Nelson and Jerry DeBruin were co-chairmen of the fund drive. The two men outlined their goals and expectations for the next three years. They planned to raise $5,000 through minor social events; $20,000 through major sponsored events; $30,000 in special gifts from the community and friends; and $45,000 in pledges from Good Shepherd Parish MCC membership. One early fundraiser was the "Winner of Hearts" Valentines Dance, held February 15, 1974 in the Sheraton-Chicago Hotel's Boulevard Room, a ballroom known for its chandelier and ornate décor. Guests paid $12 for a roast beef and chicken buffet, with a selection of French pastries, followed by dancing until 1:00 a.m. with Johnny Holiday's six-piece electronic band.

The *Shepherd's Staff*, the Good Shepherd Parish monthly newsletter, reported that the congregation moved on January 6, 1974, to the United Church of Christ at 615 W. Wellington. This was after more than three years at the Broadway United Methodist Church of Christ. The move was due to a controversy over the MCC performing same-sex "holy union" ceremonies at the Broadway church. Good Shepherd Parish considered this a temporary move until funds were raised to buy their own building. On May 1, 1974 the Rev. Arthur Green became the first paid employee of any Chicago gay community group when he began his fulltime pastoral duties at Good Shepherd Parish Metropolitan Community Church.

The Good Shepherd Parish MCC never bought a building. In 1983, what money was in the fund was spent rehabbing the United Church of Christ property at 615 W. Wellington Ave. They converted the "theater building" attached to the church offices and meeting space.

The *Chicago Gay Crusader* in 1974 reported that Good Shepherd Parish MCC had grown so fast that two pastoral assistants, Rev. Richard Babcock and Rev. Richard R. Mickley, were appointed to aid founding member Rev. Arthur Green. Babcock was a United Methodist minister who had been a missionary in Asia for twelve years. Mickley formerly the pastor of Detroit's MCC; Mickley left in mid-March to work for Phoenix MCC. One of the first events at 615 W. Wellington was a one-hour joint social on January 20 with the local chapter of Dignity, the gay Catholic group. This was followed by a united prayer service three days later at St. Sebastian's Church, 824 W. Wellington, where Dignity regularly met. This was part of an effort between Rev. Troy Perry, founder of the MCC and the national officers of Dignity in Boston, to increase cooperation between the two religious groups. Good Shepherd Parish was also honored with a visit from Rev. Troy Perry, who preached at the new venue, Ash Wednesday February 27 and on March 3, the first day of Lent. After the latter service, the Rev. Troy Perry and entourage attended an 11:00 p.m. service at the Rev. Clarence Cobbs' First Church of Deliverance, 4315 S. Wabash Ave. While in Chicago, Perry also autographed his book *The Lord Is My Shepherd and He Knows I'm Gay* at Kroch's & Brentano's, 29 S. Wabash Ave.

In February 1974, the *Chicago Tribune* published an article by Clarence Page about Good Shepherd Parish MCC. "The church's chief public spokesman," the Rev. Richard Mickley, made the following remark, "Among the stereotypes we have to erase are the idea that all gay people are leftist revolutionaries or so-called 'screaming fags.' Altho I don't oppose their existence, Communists do not represent my viewpoint. Too many people link the silly acts of the annual Gay Liberation parades with all the rest of us." This unhelpful statement may, or may not, have contributed to Mickley's abrupt departure soon afterwards. However, after leaving Chicago, Mickley went on to an illustrious career in the MCC. In 1975 he became head of the Prison Ministry in the MCC Los Angeles offices. He edited *In Unity,* the denomination's magazine, and published several books, including *Christian Sexuality* in 1975. On September 7, 1991, the Rev. Richard Mickley established MCC Manila, the Philippines's first openly gay and lesbian organization.

The Chicago Area Unitarian Universalist Gay Caucus was also active at this time. In January 1974, the *Chicago Gay Crusader* notes that on November 18, 1973, eight men and twelve women from the Caucus conducted Sunday worship services at Evanston's Unitarian Church, 1330 N. Ridge Ave. The service was in a "panel format" followed by a more traditional service with songs, poetry and a sermon. The *Chicago Gay Crusader* writes:

> "The second service opened with two taped songs, *Crossroads* by Don McLean, and *Stonewall Nation* by the gay activist Madeline Davis. A congregational hymn followed, and the caucus members were introduced by the Rev. Charles Eddis, minister of the suburban church (Evanston's Unitarian).
>
> "Caucus members read selections from the Bible's story of David and Jonathan; the ancient Greek poet Sappho; Walt Whitman's *When I Heard at the Close of the Day*; and other materials portraying gay culture and history. Helen Reddy's *Where Is My Friend?* And the hymn *Love Can Tell*, were played during the offertory."

The African American *Chicago Defender* published a piece under the headline, "'Gay Caucus' service at first Unitarian." … "'We're Gonna Be

Ourselves,' a celebration of gay love created by the Chicago Area Unitarian Universalist Gay Caucus, will be the theme of the 10:30 a.m. service, Sunday Feb. 24, at First Unitarian Church, 57th and Woodlawn." The service featured "a sharing of works of gay composers, sung by the church choir." The article reveals that the First Unitarian Church at 57th and Woodlawn, on Chicago's South Side, was where the Caucus formed one year earlier. They played a leading role in establishing an Office of Gay Concerns at Unitarian Universalist Assn. headquarters in Boston. A November 1970 editorial in the *Mt. Vernon Register-News* begins:

> "The news media has been reporting the existence of several homosexual 'churches' in California and in certain large eastern cities. During September, an Episcopal parish in Washington D.C., held a special service to meet the particular needs of homosexuals who had felt excluded and damned by the traditional church.
> 
> "Clergymen in various parts of the country have indicated their willingness to perform 'marriages' for homosexuals and lesbians seeking such a ceremony. This may sound groovy to the Gay world but it must be a basic threat to the integrity of the Christian community and its teaching about Creation, family, and the gift of life.
> 
> "... But all the Gay Power parades, and all the talk show homosexual guests are not going to change the primary direction of Christian teaching. What we really are seeing, in some instances, is the pleading of a clergyman who happens to be a homosexual and wants clearance from the religious community for his malady."

# 49
# LOYOLA U GAY GROUP AND ROGERS PARK GAY CENTER

On January 24, 1974, a gay coffeehouse opened at a bar/restaurant called David's Place, 5232 N. Sheridan Rd. *Michael's Thing* noted the, "cocktail lounge and restaurant extraordinaire" opened on November 10, 1972, with female impersonators like Wanda Lust and 1973 Best Entertainer on the North Side, Miss Ebony Carr. David's Place was owned by John Gast and Marvin Cyron.

Other gay non-alcoholic meeting places included Gay Horizons, Liberty Hall, 2440 N. Lincoln Ave., and the Blue Gargoyle at 5655 S. University Ave. The David's Place coffeehouse was started by the Loyola Gay Students group to provide, "an alternative atmosphere to the bars, in which to meet people and socialize." The quarterly journal *Psychotherapy: Theory, Research and Practice* published an article "A Peer Self-Help Group of Homosexuals on the North Side of Chicago" by Richard A. Stern. In it, Stern tells the story of "David," a twenty-two-year-old homosexual Loyola undergraduate, who was depressed by the sexually promiscuous nature of his life. During the first two years at college, David's roommates were straight, causing him to lead a dual existence. When he moved into his own apartment, his attitude toward his homosexuality changed. He began to socialize with other homosexuals who were "together." David told Stern:

> "I stopped thinking of myself as a faggot or an inferior sort of person. It was as though the weight of years of guilt was suddenly lifted. I realized that I was a whole person and a good person, and that I had a sexual identity that was unique and very natural for me. I decided not to fight what I was but to be it to the fullest extent. I rejected society's

conventional attitudes towards gayness, and sort of substituted my own set of values based on what I saw was best for me."

David formed a college gay group. As the idea of "Gay Liberation Front" was too radical for him, he named the group Loyola Gay Students. He posted flyers on bulletin boards in classrooms and dormitories, but Loyola being a deeply religious Jesuit university these were torn down. He re-posted them, installed another phone line in his apartment and began taking calls from other gay students. The problem was where to meet. It had to be off campus. David called community organizations in the Rogers Park area and found Alternatives, Inc., 5866 N. Broadway, a federally funded community drug abuse program. They allowed the gay students to hold a once-a-week two-hour meeting. Eleven people showed up to the first one. One recurring theme discussed at the meetings was the negative attitude toward gays at the college. The administration was not supportive. However, the college paper, the *Phoenix,* agreed to publish an ad, albeit under a title that angered many of the gay students. One complaining letter to the editor came from outside the group and read:

> "I just opened my November 2nd edition of the *Phoenix* and started to read the Happenings section of Page 2.
>
> "The third column contains an announcement of a Gay Liberation meeting with the headline that reads 'Say Fella.'
>
> "I think that this headline is in the worst possible taste and am quite disappointed to see such a display in the University paper. The Gay Liberation movement is working for the promotion of understanding of the homosexual and acceptance of homosexuals as humans.
>
> "To preface the article that announces their meetings with such a slanted and bigoted headline undermines their cause and reveals the ignorance of the people involved with the writing and editing of the material on that page.
>
> "As the main publication of an intellectual community, I think the *Phoenix* has a great responsibility to present if not unbiased, at least non-bigoted viewpoints on its pages.
>
> "Thank you. Nancy F. Millman."

Richard Stern, who wrote the article about "David" for the journal *Psychotherapy: Theory, Research and Practice,* never divulged the true identity of "David." Stern was, in fact, writing about himself. Richard Stern *was* "David."

One popular idea in the Loyola Gay Students group was to open a permanent gay coffee house in Rogers Park. Early on, they decided that membership would not be limited to Loyola students, but to anyone living in the Rogers Park neighborhood. An ad in the *Reader* asked if any organization would donate space for a gay coffeehouse. In *Psychotherapy: Theory, Research and Practice*, Stern writes, "as a result a local gay bar donated the use of its dining room one night a week." The gay bar in question was David's Place.

In July 1974, the *Chicago Gay Crusader* noted the Loyola Gay Students group had changed its name to the Loyola-Rogers Park Gay Association. Their coffee house meetings at David's Place were now being held again at Alternatives Inc. at 5866 N. Broadway. In the November 1974 issue of the *Chicago Gay Crusader*, an article reads:

> "NEW CENTER OPENS. Another in a series of community centers planned for gay Chicagoans was unveiled Sunday Night, Nov. 24. When the Loyola-Rogers Park Gay Students Association's storefront opened its doors at 7109 N. Glenwood Ave.
>
> "The group plans to conduct three activities there: a telephone hotline and nightly open house; a weekly meeting and rap session; and a "hot stuff" rummage sale.
>
> "Open house and hotline hours are 6 to 10 p.m. Sunday through Friday and 12 noon to 3 p.m. Saturday. The hotline is staffed by trained volunteers and can be reached at [Tel. No]
>
> "Weekly meetings of the group are held Sunday nights from 7 to 10 p.m. and are open to the public. They include a social hour followed by an informal meeting and rap session. (Meetings were formerly held at the Alternatives, Inc., headquarters, 5866 N. Broadway).
>
> "The rummage sale planned for Saturday, Dec. 14, was scheduled as the center's first fundraising event."

In February/March 1975, the *Chicago Gay Crusader* reported that the Loyola/Rogers Park Gay Center had changed its name to Giovanni's Room. It was open seven days a week from 6-10 p.m. with a coffeehouse every Sunday at 7.30 p.m. In September 1975, the word Loyola was dropped. In November 1978, the Rogers Park/Edgewater Gay Alliance opened its new center at 5823 N. Ridge and remained open until early 1981 when it disappeared from the listings in *Gay Chicago* magazine.

Mark Sherkow told the author about his involvement with the Center:

> "They had a couple of meetings at David's Place on Sheridan Road. One of the rooms in the bar. And so I went to that once, and then I happened to move up to Rogers Park and they had been meeting at a place

called Alternatives, on Broadway. It was a day care center. And it was students from Loyola and a few other people, not very many people. Then the parents found out that this gay group was meeting there and so they went to the board that was running this center and said, "We don't want this group to be here.

"Well, somebody decided to look for a storefront, so we found this storefront ... $110 a month over on Glenwood Avenue and we started a drop-in center. We would be open every night of the week 7-10 and have a phone line. And that's what we did. I think the group was in existence about 6 years. At one point they moved to Edgewater and that's when they changed the name to the Rogers Park/Edgewater Gay Alliance, so that's why they had another name there. Actually Rick (Stern) and I and a woman named Laura (Hathaway) were the leaders of the group.

"We divided our space into two sections, we put up a wall and the front part was the phoneline and we advertised it. In fact, a couple of us got trained as peer counselors at Gay Horizons, so we were running the phone service, giving people referrals and even did some counseling. Then the rest of it was set up like a living room, we had coffee and it was open every night.

"One of the issues we had to deal with early on was that some of the people who dropped in were marginal characters, and we decided we did not want to discriminate, we wanted to be open to everybody. Although, we did set up some rules of behavior. There was this one character who I'm sure had been in a mental hospital, who hadn't bathed for a long time and so we said, 'If you're in that condition, we can't let you in.' There was another fellow who just talked a lot, an incessant queen who talked a lot. He was mimicking Marilyn Monroe he told us. So we decided we didn't want to say that people can't be here, which I think was the right decision, but because of it some people stayed away. We were not a chi-chi place ... (laughs) ... In the course of the five years I was involved, we had two different leadership groups. We had about ten people that were active at one time, then eventually most of them drifted away, and then another group got formed."

In November 1977, the Rogers Park Gay Community Center moved to larger quarters at 6958 N. Glenwood. In September 1978, Vol. 1 No 2 of their newsletter *302.0* was published. (302.0 being the international medical classification number for homosexuality). Chairperson, Joe Tully, wrote this amusing report:

"Everyone should experience chairing an organization such as the Rogers Park-Edgewater Gay Alliance. I recall my first meeting of the Steering Committee. I waltzed in clutching my 50-page agenda. Two people were present. I was to have my first lesson in GST (Gay Standard

Time). After some cookies and milk, accompanied by a two hour nap, we plunged in with the introduction of guests. Seeing there were none, we proceeded with the reading of the minutes. As nothing except elections took place at the previous meeting, the minutes were waived by a unanimous vote.

"Moving right along, I asked the House Staff Director to give his report. Some qualitative suggestions for improving the staff and its functions were offered. Some of the suggestions were a) installing extra telephone lines, b) sending everyone on the staff to Azrin's Behavior Modification Training, and c) inviting Broom Hilda, Inc., to train staff in housekeeping techniques. Someone else queried, 'Isn't this a house staff matter?' Of course! Why didn't I think of that? Our conclusion was to have the house staff draw up a proposal and present it to the Steering Committee.

"I suggested that we take an ice cream break at Baskin and Robbins.

"The timely item on the agenda was moving from 7109 N. Glenwood to a better facility. It was suggested that we look for a place that was problem-free. We said that we would give it our best shot, and spent all our time talking about decorating the future center rather than dealing with finding a suitable facility. The problem was, none of us had any suggestions for funding the crystal chandeliers Scandinavian sofa, and Pierre Cardin throw rug. In keeping with realistic standards, we decided we would seek donated space (including heat, I might add).

"We proceeded on to a lengthy discussion concerning the agenda of the Gay and Lesbian Coalition of Metropolitan Chicago. As luck would have it, our representative only has to reflect our views on 39 1/2 matters. I limited the discussion time for this segment. After six motions to extend the discussion, our representative said that really only 38 1/2 of the topics needed immediate deliberation. We were all thankful for that.

"Someone interrupted and asked if I would take measures to shorten the meeting. Being the diplomat that I am, I said 'No!'

"It takes a warm, emphatic and caring person to chair the Steering Committee meetings. One must keep a level head. A good chairperson is able to store views and suggestions quickly so as to effect relevant conclusions. The best system of survival is the repetition of these words: I WILL LEAVE THIS MEETING WITH MENTAL STABILITY AND A WORKING PULSE."

# 50
# WOMEN'S COFFEEHOUSES AND MORE WOMEN'S MUSIC

Toward the end of 1973, the Women's Center, at 3523 N. Halsted St., opened and was a gathering and meeting place that sold feminist books and posters, lesbian newspapers, and offered advice on birth control, pregnancy testing, and welfare childcare. One of the first events at the new Women's Center was author Valerie Taylor speaking to the newly formed Lesbian Literature Class. In January 1974, *Lavender Woman* wrote that Taylor was "looking very grandmotherly, white braids crossed atop her head." The paper reported, "Val opened her remarks noting that it was fifty years since the publication of Radclyffe Hall's *Well of Loneliness*, which she described as one of the worst lesbian books written. Not only was Stephen described as inverted, but the sentences she was given to speak were inverted also." Taylor added that her favorite lesbian novel was *Price of Salt,* published in 1952, by Patricia Highsmith, written under the pseudonym Claire Morgan. Highsmith's first novel, *Strangers on a Train*, also had a homosexual subtext, and was made into a film by Alfred Hitchcock in 1951.

Another new lesbian/feminist space was Susan "Susie" B's at 3730 N. Broadway, Chicago's first restaurant, run by and for women. Marie Jayne Kuda in *Chicago Gay Crusader* describes the interior:

> "Graphics, posters, photographs (some of owner Eunice Militante), and macramé hangings lend much of the warm atmosphere, highlighted by white cloths, small flickering candles, and fresh flowers on each table. The bill of fare is simple to the point of originality. Hearty bowls of soup (vegetarian or meat), fresh-baked bread, herb teas or hot mulled cider, and fresh-baked dessert."

The opening of these non-alcoholic venues coincided with the rise of women's music. Even with the glitter and camp of Glam Rock, out-gay singers and musicians were few and far between. That began to change in 1973 with Alix Dobkin's *Lavender Jane Loves Women,* the first album by and for lesbians. Also 1973 saw the birth of Olivia Records, a label to promote women's music, founded by a collective of ten lesbian feminists. Chicago's contribution to women's music in the early 1970s was Linda Shear, the Chicago Liberation Rock Band and Ginni Clemens, the latter performed at a "Women Only Party" at Susie B's restaurant April 27, 1974.

In the *Chicago Tribune* Lynn Van Matre attended the first National Women's Music Festival in Champaign IL, a six-day event starting May 28, organized by women students on campus at the University of Illinois. Van Matre judged the festival badly organized, not a success, but remarkable in that it happened at all. The planned concerts, workshops, and jam sessions were billed as an effort to "give music back to its muses." During the day there were workshops on a variety of topics, including "Women and Audio Equipment," "Women as Managers" and "Sociology of Rock." Evenings were concerts by amateur and struggling musicians, with a Saturday night "name" show featuring Yoko Ono and Janis Ian. Neither turned up. It's doubtful they were ever booked to appear. The festival was open to both men and women. Van Matre wrote:

> "Night after night, day after day, radical lesbians tried to turn the whole affair into a lesbian festival (to the irritation of their straight and less militantly gay sisters), celebrating such things as 'lesbian's natural rhythm' and, in one bizarre case, women's monthly cycles. ('Get your speculum at your neighborhood clinic, learn about your cervix and what's in it, it's a new day comin' when you got the bloods again!') Not exactly your garden variety Top 40 fodder."

Van Matre was most impressed by Margie Adam, at the time an unknown West Coast singer-songwriter. Adam first performed in Chicago on September 21, 1974, at the "Woman Concert 2" show. Adam opened with low key songs of lesbian love and pain by Mary Ann Pelc. She was followed by the rock of Earth, with Sue Abod on bass, Laura DeLise on guitar, Ella Szekely on drums, and everyone on vocals. A review of Margie Adam's performance in *Lavender Woman* by BZ reads, "She speaks through her voice and through the piano as an extension of herself. She sings about not being a service station, of a house nobody lives in, of inner spaces, of friendships with unicorns – and she speaks directly to my house nobody lives in and my inner spaces."

The paper also reported on a group of women called the Dyke

Patrol who stood in front of the ticket table at "Woman Concert 2" and tried to prevent men entering the concert. They handed the following statement to each man who bought a ticket, "Men are not welcome. Rape is defined as penetration. Any man who enters this concert is a rapist – a violator of women's space. There are no exceptions: there is no such thing as an 'Exceptional Man.' All men are rapists, and that is what you are proving by 'coming' here. GO AWAY! – The Dyke Patrol."

Lavender Woman continued:

> "Some women decided to support the Patrol by not entering the concert. A great many more women seemed confused about whom to support – the women in the Patrol or the women performing, but they eventually entered. For a while, Patrol members shouted 'Rapist!' at every man who entered and at two points in the concert one Patrol member blew her whistle and invited all men to leave."

The Dyke Patrol protest may, or may not, have impacted the turnout for the next dance. *Lavender Woman* noted that "Woman Concert 3" at Liberty Hall on October 25 drew a "slim crowd," and the band, the Clinch Mountain Backsteppers, got a "lukewarm reception."

Cindy, the reviewer, writes, "The Backsteppers laid down some foot-stompin' bluegrass music at both ends of their concert and filled the rest of it with out-of-the-city ditties, music they'd learned from other west coast women, and folkified love songs for women and their Oregon mountains."

The lukewarm reception, according to Cindy, was because lesbians were falling prey to the cult of celebrity, "The fact remains that our support so far has gone overwhelmingly to individual names rather than to groups, a dangerous thing if it leads to 'star-making' instead of a new woman's culture."

# 51
# LESBIAN SEPARATISM

In March 1974, the *Lavender Woman* collective took this stand on a national story:

"COLLECTIVE STATEMENT

"On February 4, a radical group called the Symbionese Liberation Army kidnapped the daughter of Randolf [sic] Hearst, publisher, millionaire and prominent member of the American ruling class. Since then they have demanded, as preliminary ransom, a food distribution program for all California's needy people. They threaten to execute Patricia Hearst if the ransom is not payed [sic]. The establishment media has played this kidnapping for all the sensationalism it is worth, while editorials have condemned the barbarity and perversity of the SLA.

"As radical and lesbian feminists, we must express a different feeling. We are outraged by the kidnapping of Patricia Hearst. The issue is not the morality, effectiveness or appropriateness of political terrorism. We are outraged because the <u>daughter</u> of Hearst was used as a pawn in this 'revolutionary' game between the male establishment and the male left.

"For centuries, the wives and daughters of the ruling class have been used as pawns in the intricate jockeying for position and property by individual members of the male ruling class. These women, entirely without power or independence, have been the victims, hostages and passive transmitters of money, prestige and control. The SLA, by striking against the daughter of Hearst, is merely extending the centuries of male consolidation of power.

"As lesbian feminists, we absolutely condemn the act of violence carried out against a woman without power, regardless of her relationship to the ruling class (through the position of her father). The men who have perpetrated this so-called political act are maintaining the culture of violence against women and are therefore the enemies of women. The women in the SLA, who have accepted these politics, have turned against their sisters and have also become our enemies, although their treason should be understood with sadness and regret. The spectacle of one woman taking another in captivity in order to promote the cause of male radicals against the male establishment should only serve to strengthen the need for a movement of women to overthrow male supremacy."

The *Lavender Woman* collective were separatists. An editorial in the same issue of *Lavender Woman* reads, "None of us in the LW Collective work with men in 'gay rights' groups, choosing instead to work in all-woman organizations." "Separatism" was a philosophy summed up in the reprinting of a dictate called "Lesbian Separatism: An Amazon Analysis," written by four separatists in Seattle. In part, it reads:

"WHAT IS SEPARATISM?

"The premise of separatism is simple: male supremacy is the oldest, most pervasive, root cause of all oppression. Men benefit from and perpetuate the system; women suffer from it. Men are therefore the enemy. The fight to end male supremacy must be a fight to overthrow male power. Women must separate from men if we are to win. Straight and bisexual women, who give support, energy and commitment to men, are succoring their own enemy and ours. Lesbians, who have already removed themselves from the most pervasive male bond – heterosex – and committed all their love and energy to women, thus offer a role model, a road, toward the end of male oppression. The basic assumption is simple: you can't consort with the enemy if you are serious about the fight against male supremacy."

As lesbians opened more alcohol-free venues, their relationship with lesbian bars became increasingly fractious. In the spring of 1974, a rift occurred between separatists and a lesbian-owned bar called Ms., 661 N. Clark St., run by Marge Summit and Chee Chee. In the March *Chicago Lesbian Liberation Newsletter*, an article accuses Ms. of charging 75c or $1 for drinks on "All Drinks 50c night."

The following month an editorial read, "What happened to feminism? We hear that Ms. had a women [sic] stripper last Saturday night. Was that for real?"

The problems between lesbian separatists and Ms. escalated at the 1974 Gay Pride Parade when the Ms. float carried a woman naked and painted with gold body-paint. "The lady was real, I painted her gold myself," Marge Summit told the author in a August 12, 2010 email. "Some lesbians don't like nice bodies like I do."

*Lavender Woman* awarded the float, "the most insulting to women" and to the staff and owners of Ms. "The most messed up lesbians of 1974."

Prior to the 1974 Gay Pride Parade, *Lavender Woman* asked readers for their thoughts on the upcoming Gay Pride Parade:

> *"This woman is in her mid 20s and semi-out of the closet for about a year. As a lesbian she works in the straight feminist movement.*
>
> "I won't be participating in Gay Pride Week. And it's not that I'm not proud. I am proud. But I have a job. If I should march in the Gay Pride Parade, there's always the possibility I could get photographed. I think about my family and my job."

> *"This woman is in her late 30s and has been semi-out for about 4 years and is working in a lesbian organization. She considers herself first and foremost a woman.*
>
> "I will be participating in Gay Pride Week. I have marched in the parade for the last two years and will do so again. Although I do prefer to be with women, I will participate in mixed events. 'Gay Pride' to me is a social-political statement and it has changed in meaning for me in the last three years through reading. My involvement is with other women."

> *"This woman is in her mid-20s, is not directly involved in the movement. Her coming out process started four years ago – today she is completely out. She said, 'to be vulnerable in this society is terrifying. To be true to yourself feels real good.' In speaking of herself, she says she is a lesbian woman."*
>
> "No I'm not participating in Gay Pride week at all. I'm basically tired of doing anything run by the patriarchy – whether faggot pigs or straight pigs – doing what they say and when they say. My pride comes out of a lot of things – getting to know myself as a lesbian woman, being in touch as much as possible with who I am regardless of who everybody else thinks I should be. It's definitely lesbian pride. There's a thing – why are these women all participating – faggots are the denial of women having any role at all. They simply don't need women for any reason. As far as I'm concerned Gay Pride means Faggot Pride. Faggotry is an illogical extension of men's incredible hatred for women. Yes my feelings have changed about Gay Pride. I lifted some more of the fleece from my eyes."

Not all lesbians blamed "faggot pigs." In the same issue of *Lavender Woman*, Nancy Davis wrote:

> "Separatism is a phenomena which grew out of the consciousness raising sessions that destroyed the Gay Movement in the early '70s. Instead

of waging a battle against the real oppressor – heterosexuality – those active in the Gay Movement decided that they needed to 'get their heads together.' The tactics of Maoist criticism and self-criticism only served to increase sexism, and the misery of both the women and men."

Davis argued that "separatism" polarized gay men and lesbians. She explained that it forced them back into the strict heterosexual roles of men and women. "It seems so obvious that the real enemy is heterosexuality – the love of opposition – its very existence pollutes our lives. If anything, Gay women and men should see the need to unite and do some consciousness raising with straight society – the ultimate form of consciousness raising – the destruction of heterosexuality."

## 52
# CHARLES "CHUCK" RENSLOW, BATHHOUSES, THE GOLD COAST, AND THE DEWES MANSION

Men-only establishments were also opening. In the spring of 1974, the *Chicago Gay Crusader* noted two new bathhouses – the Gay Broadway Baths, 4411 N. Broadway, and the "Chicago super-bath," Man's Country. In the hip-but-straight *Reader* a ¼ page ad for the Gay Broadway Baths read, "Nocturnal and Naughty. Private anterooms. Odd jobs performed. ... No membership needed." Ten months later, the Gay Broadway Baths became a heterosexual health spa.

However, on March 20, 1974, "several hundred Chicago gay males, plus a sprinkling of lesbians and other women," attended the opening night of Man's Country/Chicago. The sprawling bathhouse, three floors high, half a block wide, located at 5015 N. Clark St., had for years been the location of the Verdandi Club, a Swedish Society recreation hall. In 1962 it became the Verdandi restaurant run by Ingrid Bergstrom, her husband Gosta, and chef Holger Larson. One year after the opening of Man's Country, Bruce Vilanch tells the history of "The Tubs" in the *Chicago Tribune*:

> "First, there was a steambath. It was in New York and it was called the Continental. Located in some converted ballrooms in an old hotel, the place was fixed up with marble fixtures and potted palms. Homosexuals gathered there to take the vapors. ... They hired two unknown performers – a singer named Bette Midler and a piano player named Barry Manilow – and they proceeded to put on small musicales. The audience would sit on the floor and cheer."

Vilanch goes on to say this "wild and freaky" idea inspired "a group of old steambath and gay bar hands" to "build the biggest, and the best, red-hot nightspot in the world":

"RUB-A-DUB-DUB. Four hundred men in a tub.

"It may sound perverse, or at the least bizarre, but that is one of the unique features of Chicago's latest watering hole, a steambath-cum-nightclub called Man's Country. ... The most exotic nightspot for blocks and blocks–if not years and years–Man's Country boasts hot and cold running showers and patrons, bedrooms, lockers, a sauna, a glass-walled steamroom, a mirrored shower that looks like something that got loose from a Stanley Kubrick set, a Jacuzzi, a multi-colored parrot that views the proceedings with serene disinterest, and a gigantic disco-music hall ... "

The one-year anniversary party, emceed by Wanda Lust, a 6ft 4inch drag queen wearing a red wig, debuted the refurbished Music Hall with a stage, lighting and sound system that cost $100,000. The star of the show was fan dancer Sally Rand. She was "at least seventy years old," and had been arrested numerous times back in 1933-1934 while performing at the Chicago World's Fair. She was on a national tour and experiencing a "camp" revival. In the *Chicago Tribune*, Vilanch points out that Man's Country isn't the sort of place you would take someone's mother, "certainly not your own." The manager, Gary Chichester, explained, "We had toyed with the idea of opening the place to women, but it just wouldn't be feasible. We are a private club, and a private men's club. ... We're a gay club and we're not ashamed of it."

Three months after the opening of Man's Country, real-estate writer Don DeBat in the *Chicago Daily News* reported that co-owner of the baths, Charles "Chuck" Renslow, was one-third of an "investment syndicate" that purchased a seventy-eight-year-old "baroque masterpiece" at 503 W. Wrightwood Ave. The Dewes mansion, built by beer baron Francis J. Dewes in 1896, was destined for the wrecking ball. It had been up for sale for some time by the Svenska Ingenjörsföreningen in Chicago (Swedish Engineers' Society of Chicago), a group founded in 1908 to support men of Swedish descent in engineering and other industrial occupations. They bought the Dewes mansion in 1921 but were forced to sell when membership dwindled from several thousand to less than 50. The "investment syndicate" comprised Renslow, his lover Dom "Etienne" Orejudos, and Herbert G. Schmid, the German owner of the Der Read Barron restaurant and bar, 2265 N. Lincoln Ave., famous for its ceiling of varnished magazine covers and sign reading, "Save Lincoln Avenue wildlife, tip the bartender." Prior to the Der Read Barron, this location had been one of Renslow's Gold Coast leather bars. The trio paid between $200,000/$250,000 for the fifteen-room mansion. Before its purchase, other potential buyers included an Indiana nudist colony owner, the Greek and Hungarian consulates, a Serbian church and social group, and the Anglican Choir School of St. Gregory. Another who almost bought the mansion was George Santo Pietro, president of short-lived *Coq* magazine (pronounced "coke"). Pietro was formerly a photographer for *Gallery*, a girlie skin magazine. The *Chicago Daily News* article suggested there was some doubt as to what the mansion would be used for as the owners disagreed: Schmid claimed "the syndicate" were opening a "French and continental" restaurant, but Phillip A. Carroll, head of Carroll Realty & Insurance, broker for the buyers, said, "Renslow told me he plans to use the mansion as a residence and showplace." Carroll went on to describe Renslow as a "mystery man," who walks "with a limp, wears blue jeans and drives around in an expensive Mercedes Benz sports car." In the June 1974, *Chicago Gay Crusader*, Renslow denied there was a restaurant opening at the Dewes mansion, pointing out that a zoning variance would have to be sought. At the time, the area was zoned for residential use only.

The *Chicago Daily News* described the Dewes mansion:

> "The lavish foyer sports a sculptured marble and iron wishing well combining figures of two lovers and Cupid. Floors are Italian mosaics and walls are made of Skogoeia marble overlaid with gilded ornamental plaster ... Hand-wrought ornamental ironwork made by the famous Krupp Iron Works in Germany was used on stairways and for chandeliers in the carved wood paneled dining room. The mansion also has a three-story stained glass window on the main stairway, a Gothic library, numerous fireplaces, a penthouse ballroom for large parties and a basement barroom."

In these opulent surroundings, on August 18, 1974, Chuck Renslow's first "White Party" was held. In *Leatherman: The Legend of Chuck Renslow* by Tracy Baim and Owen Keehnen, the authors quote an account of the first White Party from *Midwest Bar Talk*:

> "The invitation reads dress white preferred and in white they came. Chuck Renslow opened his newly acquired $250,000 mansion in Chicago [and] most everyone came. Owner of the Gold Coast bar and Man's Country bath, Chuck erected a tent in the garden to which the guests were requested to enter screening by two uniformed guards. Under the white and yellow striped [tent] the party play[ers] sipped champagne punch and sampled hors d'ouevres."

After that, the White Party was an annual event.

# CHICAGO AFTER STONEWALL

Fan dancer Sally Rand appeared in the Music Hall of Man's Country bathhouse on February 15 and February 19-22, 1975. At seventy plus years of age, Rand performed the same fan dance she was arrested for at the 1933 Chicago World's Fair in the Streets of Paris sideshow attraction at the Café de la Paix. In fact, in 1933, Rand was arrested four times in one day while shaking her ostrich feather fans over her naked body at the Chicago Theater – each time she was charged with "putting on an indecent exhibition." It was reported in the *Chicago Tribune* that she told Judge Irwin Hasten, "My dancing is art. Every seat in the theater was taken. My public wants me. There's nothing vulgar, lewd, or obscene about the dancing."

At the Chicago Theater, Rand was first arrested after her 1:30 p.m. performance, by Sgt. Harry Costello and Policewoman Bessie McShane. Arrested with Rand were her brother Harold, "her colored maid" Mattie Wheeler, Edwin Gall, and Louis Lipstone, theater production manager." In court, an amusing exchange occurred when Rand's brother Harold called out, "You have nothing on her," and Sgt. Costello corrected him, "You mean she has nothing on her." Rand and entourage were arrested again at her 3:30 p.m., 6:30 p.m. and her 8:30 p.m. performances.

At Man's Country, Rand was not arrested, and neither were her towel-clad audience.

Maggie Daly in the *Chicago Tribune* wrote, "Sally Rand, appearing at Man's Country, called us and said, 'Maggie ... Charles Renslow gave me a party, in his big house, on Wrightwood. That's the place with all the Tiffany lamps and antiques. I've been dying to get into that house for years.'"

Chicago's "Leather and Levi" biker scene was based at the Gold Coast, Chicago's first gay leather bar. The gay crowd took over the bar in 1958. In the *Chicago Gay Crusader*, Fred Alexson wrote about the Gold Coast, a "unique local business." If the stereotype of the feminine limp-wristed hairdresser scared Middle America, the notion of a group of leather-clad, Harley straddling homosexuals, riding into town à la Marlon Brando in *The Wild One* would have made them apoplectic. Introducing out-of-the-loop readers to the Chicago leather scene, Alexson wrote:

> "The search for masculine identification has even resulted in some bars becoming known exclusively as men's bars. The Gold Coast, 501 N. Clark St., is a perfect example. It has been the favorite gathering spot for many a man for years.

"It is a leather bar by definition and description. The label of leather probably stems from the fact that the bar caters to young men who enjoy wearing Levi's and leather. The bar even encourages this dress code by featuring a 'leather night.' On such a night, it is preferred that as a patron you make leather and denim part of your look. While both materials suggest the desired look of ruggedness and strength, leather can be and has been also worn as a symbol of one's 'S&M' preference."

Alexson goes on to write about the downstairs bar – backroom – the Pit:

"This part of the Gold Coast has the look, smell, and feel of ruggedness, with its brick walls, dark heavy wood and steel beams, and giant wall murals depicting masculine pride and prowess guaranteed to hypnotize any visitor.

"You may want to straddle the saddles that are used as barstools, for they fit perfectly in all the right places. This is one saddle you won't fall out of, and as your eyes ride around the room cruising they will come upon various cells with heavy steel bars looking dark and forbidding, which can't or shouldn't be entered (I'm not sure which).

"There is one cell, however, if you're not too timid, which should be explored, for it may open a whole new world of excitement and adventure for you. Just beyond the restrooms at the back of the bar, blinking red lights will direct you to another small room called the Leather Cell."

The Leather Cell was the first gay men's leather and sex-toy store in Chicago. Opened in the Pit of the Gold Coast in 1972 by Bob Maddox and Frank Goley, the store expanded upstairs. In early 1975, the two lovers opened another branch called Male Hide at 66 W. Illinois St. Although the Leather Cell offered sex toys, Male Hide confined itself to clothing. On the wall of the Leather Cell in the Pit, a sign read, "The difference between men and boys is the price of their toys." Then added underneath, "That's not true – it is the size of their toys." One popular feature of the Leather Cell was "the famous graffiti board, covered with messages and offers from all over the country: 'Looking for a buddy?' 'Would take serious S&M out West.' 'Are you into leather and rubber?' 'Wanted: a slave to serve weekend party.'"

# 53
# SYNDICATED COLUMNIST MIKE ROYKO

In March 1974 in the *Chicago Daily News,* syndicated columnist Mike Royko caused a furor with "Going bananas over liberation," a parody on the gay liberation movement. It begins:

> "Is it abnormal for a man to be in love with a monkey? Should a man conceal such a relationship and be tormented by feelings of guilt? Should man-monkey marriages be legal?
>
> "These and other such questions are now being confronted as a result of the growing Banana Lib Movement, made up of men who have had such relationships."

Royko goes on to write about "defiant Banana Pride parades, with men and monkey mates marching together." And he refers to the Rev. Rodney Treeshaker, a Banana Lib leader, as "the minister who shocked his small-town Montana congregation by revealing that for years he and a monkey had been in love."

In the *Chicago Gay Crusader,* Jim Gates, the Chicago chapter president of the group ONE, called for a mass letter-writing campaign. Chicago Gay Alliance president William B. Kelley suggested gay people mail a banana, or banana peel, to Royko as a token of their feelings. However, on March 28, a protest took place outside of the Daily News Building, 401 N. Wabash Ave. On behalf of the United Front of Gay Organizations, Michael Bergeron delivered a Phewlitzer Prize plaque in recognition of Royko's anti-gay record. The plaque read, "To Mike Royko, the top banana, for his unique way of taking the suffering of millions of homosexuals in this country and making it into a monkey story."

Along with the plaque, and a bunch of bananas, was a letter addressed to publisher Marshall Field. The letter read, "You wouldn't have printed such an article about the black movement, or the Indian-rights struggle, the women's liberation campaign, or any other similar movement. But you have the audacity to insult Gay Liberation as well as the millions of homosexuals in this country by such a verbal slap in the face."

Royko answered the protests with "Bunch of prudes":

"Chicago's gay community, as well as many liberals, say they are furious with me.

"They have bombarded me with letters and phone calls, and have picketed the building I work in to receive an apology for a column I wrote.

"Among the words they have used to describe the column are 'atrocious,' 'tragic,' 'inhuman,' 'nauseating,' 'slander,' 'lies,' 'distortion,' 'vicious,' and 'really rotten.'

"THE COLUMN raised the question of whether marriage between men and monkeys should be condoned in our society.

"The gay movement correctly deduced that it was a satirical comment on the growing demand by homosexuals that society accept their relationships as normal, and that they be permitted to marry, and adopt children.

"But they have also correctly gathered that I don't think homosexuality is normal, or that they should be permitted to marry and adopt children."

Royko also wrote a column that claimed the American Psychiatric Association's decision to delete homosexuality from the list of mental disorders was fraudulent. A theory also espoused by homophobic advice columnist Ann Landers. Royko explained:

"Before the APA voted on the homosexuality issue, a letter was received by all 18,000 members.

"The letter was signed by five prominent psychiatrists. Three are candidates for president of the APA, two are vice presidents.

"The letter urged psychiatrists to back the earlier committee contentions that homosexuality should be dropped as a mental illness.

"It didn't offer any medical reason for doing so. In fact, its most compelling argument was basically that of public relations. It said: 'We feel that it would be a serious and potentially embarrassing step for our profession to vote down a decision which was taken after serious and extended consideration by the bodies within our organization designated to consider such matters.'

"Many psychiatrists believe the letter was the deciding factor in the way the voting went.

"BUT DID THE PROMINENT PSYCHIATRISTS whose names appeared on the letter actually write it?

"They did not."

Royko claimed the letter was written by the National Gay Task Force and the APA were "subjected to as shrewd a job of hidden lobbying as you'd ever see in Washington."

A "Letter to the Editor" appeared in the *Democrat and Chronicle*, out of Rochester, NY:

> "The criticisms on the letter the National Gay Task Force sent to psychiatrists (... 'there was nothing on the letterhead, the return address, or in any part of the letter, to show that the gays had anything to do with it.'), illustrate Mr. Royko's lack of proper information. It is clear that Mr. Royko is unaware of the part gays publicly played in this 'letter.'
> 
> "For months before NGTF sent this letter to psychiatrists, in hopes of keeping the classification system's new term, gay people throughout the state were talking with individual psychiatrists and obtaining their signatures in support of the amended classification term.
> 
> "It would be ignorant for anyone to think that gays weren't behind any type of lobbying that involved their lives. For years gays have been committed to mental hospitals, given shock and chemotherapy, and have been denied civil rights, i.e. housing and employment.
> 
> "WOULD YOU THINK that an oppressed group would not be behind efforts that could end their oppression?
> 
> "Even more so, who would think that the oppressors would suddenly have a change of heart and 'liberate' the group they've oppressed for years, free of outside influence.
> 
> "Oversimplification and a lack of understanding can kill any issue. Mr. Royko has done this for Gay Liberation. First off, he has taken one group (NGTF) and one action (sending a letter) and then painted an unethical, negative picture of Gay Liberation.
> 
> "The media's influence is overwhelming. I can only hope that your paper sees the necessity in showing both sides of an issue, especially when the one shown is distorted.
> 
> "BARBARA J. BRITTON, Geneseo."

Over the years, Mike Royko remained homophobic. On April 2, 1990, the *Chicago Tribune* published Royko's column on "outing" ... "Antsy closet crowd should think twice." It begins:

> "Some militant homosexuals have come up with a new idea for improving their self-esteem, increasing political power, exaggerating their importance and getting themselves invited on TV shows that are in need of addle-brained guests.
>
> "These militants claim to know the identity of many homosexuals who go through life posing as heterosexuals. In other words, those who choose to stay in the closet.
>
> "But the militants want them to come out of the closet, whether they want to or not, and become visible members of what is known as the 'gay community.'"

Royko goes on to say that he doesn't understand the definition of "gay community." ... "Presumably, some unemployed gay drug addict would be a member of this community. So would a wealthy gay polo-playing socialite. But other than how they choose to use their sexual appendages, I don't see that they have much in common, and it's unlikely the socialite would invite the gay drug addict to cocktails."

Royko then set his sights on "outing," explaining it for his readers:

> "... homosexual militants are now using something called 'outing.' This means that if they have reason to believe, or even strongly suspect, that someone is a homosexual, they reveal it in one of their newspapers, picket his residence and make his sexual preferences public. ... In other words, what they do might appear to be an invasion of privacy, but as the saying goes, you have to break a few eggs to make an omelet. Or, as Slats Grobnik might put it, you have to peel a few fruits to make a fruit salad. (Look, don't accuse me of being insensitive. You're the ones who are poking around into someone's closet)."

In the same column, Royko commented on AIDS:

> "There is always AIDS, of course, but it has slowly sunk into the consciousness of most Americans that far more people die of cancer, heart disease and other afflictions. And that few non-homosexuals or drug-needle users are in danger. But when the President makes a speech, you don't see many cancer victims show up to screech that he is insensitive to their needs."

On April 29, 1990, a Letter to the Editor appeared in the *Chicago Tribune*, written by W. A. Verick, Chair, Chicago Area AIDS Task Force. "Mike Royko's column of April 2 ... portrayed members of the gay and lesbian community in an insulting and stereotypical manner and contributed to the burden of societal homophobia which results in a wide variety of discrimination."

Verick goes on to say:

"Mr. Royko also mentions that 'few non-homosexual or drug-needle users are in danger.'

"HIV is an infectious agent, not highly contagious but transmissible through sharing needles and sex, whether homosexual or heterosexual.

"Thousands of persons are infected through heterosexual relations yearly, but will have no indication until 10 years or more have passed when symptoms develop.

"In fact, the tragedy continues as the trend of new HIV infections has begun to shift from the gay community to communities of color where needle-sharing and heterosexual relations are major modes of transmission. And from 1988 to 1989, newly diagnosed AIDS cases among gay men increased 8 percent, while cases among heterosexuals increased 27 percent."

Mike Royko died on April 29, 1997, and was buried in the Acacia Park Cemetery, Norridge, IL.

On May 4, 1997 Clarence Page wrote in the *Chicago Tribune*:

"In his final years, critics began to wonder whether the Pulitzer Prize winner was losing his touch. Why, many wondered, was he picking on minorities, homosexuals and other less privileged groups, the sort of little guys his common man's voice used to defend?

"Maybe he isolated himself too much. He should get out more, I used to say; he needs to talk to some of the people he is writing about. Maybe he was afraid he might like them too much and lose his edge. Nothing spoils a good, well-cultivated rage like too much information."

# 54
# BECKMAN HOUSE AND GAY HORIZONS

In March 1974, Beckman House, a new gay center, opened at 3519 N. Halsted. It was named after the late gay activist Barbara Beckman. In the *Paper,* an "In Memoriam" reads:

"There is one person whose name is not on our masthead nor printed at the end of any article, yet who was as much responsible for the *Paper* as any of those who worked on it. The *Paper* was first conceived over dinner at Willoughby's with Barbara Beckman, who was insistent that Chicago needed a paper that printed news of groups who were frozen out of both the overground and underground media. ... Two days after that meeting at Willoughby's, a few days before Easter Sunday, Barbara was killed in an automobile accident."

Lesbian activist Vernita Gray told the author, "She [Beckman] and a young black woman were on the highway driving somewhere and hit a truck. Barbara was killed instantly, but her companion and friend Kathy survived."

On April 3, 1972, an article in Cedar Rapids' *Gazette* reads, "Barbara Beckman, 24, of Chicago was killed when a rented van she was driving ran off the westbound lane of Interstate 80 near Colfax Saturday."

In March 1972, Barbra Beckman, as a founding member of Radical Lesbians, attended the "Justice in America" conference at the University of Nebraska-Lincoln. A panel discussion on "third-world convocation" included Chicagoans Barbara Beckman, Susan Kahn, Linda Shear and Ortez Alderson. Beckman claimed that Nebraska law officers had harassed a group of homosexuals on their way to the conference. "A group of my gay brothers was stopped on the highway by Nebraska pigs and harassed." Alderson, who was in the car, said officers asked if they were going to the conference. He refused to comment further on the matter.

Beckman House came under the umbrella of Oscar Wilde's Children, Inc., a not-for-profit corporation founded by Michael Bergeron. It also included the *Chicago Gay Crusader*, the Chicago Gay Directory, and the Chicago Gay Switchboard. Beckman House was funded by money raised in the community. On May 11, 1974, the 21 Club at 3042 Irving Park Road celebrated their 12th anniversary with a benefit hosted by Aunt Lena and Her Original 21 Club Adorables assisted by Jay Lee at $2 a ticket. Beckman House became so popular that the *Chicago Gay Crusader* announced that on June 1, they would be renting an adjoining storefront. The expansion would double the patio's size and adding space for a library. One popular activity at Beckman House was the Gay Orientation classes, an introduction to Chicago's gay subculture for those "coming out" or new to the city. The classes included "film presentations, rap sessions, gay history, and much more."

The Grand Opening of Beckman House did not go without incident. Hosted by Michael Bergeron, veteran gay activists Dr. Franklin E. Kameny of Washington DC and Morris Kight of Los Angeles surprised the gathering by "streaking" through the reception. A photograph with strategically placed stars is on the cover of the May 1974 *Chicago Gay Crusader*. Kameny was in town to attend the Indiana Gay Awareness Conference in Bloomington and to be the guest speaker at ONE of Chicago's annual banquet. A half page photo spread entitled "The Many Faces at the ONE Banquet" appeared in the *Chicago Gay Crusader*. Those pictured were bar owner "Little" Jim Gates, Chairman, ONE of Chicago; Dr. Franklin E. Kameny, Washington DC Mattachine Society; Morris Kight, Los Angeles Gay Community Services Center; lesbian author Valerie Taylor; Jim Bradford of Mattachine Midwest; Michael Bergeron, editor of the *Chicago Gay Crusader*.

According to *Time* magazine, "streaking" was "a growing Los Angeles-area fad." *Time* went on to say, "Streakers generally race nude between two unpredictable points, and the idea is catching on among college students and other groups. Few streakers are reported to police, who are not overly concerned anyway, but passers-by have been shaken by the spectacle several times in the past few weeks, and no one knows where they might strike next."

Among the guests who witnessed the Beckman House streak were Brenda Weathers and New York gay activist Tom Smith. In 1974 Weathers founded an alcoholism and drug recovery center in Los Angeles, believed to be the first in the country aimed at lesbians. Along with alcoholism and drug addiction, venereal disease was an ever-present health issue in the gay community. The new VD Testing and Treatment Center organized jointly by the recently incorporated Gay Horizons and the Chicago Gay Medical Students Association, opened at Liberty Hall, 2440 N. Lincoln Ave. Apart from the clinic, Gay Horizons also offered a gay coffeehouse every Wednesday at 8:00 p.m. and were also sponsoring a GED high school diploma program in cooperation with the Gay Teachers Association. Gay Horizons held weekly meetings on Fridays at 7:30 p.m. in a member's first-floor apartment at 850 W. Diversey, and the group harbored ambitious plans for a community center of their own and a professional counseling service.

In May 1974, the *Chicago Gay Crusader* reported that the Chicago Gay Medical Students Association was founded in 1973 to "serve as a vehicle for communication among gay medical students, interns, physicians, and other health workers who feel that there is a need for both a better understanding within the medical community of the health problems of gay persons and to provide a responsible and professional organization to which gay persons can go for medical assistance."

The group aimed to eventually expand to have a complete health care facility for gay persons."

Visitors to the clinic picked up a leaflet that read, in part:

> "LOVE NEEDS CARE, WE CARE ABOUT YOU
>
> "We may not always have enough doctors, nurses etc. and, of course, never have enough money. Because there may be a shortage of help, you might have to wait up to an hour. Please be patient and try to understand.
>
> "ABOUT GH/GMS CLINIC
>
> "... This Clinic was founded to assure Gays of confidentiality and to give adequate treatment for those having VD problems. The Clinic opens its doors to all as we seek to erase the VD epidemic in our city.
>
> "More importantly, we function as a part of the rapidly expanding Gay Community as we demonstrate to the non-Gay establishment a positive channeling of our creative efforts!
>
> "However, this is not free or cheap. If we are to maintain our present level of service, you must help us. If we are to expand our services (to two nights or whatever), we cannot do it without the active support of you. When you are examined, treated and/or given a prescription, the value of the services rendered, including the medication, is about $35. Remember every bit helps."

## CHICAGO AFTER STONEWALL

In the book *Children of Horizons* by Gilbert Herdt and Andrew Boxer, the authors write about the genesis of Gay Horizons:

> "Horizons was an inspiration of the Stonewall revolution. It was created out of a need for a kind of 'drop-in' center like the old hippie 'crash pads' of the 1960s, where people could seek temporary shelter. Six or eight white, middle class, progressive baby-boomers got together one evening to brainstorm and dreamed up the center. The organization began in a cold-water basement, with naked water pipes and light bulbs visible on the ceiling and furnished with old sofas and hand-me-down donations."

It was important at the time for LGBT folks to have their own organizations:

> "The founders believed, as one of them has said, that, 'We could provide each other with better and more accurate information than the professionals.' In fact, many of the founders didn't trust the establishment doctors and psychologists and lawyers. Their experience as members of the third historical cohort who came out after Stonewall had shown them time and again that many of the professionals they dealt with were blatantly homophobic."

In what the *Chicago Gay Crusader* called "a surprise move," Beckman House changed hands on October 1, 1974, "After several weeks of negotiation, Oscar Wilde's Children has given Beckman House, the Gay Switchboard, and the entire operation at 2519 N. Halsted St. to Gay Horizons, Inc. Few changes in operation are expected."

Publishing the *Chicago Gay Crusader* and overseeing a gay community center's running proved too much for Michael Bergeron and Oscar Wilde's Children, the governing body. Bergeron explained, "We approached Gay Horizons with the idea of the transfer because we felt that they were certainly one of the best groups in the city to handle the center."

In an interview with the author, Lee A. Newell said:

> "That [Gay Horizons] was the first group I was involved in. They were upstairs at Clark and Diversey, and before that it was at Beckman House. They had moved out and I came in after the shit hit the fan. The original Gay Horizons was a coalition of all the different groups at Beckman House: Michael Bergeron had the phone line, and the doctors had Howard Brown Clinic, and the social workers were moving from the outreach services and the youth group, to psychotherapy services. There was no income being generated at all. From what I came to understand ... I don't really know the facts of the situation, this was before I got there ... but when they moved out of Beckman House, Howard Brown decided to

go off on their own, because they were unwilling to support the social services.

"Howard Brown had the free clinic. Everyone of a certain age remembers that you went to the 'free clinic' and it only cost $15. The first guy would come up and ask for a donation, then if you said no, then two people would come up for a donation, and if you still said no, they would take you into a side room and three people would sit you down and ask for a donation. But it was a 'free clinic,' if you could hold out long enough, you didn't have to pay.

"What happened was that Howard Brown went their own way and Gay Horizons ended up in this small suite of offices upstairs from the Astro restaurant, across the hall from Gender Services, and there was a masseur up there. It was a drop-in center, open from 7:00 PM to 11:00 PM. On Saturdays we had the youth group meeting. We had a small lobby area and the phones were there, and there was a big meeting room at the back. In the lobby there was this private office that psychotherapy used, which was just starting. This would have been '76, '77.

"Bill Krick had been vice president, and the president was a guy named Kent McClure, and he, apparently, had very bad feelings around the Howard Brown split. Kent McClure never came back. In fact, I was told I was the first chairperson who had ever served out the entire term. Bill Krick was called the 'Blessed Reverend' for a number of reasons, because he could be very hard to take. What they should have done was call elections and elected somebody to be official chairperson, but Bill didn't want that because he enjoyed running the place from being vice president. He had all of the authority and none of the responsibility."

Newell commented on his introduction to Gay Horizons:

"I first walked in there to volunteer on the phone lines, and two weeks later I was elected chairperson. It was like, 'Come to our annual meeting. Would you like to be chairperson?' I was naive enough to say yes, and they elected me.

"The guy they elected as my program director was a wonderful soul by the name of Ron Hawbaker; that's a name that will bring back shivers to a lot of people. Ron had owned a bar and he liked young men and he hung out with a lot of the street kids. Now, street kids in those days hung out at the Yankee Doodle at the corner of Clark and Schubert – it was just an old-fashioned hamburger stand.

"There were lots of runaway-throwaways, and you'd find 14, 15, 16 year old kids all the time. So our youth group was primarily street kids and there must have been 20 or 30 of them that came every Saturday. They loved it, because they ran the youth group. When they had meetings, I would come and open the facility, and they would go in and close the door and have their meeting. The adults didn't interfere with them and they really liked that."

Early on, Gay Horizons had its problems. Newell explains:

"There were all kinds of weird things that went on while Bill Krick was running the place from the second seat. One thing they had done was get together with Rogers Park Gay Center and decided they would raise money by having a raffle. They would give away $3,000 for an automobile, you could actually buy an automobile in those days for $3000, and the 2nd prize was a 10-speed bicycle, and I forget what the third prize was. It was a great idea, and they started selling tickets at a dollar a piece.

"However, when this was started, they neglected one of the basics of a benefit auction. As everyone knows when you do a benefit auction, the first thing you do is obtain the prizes. You don't plan on giving away $3,000 and then plan to get that $3,000 by selling tickets. There's a basic flaw in fundraising when you do that. Needless to say, that flaw existed in this plan.

"Me being naive and active in all kinds of Boy Scouts, youth advisory councils and all kinds of stuff through high school, I took charge. I had no qualms about going around to people and saying, 'Look, we've got this problem. Let the community sit down and figure out how to take care of it.' So we started having big meetings where we had bar owners in and we figured out how we could get tickets sold in the bars, so we could cover our costs. I think we ended up making a few thousand dollars.

"In the meantime, Ron was in charge of the tickets and he was giving them out to the hustlers to sell for us, and we ended up missing about 1,000 ticket stubs. That was probably my most difficult time; when we had the meeting and we had to fire Ron. He was fired from that, but he stuck around and helped out with Gay Horizons. It was like, 'OK this is obviously not the kind of task that Ron is good at.' That didn't make him less of a good person, to me at least. I don't know what other people thought of him."

How Charles "Chuck" Renslow bailed out Gay Horizons:

"When I was elected chairperson, we had a whole new board, and we actually had an accountant who was now going to be our treasurer, and that's when we discovered that we had no books. Howard Brown had the books. From the records that we did have, we knew that the rent had not been paid in three months, and utilities were also three months in arrears. There was a $200 long-distance phone bill that the boys had run up in the afternoons. So the question was, 'Where do we get the money to pay the rent?' They had no bank account, it was just unbelievable. What do we do?

I was told to just go over to Chuck Renslow, and he will give you the money.

"At the time, Chuck was living at the Dewes mansion, and so I walked over there to this fabulous mansion, with big stone statues holding up the front porch, rang the doorbell, and the pretty little houseboy comes and lets me in. He takes me down to see Chuck in his office, and I told him that Bill Krick said that he had been paying the rent, and I would be obliged if he would cover the rent this month. I said that in the future I fully expected Horizons to come up with some funding on its own, because we could not afford to get the reputation for being owned by any one person, or being financed by any one person. Because then, just as now, there was a tremendous amount of politics in the community. To try and stay neutral was a big effort. I'll never forget, he said, 'Not a problem.' He just stood up, took out his wallet and handed me $180. That was how I met Chuck Renslow."

Charles "Chuck" Renslow warns of Gay Horizons hustling ring.:

"They had tried to extend the hours of the phone-line to earlier in the afternoon, but the only people they could find to man the phone lines were the boys. The boys would come in and they were answering phones unsupervised from 4:00 PM to 7:00 PM. One of the first things I was told when I went to get the rent from Chuck Renslow was, 'Oh by the way, the cops called me and the boys have got a hustling service running on that number. It would be a good idea to stop that.'

Gay Horizons were quick to raise funds:

"Then at Gay Horizons we started talking about fundraising and I went around to the lawyer Paul Goldman's group, I think it was called Legacy, a senior's group. You go, you talk, they pat your head, pat your ass, and then he hands you a check for $50, and off you go. We got Marge Summit to throw a benefit auction where people donated stuff and that went very, very well. We had tons and tons of stuff; the biggest thing we ever had was Rene Hanover and Dilly, her lover, donated a piano one year. We got to auction that off."

The mysterious fire:

"I was chairperson in '77, '78. We'd moved from Clark and Diversey to Oakdale because there had been this fire in the electrical distribution closet. That mysteriously burned a little three-inch diameter hole in the floor and destroyed the fuse box for Gay Horizons. It could have been the Astro restaurant downstairs, or it could have been this guy whose name was James ___ and he was a hanger-on to the youth group. He was a sleazy type guy who must have been 20, 21, and he was very unhappy with me.

"We had the fire and we moved over to Oakdale, which is what we could afford versus what we needed. There was some friction between Joe Loundy and I. He was with psychotherapy services with the professional social workers, and they were not happy because they did not have a private separate room where they could meet with people. When we had the bridge club, they would be upset because the activity in the center was disturbing their counseling sessions. One can understand that, but that was when everyone started having very serious meetings about where do we get the money to afford the space we need?

"I don't remember exactly when I left, but I didn't go away in a huff. I know that I wanted to be chairperson for another year, to try and get Horizons really going. Joe Loundy came in and took over and did a wonderful job, an outstanding job. I then took a couple of years out to make some money in the corporate world, but I still served on the board. I was switchboard co-director, I was a peer counselor for six years, so I was around more or less until the mid '80s, then I think I just got busy with work. I'm the type of person that if I can't make my commitments, I have to resign."

# 55
# THE 5TH ANNUAL GAY PRIDE PARADE

In July 1974, the *Chicago Gay Crusader* noted the 5th Annual Gay Pride Parade "took a somewhat less militant tone this year in favor of a more festive celebration":

> "Clowns, jesters, and costumed people rode elaborately-decorated floats and marched along the 2 1/2 mile route. A shower of Mardi Gras beads and trinkets filled the air and fell to the street as a float entitled "Pennies from Heaven" rounded the corner. Beautiful drags in fabulous gowns and handsome studs in towels waved from the floats. 'Come be trashy with us' proclaimed the float from Gay Broadway [Bathhouse] and 'we'd rather be fruits than vegetables,' declared the Bistro's [a gay Disco] entry."

A "streaker" on a bicycle made it three blocks before he was arrested. The Beckman House float was a huge mock Coca-Cola carton with people inside, bearing the slogan, "Gay Love – It's the Real Thing." Controversially, a virtually naked woman painted gold was on the Ms. float, along with the bar's owners Marge Summit and Chee Chee, caused some lesbians to throw up their hands in horror. The parade followed a lavender line painted down the center of the street from Belmont Ave. to Diversey Pkwy. The line was the work of a lesbian activist who painted-by-moonlight after the city's Department of Streets and Sanitation refused her permission to do it. Another popular entry was Jo-Jo, the canine winner of the Gay Horizons Ann Landers Look-a-Like contest.

In the *Chicago Tribune,* Meg O'Connor added to the list of oddities:

> "A vampy, male homosexual, dressed in a slinky '30s dress, with furpiece over one shoulder. Bright red lips, heavily rouged cheeks, thick

false eyelashes, and a long red wig, sashayed down Broadway. ... Male bathing beauties posed in scanty swimsuits. ... A man dressed as Justice, in a white flowing robe, his skin painted gold, carried the scales of justice, showing 'straight' (heterosexual) oppression outweighing 'gay rights.'"

The 5th Annual Gay Pride Week Schedule read:

Saturday, June 22

Noon: Rally, Cook County Jail and House of Correction, 2600 S. California Blvd.

7:00 p.m.: Teach-In on "Gay People and History," apartment of Ted Berg, 452 W. Roslyn Pl.

7:00 p.m.: Artemis Players stage production (for women only), Liberty Hall, 2440 N. Lincoln Ave. Free

9:00 p.m.; Women's Sock Hop, Liberty Hall, 2440 N. Lincoln Ave., limited to 200.

Sunday, June 23

1:00 p.m.: Picnic, Lincoln Park, Clark St. and Armitage Ave., west of Chicago Historical Society.

Workshop on "Creativity" conducted during picnic.

Special Gay Pride Week services by Good Shepherd Parish Metropolitan Community Church, 615 W. Wellington Ave., and Dignity/Chicago, 824 W. Wellington Ave., both at 7:00 p.m. this Sunday and next.

7:30 p.m.: Unitarian-Universalist Gay Caucus religious service, 656 W. Barry Ave.

7:30 p.m.: Teach-in on "Gay People and Religion," apartment of Ted Berg, 452 W. Roslyn Pl.

Monday, June 24

Women's Coffeehouse (women only), Liberty Hall, 2440 N. Lincoln Ave., evening; bring instruments.

Tuesday, June 25

7:00 p.m.: Gay Pride Softball Game (between women and men), Lincoln Park, Diversey Pkwy. and Stockton Drive near Hamilton statue.

Wednesday, June 26

7:00 p.m.: Gay Horizons pot luck and Ann Landers Look-A-Like contest, Liberty Hall.

Thursday, June 27

Noon: Loop Rally and Kiss-In, Chicago Civic Center Plaza, Dearborn and Washington Sts., lunchtime gay rights demonstrations here daily.

7:30 p.m.: Teach-In on "Alternate forms of Lesbian Feminism." Apt. 2E, 6636 N. Glenwood Ave.

7:00 p.m.: Gay Pride Ecumenical Religious Service, 941 W. Diversey Pkwy. Guest speaker: Rev. Tom Maurer, Minneapolis. Topic: "Forgive But Not Forget."

Friday, June 28

7:00 p.m.: Film Festival, Liberty Hall, 2440 N. Lincoln Ave., Unity-Gay Rap, 7070 N. Ridge Ave. 8:00 p.m.

Saturday, June 29

2:30 p.m.: Workshop on "Philosophy of Heterosexuality," 2440 N. Lincoln Ave.

"Workshop for Homosexual Men," 100 E. Ohio St., 2:00 p.m.–10:30 p.m., and Sunday, 10:00 a.m. to afternoon: call _____ for details.

8:30 p.m.–12:00 p.m.: Gay Pride Week Dance, at the Post, 1720 N. Cleveland Ave.; live band; $2.50 at door.

Sunday June 30

Gay Pride Parade forms 1:00 p.m. at Belmont Ave. and Lake Shore Drive. Steps off at 2:00 p.m.; route: Belmont Ave., Broadway, Clark St., Fullerton Pkwy., Stockton Dr. to 1800 N.

Park rally at parade's end, about 3:30 p.m., followed by New Orleans fire victims' memorial about 4:30 p.m.

Buffets at co-operating bars afterward.

Special Gay Pride Week religious services 7:00 p.m.

In June 1970, one year after the Stonewall Riots, only four cities in the US celebrated Gay Pride – New York, Los Angeles, and Chicago had march's/parades and San Francisco had a Gay-In in Golden Gate Park. By 1974 Gay Pride Parades sprang up in other cities and towns. In Hackensack, NJ, Tom Masland at the *Record* wrote:

> "Undeterred by cold rain, 48 gay activists marched three times around the courthouse in Hackensack Friday night in celebration of Gay Pride Day.
>
> "Earlier, a group fostering homosexual causes, had received a letter from City Manager Joseph J. Squillace turning down a request by members to raise their flag over the courthouse.
>
> "The blue and yellow flag, with the Greek letter Lambda was forgotten Friday and an organizer had to return for it before the march began.
>
> "Squillace said the Albanians are the only group allowed to fly its flag over the city.
>
> "'The Albanians are not a minority group, but a country. If we were to allow this [the gay flag] I could have 40 flags here,' Squillace said."

Masland ends his article with, "Two uniformed policemen, several plainclothesmen, and a handful of passers-by were the only witnesses to Friday's sodden march."

The Passaic, NJ, *Herald News* wrote about the Hackensack, NJ, Pride event:

> "Some of the predominantly male group held hands and others kissed as the parade marched to chants of 'We shall overcome,' and 'Gay Pride.' Many of the marchers carried placards reading 'Gay is Good' and 'Gay Pride.' Two marchers covered their faces.
>
> "One spectator, a 47 year-year-old man, admitted to being gay also. 'I was born gay and I guess I'll die gay,' he said, 'It took a lot of courage for me to come here tonight.'"

In a "Letter to the Editor" in the *Record,* Frances J. Dilts wrote:

> "Have the people on the council sunk so low morally and spiritually that we are now asked and expected to honor a group the Bible tells us is an abomination in the eyes of God? (See Leviticus18:22)
>
> "I do not deny homosexuals the rights of all citizens – to make a living, enjoy good housing, etc. but I do strenuously object to having their sexual perversion flaunted in our faces and those of our children.
>
> "The Hackensack Council must be made up of godless men with spines of jellyfish, to be led astray by the Gay Activist Alliance."

Bad weather and media coverage affected the turn out for the Mississippi Gay Alliance Pride celebration at Riverside Park in Jackson. Mike Forester wrote in the *Clarion-Ledger*:

> "The weather, the *Clarion-Ledger* and Channel 12 News combined Sunday afternoon to minimize the turnout at a Riverside Park kickoff rally for Gay Pride Week, sponsored by the Mississippi Gay Alliance [MGA].
>
> "Eddie Sandifer, chairman of the Jackson chapter of the ACLU and MGA president, decided 'I believe that part of it was because of the weather. I had several calls before I left my place of employment that were enquiring as to whether we would still try to have the meeting, since the weather had turned out so bad.'
>
> "'And also,' Sandifer continued, 'there're several people out here in the park that would come over to this meeting that did not come over because of the television coverage and reporting that was going on. Next year probably they will; but this time they're a little leery of appearing on television and in the paper.'"

The *Boston Globe* reported that "600 gay persons march in Boston observance":

> "More than 600 homosexuals and lesbians from the New England states paraded from Copley Square to Boston Common yesterday in observance of the fifth annual Gay Pride week, which began last Sunday.
>
> "The majority of the group, some casually dressed in Levi's and T shirts, others costumed in clown suits and evening gowns, carried red, pink, green, blue and yellow balloons imprinted 'Gay Pride 1974.'
>
> "During the noon to 12:30 p.m. assembly period in Copley Square, ice cream vendors and hawkers moved among the crowd. One woman was selling tin buttons that read, 'Stars and Dykes Forever.'"

In the *Honolulu Advertiser*:

> "Hawaii will have a Gay Day in Waikiki.
>
> "Officially called Gay Pride Day, the event will begin with a parade at 11 a.m. starting at the corner of Ala Wai and McCully, then proceeding on Kalakaua Avenue to Kapiolani Park.
>
> "FOLLOWING the parade at about 2 p.m., a pot luck supper will be held at Queen's Surf Beach where the Metropolitan Community Church will conduct a memorial service for the 31 persons burned to death in an arsonist's fire at a New Orleans homosexual bar a year ago."

Rosemary Pennock in the *Austin-American-Statesman* wrote:

"A black cape and a bowler derby; a man on crutches with bright blue butterflies sprouting from his eyes; girls in slinky dresses and men in snug jeans – the crowd was a slightly flashy blend of straight and semi-flashy hip.

"The dance – a year ago – was illegal.

"This year, Gay People of Austin, a University of Texas organization, held its Gay Pride Dance at the student union with no harassment, complete legality, and a distinct lack of ostentation."

# 56
# THE CASE OF DAVID C. GARDNER

On July 1, 1974, an exclusive story by Rob Warden appeared in the *Chicago Daily News* under the headline, "High Scorer in Suburb Job Test Rejected for Teen Sex Experience." David C. Gardner, 28, married with two children, scored in the top six percent on a civil service exam, but was still rejected for a job by the Elk Grove Village Board of Fire and Police Commissioners. Warden writes that the Board's excuse was that Gardner failed a lie detector test. However, when Gardner requested the examiner's report, it read, "In the opinion of the examiner, based solely on the polygraph records, the subject told the truth to all the relevant questions."

Gardner then asked Gayle B. Bantner, chairman of the three-man village fire and police board, what the real reason was. He told him it was because he was in Chapter 13 bankruptcy and had admitted to a past homosexual encounter. Gardner said he had disclosed his Chapter 13 bankruptcy on his job application. Therefore, the board was aware of it before he had taken the Civil Service exam. The bankruptcy was caused by his wife being hospitalized thirteen times and the hospital bills mounting up. Undaunted, Gardner asked to meet with the board to tell his side of the story. He appeared at the Elk Grove Village Municipal Hall with Rob Warden from the *Chicago Daily News*. On the question of homosexuality, Gardner explained that as the polygraph report noted, when he was 19 years-old, he was paid $50 to let a homosexual "do his thing." This came to light after the polygraph examiner asked Gardner to describe the one thing he was most ashamed of. The polygraph examiner then asked Gardner if he'd had any homosexual experience in the last five years in a follow-up question. He said no. Both questions he answered truthfully.

After the hearing, one board member, H. Robert Goldsmith, agreed Gardner had been unfairly treated and voted to hire him. However, Bantner and Dr. Alan J. Shapiro voted against, admitting that Gardner's one homosexual experience nine years earlier was the sole reason for turning him down. Gardner gave Warden permission to publish his story in the *Chicago Daily News*, as he didn't want his friends to think he had failed the lie detector test.

The following day an article by Jerry Thomas appeared in Chicago's *Daily Herald*, in which Gardner explained the homosexual encounter, "It wouldn't have happened if I hadn't been drinking and I have never since had any homosexual experience." The article goes on:

> "HOWARD EGLIT, legal director of the American Civil Liberties Union said, 'Our position would be that it is unconstitutional to deprive a person of employment on the basis of his or her sexual activities. Sexual activity is as much protected as any other protected activity under the constitution and should play no role in employers' determination of whether to hire a person.'
>
> "Gardner's attorney, Leonard Groupe, said he 'is exploring all avenues – seeing which way the wind blows.' He refused to comment on further legal actions."

In October 1974, a *Daily Herald* headline read, "ACLU sues to get man fireman's job":

> "A lawsuit seeking $1,000 damages and the hiring of a Hanover Park man to the Elk Grove Fire Dept, was filed in US District Court Monday by the American Civil Liberties Union. The suit was filed on behalf of David C. Gardner, 29, who was denied hiring in July by the village's Board of Police and Fire Commissioners because he had admitted during a polygraph test to a single teen-age homosexual experience.
>
> " ... The suit seeks a court order that a policy of rejecting job applicants because of homosexual encounters is unconstitutional, that Elk Grove Village offer Gardner a job on the fire department and be barred from hiring any other fireman until Gardner is hired, as well as $1,000 damages [each] from Gayle B. Bantner and Dr. Alan J. Shapiro, the two commissioners who voted not to hire Gardner."

On January 3, 1975, the *Daily Herald* reported that the ACLU were dropping the lawsuit against Elk Grove Village:

> "Dr. Alan J. Shapiro, a member of the fire and police commission, said an agreement was reached between the ACLU and the commission which

paved the way for withdrawal of the suit that sought $2,000 in damages and a job for the rejected applicant in the village fire department.

"Dr. Shapiro said the commission agreed, in order to get the suit withdrawn, not to discriminate in the future against applicants because of isolated homosexual conducts. The agreement also emphasized, he said, that the commission was not admitting that it violated the applicant's constitutional rights or any law.

"The commission offered a fireman's job to the rejected applicant, David C. Gardner, but Gardener refused the job, Dr. Shapiro said."

# 57
# LAVENDER WOMAN SPLITS

Tensions within Chicago's lesbian community came to a head in the summer of 1974. A web of political alliances, financial shenanigans, and ideological battles between the separatist *Lavender Woman* collective and the politically moderate – by comparison – Chicago Lesbian Liberation began taking its toll. In the *Chicago Gay Crusader,* Marie Jayne Kuda documents the imbroglio leading up to the publication of a rival issue of *Lavender Woman*; titled the *Original Lavender Woman* and dated August 1974. The timeline begins:

**August 1971**

*Lavender Woman*, produced by the Women's Caucus, debuted as a single sheet in the first issue of *Feminist Voice*.

**September 1971**

The Women's Caucus open a bank account at Amalgamated Trust & Savings.

**November 1971**

The 1st Issue of *Lavender Woman* is published

**December 1971**

The secretary of the Women's Caucus files a Trade Style Account form with Amalgamated, stating that the Women's Caucus was the sole owner of the business conducted in the name of *Lavender Woman*.

**September 1972**

The Women's Caucus changes its name to Chicago Lesbian Liberation (CLL), but the bank was not informed. The account was still in the name of the Caucus.

**Early 1973**

A series of events causes a rift between Chicago Lesbian Liberation and *Lavender Woman*. Notably, when the new CLL treasurer shifted funds into her own account and used it to pay her rent, and the subsequent "creative accounting" lead to *Lavender Woman* and CLL splitting.

**March 1973**

*Lavender Woman* announced it was a collective.

**August 1973**

An editorial in *Lavender Woman* says that the Collective and CLL have severed all ties. Some women at CLL threaten legal action, and after heated discussions, a contract is drawn up whereby CLL agreed to relinquish all claims to the title *Lavender Woman* on condition that the Collective "for the life of the newspaper, will consign one full page in each issue for the sole use of CLL; that CLL will have complete control over the content, format and layout of that page."

**June 1974**

The *Lavender Woman* collective declines to publish a cartoon submitted on the CLL page.

Kuda, in her *Chicago Gay Crusader* article, describes it thus, "[The cartoon] depicted male and female characters labeled Ms. Dyke and Fairy Mary in County Jail, crying, 'Help us, sister!' to an aloof figure labeled Amazon, who says, 'Sorry! I'm a separatist.'"

In the empty cartoon frame in the June 1974 *Lavender Woman*, it reads:

"When this page was submitted by CLL there was a cartoon in this space. We found it to be of a divisive and inflammatory nature. We have rejected it because it was an irresponsible attack on individuals rather than a criticism of ideas. We attempted to contact the artist, but she was unavailable before press time. – The *Lavender Woman* Collective."

## CHICAGO AFTER STONEWALL

On July 25, 1974, Ruby Watkins, President of CLL, wrote the following letter to the Lavender Woman Collective:

> "We the women of Chicago Lesbian Liberation feel that since our contract with you has been violated by you, it leaves the contract null and void. Furthermore, your past work on the paper, *Lavender Woman*, has not reflected the views of the entire lesbian community.
>
> "All past meetings between CLL and the Collective has [sic] always been at the convenience of the Collective. This is no longer feasible, practical or acceptable with us.
>
> "Since the contract initially drawn up between us has been violated by the Collective, thus making it null and void, we the women of CLL have decided that the ownership and subject matter of the paper will revert back to the original ownership, Chicago Lesbian Liberation. We shall print and distribute *Lavender Woman* so that all the lesbian community is fully represented, rather than just representing a few select separatist groups.
>
> "Yours in Sisterhood and Solidarity
>
> "Ruby Watkins, President."

The above letter was published in the CLL produced *Original Lavender Woman* and was sent after the two letters below were handed out at a July CLL/*Lavender Woman* Collective meeting. At that gathering, the Collective refused to speak, but elected a spokeswoman instead. In *Are We There Yet? A Continuing History of Lavender Woman, a Chicago Lesbian Newspaper 1971-1976* edited by Lavender Woman Collective member Michal Brody, in "Excerpts from an Unpublished Article, October 1974" it reads:

> "We met with CLL. Our feelings were on edge and we wanted to avoid shouting matches. So we chose as our spokeswoman Claudia Scott, our levelest [sic] head and a woman who knew her herstory and CLL's. She presented copies of our statements, and after a few words back and forth, she asked CLL to consider and talk about what we'd presented and get in touch with us."

The two statements were both dated July 11, 1974, and also published in the *Original Lavender Woman*. They read:

> "RE: The CLL page in *Lavender Woman*
>
> "The LW Collective would lake [sic] to change the Aug. 1973 agreement between LW and CLL which, among other things, gave CLL the use of one page per issue of LAVENDER WOMAN.
>
> "Many things have changed for both groups in the last year:
>
> 1) CLL now has a newsletter – in effect, its own paper.

2) Both LW and the CLL newsletter serve a vital function for lesbians and have their own constituencies (though there is some overlapping).

- LW's greatest growth in distribution (in subscribers and consignment) is <u>outside</u> of Chicago.
- CLL's focus and growth seems to be <u>in</u> Chicago.

3) It appears that CLL does not need LW as it did a year ago.

4) LW, however, needs the page space. We can not increase to 20 pages because we can't afford it. To survive at 16 pages we have decided to take on advertising, which in turn will take up more space.

"We feel caught by an agreement that most of us were not party to. This agreement, made a year ago, fit the circumstances of a year ago, but it doesn't now. We want both CLL and LW to move on and keep growing.

"We propose, therefore, that CLL give the use of their page to LW in exchange for a free (normally costing $15) ½ page ad of CLL activities in every issue for the net year beginning with the July-August 1974 issue of LAVENDER WOMAN. LW will also give CLL an 18 inch unedited column in the next issue so that CLL can present its views on what has happened here–since we also will be informing readers of the change.

"The column and ad must be in by Wednesday, July 17, our deadline. AD SIZE: <u>3 ½</u> wide <u>4 ½</u> high. Ads will have to meet the standards we are developing for advertisers. At this time we have to (sic) specifications: 1) that ads come from woman-run/owned businesses and 2) that ads be visually attractive. The LW collective has final approval on all advertising. For subsequent issues of LW ads must be submitted camera-ready two Wednesdays before lay-out weekend, so we have time to discuss and approve them. We will inform you of the projected dates of lay-out weekend shortly after the distribution of the preceding issue, or by listing dates in our calendar in the preceding issue.

"As per the other agreement, this agreement is open to re-negotiation by either party at any time. – *Lavender Woman* Collective."

The 2nd letter read:

"RE: REMOVAL OF THE CARTOON.

"The decision to remove Wanda Owen's cartoon from the June 1974 LAVENDER WOMAN was a hard one for us to make, and we're well aware of the consequences in terms of hurt and angry feelings. However, there's nothing we can do about that decision now except to explain the process we went through.

"It wasn't until Sunday afternoon on lay-out weekend that enough of our collective had seen the page to be able to meet to discuss the discomfort many of us felt with the cartoon. We were not in agreement about what to do, but, at the same time, we were under pressure to make a decision quickly, since we had to finish lay-out to meet an early Monday morning deadline at the printers.

"The things we had to deal with were: 1) a bitter disagreement among ourselves about what kind of responsibility the collective should have over everything in the paper; 2) not being able to reach Milly or Wanda or Ruby by phone; 3) not having available a copy of the Aug. 1973 agreement and therefore, 4) not knowing what control, if any, we had over the page.

"Most of the collective members have joined since Aug. 1973 and have no idea what we, in fact, had agreed to do. The few who were around when the initial agreement was made thought that it had given us some kind of control.

"We resolved our internal conflict with a compromise: removal of the cartoon and insertion of a small statement in its stead. No-one was satisfied with this. The big issue for us was to survive our own differences with each other.

"We are sorry the incident happened and has caused bad feelings. – *Lavender Woman* collective."

In July 1974, the *Chicago Lesbian Liberation Newsletter* published the censored Wanda Owen cartoon. The *Original Lavender Woman* reports on an August 5 CLL meeting about the cartoon, which separatists also attended. These are some of the opinions of CLL women of the separatists at the meeting, collected by "Jamie":

"I was shocked. I am new to the movement and I didn't know the stories behind the conflicts between separatists and non-separatists. The argument became too personal and avoided the issue at hand. I thought there was more than one issue involved. The night was totally wasted for both parties. Relationships between the two groups became more strained."

"I was happy to hear their opinion and also happy to finally get a reaction from the group. But it disturbed me that they took up so much time without doing anything constructive for the Lesbian community."

"It was a stinking meeting."

---

"I don't like anyone wasting my time whatsoever. Especially when I have something else to do."

---

Rusti wrote:

"The meeting of Aug. 5 was illuminating to say the least. A controversial cartoon drawn by Wanda, which was meant to encourage a dialogue between those women who purport a separatist ideology and the women of CLL.

"Such a tizzy! You'd thought someone had Spit on their Moma! One woman was so uptight that when she was asked to give her interpretation of what a separatist was, she refused to do so. Her reasoning being that someone might inflict harm on her. Even when we assured her that she was safe and that we really wanted to dispell [sic] the myths and misunderstanding between us and them, she said she was incapable of explaining what her interpretation of separatism was. Right then and there yours truly smelled a phoney [sic] fish abroad. None of these women were able to explain or defend their beliefs at the meeting, but they all agreed the cartoon was slanderous! RIDICULOUS!"

In *Are We There Yet? A Continuing History of Lavender Woman, a Chicago Lesbian Newspaper* 1971-1976, Michal Brody explains separatist views within the Collective:

"Some separatists felt that the only solution was to go off and found a self-sufficient lesbian nation that would be as removed as possible from the rest of the world, and some separatists believed in keeping a regular job and life in the world while maintaining the greatest possible distance from men within that framework. Some separatists were willing to relate to all other women and wanted to be separate only from men, while some separatists only wanted to relate to other lesbians, leaving all men and straight women alone. And some separatists wanted to relate only to other separatists. Add to that the volatile question of how to deal with male children, in public at lesbian events, in private social situations, and as mothers and aunties. Nearly everyone had a position, and nearly every position was held with life-or-death passion."

# 58
# THE LESBIAN WRITERS CONFERENCE

On July 9, 1974, in New York City, the American Library Association's Task Force on Gay Liberation awarded 79-years-old Oak Park, IL native Jeannette Howard Foster the third annual Gay Book Award. Her long out-of-print *Sex Variant Women in Literature* (1956) is an extensive study documenting 2,600 years of overt and covert lesbian writings from Sappho to Virginia Woolf and Djuna Barnes. Foster was unable to attend the ceremony, but wrote, "I can only repeat my delight and overwhelmed gratitude at being chosen for the award, and my happy surprise that my long-respected ALA [American Library Association] is willing to admit the existence – and even honor it – of gaiety!" *Sex Variant Women in Literature* was republished by Diana Press (later renamed Naiad Press) in 1975.

Foster did not attend the Lesbian Writers Conference in Chicago either, but her spirit was felt there. In fact, in her opening address, author Valerie Taylor dedicated the conference to Foster. The conference was held over the weekend of September 13-15, 1974, the first of its kind anywhere in the world. It took place at various Hyde Park venues, including the Church of Disciples of Christ, the Blue Gargoyle coffeehouse, and the First Unitarian Church, 5650 S. Woodlawn Ave., home of the Unitarian Universalist Gay Caucus. The conference, organized by Valerie Taylor, Susan Edwards, and Rebecca Hunter of Lavender Press, Polly Adams of Mattachine Midwest, and author Marie J. Kuda, attracted 135 women to the opening night. Seventy signed up for the whole conference. The registration fee was $5.

Maria Kuda wrote about the conference for the *Chicago Gay Crusader*. Kuda writes that on the opening Friday night, Valerie Taylor, author of seven pulp fiction novels, "explored the worlds of our literary 'grandmothers' and the times in which they wrote." Saturday was a day of workshops on poetry, fiction, article writing, songwriting, and writing for newspapers. Women at the conference could also peruse a bulletin board with photographs and paintings of lesbian writers from the past and an exhibition of volumes of their work, like Radclyffe Hall's *The Well of Loneliness* and Clemence Dane's *Regiment of Women*. On hand were representatives from newspapers, small presses, and published authors to advise new writers on publishing, preparing manuscripts, contracts, copyright, agents, and distribution.

Kuda writes, "Besides learning and sharing skills, most workshops also dealt with the questions: What is women's writing? Lesbian writing? Is it enough to use traditional structures, or should we invent our own? The songwriters dealt with their music in relation to men and the politics of performing when men are present."

The final day of the conference was given over to women reading and performing their own work. Lavender Press announced they would publish an anthology of the material read. One of their books sold at the conference was *Women Loving Women* edited by Marie J. Kuda, a bibliography of lesbian-themed fiction, poetry and biography.

# 59
# THE HOWARD BROWN MEMORIAL VD CLINIC PRE-AIDS

On February 1, 1975, Peoria born Dr. Howard J. Brown, New York's first Health Services Administrator during Mayor John V. Lindsay's administration, died from heart problems aged fifty. In October 1973, Brown hit the headlines when he "came out" as gay and co-founded the National Gay Task Force (NGTF). At the time, he was quoted as saying, "You get to a point in your life where you want to leave a legacy – in a sense this can help free the generation that comes after us from the dreadful agony of secrecy."

After his death, the following letter from Bill Page of the Gay Human Rights League appeared in the *Village Voice*:

> "Dear Sir: Dr. Howard Brown, New York City's Health Services Administrator during the Lindsay administration, died February 1, 1975. Dr. Brown was a professor at the NYU School of Public Administration.
>
> "A few years ago, Dr. Brown suffered a heart attack. While in the intensive care until of the hospital, and being a doctor knowing that each moment might be his last, Dr. Brown discovered something. He discovered that the only person he loved would not be admitted to see him during this crisis.
>
> "The reason – Dr. Brown was a homosexual and this person was his lover, denied access to visitation because he was not a 'relative.'
>
> "Upon this discovery, Dr. Brown decided to take an important step. He had resigned from his city health administrator's position because of rumors that he was gay and this was going to embarrass the administration then in office.
>
> "Dr. Brown 'came out.' He publicly acknowledged his homosexuality and by so doing attempted to give emotional support to others and further

the cause of gay civil rights legislation in order to eliminate the very discrimination he had undergone during his illness.

"Because of this city's archaic approach to human rights, he became more and more active in the movement. He continually placed himself in stressful situations in order to help and encourage the gay community. A person with a history of cardiac arrests is not supposed to undergo needless stress.

"Due to the death of this brave man we are dedicating ourselves with even more vigor to obtain the necessary legislation on the city, state, and national level. This new intensity will be honoring in our way Dr. Howard Brown.

"We hope he was with his loved one when he died.

"We will *never* forget that the stress he was under was due to the uneducated public's attitude toward homosexual human beings.

"We will *never* forget that last year the city council had the chance to help us change this kind of a situation.

"We call upon all the public to aid us, as a memorial to Dr. Brown, to obtain the basic rights we are entitled to under the 14th Amendment of the Constitution. We call upon everyone, gay and straight, to contact city council members, state legislators, and members of Congress to insure passage of current pending legislation.

"It would be the best memorial. ... "

"Bill Page

"Gay Human Rights League

"Queens."

At the time of his death, Brown was slated to be the guest speaker at the April 12 One of Chicago banquet at the Como Inn, 546 N. Milwaukee Ave. One of Chicago was the local chapter of One, Inc., the Los Angeles-based gay rights group established in 1952 by Antonio "Tony" Reyes, Martin Block, Dale Jennings, Merton Bird, W. Dorr Legg, Don Slater, and Chuck Rowland. One of Chicago replaced Brown as a speaker with National Gay Task Force board member Dr. Joseph L. Norton. He was also a professor of counseling at the State University of New York at Albany.

Over three hundred people attended the annual ONE of Chicago banquet at the Como Inn. In 1975, the annual Paul R. Goldman Award was presented to gay peace activist, pulp fiction writer, and advocate for Gay Grandmothers of America, Valerie Taylor. In her speech, she accepted the award in the name of "all women" and added she was "proud to bear the name 'lesbian.'" In his speech, Dr. Joseph L. Norton related some of his "discoveries" after coming out at age 51.

> "I used to think all gays are promiscuous. Now I think I'm the only one."
>
> "Too many people dishing each other,' which is called the *Boys in the Band* or Provincetown syndrome."
>
> "Stereotypes of gay persons as sex-obsessed are just stereotypes."
>
> "Gays don't want to be the other sex."
>
> "We don't know the cause of homosexuality – I don't know or care."
>
> "All gays don't hate the opposite sex."
>
> "Some people really do go both ways. I hope the gay world will accept everybody – and I include transvestites. To the gay ones, we owe a lot. They are part of the group who helped start our revised revolution [the 1969 Stonewall Riots]."

The April-May issue of the *Chicago Gay Crusader* notes the "white-haired" Norton shocked heterosexuals, and even some gays, at the banquet with a story about the necessity of removing his cock ring for airport security screening. It must have been quite shocking to members of ONE of Chicago, a conformist, straitlaced, gay group founded in 1961 by Paul R. Goldman, a heterosexual.

Norton explained his frankness, "Until the time that I can go in a bar in Falmouth with a gay friend and a straight couple and dance without being thrown out and not be called a faggot, until that time I am going to go out and scream, 'I am gay,' and I think some of us who can be open should be open."

Shortly afterward, Dr. Howard J. Brown was honored in Chicago when the Gay Horizons sponsored VD Clinic moved to new premises at LaPlaza Medical Center 1250 W. Belden and renamed itself the Howard Brown Memorial VD Clinic. By May 1976, the clinic's 2nd anniversary, over 4,000 patients had been helped. Three months later, on August 23, the Board of Gay Horizons voted to allow the Howard Brown Clinic, now located at 2205 N. Halsted, to become a separate organization. Gay Horizons continued with its switchboard, counseling services, and gay youth efforts.

On September 5, 1979, *Gay Life* reported that the Howard Brown Memorial Clinic held a reception for City of Chicago Department of Health officials to honor the clinic's recognition as a legitimate institution serving the community. Mayor Jane Byrne had accepted the invitation to attend but was called away to represent the US at the funeral of Lord Louis Mountbatten in England. On August 27, 1979, the British royal was murdered by the

Provisional Irish Republican Army, who planted a bomb on his fishing boat, the Shadow V at Mullaghmore, County Sligo, in Ireland. Dr. Hugo Muriel, Chicago City Commissioner of Health, stood in for Mayor Byrne. At the reception, Dr. Muriel said:

> "The City of Chicago is proud of the work that the Howard Brown Memorial Clinic has done in its five years of existence. The problem of communicable diseases is a great concern of the city as it affects gay people who are part of the larger population. I am happy that the city will now be able to work directly with the clinic, and I look forward to increased cooperation and funding on the part of the city."

Prior to the city's recognition, funds for the clinic were raised in the gay community. The first big fundraiser was on February 27, 1975, with the Lincoln Park Lagooners at their Winter Carnival at the Rainbo ice arena, 4836 N. Clark St. The *Chicago Gay Crusader* writes that the upcoming Carnival "will include skating, volleyball (bring tennis shoes), gay entertainment personality Wanda Lust on ice, plus dancing, drinks, midway amusements, and door prizes." A later report estimated 1300 people attended.

In the 1970s, nobody knew about AIDS. The first mention of this mysterious disease in a Chicago paper was a small item on page 2 of the June 19, 1981 *Gay Life*:

> "ATLANTA, GA–A type of pneumonia has been found in five young men, two of whom died, and may be linked to 'some aspect of homosexual lifestyle,' according to the U.S. Public Health Service's Center for Disease Control. Between October 1980 and May 1981 the five, all active gay men, were treated for pneumonia caused by the Pneumocystis carnii parasite. The center reported in its *Morbidity and Mortality Weekly Report*: 'The fact that these patients were all homosexual suggests an association between some aspect of homosexual lifestyle or disease acquired through sexual contact and pneumocystis pneumonia.'"

The following month, Albert N. Williams wrote, "Howard Brown Clinic responds to gay cancer reports" in *Gay Life*:

> "In quick response to alarming reports of a rare and often rapidly fatal form of cancer diagnosed in homosexual men, Chicago's Howard Brown Memorial Clinic is taking steps to handle patients concerned that they may have the disease.
>
> "'We're in touch with Jim Curran at the CDC,' said the clinic's executive director Harvey McMillen, referring to Dr. James Curran of the Federal Centers for Disease Control in Atlanta, which published reports of the cancer outbreak.

"'We're being kept up to date on new information as it becomes available,' he added. The clinic is taking an active role in helping coordinate medical investigation and treatment of the cancer.

"'We're disseminating information to our doctors, and also to our telephone staff and interviewers, so that they can help people who come in or call,' said Dr. Rav Di Phillips, HBMC's medical director. Di Phillips and his staff are gathering photographs of skin lesions associated with the cancer to keep on file for identification purposes. Chicago dermatologists are being contacted to stand by as referrals for suspected lesions.

"'If any gay people in Chicago have some purplish lumps on their extremities that don't go away, they can feel comfortable about calling or coming into the clinic,' said Di Phillips. He also emphasized that people should not be unduly alarmed.

"The cancer, called Kaposi's sarcoma, was recently diagnosed in 41 men in New York and California, according to news reports. Of the 41, nine were diagnosed in California; several of those victims reported they had been in New York in the period preceding the diagnosis. Two victims have reportedly been diagnosed in Copenhagen, one of whom had visited New York.

"Kaposi's sarcoma is extremely rare in America. According to CDC estimates, the nationwide incidence of the disease is about two cases in every 3 million people. The cancer is most commonly found in black Africans in Uganda and the northern Congo, where, said Di Phillips, it can account for 10% to 20% of cancer deaths.

"The cancer usually appears first in one or more spots anywhere on the body, though Di Phillips said it is not really a skin cancer. The spots generally do not itch or cause other symptoms, often can be mistaken for bruises, sometimes appear as lumps, and can turn brown after a period of time.

"The spots range in color from a violet purple to a reddish brown. Di Phillips said this discoloration occurs because 'this kind of tumor makes lots of blood vessels. All tumors make their own blood vessels, but this one makes more than usual.' The cancer often causes swollen lymph glands and then kills by spreading throughout the body. News reports said that eight of the 41 reported victims died less than 24 months after the diagnosis was made.

"Di Phillips noted that while Kaposi's sarcoma has primarily been known to affect men over 50 in the United States, most of the 41 gay patients were under 40, with a mean age of 39. The group ranged in age from 26 to 51.

"Di Phillips also noted that the cancer has been commonly found in the hands, although in the past it had generally appeared in the feet and lower legs. 'The implication is that it may act differently,' he said, referring to what may be a new form of disease.

"Kaposi's sarcoma often seems to attack specific ethnic types, said Di Phillips, comparing it in this respect to sickle-cell anemia. In Africa, it is common among blacks but almost non-existent among whites living in the same region. American victims frequently have been Jewish or Italian, the news reports have not mentioned the ethnic backgrounds of the victims, said Di Phillips, adding. 'It would be real interesting to know what the descent of these men is.'

"However, Di Phillips was highly skeptical of conjectures that the high incidence of the cancer in a group of gay victims indicated any genetic predisposition toward homosexuality.

"According to Dr. Alvin E. Friedman-Kien of the New York University Medical Center, most of the 41 cases involved men who reportedly have had multiple and frequent sexual contacts. Friedman-Kien's reporting physicians are said by a July 3 New York Times article to have described such contacts as being with as many as 10 different partners per night as often as four times a week.

"Many of the men have also been treated for viral infections, such as hepatitis B, herpes, and the herpes-related cytomegalovirus (CMV), as well as such parasitic infections as a mebiasis and giardiasis.

"A month ago, investigators at the University of California at Los Angeles and the CDC reported outbreaks of pneumocystis pneumonia, a type of pneumonia that usually affects only people who are taking drugs to suppress their immune system. Both the pneumonia victims and the cancer victims had a high incidence of CMV infection, leading investigators to suspect that these individuals are victims of a defect in their immune system that makes them vulnerable to certain kinds of germs to which gay men often are exposed. Commenting on the hypothetical relationship between the low resistance and the reported cancer, Di Phillips noted. 'You never know whether that immune defect is a cause or an effect.'"

# 60
# RACISM AT THE LESBIAN BARS

In the spring of 1975, more Chicago gay bars were charged with discriminatory door policies. In April 1975, *Lavender Woman* reported that on Thanksgiving Day 1974, Loretta Mears and two other African American women were turned away from CK's lesbian bar, 1425 W. Diversey, after Lee, the bouncer, asked them for five ID's. While they were standing at the door, several white women entered the bar without a five ID check. On Christmas Day, the same thing happened, so Mears and her friends contacted lesbian lawyer Renee Hanover. When they all returned to the bar, Lee told them he'd had trouble with African American women, hence the five ID check. On March 10, the Illinois Liquor Control Commission issued a citation charging CK's with "inconsistent ID checking standards." Hanover stressed her aim was to get a uniform carding policy, not to close the bar. The *Chicago Gay Crusader* noted the citation required Carol Kappa, owner of CK's, to appear before the Commission to plead her case against racial discrimination charges. On April 15, after the complainants seemed reluctant to testify, the Commission dismissed the citation, stating that the "violations [of the civil rights law] as alleged were not sufficient to merit the imposition of a suspension." Kappa and the complainants entered an agreement:

> "The agreement calls for Kappa to serve all customers equally and require her to adopt new policies regarding enforcement of age restrictions for selling liquor. If Kappa believes that a prospective liquor buyer is not of lawful age, under the agreement she will be allowed to request three separate forms of ID containing proof of age. Two of the ID papers must be officially issued by a public official and the third may be any document showing age.

"The official papers may include a voter's card, a welfare card, a birth certificate, a visa or passport, a city vehicle registration receipt, student ID from a public school, or employee ID from a public agency."

That wasn't the only charge of discrimination leveled at CK's bar. A letter in issue No. 19 of the *Chicago Gay Crusader* from Manny Rosone of Elmhurst, IL was typical of many the paper received. It reads, "I would like to voice my opinion of a gay bar that discriminates against males only at weekends. The bar is CK's." Rosone goes on to say that he and friends coming from another gay bar dropped into CK's but were told at the door that no men were allowed at weekends. "I have been gay all my life and have been around the world and never ran into anything like this," wrote Rosone. "Certain dress codes I could understand, but not an out-and-out discrimination."

Some lesbians wanted all men banned from women's bars, though clearly it was a violation of the law. Arguments for excluding men were, "That there are too few lesbian bars; that gay men become the prominent clientele ('take over') a lesbian bar once admitted; and that admitting men would subject lesbian customers to unwelcome sexual overtures by non-gay men." In *Lavender Woman* the "male problem" cropped up with regard to Augie's, another lesbian bar at 3729 N. Halsted St., owned by Olga "Augie" Flanagan. Twenty women signed a petition inviting Flanagan to discuss the matter. The petition read:

"We the women of the lesbian community strongly register our complaint against the violence directed towards our sisters at Augie's Club on May 25, 1975 by a male patron.

"We demand that the past policy of the bar be enforced and that any person who assaults physically or verbally a woman patron be outlawed from further admittance to the bar.

"Because of our interests in our community and its establishments, we want to meet with the owner of Augie's Club in order to discuss issues that pertain to the bar and its clientele.

"The action that you, the owner of Augie's take concerning our safety and the safety of our sisters in your bar will determine whether we continue to patronize Augie's club."

On May 29, 1975, Flanagan met with thirty or so women at the Lesbian Feminist Center. She suggested some of the men frequenting the bar were testing her on the non-discrimination issue. One delicate issue raised was racism, as some of the men "testing" the bar were gay African American men.

## CHICAGO AFTER STONEWALL

The meeting ended with a "wait and see" policy, though Flanagan promised to ban troublemakers from the bar, both male and female. Four years later, Carol Kappa and Olga Flanagan joined forces and opened CK/Augie's, 3727 N. Broadway. In June 1980, they were repeatedly picketed by the Black Lesbian Discrimination Investigative Committee and charged yet again with implementing a racially biased door policy.

In July 1975, an anonymous doorman told another story:

"I am a doorman at one of the bars in Chicago. The primary function of a doorman is to see the patrons who enter the bar are complying with the law regarding the legal age to drink *and* that they are able to prove the compliance should the police come into the bar and request it. 'Carding' is for the protection of the individual patrons as well as the bar.

"This principle applies to all bars, gay or straight.

"On any busy evening I can find at least 15 to 20 pieces of identification that are either false or have been passed from one person to another. This is the reason for frequently checking the identification of all patrons.

"Now let me broach a subject that is not frequently acknowledged but is well known – using identification policies and techniques to exclude someone from a bar. Does it happen? Yes. Unfortunately not everyone comes to a bar for purely social and entertainment purposes. Some come to steal, some come to disrupt, some come to sell drugs, some come to vent their hostilities and prejudices. No doorman in his right mind would let this type of person into the bar to destroy the enjoyment of the patrons who are properly using the bar. This requires making a judgment about a person quickly, and no one can be 100% accurate in this type of judgement. An individual who will not properly use a bar does not fall into any one category. They can be regulars or newcomers, male or female, gay or straight, black or white. Likewise a good doorman will prohibit a person from entering the bar at the door rather than risk violence trying to remove the individual later when they have misused the bar.

"There is no bar in the country, gay or straight, that appeals to or satisfies everyone. Once established, any bar relies on its regular customers to keep its doors open. No smart bar owner is going to refuse business from newcomers of different clientele providing it does not disrupt his or her regular business. This situation raises two questions. How far must a bar owner go in being liberal and open-minded, especially in a gay bar, to new clientele when the new clientele does cast a doubt, founded or not, on the future of his business and investment? Likewise, how far must a bar owner go in being faithful to his regular clientele who have provided him with income for years? Both are very difficult questions that have no immediate answer and may never have!"

# 61
# THE 1ST ISSUE OF CHICAGO GAY LIFE AND THE 6TH ANNUAL GAY PRIDE WEEK

The first issue of *Chicago Gay Life*, with its call to unity, was published as Gay Pride Week started. It was the first year that lesbians organized their own separate women-only schedule of events. The *Chicago Gay Crusader* published both Gay Pride schedules:

The 6th Annual Gay Pride Week Schedule read:

> Saturday, June 21
>
> SOFTBALL GAME, Grant Park diamond east of the Art Institute, afternoon; men vs. women.
>
> Sunday, June 22
>
> Lincoln Park near Diversey Ave. & Sheridan Rd.; and 25c BEER at Virgo Out, 642 W. Diversey down the street, with proceeds to the [Gay Pride Week Planning Committee] GPWPC. New York activist Morty Manford will be picnic guest.
>
> Monday, June 23
>
> MOVIE: A Very Natural Thing at the Glory Hole, 1343 N. Wells, 8 p.m., $1 admission to benefit GPWPC.

# CHICAGO AFTER STONEWALL

Tuesday, June 24

CIVIC CENTER PLAZA, Dearborn & Washington Sts., noon to 2:00 p.m.–ANNUAL RALLY, with Morty Manford speaking and Act III of the annual Killer Dyke drama.

OPEN CLOSET THEATRE plays at the Drama Shelter, 2020 N. Halsted. *Love of the Artists of Bitter Suite*, *Pop People*, *One Person*, *La Répétition*, all by Robert Patrick.

EVENING WORKSHOP with Morty Manford speaking at 1221 W. Sherwin Ave., c/o Mary Houlihan.

Wednesday, June 25

COFFEEHOUSE at Beckman House, 3519 N. Halsted St., 8:00 p.m. with entertainment.

COFFEEHOUSE at the Drama Shelter, 2020 N. Halsted St., 8:00 p.m. with entertainment.

OPEN CLOSET THEATRE plays at the Drama Shelter, 2020 N. Halsted. *Kangaroo* by Bret Perry; *The Actor and the Invader*, *Cornered*, *Fred and Harold*, all by Robert Patrick; *Once Below a Lighthouse* by Ramon Del Gado.

Thursday, June 26

GAY PICNIC/RAP SESSION at Belmont Rocks, led by John Power and Don Shaw at 6:30 p.m. Alternative bad weather location is Room 200, 100 E. Ohio St., Midwest Population Center.

OPEN CLOSET THEATRE plays at the Drama Shelter, 2020 N. Halsted. *Noon* by Terrence McNally; *Cleaning House* by Robert Patrick.

Friday, June 27

COOK COUNTY JAIL VISITATION. 26th & California, A1 Cellblock at 10:00 a.m.

FILM FESTIVAL, sponsored by Good Shepherd Parish Metropolitan Community Church, at 615 W. Wellington Ave., $1 donation, at 8:00 p.m. *A Position of Faith*, *Some of Your Best Friends Are*, *Home Movie*, *Lavender*, *Gay and Proud*, *Second Largest Minority*, social hour and Stonewall re-enactment.

OPEN CLOSET THEATRE plays at the Drama Shelter, 2020 N. Halsted. *The Madness of Lady Bright* by Lanford Wilson; *Something Unspoken* by Tennessee Williams.

Saturday, June 28

GAY PRIDE WEEK DANCE, Allerton Hotel's Tip Top Tap, 701 N. Michigan Ave., 8:00 to 12:00 p.m.; $2 in advance, $2.50 at door. Disc Jockey, drinks and dancing for all.

OPEN CLOSET THEATRE at the Drama Shelter, 2020 N. Halsted. "A smash Broadway comedy"–call for details.

Sunday, June 29

GAY PRIDE PARADE, from Belmont Ave. & Halsted St.: lineup 1:00 p.m., stepoff 2:00 p.m. East Broadway, south to Clark St. and Fullerton Ave., east to Stockton Dr., south to rally area at south end of Lincoln Park's South Lagoon. Floats, prizes, music, speakers. Parade entry fee $10 for commercial establishments, free to organizations. Trophy to best commercial entry; $25 to best group entry. Mark Segal to be feature speaker at rally.

REVUE at 6:00 p.m. featuring Wanda Lust–Man's Country, 5015 N. Clark St. For this one special occasion, MEMBERSHIP WILL NOT BE REQUIRED, and both women and men are welcome. $2 admission. Sockhop dancing.

Lesbian Pride Week Schedule read:

Friday, June 20

CHILDREN'S CONCERT. Benefit for Lesbian Pride Week Committee and the Lesbian Mother's Defense Fund. Women 13 and up $2. Children $1.00; children under five free. (No males over 12 admitted). Details to be announced.

Saturday, June 21

COFFEEHOUSE, 8:00 p.m., Liberty Hall, 2440 N. Lincoln. $1.00 donations.

Sunday, June 22

TEA FOR JOANN MULERT, anti-war activist imprisoned with Jane Kennedy, 1:00 p.m., 1441 W. Farwell (Skeeter Wilson). $1.00 donation for the defense of JoAnn and other anti-war outlaws.

WOMEN'S SOFTBALL, 3:30 p.m., Diamond 21, Grant Park, Jackson and Lake Shore.

Monday, June 23

WORKSHOP, "Lesbianism and Racism," 7:30 p.m., Women's Union office, 2748 N. Lincoln. A discussion of how racism affects our lives as lesbians and what we can do about it.

Tuesday, June 24

KILLER DYKE PLAY. Civic Center, Washington and Dearborn, at noon.

WORKSHOP, "Lesbians in the Professions." Details to be announced.

Wednesday, June 25

WORKSHOP, "Lesbians in Chicago Herstory" sponsored by the New Alexandria Library. Details to be announced.

Thursday June 26

WORKSHOP, "A Mothers Workshop." Details to be announced.

Saturday, June 28

MARCH AND RALLY, "Women in Support of Lesbian Rights" in the Loop, with speakers, *Killer Dyke* play and more. 1:30 to 3:30 p.m. Details to be announced.

DANCE, Liberty Hall, 2440 N. Lincoln Ave. with Mother Right Band, 8:00 p.m.; $2.00 donation; $1.50 in advance; Women only.

Sunday, June 29

WOMEN'S SOFTBALL, 3:30 p.m., Diamond 21, Grant Park, Jackson and Lake Shore.

POTLUCK, 7:00 p.m. Lesbian Feminist Center, 3523 N. Halsted.

In July, *Chicago Gay Life* reported that Gay Pride Planning Committee officials estimated 6,000 people were either in the parade or watching it from the sidelines. Patrick Townson, the chairperson for the Pride Committee, praised the police. He sent "thank you" letters to Commander Thomas Hanley, Town Hall District, Commander Robert Sheehan, East Chicago Avenue District. He also sent letters of thanks to the Acting Commissioner

Frances Degnan of the Department of Streets and Sanitation for their help in making the parade a success.

There were two categories for "The Best Float" contest, business and organizations. In the business category, first place went to Man's Country bathhouse, with an honorable mention to the Snake Pit bar. The $25 first prize for an organization's float went to the *Chicago Gay Crusader* with an honorable mention for Gay Horizons' VD Clinic. At the rally following the parade, speakers included Mark Segal, founder of the Gay Raiders, Nancy Davis, co-author of the book *Heterosexual*, Ken Martin, pastor of MCC/Good Shepherd Parish, and a "black transvestite named Toney." Not everything went according to plan. A few eggs and "stink bombs" were thrown along the route. The rally ended abruptly when an ambulance drove through and dispersed the crowd to rescue a gay man pushed into the lagoon by an onlooker. After the rally, many parade-goers went to a free drink party at Our Den, a "boogie dance bar" that opened a year earlier. Later in the evening' Man's Country bathhouse held a Sock Hop for men and women, starring female impersonator Wanda Lust, Frannie, and a live band. Profits from the dance went to the Gay Pride Week Planning Committee.

However, Meg O'Connor in the *Chicago Tribune* thought the parade lacked its usual pizazz:

> "Bikini-clad female impersonators stopped in the center of Clark Street to pose for camera buffs, followed by a gay religious group singing, 'They will know we are Christians by our love.' That was something like last year.
>
> "But as hundreds of gay men and women marched [in the parade] ... the traditional wit and humor was mostly missing."

O'Connor described the marchers as "silent and glum":

> "Typifying last year's parade, a vampy male homosexual captured the imagination of the crowd as he sashayed down Broadway in a slinky '30s dress.
>
> "Typifying this year's parade, a female impersonator sat quietly atop a float, apparently bored with it all."

On June 20, 1975, the first issue of the bi-weekly *Chicago Gay Life* appeared. (On June 25, 1976 the name was shortened to *Gay Life*, and in December 1977, it changed from bi-weekly to a weekly publication). The paper was founded by Grant Ford, Abe Olivo, and Valerie Bouchard, owners of Lifestyle Publishers, 343 S. Dearborn #1719. The masthead read:

# CHICAGO AFTER STONEWALL

| | |
|---|---|
| Editor/Publisher: | Grant Ford |
| Associate Editor: | Valerie A. Bouchard |
| Managing Editor: | Abe Olivo |
| Editorial Staff: | Celena M. Duncan |
| | Jim Grooms |
| | Leslie Nichols |
| | Patrick Townson |
| Art: | Ed Ferguson |
| Graphics: | Pat Mielcarek |
| Legal Counsel: | Paul R. Goldman |

Explaining the beginnings of *Chicago Gay Life*, Grant Ford wrote in Vol. 1 No. 1:

> "Gay Pride Week seemed to be the greatest time to give birth to this paper. But the idea was conceived more than a year ago. It was then that I volunteered my services to another Chicago gay newspaper. I was living in Indiana at the time, and because of difficulties in working within my schedule, they concluded that my services would not be of help. But the editor told me: "Chicago could always use another gay publication. Think about it.
>
> "Think I did! But that was all, until I discussed the idea with a feminist friend, a wife and mother of two children, a person with business acumen and a great deal of person insight. It was her encouragement that pushed me into action.
>
> "*Chicago Gay Life* is the result, in great part, of the suggestion of a gay newspaper editor, and the encouragement of a straight friend. The prime reason for the paper, however, is the crying need for an open forum, published regularly, in the gay community."

Ford's remark about "published regularly" references the infrequency of recent *Chicago Gay Crusader* issues. By the June 1975 Gay Pride Week, only three issues of the paper had appeared that year: No. 18 – 1975 (dated 1974 by mistake); No. 19 – 1975; and No. 20 – June 1975. The *Chicago Gay Crusader* was born at a time when financial realities took second place to the passion, idealism and enthusiasm of the 1960s. Clearly, the owners of *Chicago Gay Life* meant "business" while, at the same time, aspiring to be the one unified voice of a diverse, and increasingly fractious community.

Associate editor, Valerie A. Bouchard, wrote on Page 1 of the premiere issue:

"What is Chicago Gay Life? What does this paper have to offer?

"Chicago Gay Life is an attempt to unite the many gay factions in Chicago and to promote dialog between gay people and the straight world. It is a forum for gay people to explore together the dimensions of what gayness means in our community and in the world.

"I came to Chicago ten months ago from the Washington D.C. area and am shocked at the separatism in gay circles. The numerous organizations in the city know little if anything about any of the others. There is no real communication among gay people, and gay life is split in factions. There is animosity between men and women.

"Who are the representatives of black gays in the city? What are the various agencies available to gay people, and what are their functions? Where can you go with all your friends, both men and women?

"Gay people talk about the discrimination and isolation imposed upon us by straight people, but within our own community we are striking discriminatory blows against each other. ...

"... Chicago Gay Life would like to focus on division within our own community and on the commonality of our lives and experiences ..."

Bouchard ended with, "We've excluded each other for too long, and it is time we included everyone in order to grow together!"

In the July 4, 1975 issue of *Chicago Gay Life*, "Name withheld by request" wrote:

"In the Bouchard editorial, comments were made about the lack of unity in gay community affairs, about 'striking discriminatory blows against each other,' 'being concerned about inclusiveness' and similar ideas. I trust this was an indirect (or possible direct) commentary on the Gay Pride Week schedule published in the same edition of the paper. Certainly, when eleven of the events were marked (W) for 'women only,' this must fall into the scope of her comments regarding unity, inclusiveness and discrimination. Surely all gay events should be open to all with each individual participating in those events that interest him or her and to which she or he can contribute. Also the organizers of these events must be sure that the events and functions are open to all who will aid in their accomplishing the ends for which they were created."

Valerie A. Bouchard answered:

"Many people have commented about the fact that I write about unity and inclusiveness in the gay community, yet, many events on the calendar were marked for women-only. There are many reasons why this happened.

"From the information I have received, the Gay Pride Planning committee had originally included men and women to represent the various factions of the gay community. However, there was tension between the men and women. Women had certain ideas and events that they wished to present. The men apparently did not agree with them, and were not open to considering new options and ideas.

"The women decided that it was not possible to work with the Gay Pride Planning Committee and withdrew to form their own activities to celebrate Lesbian Pride Week."

Little Jim's, 3501 N. Halsted, is said to be the first gay bar on Halsted Street's stretch known as Boystown. The bar is often cited as being the beginning of the gay neighborhood on Halsted, between Belmont and Grace. However, five years earlier, a gay bar – mixed men and women – was located at 3729 N. Halsted called the In Between. That location became Augie's lesbian bar. The truth is that Boystown started as Girlstown. Little Jim's closed down in 2020, but the bar's Grand Opening in June 1975 coincided with the publication of the first issue of *Chicago Gay Life*:

In Leslie Nichols "Night Life" column, it reads:

"Little Jim's, at 3501 N. Halsted, had its opening on June 5. The bar features a cleverly designed dance area with mirrored walls, flashing lights, and a strobe, plus an excellent quad sound system. Not terribly big, it leans more on the folksy ... but the go-go boys let you know you're in Chicago. The ultra-clean men's room boasts a most unusual doorknob. Pull it!"

# AFTERWORD

I spent many years working for the gay press, covering everything from porn to politics – very similar subjects, sometimes the same thing. I witnessed hirings and firings, the drama of behind-the-scenes drag shows, and all the shenanigans going on in gay groups. The only thing that kept me reasonably sane, was my determination to continue the work of pioneers like those mentioned in this book. Bill Dry, Step May, Susan Moore, Merrilee Melvin, Michael Bergeron, Marge Heinz, Nellie Tumilty, ... where are they now? Some people take a stand, are heroes in that moment, then disappear. Forgotten heroes. I believe that we should honor these young men and women who carved a path that eventually led to same-sex marriage and gays in the military. And we should also honor those who created a gay press in Chicago, to counteract the homophobia in mainstream publications.

I finished writing this book in the middle of the COVID 19 pandemic, and a most turbulent time in American history. As I finished work each day, I switched on the TV news to see the protests of Black Lives Matter over the police killing of George Floyd and others ... too many others. I watched the rise of Fascism encouraged by an unpopular President. I also saw gay businesses close down. Historically, gay bars and newspapers were where we joined together to fight for our rights. Now that's disappearing. Everything is online.

Whether we like it or not, nothing stays the same. Everything moves forward. And that's the way it's supposed to be. We keep fighting.

# BIBLIOGRAPHY

## Introduction

"4 Policemen Hurt in 'Village' Raid: Melee Near Sheridan Square Follows Action at Bar." *New York Times,* 29 Jun. 1969:33

*Come Out!* (Vol. 1 No. 1), 14 Nov. 1969

*Gay News* (Vol. 1 No. 20), 22 Jun. 1970

"Gay Revolution Comes Out." *Rat Subterranean News*, 12 Aug. 1969:7

Jeremiah. *Come Out!* (Vol. 1 No. 5) Sep./Oct. 1970

Lisker, Jerry. "Homo Nest Raided, Queen Bees Are Stinging Mad." *New York Daily News (Sunday edition)*, 6 Jul. 1969:1

"Police Again Rout Village Youths: Outbreak by 400 Follows a Near-Riot Over Raid." *New York Times*, 30 June 1969:22

Smith, Howard. "Full Moon Over Stonewall." *Village Voice*, 3 Jul. 1969:1

Truscott, Lucian. "Gay Power Comes to Sheridan Square." *Village Voice*, 3 Jul. 1969:1

## Chapter 1

Primary Sources:

McCormick Library of Special Collections at Northwestern University, Evanston, IL
Gerber/Hart Library and Archives, 6500 N. Clark St., Chicago, IL 60626

---

Blatchford, Frank. "Interrupt Police Workshop: Youths Harass Conlisk." *Chicago Tribune*, 2 Jun. 1972:4

Bradford, Jim. "The New Militancy Emerges." *Mattachine Midwest Newsletter*, Oct. 1969:2

Bradford, Jim. "The President's Corner." *Mattachine Midwest Newsletter* Jul. 1969:5

Bradford, Jim and Kelly, William B. "Cops Hit More Bars." *Mattachine Midwest Newsletter*, Oct. 1969:1

Davis, Robert. "Braasch, 18 others guilty in police shakedown trial: 4 defendants are innocent." *Chicago Tribune*, 6 Oct. 1973:S1

Davis, Robert. "Vice club list climbs to 8." *Chicago Tribune*, 17 Aug. 1973:8

"Gay bars named in cop payoff trial." *Chicago Gay Crusader* Sep. 1973:1

Howard, Mark. "Chicago Gay Scene." *Mattachine Midwest Newsletter*, Jun. 1969:2

"Justice 24, Cops 0." *Mattachine Midwest Newsletter*, Jan. 1973:1

Kelley, William B. "Eye on the News." *Chicago Gay Crusader*, Jun. 1973:10

Kelley, William B. "Gaylimaufrey." *Mattachine Midwest Newsletter*, Aug. 1969:2

Kelley, William B. "I.D. Check Escalates to Melee." *Mattachine Midwest Newsletter*, Sep. 1969:7

Kelley, William B. "Riot, Tree-Cutting Mark NYC Gay Scene." *Mattachine Midwest Newsletter*, Jul. 1969:7

Laurence, Leo. "Gays hit NY Cops." *Berkeley Barb*, 4 Jul. 1969, 5

Negronida, Peter. "Brutality Charges Key to Cop Crisis." *Chicago Tribune*, 11 May 1972:1

O'Brien, John. "Police graft probe widens." *Chicago Tribune*, 2 Jan. 1973:1

O'Brien, John. "Take set at 'hundreds of thousands.'" *Chicago Tribune*, 31 Dec. 1972:1

"OFFICER BENJAMIN RIDES (RAIDS) AGAIN!" *Mattachine Midwest Newsletter*, Jun. 1968:3

Phillips, Richard. "Ex-cop gets 3 ½ year term in Austin tavern extortion." *Chicago Tribune*, 12 Feb. 1974:9

"Police Again Rout Village Youths: Outbreak by 400 Follows a Near-Riot Over Raid." *New York Times*, 30 Jun. 1969:22

Pratt, Steven. "Conlisk Meets the People: Would Alka-Seltzer Help?" *Chicago Tribune*, 21 May 1972: 26

Smith, Howard. "Full Moon Over Stonewall." *Village Voice*, 3 Jul. 1969:1

Sneed, Michael. "Carey says Daley perils bars in bribe quiz." *Chicago Tribune*, 15 Sep. 1973:7

Stienecker, David. "Bar Patrons Plead Guilty." *Mattachine Midwest Newsletter*, Jun. 1970

"Thanasouras' tragic career." *Chicago Tribune*, 23 Jul. 1977: S8

Truscott IV, Lucien. "Gay Power Comes to Sheridan Square." *Village Voice*, 3 Jul. 1969:1

Wiedrich, Bob. "Cops, pols, mob in gay-bar payoffs." *Chicago Tribune* 4 Oct. 1973:18

# Chapter 2

Primary Sources:

McCormick Library of Special Collections at Northwestern University, Evanston, IL
Gerber/Hart Library and Archives, 6500 N. Clark St., Chicago, IL 60626
Onge, Jack. "The Gay Liberation Movement." Chicago: Alliance Press, 1971

"2 Gay Students Wanted to Share 5 Rm Unfrn. Apt." *Maroon* 3 Oct. 1969:11
*Chicago Police Star* Jun. 1969:18
Chisman, Nancy. "Gay Lib Protests Talk by Detective." *Maroon* 6 Feb. 1970:1
"City cops taking on sex harassment." *Chicago Tribune* 2 Mar. 1993:89
Dorfman, Ron. "Mattachine Editor Arrested; Gays Picket Sergeant Manley." *Chicago Journalism Review* Apr. 1970:n.p.
"Equality for Your Fellow Man." *Time* 12 May 1967:64
Ferris, Jan. "6 police officers file sex harassment suit." *Chicago Tribune* 5 Aug. 1994:301
"Gay Lib Unit at U of C." *Second City* Undated Vol. 2 No. 5:7
"GAY POWER IN 69-70." *Maroon* 24 Oct. 1969:11
"Hippie Killed by Policemen in Old Town." *Chicago Tribune* 23 Aug. 1968:C14
"Innocent Looking." *Mattachine Midwest Newsletter* Oct. 1969:3
Meisner, Jason. "Ex-cop accused of impersonating fed." *Chicago Tribune* 4 Nov. 2015:1-10
O'Brien, John. "Harassment case points a finger at police officer 'code of silence.'" *Chicago Tribune* 28 Apr. 1994: 114
Stienecker, David. "A Gay Deceiver – Or Is He?" *Mattachine Midwest Newsletter* Sept. 1969:3
"Vice Squad's Manley Infiltrates Gay Lib." *Maroon* 3 Mar. 1970:5

# Chapter 3

Primary Sources

McCormick Library of Special Collections at Northwestern University, Evanston, IL
Gerber/Hart Library and Archives, 6500 N. Clark St., Chicago, IL. 60626

---

Chicago Gay Liberation group forms." *Mattachine Midwest Newsletter* November-December 1969:3
Edelman, Murray. "Gay Lib Speaks Out." *Maroon* 24 Apr. 1970:7
"Editorial [On UC-GLF dances]" *Maroon* 14 Apr. 1970:n.p.
"Gay Lib Dances." *Maroon* 21 Apr. 1970:10
"Gay Lib Charges Prejudice." *Maroon* 17 Apr. 1970:n.p.
"Gay Liberation Supplement." *Chicago Seed* Mar. 1970:13
May, Step. "Gay Lib Dance." *Maroon* 15 May 1970:11
Thierry, David. "On the Dance ... " *Chicago Gay Liberation Newsletter* 28 Apr. 1970:2

"Up Your Alley." *Chicago Gay Liberation Newsletter* Sept. 1970:4

## Chapter 4

Primary Sources:

Gerber/Hart Library and Archives, 6500 N. Clark St., Chicago, IL 60626
McCormick Library of Special Collections at Northwestern University, Evanston, IL

---

"GAY ACTIVIST COALITION FORMED IN LOOP." *Chicago Gay Alliance Newsletter* Dec. 1971:5
"Gay group formed." *Daily Northwestern* 23 Feb. 1970:3
"Gay Liberation Supplement." *Chicago Seed* Mar. 1970:13
"Gay Liberation Week Begins This Monday." *Daily Illini* 4 May 1970:5
"'Gay' President Quits; 25-Year-Old Takes Post." *Chicago Tribune* 8 Aug. 1970:41
"Loop Gays Form." *Chicago Gay Pride CGA Newsletter* Jun. 1972:17
"New Gay Lib Groups." *Second City* Undated Vol. 2. No. 6:7
Reinhold, Robert. "Gay Students Actively Fight to Explode All the Myths." *Chicago Tribune* 26 Dec. 1971:E7
"ROOSEVELT HAS COURSE IN HOMOPHILE STUDIES." *Chicago Gay Alliance Newsletter* Dec. 1970:3
"Roosevelt U. Bans Gay Books From Display." *Chicago Gay Pride CGA Newsletter* Mar. 1972:9
Rosen, Baran. "Gay Lib hopes for liberation from prejudice." *Daily Northwestern* 5 Mar. 1970:4
Rosen, Baran. "The gay liberation movement what's it all about." *Daily Northwestern* 3 Mar. 1970:6
"RU Gay Liberation to Meet." *Roosevelt Torch* 13 Apr. 1970:3
Shelton, Lois. "Out of the Closet, Into the Street." *Roosevelt Torch* 9 Mar. 1970:5

## Chapter 5

Bicek, Margaret. "Laws inhibit homosexual activity." *Daily Illini* 16 Oct. 1971:10
Bradley, Jim. "THE HOMOSEXUAL: A Stranger in Society ... 'I Can Never Be Happy." *Daily Illini* 3 Jun. 1966:1
"Champaign passes law to protect homosexuals." *Pantagraph* 21 Jul. 1977
"FREAK-GAY ROCK CONCERT." *Daily Illini* 22 May 1970:11
Fritsch, Jane "Urbana may restudy 'gay.'" *Daily Illini* 7 Sep. 1973:3

"Gay rights bill passes Urbana panel." *Daily Illini* 28 Aug. 193:1
Gehring, Jim. "GLF continues Wigwam picketing." *Daily Illini* 18 Apr. 1972:8
Knecht, Ronald L. "Urbana dress code hit." *Daily Illini* 8 Jan. 1972:5
Miller, Greg. "Council kills gay rights proposal." Daily *Illini* 16 May 1973:3
Miller, Greg. "Council sets fund use meetings." *Daily Illini* 9 May 1973:1
"'Son' 30 Years is Adopted by Allerton." *Chicago Tribune* 5 Mar. 1960:7
Zimmerman, Jackie. "Gay Liberation Front Pickets Wigwam." *Daily Illini* 15 Apr. 1972:7

## Chapter 6

Root, Susan. "Homosexual Revolt." *Chicago Daily News* 10 Mar. 1970:22
Sampson, Paul. "The 'Gay' Life in Chicago." *Chicago Today* 22 Feb. 1970:5

## Chapter 7

Primary Sources

Gerber/Hart Library and Archives, 6500 N. Clark St., Chicago, IL 60626
McCormick Library of Special Collections at Northwestern University, Evanston, IL

---

"100 Protest Harassing of Homosexuals." *Chicago Tribune* 17 Apr. 1970:11
"The Draft Counselor–Rejecting Homosexuals." *Chicago Sun-Times* 16 Apr. 1970:98
Green, Larry and Foreman, John. "10,000 protest Vietnam War" *Chicago Daily News* 16 Apr. 1970:3
"Organist Fined $250 for Photo to Draft Board." *Fort Worth Star-Telegram* 14 Aug. 1970:14
"THE HOMOSEXUAL AND THE DRAFT-A MORAL DILEMMA." *Mattachine Midwest Newsletter* May 1966:3
Rosen, Baran. "Gay Lib Rally in Loop Protests Harassment of Oppressed Groups." *Daily Northwestern* 17 Apr. 1970:n.p.
Sanford, David. "Boxed In." *New Republic* 21 May 1966:8

## Chapter 8

Akins, Doug. "The Club Set." *Chicago Defender* 7 Nov. 1970:20

Butler, Sheryl M. "'Female Impersonator' Killed by Cop in W. Side Street Brawl." *Chicago Defender* 28 Nov. 1970:1

Claire, Arletta. *Chicago Defender* 30 Jul. 1970:14

Claire, Arletta. "Homosexual Speaks Out Society Narrow Minded." *Chicago Defender* 13 Jul. 1970:8

Claire, Arletta. "Two Readers Write in Answer to Homosexuals." *Chicago Defender* 21 Jul. 1970:8

"FOUR ARRESTED FBI Investigating Livingston Draft Board Office Damage." *The Times* 29 Jul. 1970:1

"Four Defendants Fail to Appear in Peoria Court." *The Times* 17 Nov. 1970:3

"He's Missing." *Chicago Defender* 1 May 1969:5

"Man Slain Fleeing Police in Bizarre W. Side Clash." *Chicago Sun-Times* 26 Nov. 1970:46

"On Being Black, Gay, and in Prison: 'There is No Humanity.'" *Motive* 1972:26

"ORTEZ OUT ON BAIL." *Chicago Gay Liberation Newsletter* Sep. 1970:3

"PANTHER CHIEF FAVORS GAY, WOMEN'S LIB." *Mattachine Midwest Newsletter* Oct. 1970:14

"Panthers Map Goal for U.S." *Chicago Tribune* 7 Sep. 1970:4

Simpson, June. "'Pontiac 4' Plead Guilty." *The Times* 30 Nov. 1970

"Sweet Transvestite Murdered." *Gay Flames* (Issue No 9) circa. Dec. 1970

"TRANSVESTITE KILLED IN WEST SIDE CLASH." *Chicago Gay Alliance Newsletter* Dec. 1970:2

Victor, Joe, Peter, Art, Robbie and Michael. "GAYS DISCOVER REVOLUTIONARY LOVE." *Chicago Gay Liberation Newsletter* Oct. 1970:3

Weaver, Audrey. "Gay Guys Movement in Midwest is Going Strong." *Chicago Defender* 31 Oct. 1970:8

# Chapter 9

Primary Sources:

Gerber/Hart Library and Archives, 6500 N. Clark St., Chicago, IL 60626
McCormick Library of Special Collections at Northwestern University, Evanston, IL

---

"Gay Liberation Supplement." *Chicago Seed* Mar. 1970:13
"GAY WOMEN." *Maroon* 6 Mar. 1970:11
"H. Horowitz Co. Jewelers." *Playbill* Jan. 1970:25

Landfield, Jerome. "Does 'The Boys' Tell It Straight?" *Chicago Daily News* 10 Jan. 1970:19

Leonard, William. "Crowley's 'Boys in the Band' Realistic Look at Homosexuality." *Chicago Tribune* 30 Nov. 1969:E1

"MY SIN by Lanvin." *Playbill* Jan. 1970:8

## Chapter 10

Primary Sources:

Gerber/Hart Library and Archives, 6500 N. Clark St., Chicago, IL 60626

McCormick Library of Special Collections at Northwestern University, Evanston, IL

---

"Chicago Gay Liberation." *Chicago Seed* undated circa. Jun. 1970 Vol. 5 No. 5:21

Larsen, Richard. "Gay Pride Week." *Chicago Seed* undated circa. Jul. 1970 Vol. 5 No. 7:9

Larsen, Richard. "Ho-Ho-Homosexual." *Chicago Seed* undated circa. Jul. 1970 Vol. 5 No. 7:7

## Chapter 11

"20,000,000 GAY PEOPLE CURED! PSYCHIATRISTS DROP 'SICK' LABEL." *Chicago Gay Crusader* Jan. 1974:1

"Ann slanders less." *Chicago Gay Crusader* Jan. 1974:1

Bayer, Ronald. "Homosexuality and American Psychiatry: The Politics of Diagnosis." New York: Basic Books Inc., 1981

Bell, John. "Howard Miller to the Rescue!" *Chicago Daily News* 15 Jan. 1971:1

Bergler M.D. Edmund. "Homosexuality: Disease Or Way of Life." New York: Hill and Wang, 1957

Bieber, M.D., Irving. "Homosexuality: A Psychoanalytic Study of Male Homosexuals." New York: Basic Books, 1962

"Broward Celebrity Line." *Miami Herald* 19 April 1970:114

Christmas, Faith C. "Mental Illness Is High." *Chicago Defender* 13 Jun. 1970:1

Crane, George W. "The Worry Clinic." *Dixon Evening Telegraph* 2 Dec. 1971:20

Crane, George W. "The Worry Clinic." *Dixon Evening Telegraph* 31 Dec. 1971;6

Crane, George W. "The Worry Clinic." *Dixon Evening Telegraph* 9 Jul. 1973:20

"Dear Abby." *Mt. Vernon Register-News* 3 May 1972:9

# CHICAGO AFTER STONEWALL

"Dear Abby." *Mt. Vernon Register-News* 22 Oct. 1973:3

"Dear Abby." *Pantagraph* 22 Oct. 1975:40

Delaplane, Stan. "Around the World." *Chicago Tribune* 4 Mar. 1973:102

Ellis, PH. D., Albert. "Homosexuality, it's Causes and Cures." New York: Lyle Stuart, 1964.

Gulian, Larry. "GAYS MARCH ON ANN LANDERS." *Chicago Gay Crusader* Jun. 1973:4

Hatterer, Lawrence J. "Changing Homosexuality in the Male: Treatment for Men Troubled With Homosexuality." New York: McGraw-Hill Book Co., 1970.

Hauck, PH. D., Paul A. "Many adults are afraid to grow up." *Dispatch* 5 Nov. 1973

Helen Help Us." *Daily Chronicle* 12 May 1970:10

Hines, William. "Homosexuality Off Illness List." *Chicago Sun-Times* 16 Dec. 1973:3

Hines, William. "Militants Shrink the Shrinks." *Chicago Sun-Times* 15 May 1970:5

"Homosexuality Not Moral Issue Says Med Prof." *Chicago Defender* Jun. 2 1970:18

Landers, Ann. "Ask Ann Landers." *Chicago Sun-Times* 24 Apr. 1973:4 Section Two

Landers, Ann. "Ask Ann Landers." *Chicago Sun-Times* 8 Jan. 1974:4 Section Two

Landers, Ann. "Ask Ann Landers." *Chicago Sun-Times* 5 Mar. 1973:4 Section Two

Landers, Ann. "Ask Ann Landers." *Chicago Sun-Times* 23 Jul. 1976:4 Section Two

Lardine, Bob. "Homosexuality CAN be 'cured.'" *New York Daily News* 23 Aug. 1970:242

"Love solves problems." *Chicago Defender* 29 Jun. 1971:20

May, Step. "GAY LIBERATION meets the SHRINKS." *Gay Flames* (Pamphlet No 6) undated

"New Ideas In Sex Problems Are Discussed." *Dispatch* 10 Mar. 1969.

Ovesy, Lionel. "Homosexuality and Pseudohomosexuality." New York: Science House, 1969

Payne, Ethel L. "Homosexual Rights–How Far Can They Go?" *Chicago Defender* 15 Jun. 1974:8

Petersen, Clarence. "Miller Show 'Assault' Is Exaggerated." *Chicago Tribune* 19 Jan. 1971:16

Reuben, David. Everything You Always Wanted to Know About Sex* (*But Were Afraid to Ask)." Philadelphia: David McKay Publications, 1969

Roberts, Steven V. "Homosexuals in Revolt." *New York Times* 24 Aug. 1970:1

Socarides, Charles W. "The Overt Homosexual." New York and London: Grune and Stratton, 1968

Socarides, Charles W. "Homosexuality and Medicine." *Journal of the American Medical Association* 18 May 1970; n.p.

Weimhoff, Henry. "The 'Problem' of Homosexuality." *Maroon-Grey City Journal* 30 Jan. 1970:1

# Chapter 12

Primary Sources

Gerber/Hart Library and Archives, 6500 N. Clark St., Chicago, IL 60626
Interview with Ronnie D.
McCormick Library of Special Collections at Northwestern University

---

"A Gay Office at University of Chicago." *Chicago Gay Alliance Newsletter* May 1971:5
"ALLIANCE ALIVE AND WELL IN CHI!" *Chicago Gay Alliance Newsletter* Nov. 1970:1
"Dance Troup to Perform for Cuban Brigade." *Chicago Gay Liberation Newsletter* Aug. 1970:3
"Gay Legal Action to be Sought Against Astro." *Chicago Gay Liberation Newsletter* Sep. 1970:1
"march on! GAY LIB JOINS IN HIROSHIMA DAY PARADE." *Chicago Gay Liberation Newsletter* Sep. 1970:1
"picket spanish pigs." *Chicago Gay Liberation Newsletter* 28 Apr. 1970:1
"RING OUT THE OLD – RING IN THE NEW!!!" *Chicago Gay Liberation Newsletter* Sep. 1970:3
"SCHISM IN CHICAGO GAY LIB!" *Chicago Gay Liberation Newsletter* Oct. 1970:1

# Chapter 13

Covelli, Judy. "Seniors Hear Homosexuality Talk." *Daily Herald* 20 Mar. 1970:59
Taylor, Valerie. "THE WORD GETS AROUND." *Mattachine Midwest Newsletter* Nov. 1970:5
Wellman, Tom. "This Novice is Determined." *Daily Herald* 3 Apr. 1970:59
"Will 135 Kids Fight to Love Same Sex?" *Daily Herald* 17 Apr. 1970:60

# Chapter 14

"A MERRY CHRISTMAS TO ALL." *Chicago Gay Alliance Newsletter* Dec. 1970:1
"POLL OF ALDERMANIC CANDIDATES!" *Chicago Gay Alliance Newsletter* Feb. 1971:4

## Chapter 15

Primary Sources

Gerber/Hart Library and Archives, 6500 N. Clark St., Chicago, IL 60626
McCormick Library of Special Collections at Northwestern University, Evanston, IL

---

"K.U. Gay Group Not Recognized." *Great Bend Tribune* 6 Sep. 1970:1
Osweiler, Marilyn. "The Gay in Iowa City." *Quad City Times* 31 Jan. 1971:48
Robinson, Charlotte. "At U.W. Teach-In 'Gay Lib" Idea Comes Out from Underground." *Capital Times* 1 May 1970:27

## Chapter 16

Primary Sources:

Gerber/Hart Library and Archives, 6500 N. Clark St., Chicago, IL 60626
McCormick Library of Special Collections at Northwestern University, Evanston, IL

---

Capricorn. "IT'S NOBODY'S BUSINESS: AN EDITORIAL." *Chicago Gay Alliance Newsletter* Nov. 1971:2
*Chicago Gay Pride* Jun. 1971
Chin, Richard. "GAY NOT GUILTY." *Chicago Seed* (Vol. 7 No. 4) 30 Jul. 1971:n.p.
"Gay lib fights job bias." *Chicago Daily Defender* Oct. 28 1971:14
"GAY VICTORY [Alvin Golden Case]" *Chicago Seed* 14 Jul. 1971:n.p.
Virginia. "GAY PRIDE KISS-IN." *Chicago Seed* Circa. Jun. 1971:5

## Chapter 17

Bierce, Harley R, and Thrasher, Donald K. "Porn Dealer Slaying Believed Mob-Linked." *Indianapolis Star* 23 Sep. 1976:1
Branegan, Jay. "Sex shop raids net 10 arrests." *Chicago Tribune* 27 Oct. 1974:B18
"City acts against 7 X-movie theaters." *Chicago Tribune* 27 Sep. 1973:B9
Davis, Robert. "Crackdown by U.S. Attorney Judge OKs Smut Film Seizures." *Chicago Tribune* 1 Aug. 1972:15

Davis, Robert. "U.S. to Probe Showing of 'Adult' Movies Here." *Chicago Tribune* 25 Jul. 1972:1

"Film Given to FBI; Owner Is Set Free." *Chicago Tribune* 3 Aug. 1972:A8

Fitzgerald, Tom. "Fitz Column." *Chicago Sun-Times* 25 Jun. 1973:3

"From bomb threats to dynamite." *Chicago Tribune* 2 Dec. 1973:H100

Gibson, Ray. "Missing porn-theater owner found dead in car trunk." *Chicago Tribune* 27 Jul. 1985:5

"Hanrahan Tells of Film Probe." *Chicago Tribune* 26 Jul. 1972:A1

Janet. "BIJOU THEATRE." *Chicago Seed* Aug. 1971:18

Larie, Larry. "THEATERS EXPLOIT GAY PEOPLE." *Chicago Seed* 18 May 1972:18

Locin, Mitchell and Marks, Howard. "Bombs rock 3 porno houses; dynamite sticks found in 4th." *Chicago Tribune* 15 Nov. 1974:1

"Mob tie suspected in bomb at nude shop." *Chicago Tribune* 22 Oct. 1974:A12

O'Brien, John. "Mob enforcer gets 13 years for threatening shop owner." *Chicago Tribune* 17 Feb. 1990: S5

O'Brien, John. "Porn theater owner reported missing." *Chicago Tribune* 26 Jul. 1985:C2

"Three Face Obscenity Counts." *Chicago Tribune* 17 Oct. 1972:A4

Wattley, Philip. "Police say hoodlum asked sex theater exec for money." *Chicago Tribune* 25 Sep. 1976:N3

Wattley, Philip. "Probe theater bombings." *Chicago Tribune* 16 Nov. 1974:N9

Wattley, Philip and O'Brien, John. "Mob, union motives studied 2 theories in death of sex-film vendor." *Chicago Tribune* 23 Sep. 1976:3

Wattley, Philip and Siskel, Gene. "Sex film chain owner slain. Hint mob attempt to muscle in." *Chicago Tribune* 22 Sep. 1976:1

# Chapter 18

"CGA Center is open for you." *Chicago Gay Pride* Jun. 1971:3

Ettorre, Barbara. "Gay Men Discuss Their Lives, Parents, Images." *Chicago Today* 27 Jun. 1972:26

"GAY COMMUNITY CENTER TO CLOSE." *Chicago Gay Crusader* Sep. 1973:1

"Gay Raid." *Chicago Seed* Circa. Nov.-Dec. 1971:6

"OPEN HOUSE AT CENTER MAY 1st!" *Chicago Gay Alliance Newsletter* Apr. 1971:1

"OPEN HOUSE HIGHLIGHTS." *Chicago Gay Alliance Newsletter* May 1971:2

Schultz, Terri. "Homosexual Discusses Struggle for Legal Equality" *Chicago Tribune* 12 Dec. 1971

"Understanding the Other Side." *Chicago Tribune* 3 Sep. 1971:38

# Chapter 19

Primary Sources:

Gerber/Hart Library and Archives, 6500 N. Clark St., Chicago, IL 60626
McCormick Library of Special Collections at Northwestern University, Evanston, IL

---

Brody, Michal. "Are We There Yet? A Continuing History of Lavender Woman, a Chicago Lesbian Newspaper 1971-1976." Iowa City: Aunt Lute Book Co., 1985
*Daughters of Bilitis/Chicago Newsletter* Jan. 1970
"Gloria Steinem Coming To NIU" *Daily Chronicle* 6 Mar. 1972:10
*Lavender Woman* Nov. 1971
"Men aren't necessary." *Reno Gazette-Journal* 10 Oct. 1969:11

# Chapter 20

Fish, Bob and Nelson, Ray. "An Interview with Allen Ginsberg and William Burroughs." *Chicago Gay Crusader* Jun. 1975:6
"Gays Zap Foran." *Chicago Seed* Circa. Nov.-Dec. 1971:n.p.

# Chapter 21

Primary Sources:

Cook County Law Library in the Richard Daley Center
McCormick Library of Special Collections at Northwestern University, Evanston, IL
Gerber/Hart Library and Archives, 6500 N. Clark St., Chicago, IL 60626

---

Andrew, Christopher and Mitrokhin, Vasili. "The World Was Going Our Way: The KGB and the Battle for the Third World" New York: Basic Books, 2005
Jay, Karla and Young, Allen. "Out of the Closets: Voices of Gay Liberation" New York: New York University Press, 1972
Reports of the Committees (January 17, 1978) at the Cook County Law Library
Reports of the Committees (January 25, 1943) at the Cook County Law Library
Young, Allen. "Gays Under the Cuban Revolution" San Francisco: Grey Fox Press, 1982

## Chapter 22

Primary Sources:

Gerber/Hart Library and Archives, 6500 N. Clark St., Chicago, IL 60626
McCormick Library of Special Collections at Northwestern University, Evanston, IL

## Chapter 23

Primary Sources:

Gerber/Hart Library and Archives, 6500 N. Clark St., Chicago, IL. 60626
McCormick Library of Special Collections at Northwestern University, Evanston, IL

---

"An interview with Michael Bergeron." *The Paper* Sept/Oct. 1972:4

## Chapter 24

Primary Sources

Author's interview with Rev. Charles Lamont.
Gerber/Hart Library and Archives, 6500 N. Clark St., Chicago, IL 60626

---

"A special minister bids for a special ministry." *Chicago Sun-Times* 16 Nov. 1971:34
"Chicago minister faces suspension." *Advocate* 29 Mar. 1972:13
"Eye Ministry to homosexuals." *Chicago Tribune* 10 Jun. 1971:B18
"Lamont suggests forcing church "confrontations.'" *Advocate* 5 Jul. 1972:10
"Methodists due challenge." *Advocate* 29 Mar. 1972:13
"Minister Fights Suspension." *Chicago Gay Pride CGA Newsletter* Mar. 1972:3

## Chapter 25

Primary Sources:

Author's interview, personal documents and journal entries of Denny Halen

Gerber/Hart Library and Archives, 6500 N. Clark St., Chicago, IL 60626

---

"End Celibacy Rule, Priest Group Asks." *Chicago Tribune* 16 Mar. 1972: B23

"GAYS INVITED TO ROMAN CATHOLIC MASS." *Chicago Gay Alliance Newsletter* Jan. 1971:3

Gilun, Rev. John E. "End 'Black Sheep' Mass." *Chicago Pride CGA Newsletter* Mar. 1972:n.p.

Larson, Roy. "Ministry to homosexuals brings action, little talk." *Chicago Sun-Times* 7 Apr. 1973:50

"National Conference of Catholic Bishops' Committee on Pastoral Research and Practices, Principles to Guide Confessors in Questions of Homosexuality." Washington, DC: USCCB, 1973

Pick, Grant. "Does God Love Gay Catholics?" *Reader* 10 Jun. 1977: 1

## Chapter 26

"Benefit Concert [The Family of Women]." *Lavender Woman* (Vol. 1 No. 5) Sep. 1972:5

"Gay Women's Caucus." *Chicago Seed* Apr. 1972:8

Kuda, Marie. "Linda Shear: Lesbian/Feminist/Folksinger." *Paper* Sep.-Oct. 1972:6

Landis, Linda Lee. "Women's Rights Proviso Work." *Chicago Tribune* 6 Jun. 1972:B1

Leigh. "Family of Women." *Lavender Woman* (Vol. 1 No. 6) Nov. 1972:3

Lightfoot, Barbara. "Benefit Feedback." *Lavender Woman* (Vol. 1 No. 4) Jul. 1972:n.p.

Lumen, Patricia. "An Evening Wit Linda Shear Onstage at the Aisle 5." *Paper* Sep-Oct. 1972:8

Schultz, Terri. "Women's Lib Band Rocks, Raps Oppression." *Chicago Tribune* 30 Jan. 1972:343

"Why We Left Chicago Gay Alliance." *Lavender Woman* (Vol. 1 No. 2) Dec. 1971:n.p.

## Chapter 27

"American Library Task Force: A Gay Force of Liberation." *Chicago Gay Pride* Aug. 1972:2

Ettorre, Barbara. "Gay Men Discuss Their Lives, Parents, Images." *Chicago Today* 27 Jun. 1972:26

Ettorre, Barbara. "Lesbians Live in a Twilight Zone." *Chicago Today* 28 Jun. 1972:35

Galliette, Dick. "Gay Pride Week." *Mattachine Midwest Newsletter* 4 Aug. 1972:1
"Successful Gay Pride Week celebration." *Paper* Jul. 1972:1

## Chapter 28

"Ad for Roby Landers at the Aragon Ballroom." *Chicago Tribune* 1 Nov. 1969:77
"Ad for Roby Landers at the Colony Club." The *Kansas City Times* 26, Feb. 1963:18
Alexson, Fred. "Looking around at Chicago." *David* Aug. 1973:21:
Barker, Bobby. "Bobby Barfly." *Chicago Gay Crusader* Aug. 1974:7
"The Birds of Sparrows." *Paper* Jul. 1972:11
Brody, Michal. "Are We There Yet? A Continuing History of Lavender Woman, a Chicago Lesbian Newspaper 1971-1976." Iowa City: Aunt Lute Book Co., 1985
"CHEZ RON AD." *Mattachine Midwest Newsletter* Nov. 1970:4
"Chicago Bar Guide." *Tuffy* (Vol. 1 No. 1) Aug. 1972:n.p.
Ettorre, Barbara. "Gay Men Discuss Their Lives, Parents, Images." *Chicago Today* 27 Jun. 1972:26
Fish, Bob. "Punchinello's." *Paper* Jul. 1972:17
"Gay lib pickets." *Maroon* 23 Feb. 1973:5
Herman, Edith. "Restaurant Fire Routs High Rise Tenants" *Chicago Tribune* 11 May 1975:3
"Michael's Thing." *Mattachine Midwest Newsletter* Aug. 1972:3
"NEW GAY SPOTS LIVEN CITY." *Mattachine Midwest Newsletter* Dec. 1970-Jan. 1971:16
"PQ's Grand Opening." *Mattachine Midwest Newsletter* 8 Sep. 1972:9
Townson, Patrick. "Jamies raided by cops." *Chicago Gay Life* 29 Oct. 1975:1
Vilanch, Bruce. "A Comet Named Sokol is About to Become a Star." *Chicago Tribune* 25 Apr. 1975:B2

## Chapter 29

Primary Sources:

Cook County Law Library in the Richard Daley Center.
Gerber/Hart Library and Archives, 6500 N. Clark St., Chicago, IL 60626

---

"2 others also shut? Mayor tries to close Bistro." *Chicago Gay Crusader* (Issue No. 18) 1974:6

Barker, Bobby. "Bobby Barfly." *Chicago Gay Crusader* Nov. 1973:8

"Bistro wins license case." *Chicago Gay Crusader* (Issue No. 24) 1975:1

DiVito, Lou. "THE BISTRO." *Gay Chicago* 13 May 1982:18

DUGAN'S BISTRO, INC. and Edward Davison v. Richard J. Daley, Mayor of the City of Chicago (56 Ill. App.3d 463 14 Ill.Dec. 63)

Kelley, William B. "Bar accused denies bias." *Chicago Gay Crusader* Aug. 1974:1

Kelley, William B. "Eye on the News." *Chicago Gay Crusader* Nov.-Dec. 1974:8

Reiff, Nancy and Paul, Ralph. "Here's looking at you." *Gay Chicago* 3 Jun. 1983:4

Van Matre, Lynn. "Secure sexuality ... and the scene sells." *Chicago Tribune* 7 Apr. 1974:E3

## Chapter 30

Cassidy, Claudia. "Luchino Visconti's 'Death in Venice.'" *Chicago Tribune* 9 Aug. 1971:B9

"Director and Cast of Play Are Arrested Here." *The Atlanta Constitution* 1 Feb. 1975:10

Drake, Sylvie. "'Puppy Dogs Tails' at After Dark." *Los Angeles Times* 14 Mar. 1975:74

Freedman, Richard. "The importance of not getting caught." *Chicago Tribune* 28 Jun. 1970:L3

Kramer, Carol. "Leftist Visconti Lives Right, But Not Under a Bridge." *Chicago Tribune* 11 Jul. 1971:125

Leonard, Will. "Brainless gay farce fizzles." *Chicago Tribune* 10 Apr. 1974:C3

Lynch, Jody. "Peter Pan." *Lavender Woman* Mar. 1973 (Vol. 2 No. 2):n.p.

Lynch, Jody. "Trevor." *Lavender Woman* Aug. 1973 (Vol. 2 No. 5):n.p.

"Mommy's Boys." *Chicago Tribune* 23 Aug. 1970:Q7

Offen, Ron. "Nay Love for Gay Love." *Reader* 27 Oct. 1972:N2

Reed, Rex. "Cannes Men: Rich Boy Segal and Arrogant Visconti." *Chicago Tribune* 6 Jun. 1971:133

Stark, John. "Lesbian play tries hard for laughs." *San Francisco Examiner* 24 Jun. 1975:24

Storr, Anthony. "Eligible Bachelors." *Chicago Tribune* May 21 1972:J3

## Chapter 31

Primary Sources:

Gerber/Hart Library and Archives, 6500 N. Clark St., Chicago, IL 60626

McCormick Library of Special Collections at Northwestern University, Evanston, IL

Banks, Nancy. "'Sexual Orientation' at City Hall." *Reader* 2 Nov. 1973:10
"Governor Walker Booed." *Mattachine Midwest Newsletter* 2 Mar. 1972:1
"Illinois Gay for Legislative Action." *Chicago Gay Pride* Dec. 1972:5
Kelley, William B. "SIX CONFRONTATIONS When will Walker get the message?" *Chicago Gay Crusader* May 1973:1

## Chapter 32

Primary Sources:

October 29, 2010, interview with the Rev. Charles Lamont.
Gerber/Hart Library and Archives, 6500 N. Clark St., Chicago, IL 60626

---

Cole, Rob. "McGovern Denial." *Advocate* 8 Nov. 1972:1
"Demos veto abortion plank." *Miami News* 27 Jun. 1972:7
"McGovern Backs Gays." *Chicago Gay Pride* Jun. 1972:7
"McGovern Gays Badly Shaken Up." *Advocate* 2 Aug. 1972:3.
"Miami Transvestite Law Struck Down." *Asheville Cirizen-Times* 23 Jun. 1972:1
"National Coalition of Gay Organizations." *Miami News* 7 Jul. 1972:73
"PROTESTORS MARCH ON CONVENTION-EVE GALA." *Times* 21 Aug. 1972:1
Warden, Philip. "McGovern Gets His Platform." *Chicago Tribune* 13 Jul. 1972:12
"Zippies Flight Hoffman, Rubin for Yippie Power." *Chicago Tribune* 8 Jul. 1972:S5

## Chapter 33

Banks, Nancy. "'Sexual Orientation' at City Hall." *Reader* 2 Nov. 1973:n.p.
D.C. PASSES RIGHTS BILL; CHICAGO PROPOSALS STILL PENDING." *Chicago Gay Crusader* Nov. 1973:15
Enstad, Robert. "Trouble Foreseen Enforcing Proposed Rules on Job Bias." *Chicago Tribune* 15 Jul.1972:20
Kelley, William. "Gay Rights Bills Filed in City Council." *Chicago Gay Crusader* Jul. 1973:4
Kelley, William. "Rights setback stirs controversy, new plans." *Chicago Gay Crusader* Jun. 1974:3

Kramer, Carot. "Opposed in New York: Gay rights bill appears doomed. *Chicago Tribune* 5 May 1974:44
"Legislative Action." *Chicago Gay Pride* Aug. 1972:3
"Putting it to City Hall." *Lavender Woman* Nov. 1973:n.p.
"Rights bills: alive but ailing." *Chicago Gay Crusader* Aug. 1974:1
Trotter, Leslie A. "Nay to gays." *Chicago Defender* 26 Jun. 1974:15

## Chapter 34

Primary Sources:

Gerber/Hart Library and Archives, 6500 N. Clark St., Chicago, IL 60626

"19 Homosexuals Arrested in Fla." *Akron Beacon Journal* 7 Jul. 1974:16
"34 Seized In Drive On Homosexuals." *Indianapolis News* 27 Oct. 1969:2
*Chicago Gay Listings* (Vol. III No. 1) Jan. 1973
"Homosexuals Arrested." *Tampa Times* 18 Aug. 1972:57
"Homosexuals arrested in Dallas." *Corsicana Daily Sun* 29 Aug. 1975:1
"Police make 30 arrests of homosexuals." – *Daily Herald* 17 Jun. 1975:2

## Chapter 35

Primary Source:

Gerber/Hart Library and Archives, 6500 N. Clark St., Chicago, IL 60626
McCormick Library of Special Collections at Northwestern University, Evanston, IL

"Letters to the Editor." *Tucson Daily Citizen* 9 May 1973:29
Shapiro, Howard S. "Homosexuals Should They Teach?" *Chicago Tribune* 23 Aug. 1972:B3

## Chapter 36

Primary Sources:

Gerber/Hart Library and Archives, 6500 N. Clark St., Chicago, IL 60626

---

"Book on Homosexuality Issued by Church Press." *Bensenville Register* 22 Dec. 1969:13

"Church Suspends Homosexual Pastor." *Chicago Tribune* 2 Jun. 1971:B10

"Ordaining of Homosexual OKd." *Chicago Tribune* 2 May 1972:3

Pratt, Steven. "Presbyterian Assembly Accepts Report on Sex and Abortion." *Chicago Tribune* 26 May 1970:4

Sindt, David. "Minister rejected." *Chicago Gay Crusader* May 1973:1

## Chapter 37

Primary Sources:

Gerber/Hart Library and Archives, 6500 N. Clark St., Chicago, IL 60626

---

"Barred gays to picket church." *Chicago Sun-Times* 19 May 1973:n.p.

Gulian, Larry and Hockemeyer, Alan. "We're Not Good Enough. Gays Shut Out, Picket Ward Fair." *Chicago Gay Crusader* Jun. 1973:8

## Chapter 38

Primary Sources:

Gerber/Hart Library and Archives, 6500 N. Clark St., Chicago, IL 60626

---

"Borchers condemns ISU's gay support." *Vidette* 1 May 1973:8

" ... but is it worth $1,400? *Vidette* 1 Dec. 1972:4

"Campus News." *Vidette* 6 Mar. 1970:7

Elmer, John. "Theft conviction overturned: Former legislator wins appeal." *Chicago Tribune* 21 Sep. 1977:4

Elmer, John. "Mandatory Sterilization Bill Offered." *Chicago Tribune* 5 Mar. 1971:2

"Gay Alliance is a learning experience." *Vidette* 1 Dec. 1972:4

"GLF organizes at Illinois State." *Vidette* 2 Apr. 1970:1

"Heterosexuals ask for $68,000 orgy." *Vidette* 6 Dec. 1972:4

Kelley. William B. "House committee kills anti-gay measure." *Chicago Gay Crusader* Jun. 1973:8

"Replace Waters with monkey." *Vidette* 7 Dec. 1972

Waters, Mike. "Clubs left without funding." *Vidette* 16 Nov. 1972:4

## Chapter 39

Primary Sources:

Gerber/Hart Library and Archives, 6500 N. Clark St., Chicago, IL 60626

---

"29 die in New Orleans fire." *Chicago Tribune* 25 Jun. 1973:1

Alexson, Fred. "Looking Around at Chicago." *David* Aug. 1973:20

"Ann Landers." *Dixon Evening Telegraph* 9 Oct. 1973:4

"Chicago Gay Arbitration Board." *Lavender Woman* Mar. 1973:n.p.

Fitzgerald, Tom. "Fitz Column." *Chicago Sun-Times* 25 Jun. 1973:3

"GAY PRIDE HUGE SUCCESS 2500 March." *Chicago Gay Crusader* Jul. 1973:1

LaVelle, Mike. "How Uptown Reacts to Crisis." *Chicago Tribune* 13 Sep. 1973:26

## Chapter 40

Primary Sources:

Gerber/Hart Library and Archives, 6500 N. Clark St., Chicago, IL 60626

---

Banes, Sally. "Jill Johnston in Chicago. Grande Dame of Dykes." *Reader* 6 Jul. 1973:3

Flynn, Betty. "Jill Johnston: Crusader for Lesbianism." *Chicago Daily News* 29 Jun. 1973:25

Kelley, William B. "Letters to the editor." *Chicago Gay Crusader* Jul. 1973:2

Lightfoot, Barbara. *Cries From Cassandra* (Vol. 1 No. 1) Jun. 1973:n.p.

Thompson, Sara. "The Politics of Drag." *Lavender Woman* Mar. 1973:n.p.

# Chapter 41

Primary Sources:

Reports of the Committees (January 25, 1943) at the Cook County Law Library
Reports of the Committees (January 17, 1978) at the Cook County Law Library

---

"Appeal planned: Two convicted of wearing drag." *Chicago Gay Crusader* Sep.-Oct. 1974:6
"BEWARE: Enticement." *Mattachine Midwest* Newsletter Feb. 1969:3
Charles, W.S. "Ladies in Pants." *Chicago Tribune* 17 Jul. 1943:10
"Cross-sex dress ban overruled." *Chicago Tribune* 21 Sep. 1973:17
Davis, Robert. "Teacher Challenges 'Drag Law." *Chicago Tribune* 14 Apr. 1972;35
Hirsley, Michael. "'Vice versa squad fights male hookers." *Chicago Tribune* 25 Jul. 1976:38
"Impersonator is jailed for prostitution." *The Argus* 5 Sep. 1974:16
Smith, Cecil. "This is a Show! Berlin and Army Get the Credit." *Chicago Tribune* 5 Jan. 1943:11
Weintraub, Larry. "Transvestite Law Held Illegal; 4 Juveniles Freed." *Chicago Sun-Times* 21 Sep. 1973:6

# Chapter 42

Franks, Lucinda. "Homosexuals As Foster Parents." *New York Times* 7 May 1974:n.p.
Gorner, Peter. "The Growing Furor Over the State's Children." *Chicago Tribune* 25 Jul. 1973:D1
Kelley, William B. "STATE WAVERS ON GAY FOSTER PARENTS." *Chicago Gay Crusader* Aug. 1973:3
Koch, Joanne and Lew. "Gays foster lonely futures for children." *Dixon Evening Telegraph* 17 Jul. 1974:6
"No Sissies." *Chicago Defender* 25 Jul. 1973:4
Shore, Warren and Banis, Diane. "Study Child Placement in Homosexual Homes." *Chicago Today* 19 Jul. 1973:7
Shore, Warren and Banis, Diane. "Placement Ruling Stirs Protest." *Chicago Today* 23 Jul. 1973:12

## Chapter 43

"2 teens tell of 25 slayings: Police unearth 19 bodies, hunt more." *Chicago Tribune* 10 Aug. 1973:1

"'GAY' ANGLE IN HOUSTON MURDER STORY EXPLOITED." *Chicago Tribune* Aug. 1973:3

"Gays denounce media treatment of Houston murders." *Chicago Tribune* Sep. 1973:1

Goldman, Paul R. "Homosexuality, Homicide." *Chicago Tribune* 16 Aug. 1973:16

"The Houston horror story." *Chicago Tribune* 11 Aug. 1973:S6

Janes, Jeanne. "Houston Police Deny Laxity on Runaway Cases." *Chicago Tribune* 14 Aug. 1973:3

## Chapter 44

"GAY ANTHROPOLOGISTS FORM." *Chicago Gay Crusader* Oct. 1973:5

Merridew, Alan. "World scientists to meet here for anthropology congress." *Chicago Tribune* 27 Aug. 1973:19

Nichols, Jack and Clarke, Lige. "He-Man Horseshit." *Screw* 23 May 1969;n.p.

Petersen, Clarence. "Homophobia: Fear and Loathing on the Sexual Trail." *Chicago Tribune* 30 Sept. 1973:F8

## Chapter 45

Crane, Dr. George W. "The Worry Clinic." *Dixon Evening Telegraph* 12 Dec. 1969

"EDITORIAL: In Memoriam James Clay." *Chicago Gay Crusader* Nov. 1973:2

"FELICIA'S 7TH ANNUAL COSTUMES ON REVIEW." *Chicago Gay Crusader* Nov. 1973:10-11

Gold, Aaron. "Tower Ticker." *Chicago Tribune* 15 Oct. 1973:A2

"IDENTIFY DEAD WOMAN ACCUSED OF BAR SHOOTING." *Chicago Gay Crusader* Nov. 1973:1

Kotulak, Ronald. "Surgeon Claims 95-98% Success Rate in Sex Change." *Chicago Tribune* 17 Oct. 1973:A14

"Letters to the Editor." *Chicago Gay Crusader* Jul. 1974:2

"New York Dolls." *Chicago Tribune* 23 Sep. 1973:E20

Pesmen, Sandra. "A Day at Chicago's Sex-Change Clinic." *Chicago Daily News* 7 Mar. 1974:48

"Popiwchak." *Chicago Tribune* 30 Oct. 1973:36

"ROUNDUP television David Bowie at midnight." *Chicago Tribune* 10 Nov. 1973:34

Reed, Rex. "A Dazzling Italian Farewell ... " *Chicago Tribune* 20 Jan. 1974:E20
Schultz, Terri. "Our Town." *Chicago Tribune* 14 Feb. 1971:416
Van Matre, Lynn. "All Dolled Up–But That's All, Man." *Chicago Tribune* 13 Oct. 1973:W_B32
Van Matre, Lynn. "Music: The Dolls: Sophomoric Gimmickry." *Chicago Tribune* 12 Oct. 1973:A3
Vilanch, Bruce. "Behind the Makeup of the 'Dolls'" *Chicago Today* 26 Oct. 1973:29
Wilson, Margaret. "Lesbian Lore." *Chicago Gay Crusader* Dec. 1973:17
"Woman is slain in bar dispute." *Chicago Tribune* 24 Oct. 1973:A5

## Chapter 46

"40 men vie for Miss Gay America." *Times Standard* 4 May 1973:11
Alexander, Alice. "The Rebirth of Shawn Luis." *Tennessean* 5 Oct. 1975:168
"CHICAGO FEMALE IMPERSONATOR CROWNED MISS GAY." *Jacksonville Daily Journal* 15 May 1973:7
"Female Clothes, Makeup ... " *Tennessean* 29 May 1972:2
"No One Wants Gay Loot." *Daily News-Journal* 7 May 1973:6
"Several come from closet to accept Miss Gay funds." *Johnson City Press-Chronicle* 8 May 1973:14
"There she – er, he is." *Chicago Tribune* 7 May 1974:33

## Chapter 47

"Gays outraged by 'Welby.'" *Chicago Gay Crusader* Aug. 1974:12
"GAYS ZAP NBC AND GILLETTE." *Chicago Gay Crusader* Dec. 1973:1
Kloss, James. "Gay Raiders' Leader Presses TV Campaign." *Chicago Daily News* 4 Mar. 1974:39
Vilanch, Bruce. "Tube fails again with gay issue." *Chicago Tribune* 8 Oct. 1974:40

## Chapter 48

"A church for homosexuals." *Chicago Tribune* 7 Jun. 1970:270
"editorial ... The Homosexual A 'Cross' To Bear." *Mt. Vernon Register-News* 19 Nov. 1970:4
"'Gay Caucus' service at first Unitarian." *Chicago Defender* 23 Feb. 1974:39
"Gay Unitarians conduct Evanston church services." *Chicago Gay Crusader* Jan. 1974:2
"[Homosexual Church]" *Time* 13 July 1970:n.p.

"Homosexuals Have Own Church In South State." *Sacramento Bee* 13 Dec. 1969:4

Kosman, Bill. "ART MOVIE HOUSE THEIR CHURCH: Homosexuals' Spiritual Home 25 Mar. 1970:25

"Letter to the Editor." *Chicago Tribune* 2 Aug. 1970:152

"Local church gets new home, staff members." *Chicago Gay Crusader* Jan. 1974:5

"NEW CHURCH HOME." *Shepherd's Staff* (Vol. 4 No. 8) Dec. 1973:1

Page, Clarence. "Gay Church Offers Refuge in Straight World." *Chicago Tribune* 24 Feb. 1974:30

"Religion, Law, Homosexuality." *Dispatch* 13 Jul. 1970:4

## Chapter 49

"David's Place." *Michael's Thing* 9 Nov. 1972:n.p.

Kelley, William B. "Eye on the News." *Chicago Gay Crusader* Jul. 1974:9

"NEW CENTER OPENS." *Chicago Gay Crusader* Nov. 1974:1

Stern, Richard A. "A PEER SELF-HELP GROUP OF HOMOSEXULS ON THE NORTH SIDE OF CHICAGO." *Psychotherapy, Theory, Research and Practice* (Vol. 12 No. 4) Winter 1975:418

Tully, Joe. "CHAIRING" *302.0* Sep. 1978:2

## Chapter 50

BZ. "The Performance." *Lavender Woman* Oct. 1974:6

Cindy. "Clinch Mountain Backsteppers." *Lavender Woman* Dec. 1974:n.p.

Kuda, Marie Jayne. "Women's Restaurant Opens." *Chicago Gay Crusader* Dec. 1973:5

"Writer speaks to lesbian lit class." *Lavender Woman* Jan. 1974:n.p.

Van Matre, Lynn. "Women's Festival: Muses Try Their Hand." *Chicago Tribune* 9 Jun. 1974:E10

## Chapter 51

"ARE WE RIPPED OFF IN THE BARS ON FIFTY-CENT NIGHT." *Chicago Lesbian Liberation Newsletter* Mar. 1974:1

"Collective Statement." *Lavender Woman* Mar. 1974:n.p.

"[Editorial]" *Chicago Lesbian Liberation Newsletter* 4 Apr. 1974:1

"LW INTERVIEWS THE COMMUNITY: lesbian thoughts on gay pride." *Lavender Woman* Jun. 1974:1

## Chapter 52

"Ad for Gay Broadway." *Reader* 7 Jun. 1974:n.p.
Alexson, Fred. "Unique local business: Leather and things: one man's viewpoint." *Chicago Gay Crusader* Feb.–Mar. 1975:12
Baim. Tracy and Keehnen, Owen. "Leatherman: The Legend of Chuck Renslow." Chicago: Prairie Avenue Productions, 2011.
"Chicago super-bath opens." *Chicago Gay Crusader* Mar.-Apr. 1974:13
Daly, Maggie. "Sally Rand." *Chicago Tribune* 13 Feb. 1975:29
DeBat, Don. "Mystery Man Buys Dewes Mansion." *Chicago Daily News* 7 Jun. 1974:23
Kelley, William B. "Mansion buyer called 'mysterious.'" *Chicago Gay Crusader* Jun. 1974:1
"Man's Country, hottest spa in town." *Chicago Tribune* 14 Feb. 1975:B9
"Sally Dances in Loop; Arrest Her 4 Times." *Chicago Tribune* 5 Aug. 1933:1

## Chapter 53

"GAYS PROTEST ROYKO'S INSULTS." *Chicago Gay Crusader* Mar.-Apr. 1974:1
Royko, Mike. "Bunch of prudes." *Billings Gazette* 2 Apr. 1974:8
Royko, Mike. "Going Bananas Over Liberation." *Chicago Daily News* 22 Mar. 1974:3
Royko, Mike. "Propaganda First Class." *Chicago Daily News* 17 May 1974:3
"Royko's criticism errs." *Democrat and Chronicle* 18 Jun. 1974:6

## Chapter 54

Primary Sources:

McCormick Library of Special Collections at Northwestern University, Evanston, IL
Gerber/Hart Library and Archives, 6500 N. Clark St., Chicago, IL 60626

---

"A MOVE TOWARD UNITY: BECKMAN HOUSE CHANGES HANDS." *Chicago Gay Crusader* Sep.-Oct. 1974:1
"Beckman House Expands." *Chicago Gay Crusader* May 1974:1
"Eleven Killed in Iowa Easter Weekend Crashes." *Gazette* 3 Apr. 1972:4
*Gay Horizons Volunteer* (Vol. 1 Issue No. 2.) Dec. 1974:n.p.

Herdt, Gilbert and Boxer, Andrew. "Children of Horizons." Boston: Beacon Press, 1993

"In Memoriam [Barbara Beckman]." *Paper* Jul. 1972:2

"THE MANY FACES AT THE ONE BANQUET." *Chicago Gay Crusader* May 1974:13

"The Nation: Takeoff." *Time* 10 Dec. 1973:n.pag.

"Streakers." *Chicago Gay Crusader* May 1974:1

Wall, Milan. "Feminist Finds Little in Common with Marxist Lesbians." *Lincoln Star* 11 Mar. 1972:3

Wall, Milan. "Justice Conference set to Open at NU Monday." *Lincoln Star* 3 Mar. 1972:10

## Chapter 55

"600 gay persons march in Boston observance." *Boston Globe* 23 Jun. 1974:19

"Bergen march hails 'Gay Day'" *Herald-News* 29 Jun. 1974:1

"Gay Day parade June 30." *Honolulu Advertiser* 22 Jun. 1974:24

Forester, Mike. "Small Turnout For Gay Pride Rally." *Clarion-Ledger* 24 Jun. 1974:11

"Letter to the Editor." *Record* 1 Jul. 1974:29

"MARDI GRAS OF THE MIDWEST CHICAGO'S FIFTH ANNUAL GAY PRIDE PARADE." *Chicago Gay Crusader* Jul. 1974:1

Masland, Tom. "Gays march in Bergen." *Record* 30 Jun. 1974:20

O'Connor, Meg. "But few raise eyebrows: Gay parade stops traffic." *Chicago Tribune* 1 Jul. 1974:A1

Pennock, Rosemary. "Dance at UT." *Austin American-Statesman* 1 Jul. 1974:7

## Chapter 56

"ACLU drops suit against Elk Grove." *Daily Herald* 3 Jan. 1975

"ACLU sues to get man fireman's job." *Daily Herald* 22 Oct. 1974:30

Warden, Rob. "High Scorer in Suburb Job Test Rejected for Teen Sex Experience." *Chicago Daily News* Jul. 1974:18

## Chapter 57

Brody, Michal. "Are We There Yet? A Continuing History of Lavender Woman, a Chicago Lesbian Newspaper 1971-1976." Iowa City: Aunt Lute Book Co., 1985

"CARTOON DRAWS CONTROVERSEY [sic]." *Original Lavender Woman* Aug. 1974:n.p.

"FROM THE PRESIDENT'S PEN." *Original Lavender Woman* Aug. 1974:n.p.

Kuda, Marie Jayne. " ... and then there were two: Second 'Lavender Woman' appears." *Chicago Gay Crusader* Sep.-Oct. 1974:1

"[Missing Cartoon]" *Lavender Woman* Jun. 1974:14

"[Wanda Owen cartoon]." *CLL Newsletter* Jul. 1974:3

## Chapter 58

Kuda, Marie J. "Lesbian writers meet." *Chicago Gay Crusader* Sep.-Oct. 1974:1

## Chapter 59

Anderson, Ron. "Second Winter Carnival March 14th–sponsored by Lincoln Park Lagooners." *Chicago Gay Life* 5 Mar. 1976:1

"Annual ONE banquet honors Valerie Taylor." *Chicago Gay Crusader* Apr.-May 1975:4

"City recognizes Howard Brown Clinic: Opening ceremony highlighted by ribbon-cutting." *Gay Life* 14 Sep. 1979:3

"Dr. Howard Brown." *Village Voice* 24 Feb. 1975:3

"Ice Carnival benefit Feb 23." *Chicago Gay Crusader* Feb.-Mar. 1975 (incorrectly dated 1974 on cover):1

"New pneumonia linked to gay lifestyle." *Gay Life* 19 Jun. 1981:2

Peters, Tom. "Clinic splits from Gay Horizons." *Gay Life* 3 Sept. 1976:1

Pfeiffer, Richard. "THIS MONTH." *Chicago Gay Crusader* Feb.-Mar. 1975:13

Williams. Albert N. "Howard Brown Clinic responds to gay cancer reports." *Gay Life* 10 Jul. 1981:1

## Chapter 60

"C.K.'s settles race bias charges." *Chicago Gay Crusader* (Issue No. 19) 1975:3

"DISCRIMINATION CHARGED AT CK'S" *Lavender Woman* Apr. 1975:n.p.

"Exclusion: Letter to the Editor." *Chicago Gay Life* 4 Jul. 1975:4

June. "AUGIE'S CONTROVERSY." *Lavender Woman* Jun. 1975:n.p.

## Chapter 61

Bouchard, Valerie A. "Associate Editor Speaks Out." *Chicago Gay Life* Jun. 20, 1975:1

"Exclusion: Letter to the Editor." *Chicago Gay Life* 4 Jul. 1975:4

Ford, Grant A. "Born in Gay Pride." *Chicago Gay Life* 20 Jun. 1975:6
"GAY PRIDE WEEK SCHEDULE." *Chicago Gay Crusader* Jun. 1975:3
"LESBIAN PRIDE WEEK SCHEDULE." *Chicago Gay Crusader* Jun. 1975:3
Nichols, Leslie. "Night Life." *Chicago Gay Life* 20 Jun. 1975
O'Connor, Meg. "Wit, humor missing." *Chicago Tribune* 30 Jun. 1975:C11

# INDEX

3 Penny (Adult Movie Theater), 107

## A

*& Puppy Dog Tails*, 182-183
Aardvark (Adult Movie Theater), 106-107
Aaron, David, 177
Aaron, William, 180-181
Abernathy, Ralph (Reverend), 8, 60
Abney, John Thomas, 103, 114, 157, 191
Abod, Susan, 148, 282
Acanfora, Joe, 208-209
Adam, Margie, 282
Adams, Polly, 321
Admiral (Adult Movie Theater), 107-108, 110
Adron's, 164
*Advocates* (TV Show), 77
Advocates for Gay Action, 132, 187
Afro-American Patrolman's League, 8
Ahmad, Maher, 26, 28
Akiko, Yosano, 148
Alameda Club, 5, 101, 158, 164
Alderisio, Felix "Milwaukee Phil," 107
Alderson, Ortez E, 49, 85, 183, 298
*A Lesbian Portrait*, 145
Alexander, George, 188
Alfie's (Gay Bar), 11
Allen, Ben, 272
Allen, Naomi (Aldermanic Candidate), 92-93
Allerton, Robert, 35-36
Allison, Keith, 108
Alternatives, Inc, 277-279
American Civil Liberties Union, 192, 313
American Legion Post, 152, 223
American Library Convention, 152, 154
American Medical Association, 66
American Psychiatric Association, 66, 72, 83, 294
Andrew, Christopher, 127
Annex (Gay Bar), 3-4, 12, 101, 158, 160, 164

Another Place (Gay Bar), 164
Anti-Women's Liberation League, 150
*A Position of Faith*, 229
Appel, Kenneth, 39-40
*Are We There Yet? A Continuing History of Lavender Woman, a Chicago Lesbian Newspaper 1971-1976*, 116, 161, 317, 334
Argiris, Nick, 11
Arrigo, Victor, 220
Artemis Players, 149, 184-185, 307
Astro (Restaurant), 82-85, 302
Athenaeum Theater, 216
Atkins, Tom, 77
Augie's (Gay Bar, 164, 330-331, 339
Avondale United Methodist Church/Logan Square, 88, 134, 191

## B

Babcock, Richard (Reverend), 273
Baker, Jack, 102, 154
Baldwin, Helen, 118
Banis, Dianne, 243
Bantner, Gayle B, 312-313
Barber, John (Aldermanic Candidate), 92
Barnard, Ronald L. (Lawyer), 50-51
Barnett, William (Alderman), 199, 240
Barrett, Andrew C, 8
Barry, Robert, 192
Barta, Michael, 63, 88
Bash, Johnny, 178
Basile, Sophia, 90
Baton (Drag Bar), 11, 160-161, 164, 228, 251, 256, 259, 264
Bayer, Ronald, 73-74
Bearded Lady, 173, 175-176, 178
Beckman, Barbara, 298
Beckman House, 298-299, 301, 306, 333, 366
Begun, Jeffrey S, 107-110
Behnen, Robert "Father Max" (Reverend), 139-140, 199
Belfry (Restaurant), 163

Belmont Rocks, 151, 153, 206, 333
Benedict, Ruth, 251
Benjamin, Eugene J. (Vice Coordinator), 12
Bentley's (Gay Bar), 158
Bergen, Candice, 45
Bergeron, Michael, 132-133, 154, 160, 163, 223, 227, 230, 265, 293, 299, 301, 341
Bergler, Edmund, 66
Berlin, Irving, 238
Bicek, George, 242
Bieber, Irving, 65-66, 73, 97
Big Basket (Juice Bar), 88
Bijou Theater (Adult Movie Theater), 105-109, 111
Birch, Robert, 26-27
Bird, Merton, 324
Birk, Lee (Doctor), 255
Biscotto, Tom, 86
Black Panthers, 44, 49, 53, 55, 60, 69, 86
Blake, Arthur, 2, 165
Bland, William (Mayor), 40
Block, Martin, 324
Blondina, 9
Blue Dahlia (Drag Bar), 2, 12, 164
Blue Gargoyle (Coffee Shop), 15, 87, 225, 276, 321
Blue Pub (Gay Bar), 5-6, 158, 164
Blue, Romy, 2
Bogarde, Dirk, 181
Bolling, Thomas (Patrolman), 55
Borchers, Webber A. (State Representative), 218, 220-221
Bouchard, Valerie, 336-338
Bowen, John, 184-185
Bowie, David, 173, 257
Boyer, Judy, 220
Boyette, Betsy, 119
Boyle, Edward F. (Alderman), 93
Boyle, Eugene (Reverend), 138
Boys at Sea (Gay Bar), 164, 272
*Boys in the Band* (Film), 59-60
*Boys in the Band* (Play), 41
Braasch, Clarence E. (Captain), 9-11, 161
Brabeck, Judy, 227

Bradberry (Lesbian Bar), 161, 164
Bradford, Jim, 2, 5, 6, 21, 31, 45, 154, 230, 299
Britt, John, 272
Broadway Sam's (Gay Bar), 158, 160, 164, 272
Broadway United Methodist Church of Christ, 272-273
Brody, Michelle "Michal," 21, 58-59, 116, 149, 161, 317, 320
Brooks, David Owen, 248
Brown, Howard J. (Doctor), 323-326
Brown, Michael, 228
Bruce, Lenny, 105
Bryant, Audrey, 160
Bryant, Ronald F, 204
Bughouse Square, 63, 123, 151
Burden, Carter, 198
Burk, Michael P, 188
Burke, Edward (Alderman), 199, 202
Burke, Phyllis J, 49
Burt, William (Illinois State Police), 205
Burton Place (Restaurant), 160, 163
Bush, Irving M. (Doctor), 260
Byrne, Jane (Mayor), 325-326

## C

Cahill, Andy, 165
Cameron, Stuart (Reverend), 214
Cantrell, John, 103, 154
*Can't Stop the Music*, 165
Capra, Joan, 149
Capri (Adult Movie Theater), 107
Cardwell, David, 160, 162
Carey, Bernard (States Attorney), 10
Carnegie Theater, 59
Carr, Ebony, 160, 276
Carradine, Robert, 110
Carson, Pirie Scott & Co, 102
Carter, Raymond (Captain), 42
Cello, John (Police), 10
Chain (Gay Bar), 160, 164
Chalmers, E. Laurence Jr. (Chancellor), 100
*Changing Homosexuality in the Male*, 66
Channing, Carol, 159

Charles, Sara (Doctor), 74
Checkmate (Gay Bar), 158, 160, 164
Chesterfield (Gay bar), 3, 12
Chez Ron (Lesbian Bar), 161, 164
Chicago Area Unitarian Universalist Gay Caucus, 274-275, 307, 321
Chicago Committee on Gay People and the Law, 102
Chicago Gay Alliance, 63, 70, 86, 96, 101, 102, 113-115, 128, 134, 136, 142, 154, 188, 191, 197, 199, 202, 214, 216, 227, 229, 249, 265-267, 293
Chicago Gay Law Students Association, 224, 231
Chicago Gay Medical Students, 300
Chicago Gay Men's Chorus, 216
Chicago Gay People's Legal Committee, 188, 226, 228
Chicago Gay Social Work Association, 188, 224, 226, 229
Chicago Gay Teachers Association, 76, 208, 224, 226, 229-300
Chicago Gay Youth, 188
Chicago Lesbian Liberation, 148-149, 151-154, 161, 188, 225-227, 229-230, 232, 235, 256, 315-317, 319
Chicago Mental Health Association, 69
Chicago Moving Picture Operators Union, 108
Chicago Peace Council, 85
Chicago Women's Liberation Rock Band, 145, 148, 151, 282
Chichester, Gary, 83, 87, 93, 289
Childs, Kitch, 63-64, 199-200
Chinn, Richard, 21, 103, 154
Churchill, Wainwright, 252
CK's (Lesbian Bar), 329-330
Clarke, Lige, 252
Clark, Kevin M, 49
Clark, Ronald J (Lawyer), 236
Clay, James, 49, 55-56, 256
Cleaver, Eldridge, 53
Clemens, Ginni, 282
Clinch Mountain Backsteppers, 283
Clingan, Eldon, 198
Closet (Gay Bar), 164

Club 69 (Gay Bar), 5
Club Yoyo (Gay Bar), 164
Cobbs, Clarence H. (Reverend), 272, 274
Coconuts (Gay Bar), 178
Cody, John Patrick (Cardinal), 139, 199, 202
Cogdill, Ray, 262
Cohen, Irving, 2
Cohen, Jerry, 87
Coliseum Ballroom, 23-24, 35, 55, 96
Collins, Chuck, 101
Columbia University, 14, 29-30, 257
Coming Out Pub, 160, 164, 272
Conlisk, James B (Police Superintendent), 6, 8, 10-11, 17
Cook County Jail, 152, 224, 228-229, 307, 333
Cooper, Alice, 257
Cooper, Jeff, 230
Corll, Dean Allen, 248-249
Corman, Roger, 110
Cornell University, 15, 30
Cousins, William (Alderman), 198
Crane, George W. (Doctor), 78, 253
*Cries from Cassandra*, 235
Cronkite, Walter, 192, 266
Crowley, Mart, 59-60
Curran, James (Doctor), 326

**D**

Daley, Richard J (Mayor), 6-7, 10-11, 15, 17, 56, 92, 133, 167-168, 175, 187-188, 206
D'Allesandro, Nick, 3-4
Daughters of Bilitis, 2, 62, 116, 118
David, Jack, 162, 230, 272
David's Place (Drag Bar), 160, 230, 259-260, 276, 278
Davilo, Marc (Police), 239-241
Davis, Angela, 52
Davis, Madeline, 193, 274
Davis, Nancy, 203, 286, 336
Davison, Edward aka Eddie Dugan, 167-168, 173-178
Davis, Rennard Cordon "Rennie," 45

372

Davis, Richard (Aldermanic Candidate), 62
*Death in Venice*, 181-182
DeBruin, Jerry, 273
*Deep Throat*, 107
Dee, Tony, 2
Del Gado, Ramon, 333
DeLise, Laura, 282
Dellinger, David, 45, 121
Democratic National Convention 1968, 2, 44-45, 133, 190
Democratic National Convention 1972, 128, 132-133
Denenberg, Kenneth (Doctor), 245
Depres, Leon M. (Alderman), 198
Der Read Barron (Restaurant), 289
Devil's Den (Gay Bar), 160
DeVito, Lou, 178
Dewes Mansion, 288-290, 304
Dierstein, M. Lois, 16
Dignity, 139-140, 217, 273, 307
Di Leonardi, Joseph (Police Commander), 109
Di Phillips, Rav (Doctor), 327-328
DiVarco, Joseph, 12
Dobkin, Alex, 282
Donaldson, Stephen, 14
Drama Shelter, 182, 333-334
Drantz, Ronnie, 82
Dry, Bill, 16, 26-28, 45, 341
Dugan, Kenneth (Councilman), 38
Dugan's Bistro (Disco), 160, 164, 167-178, 226, 228, 251, 306
Duncan, Celena M, 337
Dyke Patrol, 282-283

# E

Eddis, Charles (Reverend), 274
Edelman, Murray, 21, 23, 69-70, 96, 154
Edwards, Susan, 321
Eighmey, George (Alderman), 39
Elk Grove High School, 88-90
Elk Grove Village Board of Fire and Police Commissioners, 312
Ellis, Albert, 66
Encore Theater, 270-271

Episode (Gay Bar), 164
Ervanian, Harry (Captain), 17
Evans, Timothy C. (Alderman), 202
Evans, Wayne, 139
*Everything You Always Wanted to Know About Sex (But Were Afraid to Ask)*, 69

# F

Family of Women, 149, 228, 232
Farnham, Richard, 272
Farrelly, Terry, 220
Feminist Lesbian Intergalactic Party, 104, 154, 228
Feminist Lesbian Party, 132, 188
Ferguson, Drew, 109
Ferguson, Ed, 337
Festival (Adult Movie Theater), 106-107, 110
Field, Irwin (Judge), 7
Fields, Michael, 69
Fiery Flames Collective, 101, 103-104, 132, 154
Finnelly, James (Patrolman), 55-56, 256
Finnie's Ball, 55
Finochio's (Gay Bar), 160
First Church of Deliverance, 272, 274
Fisher, Peter, 29, 155
Fishman, Israel, 154
Flanagan, Olga "Augie," 330-331
Fleishman, Julius, 11
Fleishman, Walter, 11
Flint, Jim "Felicia," 161
Follies (Adult Movie Theater), 108
Foran, Tom, 121-124
Forcade, Thomas, 190
Ford, Grant L, 337
Fordley, Harold F, 107
Foster, Jeannette Howard, 95, 321
Foster, Jim, 193
Foxx, Redd, 265
Frankie Da Kat, 177
Fraser, Donald, 190-191
Freedman, Alfred M. (Doctor), 73
Freedman, Linda, 101
Friedman-Kien, Alvin E. (Doctor), 328

Froines, John, 45, 121

## G

Gaard, David, 182, 184
Gacy, John Wayne, 248
Gallimore, William, 115
Gardner, David C, 312-314
Garwood, Nancy, 16
Gate (Gay Bar), 164
Gates, Jim, 299
Gay Activist Alliance, 63, 86, 96, 101-102, 113-115, 128, 134, 136, 140, 142, 154, 188, 191, 197, 199, 202, 214, 216, 224, 226-227, 229, 249, 265-266, 293
Gay Activist Alliance of Miami, 191-192, 195
*Gay and Proud* 333
Gay Anthropologists 251
Gay Broadway (Bathhouse), 288
Gay Caucus Against War and Fascism, 76, 224, 228-229
Gay Center on Elm Street, 101-102, 112-115, 128, 268
Gay Committee of Returned Brigadistas, 126
*The Gay Crusaders*, 155
Gay Horizons, 115, 276, 279, 298, 300-306, 308, 325, 336
Gay Liberation Front
    Illinois Institute of Technology, 94-95, 98
    Loop College, 30
    Northern Illinois University-DeKalb, 29-30, 94-95, 97, 98
    Northwestern University, 26-28, 45
    Oberlin College, 94, 96
    Roosevelt University, 28-29
    Southern Illinois University, 43, 94-96, 98
    University of Chicago, 14-18, 23, 26, 28, 43-45, 58, 69, 87, 122, 124, 127
    University of Illinois Chicago-Circle Campus, 29, 44
    University of Illinois Urbana-Champaign, 32-34, 37-39
    University of Iowa, 94, 96, 100, 153
    University of Kansas, 31, 94-96, 98, 100
    University of Louisville, 94, 95, 96, 98
    Wisconsin State University, 94, 96, 98-99, 191
Gay Human Rights League, 323-324
*The Gay Mystique,* 29, 155
Gaynor, Gloria, 173
Gay Pride Planning Committee, 332, 335-336
Gay Raiders, 266, 336
Gay Speakers Bureau, 265
*Gays Under the Cuban Revolution*, 124
Gay Switchboard, 299, 301, 305, 325
Gay Unity Council of Chicago, 63
Gay Women's Caucus, 116, 142-144
Genesen, Lawrence (Judge), 236
Gerry's Club (Gay Bar), 11
Gertz, Thomas Erwin (Doctor), 6, 88, 134
Giancana, Sam "Momo," 109
Gill Community Arts Center, 184
Gilmore, Bill, 191
Gilun, John E. (Reverend), 139
Ginsberg, Allen, 105, 121, 195, 222
Gittings, Barbara, 83, 154-155
Glass, Charles (Patrolman), 17
Glass Menagerie, 263
Glory Hole (Gay Bar), 160, 164, 226, 228, 272, 332
Gold Coast (Gay Bar), 11, 158, 160-161, 163-164, 226, 228, 288-292
Golden, Alvin, 102
Goldman, Paul (Lawyer), 7, 245, 249, 304, 324-325, 337
Gold, Ron, 266
Goldsmith, H. Robert, 313
Gonsky, Paul, 107-111
Goodell, Charles (US Senator), 44
Good Shepherd Parish, 230, 272-274, 307, 333, 336
Gouze-Rénal, Christine, 30
Grace Lutheran Church, 139, 224
Granato, Robert C. (Doctor), 257
Graubert, Jeffrey, 32, 37-38, 203
Gray, Vernita, 154, 298
Green, Arthur, 273

Gregg, John Wyatt, 35-36
Grooms, Jim, 337
Groupe, Leonard (Lawyer), 313
Grubstake (Restaurant), 163
Gruenberg, Ira, 11
Gulian, Larry, 76, 188, 198-199, 202
Gullatte, James (Aldermanic Candidate), 92

## H

Hacker, Iberus (Reverend), 227
Haig (Gay Bar), 11, 158, 160, 164
Halen, Denny, 139
Hall, Joel, 85
Hanover, Renee (Lawyer), 15, 24, 26, 41-42, 45, 88, 96-97, 102, 239, 304, 329
Hanrahan, Edward V. (State's Attorney), 107
Harris, Edward (Alderman), 39
Hatterer, Lawrence J. (Doctor), 66, 71
Hauck, Paul A. (Psychologist), 72
Hawbaker, Ron, 302
Hayden, Tom, 45, 121
Hayride aka Wagon Wheel (Gay Bar), 11
Healey, Edward F. (Judge), 168
Hedlund, Marilou (Alderman), 198
Heinz, Marge, 119
Henley, Elmer Wayne, 248
Henritze, Jim, 3
Hesseman, Howard, 110
Hewitt, Ronald, 57
Hideaway II (Gay Bar), 164
High Chaparral (Gay Bar), 164
Himmel, Mary, 230
His 'n' Hers (Gay Bar)
Hitching Post (Gay Bar), 164
Hoffman, Abbie, 45, 121, 190
*Holding* (Film), 229
Holzman, James (Police District Commander), 10
*Home Movie*, 333
Homophile Liberation Alliance, 21
Homophile Youth Movement, 2
*Homosexuality* (Book), 66
*Homosexuality and American Psychiatry: The Politics of Diagnosis*, 73

*Homosexuality and Pseudohomosexuality*, 66
*Homosexuality: A Psychoanalytic Study of Male Homosexuals*, 65
*Homosexuality: Disease or Way of Life*, 66
*Homosexuality, Its Causes and Cures*, 66
Homosexuals Organized for Political Education, 63, 132
Honegger, David, 176
Hopper, Dennis, 45
Houlihan, James, 220
Houlihan, Mary, 138-141, 333
House of Landers (Drag Bar), 160, 230, 272
Howard Brown Memorial VD Clinic, 323, 325-326
Howard, Mark, 2
Hubbard, Maceo (Supervisory Trial Attorney Criminal Section), 57
Huber-Zoch, Vickie (Police), 19
Hugel, Bob, 272
Hughes, Sue, 272
Hullman, Leonard (Psychologist), 72
Human Awareness Institute, 21
Hunter, Rebecca, 321
Hursey, Paul (Alderman), 39
Hutson, Paul G, 100
Hyde Park Homophile League, 14

## I

Ida Noyes Hall, 17, 87
Ifs, Ands and Burt's (Gay Bar), 11
Illinois Fair Employment Practices Commission, 102, 189, 197-198
Illinois Foster Parents' Association, 245
Illinois Gay Rights Task Force of the Alliance to End Repression, 198
Illinois Gays for Legislative Action, 188-189, 198-199, 202, 216-217, 227, 265
Illinois Liquor Control Commission, 7, 156, 167, 174, 329
Illinois State University Gay People's Alliance, 188, 218-220
In Between (Gay Bar), 226
*Inga, the Animal Lover*, 107
Inner Circle (Gay Bar), 11

Inner Circle on Erie (Gay Bar), 164-165
Institute of Juvenile Research, 26
Isle of Capri (Gay Bar), 164
Ives, William C, 197

## J

*Jackson County Jail*, 110
Jackson, Jesse, 133
Jacobs, Dina, 230
Jacobs, Elaine, 149
James, Sharon, 118-119
Jamie's (Gay Bar), 11, 158, 160, 162-163, 164
Jayaram, Bangalore (Doctor), 260-261
Jay, Karla, 124
Jeffers, Thomas, 244
Jeffrey's Pub, 164
Jemilo, John (Lawyer), 19
Jenkins, Sherry, 148-149
Jennings, Dale, 324
Jessie's (Gay Bar), 164
Jett-Blakk, Joan, 179
Johansen, David, 258
Johnson, Dean, 17
Johnson, Tony, 154, 228
Johnson, William (Reverend), 227, 229-230
Johnston, Jill, 225, 232-234
Johnston, Ralf L, 156
Jones, Norman, 262
Jones, Tommy Lee, 110

## K

Kahn, Susan, 298
Kaineg, Sue, 89
Kameny, Frank, 74, 77, 79, 83, 299
Kappa, Carol, 329, 331
Karlin, Mike, 158
Keller, John R, 188
Kelley, Clifford P. (Alderman), 198-199, 201, 203
Kelley, William B, 1-2, 4-5, 9, 115, 154, 174, 189, 197-198, 216, 230, 232, 245-246, 249, 265, 266-267, 293
Kelly, Nick, 87, 177
Kempton, Murray, 250

Kennedy, Florynce, 266
Kerouac, Jack, 105
Kerr, Patricia, 149
Kight, Morris, 299
Killer Dyke, 104, 228, 230, 333, 335
Kimberley, Kim, 239-240
King's Ransom (Gay Bar), 2, 11, 101, 158, 160, 164
King, Sunny, 63
Kinsey, Alfred (Doctor), 114
*Kiss This Miss*, 107
Kitty Sheon's (Gay Bar), 2, 158, 160, 164
Klepak, Ralla, 15
Kmetko, Tom, 244
Knight Out (Gay Bar), 160, 164, 226, 228
Knight, Thomas (Prosecutor), 111
Koch, Joanne, 246
Koch, Lew, 246
Kolberg, Dean T, 156
Krick, Bill, 302-304
Kronengold, A.J, 184
Kuda, Marie Jayne, 148, 281, 315-316, 321-322

## L

Lady Baronessa, 262, 264
Lamont, Charles (Reverend), 88, 134-137, 191-192, 212
Landers, Ann, 74-76, 78, 80, 231, 294, 306, 308
Landers, Roby, 159-160, 230
Landt, Skip, 23
Langford, Anna R. (Alderman), 198, 202
La Noche de Ronda (Gay Bar), 160, 226
LaPorte, Rita, 119
Larsen, Richard, 62-63, 139
*Lavender* (Documentary), 149, 229, 333
*Lavender Woman*, 116-119, 142-144, 149, 161, 184, 200, 231, 234-235, 281-283, 284-286, 315-320, 329-330
Lawrence, Helen, 111
Lear, Norman, 265
Leather Cell, 292
Leather Toy Store, 160
Legacy 21 Club, 4-5, 7, 162, 272
Leggett, Gene, 211-212

Legion of Mary, 139-141
Leonard, Jerris (Assistant Attorney General Civil Rights Division), 57
Le Pub (Gay Bar), 163, 260
*Les amitiés particulières*, 30
Lesbian Feminist Center, 330, 335
Lesbian/Feminist Theatre of Chicago, 184
Lesbian Mother's Defense Fund, 334
*Lesbian Nation*, 232-233
Levey, Robert, 272
Levine, Larry, 245
Levin's Inn, 164
Lewis, Tony, 230
Lightfoot, Barbara, 144, 235
Lincoln Park Lagooners, 326
Lincoln Park Presbyterian Church, 62, 88, 93
Linghorn, Harry, 266
Lisowski, Ed, 33-34
Litman, Fay, 261
Little Jim's, 339
Livingston County Draft Board, 49-50
LoBue, Anthony (Police), 239, 241-242
Lonnquist, Judy, 199
*The Lord Is My Shepherd and He Knows I'm Gay*, 274
*The Love That Dared Not Speak Its Name: A Candid History of Homosexuality in Britain*, 180
Louis Gages Fun Lounge, 5, 7
Louÿs, Pierre, 118
Loyola-Rogers Park Gay Students Association's, 276
Luis, Shaun, 262
Lust, Wanda, 160, 226, 228, 276, 289, 326, 334, 336
Lyon, Phyllis, 155

# M

Machine Juice Bar, 164
Madison Alliance for Homosexual Equality, 99
Male Hide, 292
Manford, Morty, 201, 230, 332-333
Manilow, Barry, 159, 288
Manley, John (Police), 14-20, 26, 45-46
Manley, John J "Cap'n Jack," 17
Mann, Thomas, 55, 181
Man's Country, 288-291, 334, 336
*Marcus Welby, M.D*, 266-267
Mark III (Gay Bar), 164
Marovitz, Abraham L. (Judge), 237
Martin, Del, 155
Martin, Ken (Reverend), 336
Mascolino, Salvatore (Police), 10
Massachusetts Mental Health Center, 255
Mattachine Midwest Chicago, 6, 14, 21, 31, 45, 62-63, 88, 134, 230, 299, 321
Mattachine New York, 2
Maurovich, Walter (Police District Commander), 10
Maybauer, John, 84, 139, 154
May, Step, 16-17, 22-23, 44, 67, 124, 188
McClain, James Michael, 47-48
McClure, Kent, 302
McConnell, Michael, 154
McDermott, John (Police District Commander), 10
McMillen, Harvey, 236
McCormack, David (Deputy Fire Chief), 201
McGee, Edward (Patrolman), 9
McGovern/Fraser Commission, 190-191
McGovern, George (Senator), 133, 193-195
McNally, Terrence, 333
Mead, Margaret (Doctor), 251
Mehrtens, William O. (Judge), 192
Melvin, Merrilee, 117, 341
Merrill, Laura, 230
*Meshes of the Afternoon*, 229
Metropolitan Community Church, 226, 230, 270-271, 273, 307, 310, 333
Miami Beach City Council, 190
Miami Sexual Identity Crisis Center, 75
Michas, Christopher (Alderman), 93
Mickley, Richard R. (Reverend), 273
Midler, Bette, 159
Midwestern Gay Lib Conference, 63
Midwest Regional Gay Liberation Convention, 94, 98

Mielcarek, Pat, 337
Mike's Aragon (Gay Bar), 164
Mike's Terrace Lounge, 164
Mikva, Abner (Representative), 45
Miller, Howard, 69-70
Miller, Jerome, 243-246
Mimieux, Yvette, 110
Minuskin, Myron, 11
Miss Gay America, 262-264
Miss Gay Chicago, 259
Mitrokhin, Vasili, 127
Molly's (Juice Bar), 12
Monahan, Colleen, 149
Monroe Theater, 241-242
Montalvo, Fanny, 148
Ms (Lesbian Bar), 158, 162, 164, 285, 306
Muriel, Hugo (Doctor), 326
Murphy, Claudia, 11, 181, 183
Murray, Bill, 182
My Brother's Place (Restaurant), 164

**N**

Name of the Game (Gay Bar), 164
Napier, Lowell (Police), 10
*Narcissia*, 229
Natarus, Burton (Alderman), 199, 240
National Association for the Advancement of Colored People, 8
National Conference of Catholic Bishops, 138
National Democratic Convention (1968), 2, 17, 44-45, 190
National Federation of Priests' Councils, 138
National Gay Convention, 128-131
National Lawyers Guild, 96-97
National Organization of Women, 199
Neal, Sanford (Police Sergeant), 236
Nelson, Bruce, 273
Nelson, Cathy, 117
*Never Can Say Goodbye*, 173
Newberry (Adult Movie Theater), 106-108
New Haven Women's Liberation Rock Band, 145
Newton, Huey, 51, 53, 55

New York Dolls, 257-258
New York Gay Activist Alliance, 128, 191
Nichols, Jack, 252
Nichols, Leslie, 337, 339
*Nightline*, 134
Nite Life (Drag Bar), 10, 158, 164
Nixon, Richard M, 105, 187-188
Nobel, Muffie, 117, 155
Noble, Tommy, 176
Noche de Ronda, 160, 226
Normandy (Gay Bar), 11, 24-25-26
Northern Illinois Conference of the United Methodist Church, 134-137
Northwestern University Legal Assistance Clinic, 240
Norton, Joseph L. (Doctor), 324-325

**O**

O'Banion's (Gay Bar), 158
O'Connell, Brian, 69
Odom, Jack (Police Sergeant), 205
Office (Gay Bar), 158, 160, 164
Ogilvie, Richard, 187-188
Old Marlene, 5
Oliver, Frank, 107
Olivo, Abe, 336-337
ONE of Chicago, 62, 151, 299, 324-325
Onge, Jack, 139
Orange Cockatoo (Drag Bar), 12
Orejudos, Dom "Etienne," 289
Oscar Wilde's Children, 299, 301
Our Den (Gay Bar), 336
Our Place (Gay Bar), 164
*Out and Proud*, 101
*Out of the Closets: Voices of Gay Liberation*, 124
*The Overt Homosexual*, 66
Ovesy, Lionel, 66, 69
Owens, Georgia, 5-6
Owen, Wanda, 318, 319-320

**P**

Page, Bill, 323
Palermo, Mark, 176
Paley, Hiram (Mayor), 39-40
Palumbo, Michael, 109

# CHICAGO AFTER STONEWALL

Parkside (Gay Bar), 164
Patch (Lesbian Bar), 164
Patrick, Robert, 333
Peanut Butter and Jelly (Gay Bar), 164
Pearson, Theodore (Aldermanic Candidate), 92
Peek, Jerry, 262-263
Peeping Tom (Adult Movie Theater), 111
Pelc, Mary Ann, 282
Pellegrini, Norman, 249
Penguin (Gar Bar), 164
Pepper's (Gay Bar), 158, 160, 164
Perry, Troy (Reverend), 266, 270-271, 273-274
Peters, Betty, 117, 235
Peterson, John (Alderman), 39
Petretti, Paulette (Assistant Corporation Council), 19
Peyrefitte, Roger, 30
Pfeiffer, Richard, 265
Pierce, Harriet, 150
Pittenger, John, 209
*Playboy*, 45, 153
Playboy Mansion, 45
Plomin, David, 176
Pollack, Mary (Councilmember), 39
Polley, Anthony aka Joy, 236
Ponwrance, Rocky, 192
PopiwChak, Joanne, 256
Pottinger, Patricia J, 49
Pour House (Gay Bar), 164
Power, Joseph A. (Judge), 107
PQ's (Gay Bar), 157-158, 177
Prescott, Suzanne, 148
Prince, Virginia, 254-255
Pryor, Thomas M. (Bishop), 134-135
Punchinello's (Gay Bar), 158-159, 164

## Q

Queen's Surf (Gay Bar), 158

## R

Radical Drags, 128-129
Radical Lesbians, 298
Rae, Ronald (Police Commander), 8
*Ranch Slaves*, 107

Rand, Sally, 289, 291
Rechy, John, 182
Red Butterflies, 63, 69
Reese, Della, 159
Reiff, Nancy, 159, 175
Reilly, Danny, 165
Renslow, Charles "Chuck," 11, 85, 161, 288-291, 303-304
Renslow, Patrick, 162
REO Speedwagon, 45
Republican National Convention 1972, 190
Reuben, David (Doctor), 69-70, 114
Reyes, Antonio, 324
Rhodes, Rusty, 165
Rialto (Adult Movie Theater), 108
Ricciardi, Patrick "Patsy," 107-108, 111
Richardson, Mary, 154
Rifkin, Edward (Police), 10
Rising Up Angry, 8
Ritz (Gay Bar), 101, 158, 164
Robbins, Bruce, 159
Robinson, Frank M, 152-153
Robinson, Renault, 8
Rochford, James M. (Acting Superintendent), 11-12
*Rocky Horror Picture Show*, 258
*Rocky Horror Show* 258-259
Rodriguez, Jose, 5
Rodriguez, Matt (Police Superintendent), 18-20
Rodwell, Craig, 2
Rogers Park Gay Center, 276, 278, 279, 303
Rogow, Bruce, 192
Rohn, Allan (Chief of Police), 49
Rojek, Charles, 165
Rosone, Manny, 330
Rowland, Chuck, 324
Rowley, Kathy, 148
Royko, Mike, 299-303
Rubin, Jerry, 45, 121
Rule, Elton, 267
Ruthie's (Gay Bar), 158

379

## S

Sadoughi, Wanda (Psychologist), 260
Sam's (Gay Bar), 11
Samuelsohn, Howie, 101
*Sanford & Son*, 265
Sawyer, Eugene (Alderman), 198
Sawyer, Jack (Professor), 26
Schmid, Herbert G, 289-290
Schoenfield, Mark, 240
Schweihs, Frank, 111
Scortia, Thomas N, 152
Scott, Claudia, 317
Seale, Bobby, 45, 53, 121
*Second Largest Minority*, 333
Segal, Mark, 266, 334, 336
Seno, Steve L. (Patrolman), 9
Serling, Rod, 45
*Sexual Behavior in the Human Male*, 114
*Sex Variant Women in Literature*, 321
Shainess, Natalie (Doctor), 75
Shakur, Afeni, 52
Shakur, Tupac, 52
Shane, David, 216
Shannon, William H. (Alderman), 198, 202
Shapiro, Alan J. (Doctor), 313-314
Shari's (Gay Bar), 158, 160, 164
Shaw, Don (Reverend), 199, 333
Shearer, Del, 119
Shear, Linda, 117, 142, 144-145, 148-150, 282, 298
Shelley, Martha, 45
Sherkow, Mark, 278
Shields, David (Judge), 239
Shin, Roger L. (Doctor), 212
Shirley's Set Lounge, 164
Shoreline (Gay Bar), 164
Shoreline 7 (Gay Bar), 9
Shore, Warren, 243
Shusterman, Harold (Rabbi), 110
Simon, Seymour (Alderman), 198, 202
Simon, Tobias (Lawyer), 77
Simon, Seymour (Alderman), 198, 202
Simon, William (Psychologist), 26
Simpson, Dick (Alderman), 216
Sindt, David, 115, 154, 188, 211-213, 215, 224
Singer, June (Doctor), 245
Singer, William (Alderman), 93, 198
Skeist, Robbie, 124, 127
Slater, Don, 324
Sloan, Margaret, 117-118
Small, Patrick, 190
Smith, Gary, 100
Smith, Jonathan (Lawyer), 24, 63
Smith, Tom, 299
Snake Pit (Gay Bar), 164, 336
Socarides, Charles (Doctor), 66-68, 73, 77
*Society and the Healthy Homosexual*, 252
Sokol, Marilyn, 164-165
*Some of Your Best Friends*, 333
*Songs of Bilitis*, 118
Southern Christian Leadership Conference, 8
Spangler, Virgil, 191
Sparrows (Gay Bar), 85, 158-160, 162
Sperling, Jack (Judge), 237-240
Spitzer, Robert L. (Doctor), 72
Springer, Norbert, 11
Springfield Gay Liberation, 188
St. Alphonsus Catholic Church, 216
Stan Dale Show, 21
St. Andrew's Catholic Church, 8
Stanley, William, 32, 34, 38
Steinem, Gloria, 118
Stensland, Paul, 30
Stern, Richard A, 276-278, 279
Stevenson, H.L, 250
Stienecker, David, 7, 15, 45-46
St. John, Jeffrey, 250
Stonewall Riots, 1-2, 15, 32, 62, 83, 118, 151, 180, 182, 230, 269, 301, 308, 325
Storr, Anthony (Doctor), 180-181
*Straight: A Heterosexual Talks About His Homosexual Past*, 180
Strazzante, Salvatore, 11
Stroud, Jean, 119
St. Sebastian's Church, 138-140, 217, 273
Studebaker Theatre, 59-60
Student Homophile League, 15

Student Mobilization Committee, 44-45, 85
Sue and Nan's (Gay Bar), 272
Summit, Marge, 51, 158, 162, 164, 285, 304, 306
Susan "Susie" B's (Restaurant), 281-282
Swank, Bill, 163
Swartzman, Dan, 240
Szekeley, Ella, 144, 149
Szwedo, Frank (Police), 17-18

**T**

Tabin, Morton S. (Doctor)
Task Force on Gay Liberation, 154, 321
Taylor, Valerie, 21, 88, 230, 281, 299, 321, 324
Telow, Stephen J. (Aldermanic Candidate), 92
Tenement Square (Gay Bar), 164
Terkel, Studs, 21, 217
Termite (Adult Movie Theater), 107
Terrell, Tanya, 160
Thanasouras, Mark (Captain), 12
Thierry, David, 23-24, 88
Third World Gay Revolutionaries, 25, 49, 51, 86, 102, 155
*This Day's Death*, 182
*This is the Army*, 238
Thomas, Ray, 176
Thomas, Ron, 158
Thompson, James R. (US Attorney), 9-12
Tiffany's Manicure Parlor, 109
Tillie the Dirty Old Lady, 3
Tobin, Kay, 155
Togetherness (Gay Bar), 11, 158
Tosswill, Susan, 23
Toushin, Steven H, 107-110
*The Towering Inferno*, 152
Town Hall District, 335
Townson, Patrick, 84, 162, 335, 337
*Transvestia*, 255
*The Transvestite and His Wife*, 255
Transvestite Legal Committee, 132
*Trevor*, 184-185, 223-225
Trip (Gay Bar), 156, 158, 163-164, 226
Troche, Confesor (Patrolman), 9

Trotter, Leslie A, 188, 202-203
*Tubstrip*, 184
Tully, Joe, 279
Tumilty, Nellie, 119
Turkington, Edward, 22

**U**

*Underground News*, 101
Uniformed Fire Officers Association, 201
United Church of Christ, 229, 273
Up North (Restaurant), 158, 161-163, 226, 228, 230-231, 272
Upper Mississippi Valley Psychological Association, 72
Upstairs (Gay Bar), 229-230

**V**

*Vacation in Hot Pants*, 107
Van Buren, Abigail, 80-81
VanderMeer, Abram (Doctor), 209
Venceremos Brigade, 82, 124-127
Vice Control Division, 2
Vietnam War, 2, 17, 21, 44-46, 49, 85, 101, 190, 195
Village People, 165
*Village Voice*, 1, 225, 232-233
Vincenz, Lilli, 101
Visconti, Luchino, 181
Voeller, Bruce, 128, 194

**W**

Walker, Daniel (Governor),187-189
Wallender, Raymond, 230
Washington, Jimmy L. (Alderman), 198
Watch Your Hat & Coat Saloon, 262
Waters, Mike, 218-220
Watkins, Ruby, 117, 317
Wayne, Candace (Lawyer), 19
*Wax Museum*, 21
Weathers, Brenda, 299
Weimhoff, Henry, 14, 21, 42-43, 45, 63, 65-66, 251
Weinberg, George
Weiner, Lee, 45, 121
Weisstein, Naomi (Doctor, 148)
Welles, Artesia, 160

Wellman, Joseph, 89
Weltge, Ralph W. (Reverend), 212
Wemette, William "Red," 111
Whalen, John, 208
White, Georgia, 5-6
Whittle, Paul O, 135
Wicker, Eileen, 30, 188
Wicker, Randy, 155
Wigwam (Restaurant), 37, 38
Wilinski, Robert (Alderman), 198
Williams, Tennessee, 334
Willoughby's (Gay Bar), 164
Wilson, Demond, 265
Wilson, Lanford, 334
Wilson, Margaret "Skeeter," 76, 208, 227, 334
Wilson, Peter, 188
Wilson, Wallace, 239
Women Identified Women, 63
*Women Loving Women*, 322
Women's Bar Association of Illinois, 15, 26
Women's International Terrorist Conspiracy from Hell, 89
Women's Liberation Movement, 259
Wooden Barrell (Gay Bar), 160, 226
Woodlawn, Holly, 164
Woods, Alfred, 29
*The World Was Going Our Way: The KGB and the Battle for the Third World*, 127

# Y

Yippies, 121, 190, 195
Young, Allen, 122, 124

# Z

Zippies, 190
Zipprodt, Charles M. (Mayor), 37

# CHICAGO AFTER STONEWALL

# ABOUT THE AUTHOR

St Sukie de la Croix has been a social commentator and researcher on Chicago's LGBT history for three decades. He has published oral-history interviews; lectured; conducted historical tours; documented LGBT life through columns, photographs, humor features, and fiction; and written the book *Chicago Whispers* (University of Wisconsin Press, 2012) on local LGBT history. St Sukie de la Croix, the man the *Chicago Sun-Times* described as "the gay Studs Terkel," came to Chicago from his native Bath, England, in 1991. He has had columns in local publications or online news and entertainment sources such as *Chicago Free Press, Gay Chicago, Nightlines/Nightspots, Outlines, Blacklines, Windy City Times*, and *GoPride*.com as well as numerous others outside the city. In 2008 he was a historical consultant as well as an on-screen interviewee for the WTTW television documentary *Out & Proud in Chicago*. In 2005 and 2006 he had two of his plays, *A White Light in God's Choir* and *Two Weeks in a Bus Station with an Iguana*, performed by Chicago's Irreverence Dance & Theatre Company. A popular and engaging lecturer, he has spoken at an array of venues from Chubb Insurance to Boeing and from Horizons Gay Youth Services to the Chicago Area Gay and Lesbian Chamber of Commerce. His crowning achievement came in 2012 when the University of Wisconsin published his in-depth, vibrant record of LGBT Chicagoans, *Chicago Whispers: A History of LGBT Chicago Before Stonewall*. With a foreword by noted historian John D'Emilio, the book received glowing reviews and cemented de la Croix's deserved position as a top-ranking historian and leader. In 2012 de la Croix was inducted into the Chicago LGBT Hall of Fame. Two years later he moved to Palm Springs, California, and in 2017 published *The Blue Spong and the Flight from Mediocrity*, a novel set in 1924 Chicago, followed by *The Orange Spong and Storytelling at the Vamp Art Café* in 2020. In 2018 he published *The Memoir of a Groucho Marxist*, a work about growing up Gay in Great Britain, and in 2019, *Out of the Underground: Homosexuals, the Radical Press and the Rise and Fall of the Gay Liberation Front*. Also in 2019 he published *St Sukie's Strange Garden of Woodland Creatures* with celebrated illustrator Roy Alton Wald. It was in 2019 that St Sukie de la Croix and Owen Keehnen launched their Tell Me About It Project, which led to the 2019 publication of *Tell Me About It, Tell Me About It 2*, and in 2020, *Tell Me About It 3*.

www.ingramcontent.com/pod-product-compliance
Lightning Source LLC
Chambersburg PA
CBHW020941230426
43666CB00005B/106